P9-CCH-561

SHORT-TERM PSYCHOTHERAPY

HANDBOOK OF

SHORT-TERM PSYCHOTHERAPY

LEWIS R. WOLBERG, M.D.

Clinical Professor of Psychiatry, New York University School of Medicine
Founder and Emeritus Dean, Postgraduate Center for Mental Health, New York

1980
Thieme-Stratton Inc.
New York

Georg Thieme Verlag
Stuttgart · New York

Thieme-Stratton Inc.
381 Park Avenue South
New York, NY 10016

LC 79-29757 / ISBN 0-913258-67-9
Georg Thieme edition: ISBN 313 5951 01-4
Printed in U.S.A.

Contents

Preface

In 1959, I chaired a seminar at the Postgraduate Center for Mental Health in New York City, during which a number of participants presented material detailing their thoughts about and experiences with short-term therapy. Helen Avnet, Director of Research, Group Health Insurance Company, revealed the results of a project that lasted two and one-half years, in which a panel of 1,139 psychiatrists treated patients on a short-term basis. On termination, 70 percent of the patients were rated by the panel as improved or recovered. It was concluded that a large portion of the community's psychiatric needs could be met by short-term treatments. Jules Masserman detailed the historical-comparative and experimental roots of short-term therapy, tracing its origins in the past. Sandor Rado presented material on motivational factors that could provide guidelines for techniques in short-term therapy. Paul Hoch differentiated the characteristics of short-term versus long-term therapy. Franz Alexander dealt with psychoanalytic contributions to short-term therapy in facilitating a corrective emotional experience. Lothar Kalinowsky lectured on the use of somatic treatments in short-term therapy. Alexander Wolf dealt with short-term group psychotherapy. Molly Harrower described a research project related to outcome of long-term and short-term therapy. Arlene Wolberg discussed the incorporation of case-work procedures in a short-term program. I gave two lectures, one on general aspects of technique and the other on the employment of hypnosis as an adjunct in short-term therapy. The seminar was published later by Grune & Stratton under the title *Short-term Psychotherapy*.

It is interesting in reviewing the current literature that independent studies have validated an astonishingly large percentage of the ideas and observations of this seminar. It is relatively recently, however, that there has been a swing toward short-term therapy as a primary and preferred treatment rather than as an expedient. Even national psychoanalytic organizations, strongholds of long-term treatment, have begun to preach its virtues and have organized continuing-education courses on the subject. A host of articles and a number of interesting books have appeared, outlining philosophies, goals, selection procedures and techniques that the authors have found valuable in their attempts to abbreviate treatment. In the main, similarities of concepts have exceeded differences. Nevertheless, a great number of questions remain unanswered, and it is the purpose of the present volume to contribute to the resolution of some of these.

One of the most critical questions is related to the value of dynamic approaches in short-term therapy. Most importantly, can we empirically prove the effectiveness of a dynamically based short-term therapy? Controlled experiments have been few, and even in these the difficulties that shadow outcome studies tend to obscure results. Yet with all our skepticism about quantifying brief clinical operations sufficiently to satisfy the criteria of objectivity, validity, and reliability so essential in scientific studies, discriminating experience establishes beyond reasonable doubt the usefulness of a dynamic orientation in any form of short-term psychotherapy. This applies whether we are helping a person recognize and then to come to terms with his past, as in insight therapy, or eliminating effects of the past through reinforcement of adaptive behaviors, as in behavior therapy, or squeezing the past out of muscles and tissues as in the "new body therapies," or gaining a perspective on inner emotional effects of the past through sensory awareness techniques, or correcting habitual past modes of thinking, as in cognitive therapy. Indeed, a dynamic approach, in my opinion, is the best design to follow in all forms of psychotherapy, however brief they may be, and while it may not have an immediate dramatic influence on the personality structure, it can catalyze such changes eventually through its continuing influence on cognition.

In this volume I have attempted to bring together common elements in the chief models of short-term therapy currently in use and to evolve principles that can be employed by individual therapists, irrespective of their theoretical biases and styles of operation. How a dynamic viewpoint may practically be introduced in any form of psychotherapy is one of my goals. The short-term method that I will describe is not presented with illusion that it is flawless, infallible, or universally applicable. Nor may it prove equally helpful to all therapists or curative in every case. It is, nevertheless, in my opinion, (and in the judgment of therapists who have utilized the method), an easily learned and effective technique serviceable for the great majority of patients seen in clinics and private practice. The method also takes into consideration the fact that there will be patients who are not good subjects for short-term treatment and who will require other forms of help. Under these circumstances, the method will function as a useful initial diagnostic procedure, enabling the therapist to select modalities that will serve the patient best.

The method also contains a means of providing continuing therapy for the patient through assigned homework and the use of a casette tape, the making of which will be described in detail. It has always confounded me that so many therapists assume that when the last formal treatment session has ended, the patient can sally forth like the fabled prince and princess to live happily ever after. The facts on the follow-up are a grim denial of this fantasy. For example, in follow-up research of patients who had been treated in a comparison study with two forms of brief psychotherapy (behavior therapy and psychoanalytically oriented psychotherapy) and who were discharged as improved, Patterson, et al (1977) found that one year after termination, fully 60 percent had sought out and obtained further treatment. These figures are probably low because many discharged patients who do not seek formal therapy utilize other forms of help or self-help to reduce their tension and better their adjustment. Life, after satisfactory psychotherapeutic treatment, continues to present a never ending series of challenges that can tax coping capacities of even "cured" patients. This is not altogether bad, for in meeting these challenges the individual has an opportunity of strengthening adaptive patterns, much like a booster shot can enhance the effect of a prior vaccination. Short-term psychotherapy offers the patient a means by which one's future may be regulated, provided the therapist prepares the patient for anticipated events and contingencies and teaches a way of dealing with these, should they appear.

As a handbook, this volume provides an outline of process in short-term therapy. Should extensive details of technique be sought, they may be found elsewhere, including the third edition of my book *The Technique of Psychotherapy*. It is recommended that the reader if not already acquainted with some techniques other than individual psychotherapy experiment with these to see whether they accord with one's individual styles of working. In my opinion, a therapist's usefulness is especially enhanced by knowledge of group therapy (see *The Technique of Psychotherapy*, 3rd ed, pp. 702–729), family therapy (pp. 729–733), marital (couple) therapy (pp. 733–740), behavior therapy (pp. 685–701), relaxation procedures (pp. 761–766), and somatic therapy (pp. 767–789). Other techniques may periodically be useful such as hypnosis (pp. 791–809), sex therapy (pp. 809–817), and bibliotherapy (pp. 817–833). It goes without saying that knowledge of the therapeutic process from the initial interview to termination (pp.

353–684; 743–758) and especially interviewing techniques (pp. 360–382) are indispensible.

A final word of caution may be indicated. One should not assume that it is always possible to duplicate or surpass with short-term approaches what can be done with *appropriately selected patients* through longer-term treatment. But, for the great majority of people seeking help for emotional problems, the time element is not the most important variable in psychotherapy. Time is too frequently considered a magical device that acts like a detergent, washing away accumulated neurotic residues. It is assumed traditionally that the longer a patient remains in psychotherapy, the greater the benefits he will derive from it. Common practice, however, convinces that this is true only up to a certain point. Beyond such a point, resistances pile up in a disturbing number of patients, gains are neutralized, and a setback ensues. Peering into the causes of these misfortunes, we observe in therapy that goes on for too protracted a period an emerging sense of helplessness that may be concealed by various reaction formations. The consequence is a sabotage of progress and ultimately an exacerbation of symptoms. The therapist then becomes for the patient a crutch; without whom independent steps are avoided. This is particularly the case in sicker patients whose dependency needs are hallmarks of their basic personality structure, or who have, because of persistent anxiety, lost their sense of mastery and distrust their own capacities to function. Whatever gains may accrue from any evolving insights are neutralized by the crippling influence of the prolonged sheltered relationship. Playing a waiting game in the hope that time will eventually dislodge a neurosis too frequently results in patient paralysis and therapist frustration.

Such disconcerting phenomena give impetus to our efforts to shorten the therapeutic process without devitalizing its effect. This is not to depreciate economic and other practical reasons for abbreviating short-term therapy. But apart from cost effectiveness and the need to minister to the growing multitudes of people who seek help, dynamic short-term treatment is justified only if it can prove itself to be a truly useful means of dealing with emotional problems in the vast majority of cases. In my opinion, this proof has now been established.

Acknowledgment is made to the Postgraduate Center for Mental Health, under whose auspices this book was written, and to its Staff for the stimulation they inspired. Thanks are due to Grune & Stratton, the publishers of my books *Short-term Psychotherapy* and *The Dynamics of Personality* (with John Kildahl) for permission to utilize some material from these volumes in Chapters 7, 8, 9 and 16. Credit is also due to my secretary, Ann Kochanske, for her effective help with the physical preparation of the book and the checking of references.

Lewis R. Wolberg, M.D.

New York, New York
November 1, 1979

CHAPTER 1

Models of Short-term Therapy

Brief treatment is no newcomer on the psychotherapeutic scene. Chronicled in primitive archives of earliest recorded history, particularly in Egypt and Greece, are accounts of what we may consider species of short-term psychotherapy. In these ancient documents there are transcribed elaborate rituals to heal the afflicted, to solace troubled souls, and to assuage anguish and distress. Among such interventions are tranquilizing nostrums, bodily manipulations, trance incantations, persuasive suggestions, and even rudiments of reinforcement therapy, emotional catharsis, and interpretation of fantasies and dreams. Elaborations of these therapies continue to this day draped in the sophistication of modern theories. Up to the beginning of the twentieth century methods of treatment were short term; even the original Freudian techniques were implemented over a period of a few months. Gradually psychoanalytic methods stretched out in time, and the number of weekly sessions increased as efforts were directed at the task of resolving resistance to unconscious conflict. A few contemporaries of Freud, notably Adler, Ferenczi, Stekel, and Rank, tried heroically to shorten the protracted time of psychoanalysis, but their methods were repudiated by the official analytic establishment. Some Rankian and Stekelian strategems survived, nevertheless, and have been adapted to fit in with present-day styles and contemporary ideologies.

Psychoanalytic Modifications in Brief Dynamic Therapy

It was Franz Alexander in 1946 who most strikingly challenged the validity of prolonged time as a necessary component of treatment methods directed at reconstructive goals. Reaction to Alexander's unorthodoxy was at first harsh, and although he was accused of abandoning the psychoanalytic ship, it is to his credit that he resisted recanting his convictions. Along with French he published a pioneer work on brief therapy (Alexander & French, 1946) that questioned many of the assumptions of long-term classical psychoanalysis.

In their volume the authors describe experimenting with varying the frequency of interviews, the alternative use of the chair and couch, deliberate interruptions of treatment prior to termination, strategic playing of studied roles, and combined use of psychotherapy with drug and other treatments. At the time their experiments were considered as daring and innovative. Particularly regarded as aberrant were the emphasis on problem solving and the consideration of therapy as a corrective emotional experience that functioned to break up old reaction patterns. "In some cases," they wrote, "the development of a full-fledged transference neurosis may be desirable; in others it should perhaps be avoided altogether. In some it is imperative that emotional discharge and insight take place gradually; in others, with patients whose ego strength is greater, interviews with great emotional tension may be not only harmless but highly desirable. All this depends upon the needs of the patient in a particular phase of the therapeutic procedure." The modifications suggested were forms of psychoanalysis based on dynamic principles that attempt to secure a more harmonious environmental adjustment with enhanced development of one's capacities.

Frequent interviews over a long-term period, they insisted, had a regressive consequence often gratifying the patient's dependency needs. "The initial soothing effect of the prolonged outlook gradually becomes corruptive, and the therapist, faced with the task of driving the patient from his comfortable infantile position, realizes anew how difficult it is to force anyone to give up acquired rights." It was a fallacy, they contended, to assume that an analysis oriented around regressive material was more thorough than one focused on the immediate life conflict. Indeed, regressive material was usually a sign of neurotic withdrawal from a difficult life situation. It was the duty of the therapist to divert this retreat toward new attempts to solve problems from which the patient had fled in the past. Another disadvantage of too frequent sessions was that transference was not allowed to accumulate, being drained off in small quantities at each session, thus lessening the emotional participation. They advised manipulation of the frequency of sessions to intensify emotional reactions. A focus on the present helped reduce the evolvement of a transference neuroses and the substitution of transference gratifications for real-life experiences. Putting into practice what had been learned in therapy encouraged the bolstering of self-confidence and the overcoming of neurotic impairment. The patient during the course of his experimenting with new patterns was to be forewarned of failures and the need to analyze the reasons for these should they occur, thus turning them to advantage.

With the development of community mental health facilities and the servicing of increasing groups of patients by staffs depleted through shrinking budgets, the necessity of limiting time devoted to treatment without destroying its effectiveness has rekindled interest in the observations of Alexander and French. Moreover, restriction of payments to a designated number of sessions by insurance companies has forced even those therapists who by training and conviction are dedicated to long-term therapy to modify their tactics and to bring treatment to a halt within the confines of the alloted reimbursement term. Economics has thus had a corrosive effect on ideology, which is probably all to the good in a field where bias and opinion have frozen professionals to postulates that could never have been otherwise thawed out and revised.

The work of Alexander and French provided the foundation for other developing systems of dynamic short-term therapy and inspired a number of analysts who though loyal to the teachings of Freud refused to consider them as divine revelations (Marmor, 1979). While challenging classical analytic concepts, they vouchsafed the validity of the dynamic design. Among the best known of contemporary contributions to dynamic short-term therapy are the writings of Malan, Sifneos, and Mann.

In the study by Malan (1963) at the Tavistock Clinic in London, the patients treated were those who were able to explore their feelings and who gave the impression they could work with interpretive therapy. All of the therapists involved were psychoanalytically oriented and willing to employ an active interpretive technique. Sessions totaled from 10 to 40. It was possible, Malan wrote, under these conditions "to obtain quite far-reaching improvements not merely in symptoms, but also in neurotic behavior patterns in patients with relatively extensive and long standing neuroses." The best results were achieved when (1) the patient was highly motivated, (2) the therapist demonstrated high enthusiasm, (3) transference developed early, especially negative transference, and was interpreted, and (4) grief and anger became important issues as termination approached. The prognosis was also best where the patient and therapist showed a strong willingness to get involved—the former with an intense desire for help through understanding, the latter with sympathy while interacting objectively and not with countertransference. Even deep-seated neurotic behavior patterns could be lastingly changed. The technique if properly used carried few dangers, even where penetrating interpretations were made from dreams, fantasies, and the therapist-parent link of the transference that connected the present with childhood experiences. Malan modestly suggested that a crucial ingredient in change might not be the technique employed, but the nonspecific factor of the analyst applying himself enthusiastically to his technique irrespective of whether it was analytic or nonanalytic.

In a later study published in his book *Frontier of Brief Psychotherapy,* Malan (1976) confirmed his previous conclusions regarding the utility of dynamic short-term therapy and described some principles of selection of suitable patients for this form of treatment. In Malan's sample the patients were carefully screened. Chosen were those who appeared "to have the basic strength to stand up to uncovering psychotherapy," "who were responsive to interpretation," and who could help formulate a circumscribed focus around which therapy could be done. Severity of pathology or chronicity were not considered. Of all factors in prognosis, motivation for insight and the ability to focus on significant material seemed to be of primary importance. These were considered to be measures of successful interactions between patient and therapist. Patients who were excluded were alcoholics, homosexuals, drug addicts, those who had at one time made serious suicidal attempts, who had a period of long-term hospitalization, who had more than one course of ECT, who suffered from incapacitating chronic obsessional or phobic symptoms, and who were grossly destructive or self-destructive in acting-out. As was predicted, reasons for rejection were that the patient would have difficulty in making contact, that a great deal of work would be needed to develop proper motivation for therapy, that rigid and deep-seated issues required more work than the limited time could allow, that severe dependence and other unfavorable intense transference feelings would be too obstructive, or that depressive or psychotic disturbances might be precipitated or intensified.

Sifneos (1972), confirming many of Malan's findings, adds some other criteria of selection for this form of dynamic "anxiety-provoking" therapy that lasts from 2 to 12 months. Suitable patients are those who possess five qualities: (1) existence of above-average intelligence, (2) possession of at least one meaningful relationship in the past, (3) ability to interact with the initial interviewer while manifesting appropriate emotions and a degree of flexibility, (4) ability to identify a specific chief complaint, (5) willingness to understand oneself, to work on oneself, to recognize one's symptoms as psychological, to be honest in revealing things about oneself, to participate actively in therapy, and to make reasonable sacrifices (Sifneos, 1978).

For patients who are selected, sessions are held once weekly for 45 minutes in face-to-face interviews. The initial interview deals with history taking, particularly "a judicious confrontation by open-ended and forced-choice type of questions." As areas of conflict and maladaptive reactions open up, the therapist asks questions that will give him a clearer picture of the psychodynamics. He may then be able to make a connection between the underlying conflicts and the superficial complaints. Before long, transference feelings are apt to emerge. "The therapist must then confront the patient with his transference feelings and use them as the main psychotherapeutic tool." This facilitates tracing of one's emotional problems in the past and recognizing how conflicts give rise to one's symptoms. Sooner or later resistance appears. "The whole tone of the interviews start to change," silences appear, "the whole interview seems fragmented." Confrontation and clarification are employed as tools, but a transference neurosis is avoided. The patient must be confronted with his anger and his negative feelings, and these may flair up with the therapist's anxiety-provoking questions. Interpretations help clarify the patient's reactions. Awareness of his own countertransference is vital, and the therapist must make sure he is not using the patient to gratify his own needs. Repeatedly demonstrating how the patient deals with his conflicts and the adverse effects on him, the therapist acts as "an unemotionally involved teacher." Tangible evidence of progress is shown by the patient's ability to relate what is going on to past sources and by improvement in his interpersonal relationships. The therapist must work uninterruptedly toward termination, handling his countertransference and realizing that "there are certain behavior patterns which cannot be altered by psychotherapy." At a propitious time termination must be discussed. The patient's reactions such as anger, depression, and fear must be anticipated and handled.

The following outlines technical processes in Sifneos's technique:

1. The patient is asked to list in order of urgency the problems that he would like to overcome.
2. It is essential to develop a rapid therapeutic alliance with patient, since the patient's positive feelings toward therapist constitute a chief therapeutic tool. Agreement must be reached regarding the problem to be solved.
3. The therapist rapidly arrives at a tentative psychodynamics and the underlying emotional conflicts.
4. The focus in therapy is on these conflicts, the object being to help the patient learn new modes of solving difficulties.
5. The therapist must confront patient with anxiety-provoking questions, helping him to face and examine areas of difficulty rather than to avoid them, and enabling him to experience his conflicts and to consolidate new solutions for them.
6. If successful in reaching the goals set forth, the patient should be able to utilize his learning "to deal with the new critical situations in the future."

It must be remembered that the basis of Sifneos' approach was work with a clinic population of self-referred, relatively well-educated young people "who gave freely of their time and were eager to help." While these requirements are ideal, the average therapist will see a good number of less suitable patients urgently demanding symptom relief whose problems are linked to inner conflicts and who do not fulfill the selection requirements of Sifneos. They might still be considered for dynamic therapy, but anxiety-provoking tactics may have to be avoided.

Sifneos has not neglected consideration of other classes of patients not qualified for the anxiety-provoking technique but amenable to an "anxiety-suppressive" form of therapy. Such therapy is designed for patients with weak ego structures who habitually have poor interpersonal relations and are disposed to lifelong emotional difficulties. Here the goal is to dissipate anxiety by such tactics as reassurance, advice giving, emotional catharsis, environmental manipulation, persuasion, hospitalization, or medication. Where the patient has adequate motivation to receive help, recognizes that his symptoms are psychological, is able to maintain a job, and is willing to cooperate with the therapist, he has the best opportunity for relief. Sessions last from a few minutes to an hour and are spaced every week, twice a week, or oftener. Brief crisis supportive therapy lasts up to 2 months and is aimed at overcoming the emotional decompensation. Patients with serious difficulties, however, may require support for a prolonged period.

An interesting form of dynamic brief therapy has been detailed by Mann (1973). A few of the principles were originally described by Rank (1936, 1947). Stressing the subjective and objective meanings of time (e.g., separation, loss, death, etc.) both to the patient and therapist, Mann contends that ambiguity about time limitations of therapy may act as a deterrent to acceptance of reality and the work to be done. Patients, he avows, are bound to "child time," an unconscious yearning for eternity, and must be brought to the acceptance of realistic limited "adult time." He outlines a *fixed* 12 session form of treatment based on psychoanalytic concepts around which he has structured a methodology. "Experience has demonstrated that 12 treatment sessions is probably the minimal time required for a series of dynamic events to develop, flourish, and be available for discussion, examination, and resolution."

The limited interview is concerned with clarifying what the patient seeks from therapy. Two or more sessions may be required here. In the course of this inquiry "a formulation of the central conflict productive of the present manifestations of distress can be made . . . [the therapist] telling the patient what is wrong with him." This may or may not accord with the patient's incentive for seeking help. A delineation of other unconscious determinants is attempted by examining past sources of the central conflict. A diagnosis is made, and there is an assessment of the patient's general psychological state. There is then an estimate of how 12 hour sessions should be distributed: 12 full sessions once weekly, 24 half-hour sessions over 24 weeks, or 48 sessions of 15 minutes over 48 weeks. The therapist expresses to the patient his opinion of the patient's chief problem and what he believes should be done. He consults his calendar and announces the *exact* date of termination. He settles dates and times of appointments and discusses the fee. He assures the patient that if they find the chosen central issue erroneous, they will move on to another issue. The patient is then given the privilege to accept or reject the stated conditions. Assuming that the patient has sufficient ego strength to negotiate a treatment agreement and to tolerate a structured schedule, arrangements for therapy are concluded.

The interviews are conducted on as high an emotional level as possible, moving from adaptive issues to defenses to genetic origins of conflicts. This, of course, requires that the therapist be empathic and that he have a high degree of comprehension of dynamics. The choice of the central issue will vary with the therapist's understanding and experience. Since free association is impractical in short-term therapy, some other form of communication is needed. Mann recommends Felix Deutsch's "associative anamnesis" (Deutsch, 1949) as one way of working.

Even though a number of conflictual themes vary, a common one, "the recurring life crisis of separation-individuation is the substantive base upon which the treatment rests." Mastery of separation anxiety serves as a model for overcoming other neurotic anxieties. Among basic universal conflict situations that relate to the separation-individuation theme are (1) independence versus dependence, (2) activity versus passivity, (3) self-sufficiency versus inadequate self-esteem, and (4) "unresolved or delayed grief." Mastery of separation-individuation influences the mastery of all of the latter conflicts. During termination of therapy the patient will undergo a degree of anxiety reflective of the adequacy of his resolution of the separation-individuation phase of his early development. One or another of the four basic universal conflicts will be activated during the termination phase.

Mann advises not to compromise the 12-session time limit by making any promises to continue therapy after the allotted period has ended. In this way a fixed time structure is presented to the patient in which the drama of establishing a dependent relationship and of working through the crisis of separation and achievement of autonomy is repeated in a setting that permits a more satisfactory solution than the individual realized in his past early relationships. In other words, we are provided with two themes in therapy: the first, the central issue for which the patient seeks treatment, and the second, the more basic separation-individuation theme. The fact that we focus on an agreed area of investigation and that the patient possesses knowledge of imminent termination limits the extent of regression in the transference. The rapid mobilization of a positive transference in the first few sessions will bring symptom relief and an outpouring of material. Although the focus is on the central issue, the adaptive maneuvers of the patient and the genetic roots of the central issue will soon become apparent. The therapist, however, must resist the temptation to deviate from the central theme. At all times, the therapist is active in "supporting, encouraging, and educating the patient." This does not mean giving advice or guidance. About the seventh session the patient will begin to sense disappointment in therapy since he is not allowed to talk about all of the things he wants to bring up and must confine himself to the central issue. At this point negative transference will appear, and ambivalence replaces positive transference. Resistance rears its head, and symptoms may return. Despite these reactions the therapist must work toward termination. This will be difficult for both patient and therapist since the emotions of termination and separation (such as grief and anger) will be disconcerting. The patient will show many defenses against termination that will have to be handled.

Interpretation of the patient's reactions is important as the patient expresses his ambivalent feelings, the therapist enunciating the idea that the patient's responses are understandable since his expectations are not being fulfilled. Data from the patient's past will allow for a relating of the patient's reactions to early experiences with parental figures. The last three sessions at least should be devoted to dealing with the patient's feelings about termination.

As to selection of patients for this type of therapy, according to Mann, most patients are candidates except those with borderline or psychotic problems. Young people in a maturational crisis have difficulties "exquisitely related to the separation-individuation process." Regarding therapists who can work with this method, Mann says: "It is evident that this kind of psychotherapy requires a high degree of skill, knowledge, and experience. Knowledge of the psychoanalytic theories of mental functioning heavily buttressed by experience in the long-term treatment of patients is the first preparation for this treatment plan."

Another system of dynamic short-term therapy is described by Lewin (1970), who, following the lead of Bergler (1949), considers symptoms a consequence of psychic masochism, which is a universal ingredient of neuroses. The need to appease guilt through suffering, he avows, can prevent progress in therapy. "Ideally, the core of the patient's masochism, his bad introject, should be exposed and replaced, along with his sadistic conscience." While this may not always be possible, the least the therapist can do is to confront the patient with his masochism. Assigning all of his problems and symptoms to self-punishment for guilt feelings in relation to parental figures provides the patient with a focus that, according to Lewin, helps shorten the therapeutic process.

Eclectic Systems

Spurred on by community need, by strictures on the number of sessions financed by third-party payments, and by dissatisfaction with the results of long-term treatment, therapists of all denominations have experimented with briefer methods and contributed writings to short-term theory and practice. Some of the techniques are a revival of the methods employed in the preanalytic and early analytic period. Some are replicas of established casework and counseling procedures. Others are more innovative, being influenced by behavior therapy, by the contemporary emphasis on ego functions, by an increasing interest in problem solving as a primary means of enhancing adaptation, as well as by a resurgent flexible eclecticism (Grayson, 1979). Accordingly, a number of models of short-term therapy have been introduced, and some of these will be cited as examples. Other excellent models undoubtedly exist, but they cannot be included because of lack of space. An example of how florid the writings have become in short-term therapy is the annotated bibliography of Wells (1976), who in reviewing the literature up to 1974 details 243 citations covering major journals in psychiatry, psychology, and social work. These articles are categorized into theoretical and review articles, individual adult therapy, individual therapy of children and adolescents, group therapy, family therapy, marital therapy, and treatment of hospitalized patients.

In 1965 Bellak and Small wrote a book (the second edition of which appeared in 1978) that differentiated emergency from brief psychotherapy. They contend that emergency treatment is a temporary approach utilized in crisis, while brief psychotherapy is a "foreshortened application of traditional psychotherapy, called into being either by the life situation of the patient or by the setting in which treatment is offered." They offer a form of brief psychotherapy that is rooted in orthodox psychoanalytic theory and directed at symptoms or maladaptations, avoiding the reconstitution of personality that may, nevertheless, come about autonomously. Brief psychotherapy may stabilize the individual sufficiently so that "he may be enabled to continue with more extensive psychotherapy." The time span allotted for treatment is one to six sessions. A positive transference is fostered, free association avoided, and interpretation tempered, being coupled with other types of intervention like medical, environmental, etc. Brief therapy, they observe, is useful in nearly every kind of emotional disturbance, even psychosis. While extensive restructuring of the character is desired and possible, or where acting-out exists, however, it is not suitable.

A detailed history is essential with a complete exploration of the presenting problem, the precipitating factors, the contemporary life situation, and the developmental history, including family relationships. The object is to understand the present illness "in dynamic terms and related to preceding genetic, developmental, and cultural events." Out of this, some immediate therapeutic help may be rendered that can take the form of a minor interpretation. Psychotherapy is planned "within the framework of what the patient is willing to engage in," in contrast to the position taken by some therapists like Sifneos to the effect that "the patient must fit the treatment chosen for him by the expert." In Bellak and Small's method dreams may be elicited, projective testing like the Thematic Apperception Test used, and hypnosis employed to bring out repressed material. An attempt is made to establish causal factors in relation to precipitating incidents and specific historical events and structures. Judicious use of interpretation to impart insight, reassurance and support when necessary, counseling, guidance, conjoint family therapy, group therapy, drugs, electroconvulsive therapy (as in suicidal depressions), and environmental manipulation will call for a good deal of flexibility, diagnostic acumen, and clinical judgment on the part of the therapist. Emphasis in working-through is upon immediate learning. "The maintenance of the positive relationship," they state, "avoids a sense of rejection in the terminating process and permits the patient to retain the therapist as a benign, introjected figure." Treatment is ended by informing the patient that the therapist is available in the future when needed.

The literature is replete with descriptions of special techniques vaunted by the authors as uniquely effective for short-term therapy. Their enthusiasm is understandable because therapists become skilled in certain methods to which they are by personality, operational style, and theoretical bias attuned. Lest we become too rhapsodic over any set of methods, however, we must remember that while they may be effective in the hands of some, they may not be useful for all therapists. Matching patient and method is also a challenging problem (Burke et al, 1979). Except for a few syndromes, such as behavior therapy for phobias and pharmacotherapy for psychoses, outcome studies fail to credit any special interventions with global superiority over other approaches. Indeed, statistics indicate equivalent improvement rates for a host of available techniques. Nevertheless, a study of the various modalities in contemporary use is rewarding if no more than to provide us with models that may selectively be useful.

Among the most common techniques, in addition to those previously cited under dynamic therapies, are *interpretive methods* that draw their substance from classical (Freudian) and nonclassical (Adlerian, Stekelian, Rankian, Jungian, and Reichian) psychoanalysis as well as from *behavioral models.* The list that follows includes the more formal modalities currently in use:

1. *Autogenous training* (Crosa, 1967; Luthe, 1963; Schultz & Luthe, 1959).
2. *Behavioral models* (Ayllon & Azrin, 1968; Bandura, 1969; Crowe et al, 1972; Ferber et al, 1974; Ferster, 1964; Franks, 1964; Franks & Wilson, 1975; Ghadirian, 1971; Hand & LaMontagne, 1974; Hofmeister, 1979; Lazarus, 1976; Lick & Bootzin, 1970; Patterson, 1973a, 1973b, 1974; Richardson & Suinn, 1974; Stuart, 1969; Suinn et al, 1970; Wolpe, 1964).
3. *Bioenergetics* (Lowen, 1958; Palmer, 1971).
4. *Biofeedback* (Blanchard & Young, 1974; Glueck & Stroebel, 1975; Stroebel & Glueck, 1973).
5. *Casework therapy* (Kerns, 1970; Upham, 1973; Wattie, 1973; A. Wolberg, 1965).
6. *Cognitive learning* (Bakkar & Bakkar-Rabdau, 1973; Greene, 1975).
7. *Cognitive therapy* (Beck, 1971, 1976; Ellis, 1957, 1965, 1973; Glicken, 1968; Rush, 1978).
8. *Confrontation methods* (G. Adler & Buie, 1974; G. Adler & Myerson, 1973; Garner, 1970a, 1970b; Godbole & Falk, 1972; Kaswan & Love, 1969; Sifneos, 1972).
9. *Counseling methods* (Gross & Deridder, 1966).
10. *Dance and movement therapy* (Smallwood, 1974).
11. *Decision therapy* (Greenwald, 1974).
12. *Emotional catharsis* (Nichols, 1974).
13. *EST* (Kettle, 1976).
14. *Gestalt therapy* (Perls, 1969; A. C. Smith, 1976).
15. *Goal attainment scaling* (La Ferriere & Calsyn, 1978).
16. *Guided affective imagery* (Koch, 1969).
17. *Hypnosis* (Crasilneck & Hall, 1975; Frankel, 1973; Morra, 1967; Rabkin, 1977; Spiegel, 1970; Spiegel & Spiegel, 1978; Stein, 1972; Wolberg, 1948, 1964, 1965).
18. *Interpretive methods* (K. A. Adler, 1972; Ansbacher, 1972; Barten, 1971; D. Beck, 1968; Davanloo, 1978; Davanloo & Benoit, 1978; Gillman, 1965; M. Moreno, 1967; Small, 1971; Wahl, 1972).
19. *Mediation* (Carrington, 1977; Carrington & Ephron, 1975).
20. *Milieu therapy* (Becker & Goldberg, 1970; Clark, 1972; Goldberg, 1973; Knobloch, 1973; Raskin, 1971; Stainbrook, 1967; Visher & O'Sullivan, 1971; Wilkins, 1963).
21. *Multimodal therapy* (Lazarus, 1976).
22. *Persuasion* (Maltz, 1960).
23. *Primal therapy* (Janov, 1970).
24. *Programmed psychotherapy* (H. Young 1974).
25. *Psychoimagination therapy* (Shorr, 1972).
26. *Psychosynthesis* (Tien, 1972).
27. *Reality therapy* (Glasser, 1965; Glasser & Zunin, 1972).
28. *Relaxation* (Benson et al, 1974).
29. *Scream therapy* (Casriel, 1972).
30. *Sensitivity training* (Quaytman, 1969; Schutz, 1967).
31. *Social therapy* (Bierer, 1948; Fleischl & Wolf, 1967).
32. *Somatic therapy* (Dasberg & Van Praag, 1974; Hayworth, 1973; Hollister, 1970; Kalinowsky & Hippius, 1969; Ostow, 1962).
33. *Structural integration* (Rolf, 1958; Sperber et al, 1969).
34. *Symboldrama* (Leuner, 1969).
35. *Transactional analysis* (Brechenser, 1972; Hollensbe, 1976; Johnson & Chatowsky, 1969; Sharpe, 1976).
36. *Videotape playback* (Alger, 1972; Berger, 1970, 1971; Gonen, 1971; Melnick & Tims, 1974; Silk, 1972).

Less formal therapies have drawn on the following techniques:

1. *Buddhist Satipatthana,* or *"mindfulness meditation"* (Deatherage, 1975).
2. *Communication theory* (Kusnetzoff, 1974; R. C. Martin, 1968).

3. *Dream analysis* (Merrill & Cary, 1975).
4. *"Emotive - reconstructive psychotherapy" (ERP),* which combines the use of imagery with hyperventilation (Fulchiero, 1976; Morrison & Cometa, 1977).
5. *"Fischer-Hoffman process* (A. C. Smith, 1976).
6. *"Flomp method"* (Hagelin & Lazar, 1973).
7. *Morita therapy* (Reynolds, 1976).
8. *Naikan* (Ishida, 1969).
9. *"Paradoxical intention"* (Frankl, 1965, 1966).
10. *Social skills training* (Argyle et al, 1974).
11. *Social systems approaches* (Clark, 1972).
12. *Story telling* (De La Torre, 1972).
13. *Team systems approaches* (Dressler et al, 1975).
14. *"Therapeutic paradox" technique* (Fulchiero, 1976).

Special techniques have also been recommended for particular syndromes:

1. *Conversion reactions* (Dickes, 1974).
2. *Depressive reactions* (Campbell, 1974; Neu et al, 1978; Regan, 1965; Sokol, 1973).
3. *Hysterical personality disorders* (Seibovich, 1974).
4. *Obsessive-compulsive disorders* (Suess, 1972).
5. *Phobias* (Skynner, 1974).
6. *Psychosomatic conditions* (Mentzel, 1969; Meyer, 1978; Meyer & Beck, 1978).
7. *Sexual problems* (Kaplan, 1974; Levit, 1971; Mears, 1978; Springman, 1978).
8. *Smoking habits* (Marrone et al, 1970; H. Spiegel, 1970).
9. *Unresolved grief* (Volkan, 1971).
10. *Untoward reactions to physical illness* (E. H. Stein et al, 1969; Tuckman, 1970).
11. *War neuroses* (Pruch & Brody, 1946).

Moreover, selected interventions have been advised for specific categories of patients:

1. *Alcoholics* (Krimmel & Falkey, 1962).
2. *Dying patients* (Cramond, 1970).
3. *Geriatric patients* (Godbole et al, 1972; Goldfarb & Turner, 1953).
4. *University students* (Bragan, 1978; Killeen & Jacobs, 1976; Loreto, 1972; W. Miller, 1968).

The use of short-term approaches in primary care and medical settings has been described by Bleeker (1978), Budman et al (1979), Conroe et al (1978), and Kirchner et al (1978). Although not focused directly on short-term therapy, the contributions of Strupp (1972) and Frank (1973) to related aspects of treatment are noteworthy.

Short-Term Therapy in Outpatient Clinics

The urgency in many clinics to alter tactics of psychotherapy in line with the requirements of the patients being treated as well as the disposition of the community has resulted in the shifting from long-term treatment toward eclectic short-term programs. For example, at the Montreal General Hospital in Canada a change in the treatment philosophy away from the long-term objective of personality reconstruction was necessary for practical reasons: (1) because the kind of patient population the clinic dealt with was unable to utilize a prolonged therapeutic relationship and (2) because some of the therapists were not fittingly trained or were unable to spend a sufficiently long time to follow through with appropriate treatment measures (Davanloo, 1978; Straker, 1968). The result was a "high dropout rate or the rapid development of chronic clinic dependency." In addition, waiting lists became so great that acute emotional crises could not receive needed help. A brief psychotherapy program was started in 1961 based on psychodynamic formulations. Patients who did not qualify for the program received supporttive kinds of help, pharmacotherapy, social service assistance, ward care, and so on, according to their needs. With this pragmatic change the dropout rate decreased over five times, and staff interest and morale were greatly strengthened. Follow-up studies 2 years after intake revealed that 66 percent of the total case load had benefited sufficiently to need no further therapy. Patients selected for and treated with brief psychotherapy showed an 84 percent remission rate.

Largely through Davanloo's efforts three International Symposia were organized, in 1975, 1976, and 1977, bringing together professionals interested in brief approaches. Davanloo's methods resemble those of Sifneos and Malan. Evaluation criteria for dynamic therapy are, first, the assay of the ability to establish meaningful relationships based on the patient's having had previous emotional ties with other people. Even in the first interview the patient's capacity to interact with the therapist will be obvious. Second, there is an estimate of the ego's capacity to experience and tolerate anxiety that will be mobilized in the interview. Third, motivation for true change must be differentiated from a desire to satisfy an infantile need in therapy. Fourth, psychological mindedness and capacity for introspection are judged carefully. Fifth, the most crucial criterion is the patient's ability to respond constructively to interpretation during the evaluation interview. Sixth, the degree of intelligence is an important factor in the choice of approach. Seventh, the evaluator must determine the richness and flexibility of available defenses since these correlate with effective utilization of dynamic therapy. Davanloo is wedded to classical analytic formulations, such as the structural hypothesis, and frames his language in these terms. There is general agreement among most therapists with Davanloo's belief that selection of a psychotherapeutic focus is vital in short-term therapy and that "identification and understanding of the psychodynamics and psychological processes underlying the patient's psychological problems is the key issue in the evaluation process."

Other clinics that have remodeled the structure of their services along short-term lines also report an improved remission rate among patients and a heightened staff moral. The number of sessions devoted to treatment is considered arbitrary and has tended to cluster around lower limits, which in some studies have yielded results equal to treatment with numerically higher sessions. Errera et al (1967) compared the results of patients at the Yale-New Haven Medical Center Psychiatric Outpatient Clinic who were in therapy for from 6 to 10 sessions with a similar population who received 21 or more treatment sessions and found that "there was no significant difference in the improvement rates, neither as recorded by the therapists nor evaluated by the raters."

Lingering doubts as to the extent of help patients receive has been all but dissipated by the experience of clinics that have converted their services along short-term lines and conducted follow-up inquiries. At the Boston University Medical Center Psychiatric Clinic, for example, a study was conducted by Haskell et al (1969) as to what happened to patients after 12 weeks in short-term therapy. Significant changes were found in the group as a whole (about 71 percent) on five measures of depression, anxiety, and overall improvement. Even though it was felt "that the type of patient who responds to time-limited therapy differs markedly from the type who responds to long-term therapy," no clear-cut criteria were apparent.

Clinics associated with colleges have also noted excellent results with a small number of sessions (Miller, 1968; Speers, 1962; Whittington, 1962). Because college students are at an age level where problems in identity, resolution of dependency with emergence of autonomy, and firming of sexual role are being worked through, they are, as a group, bound to experience a good deal of stress. The presence of a facility that can offer them crisis-oriented psychological services can be extremely helpful in fostering a better adjustment. Experience indicates that relatively few sessions are necessary for the great majority of students. For example, a review of 3,000 students who applied for help at the City College of San Francisco showed that the average number of contacts was below three (Amada, 1977).

Walk-In Clinics and Crisis Intervention

The growth of community psychiatry has encouraged a multitude of short-term programs organized for purposes of crisis intervention and the dealing with emergencies (Annexton, 1978; Donovan et al, 1979; D. Goldstein, 1978; Robbins, 1978). Walk-in clinics that bring help to virtually thousands of people have sprouted throughout the country. An example is the Intake Reception Service at the Psychiatric Clinic of the Maimonides Medical Service in Brooklyn, N.Y., which functions as a walk-in clinic offering immediate help to anyone applying (Gelb & Allman, 1967). Four to eight individual sessions are given. If more therapy is needed, maximal use is made of group and family therapy. Professionals from different disciplines are used, including psychiatrists, psychologists, psychiatric social workers, and psychiatric nurses. An experienced therapist may be accompanied by a therapist in training, who participates as an observer. Thus the session operates as a training tool. Indications for referring a patient to a psychiatrist therapist are any of the following: (1) somatic symptoms, (2) mental illness in a patient who is dangerous to himself or others, (3) a need for medications, (4) history of attempted or threatened suicide, or (5) a special request for a psychiatrist. The approach utilized is dynamically oriented and is not considered, in the words of Gelb and Allman (1967) "an emergency shortcut or a poor substitute for an unattainable ideal but is, in itself, the most effective and human approach to our patients. . . ." Immediate, active, emphatic and accurate confrontation with neurotic functioning is more effective than "years of passive working-through." Patients who require more help after therapy ends are invited to return "anytime the need arises," but not on a continuing basis. This approach has resulted in a 60 percent improvement rate within five visits.

This improvement rate, that is about two-thirds of the patients receiving therapy, is substantiated by many other walk-in clinics (Gottschalk et al, 1967; Jacobson & Wilner, 1965). In a large study of over 8,000 patients treated on an emergency basis only 10 percent required continuing long-term therapy (Coleman & Zwerling, 1959). The value of short-term group crisis intervention has also been demonstrated. In a study of 78 cases receiving six group sessions compared with 90 control cases in unlimited groups or individual therapy, the short-term group cases demonstrated greater improvement on a 5-point scale of functioning (Trakas & Lloyd, 1971).

Walk-in clinics designed to provide immediate goal-limited help (Bellak, 1964; Coleman & Zwerling, 1959; Jacobson et al, 1965; Normand et al, 1967; Peck et al, 1966) generally concern themselves with crisis intervention and usually restrict the total number of sessions to six or less. Referral for more extended care is provided where necessary. Although the work-up done in different clinics will vary, it generally includes some dynamic formulation of the problem, an assay of existing ego strengths and weaknesses, and an estimate of the degree of pathogenicity of the current environment. Toward this end Normand et al (1967) have described a joint initial interview conducted by a psychiatrist–social worker team. Such a team maximizes the selection of an approach to the existing problem and outlines a blueprint for action. A working hypothesis is formulated attempting to relate intrapsychic and/or environmental aspects to the disturbed behavior or the symptoms, and it is around this hypothesis that choice of interventions is made from a wide range of supportive, educational, and insight-oriented approaches. Should no improvement occur, the working hypothesis is reformulated. This approach has proven itself to be practical "as an aid to providing high quality mental health services for the poor" in the face of even overwhelmingly impossible environmental deprivations. There is a feeling that patients from lower socioeconomic classes do better with short-term crisis intervention therapy than with any other approach (Haskell et al, 1969; Meyer et al, 1967; Sadock et al, 1968.)

Walk-in clinics thus provide a vital need in the practice of community psychiatry by making treatment immediately and easily accessible to all classes of patients. Many problems can be managed through this means that otherwise would go unattended. On the basis of an analysis of many interviews in the psychiatric walk-in clinic of the Massachusetts General Hospital in Boston, which handles about 40 walk-in patients each day (15,000 visits per year), Lazare et al (1972) have listed 14 categories of patients.

1. Patients who want a strong person to protect and control them. ("Please take over.")
2. Those who need someone who will help them maintain contact with reality. ("Help me know I am real.")
3. Those who feel so empty they need succorance. ("Care for me.")
4. Those who need some clinic or person around for security purposes though the contact be occasional. ("Always be there.")
5. Those ridden with guilt who seek to confess. ("Take away my guilt.")
6. Those who urgently need to talk things out. ("Let me get it off my chest.")
7. Those who desire advice on pressing issues. ("Tell me what to do.")
8. Those who seek to sort out their conflicting ideas. ("Help me put things in perspective.")
9. Those who truly have a desire for self-understanding and insight into their problems. ("I want psychotherapy.")
10. Those who see their discomfort as a medical problem that needs the ministrations of a physician. ("I need a physician.")
11. Those who really seek some practical help like disability assistance, legal aid, or other intercessions in their life situation. ("I need your legal powers.")
12. Those who credit their difficulty to ongoing current relationships and want the clinic to intercede. ("Do it for me.")
13. Those who want information as to where to get help to satisfy various needs, actually seeking some community resource. ("Tell me where I can get what I need.")
14. Nonmotivated or psychotic persons who are brought to the clinic against their will. ("I want nothing.")

Where the therapist is perceptive enough to recognize the patient's desire and where he is capable of gratifying or at least acknowledging that he understands the request, he will have been able to start a working relationship. Should he bypass the patient's immediate plea for help or probe for conflicts and other dynamic forces underlying the request, therapy may never get started. Obviously, fulfilling the patient's desire alone may not get to the bottom of the patient's troubles, but it will be an avenue through which one will be able to coordinate and utilize the data gathered in the diagnostic evaluating interview. In clinics or private therapy where there is lack of congruence between what the patient seeks and what the therapist decides to provide, the dropout rate after the first interview is as high as 50 percent (Borghi, 1968; Heine & Trosman, 1960).

The claim that short-term treatment accords with superficiality of goals has not been proven, especially where therapy is conducted along even modest dynamic lines. Thus, a type of crisis intervention that aims at more than symptom relief is described by M. R. Harris et al (1963), who treated a group of 43 patients with up to seven sessions with the objective of (1) resolution of the stress factor precipitating the request for help and (2) clarifying and resolving, if not the basic conflict, the secondary derivative conflicts activated by the current stress situation. "Our hypothesis is that such exploration and working through facilitated the establishment of a new adaptive balance." During therapy the motivation for further treatment was also evaluated. Thirty-eight (88 percent) of the patients were helped by brief therapy. Thirteen (30 percent) of the patients continued in long-term treatment. Three patients (7 percent) returned for a second brief series of contacts. During interviewing with this treatment, efforts were made to establish connections between conflicts and the precipitating stress since this enabled the patient to "be better able to cope with his distress and achieve a new psychic equilibrium." Historical material was utilized only when it was spontaneously brought up and related directly to the current difficulty. The authors declare that where long-standing vexations exist, motivation for further treatment "may in fact be increased by the experience of a successful brief therapeutic transaction." Adoption of a psychodynamic stance in crisis intervention can enhance the quality of results, as Louis (1966) and others have pointed out.

Of all devastating stressful experiences, the death of a loved one, or a person on whom the survivor is dependent, is perhaps the most mismanaged. Apart from token consolations, a conspiracy of silence smoulders under the assumption that time itself will heal all wounds. That time fails miserably in this task is evident by the high rate of morbidity and mortality among survivors following the fatal event (Kraus & Lilienfeld, 1959; Rees & Lutkins, 1967; M. Young et al, 1963).

Recognition of these facts has led to some crisis intervention programs to provide short-term help for the bereaved in the service of both prevention and rehabilitation (Gerber, 1969; Silver et al, 1957; P. R. Silverman, 1967). Success of these programs presages their further development and expansion. Gerber (1969) has described some methods for fostering emancipation from the bondage of grief and readjustment to present realities. These include (1) helping the client to put into words his or her feelings of suffering, pain, guilt, notions of abandonment and anger as well as the nature of the past relationship with the deceased, good and bad; (2) organizing a plan of activities that draws upon available resources and friends; (3) lending a hand in resolving practical difficulties involving housing, economic, legal, and family rearrangements; (4) making essential referrals for medical assistance including prescription of drugs for depression and insomnia and offering future assistance. Service to a bereaved person is often best recommended by the family physician, and such recommendations may be a requirement. An initial home visit by a social worker or other professional or trained paraprofessional may be necessary before the client will accept office visits.

Dealing with Unresponsive Patients

Despite our best efforts to shorten therapy there will be some patients who will need continuing treatment. Clinics only too often become clogged with such chronic patients whose treatment becomes interminable. This can result in long waiting lists and an end to ready access to therapy for even emergency problems. This is not to depreciate the value of prolonged treatment in some long-standing emotional problems. However, from a pragmatic standpoint, for the great majority of chronic patients other modes of management are not only helpful, but actually are more attuned to the continuing needs of these patients. Such alternative methods involve, perhaps for the remainder of a patient's life, occasional short (10- to 15-minute) visits with a professional person on a monthly or bimonthly basis, supervision of drug intake, introduction into a group (therapeutic, social, or rehabilitative), and utilization of appropriate community resources. What the therapist tries to avoid for such a patient is stimulating dependency on himself personally.

An eight-year experiment at an outpatient clinic dedicated to the therapy of the chronically ill at the University of Chicago Hospitals and Clinics is reported by Rada et al (1969). The clinic is open every Thursday afternoon for 2½ hours, patients being seen in order of arrival. Patients are accepted only after a diagnostic evaluation and initial work-up by the referral sources to make sure they will be suitable for the clinic routines. The staffing is by psychiatric residents, medical students, a social worker, receptionist, and two attending staff supervisory psychiatrists, the latter four being the only permanent staff. Upon arrival, the receptionist greets the patient—and if they come, the family—and brings the patient into the waiting room, where light refreshments (cookies and coffee) are served. Patient interactions are encouraged. Individual interviews are for 15 to 25 minutes to ascertain the present physical and emotional state, to regulate the drug intake if drugs are taken, to offer recommendations for intervening activities, and to make an appointment for the next time. The patients are then returned to the waiting area for more coffee and socialization. Family and couples therapy are done if necessary. Frequency of visits range from weekly sessions to once every 6 months although patients may return voluntarily if they need help. Should the patient drop out of therapy, he is permitted to return in times of stress without having to go through a readmission procedure. After the clinic hours the staff meets briefly (30 to 45 minutes) to discuss the day's problems. The two attending psychiatrists do not see individual patients (except in emergencies); they serve as administrative supervisors and active participants in the waiting area experience and the staff group meetings. Patients see the same therapist (a resident) for 3 months to a year and know that they will be transferred to another professional from time to time. Diagnostic categories vary, approximately half being psychotic, the remainder having severe neuroses and personality disorders. Fees generally support the clinic and are relatively low.

Short-term Hospitalization and Its Alternatives

Shrinking budgets have made it mandatory to take a hard look at costs versus benefits not only in regard to psychotherapy, but also protracted psychiatric hospitalization. Apart from pragmatic disadvantages or impracticalities of cost/benefits, prolonged institutionalization fosters regression and paralyzing dependencies—plus extended separation from community life. These unfortuante contingencies have sponsored shifts from long-term confinement to short-term detention organized around the objective of early discharge. Alternatives to hospitalization have also been explored. For example, in an experimental program Davis et al (1972) demonstrated that a team led by visiting nurses going to the homes of patients to oversee proper medication could prevent hospitalization and improve relationships within the family. Another example is the finding by Zwerling and Wilder (1962) that a day-care treatment facility could often act as an adequate substitute for an inpatient unit. There are, nevertheless, situations when hospitalization is essential, for example, to provide security for disturbed or suicidal patients or where crisis-oriented therapy is needed and it cannot be done on an outpatient basis. A limited hopsital stay may be all that is required. Even in children short-term hospitalization is sometimes considered (Shafii et al, 1979).

That it is possible to reduce the time of hospitalization of patients admitted to an institution through a crisis intervention program utilizing a wide range of treatment modalities has been demonstrated by Decker and Stubblebine (1972) in a 2½ year study of 315 young adults. At the Connecticut Mental Health Center a program of brief (3-day) intensive hospitalization and 30-day outpatient care has been used to deal with patients requiring hospitalization (Weisman et al, 1969). In the hospital, crisis intervention methods are employed toward restoring the patient to the previous level of functioning. On discharge there is a 1-month outpatient period of treatment, which is considered a follow-up measure. An agreement is made in advance as to this limited time arrangement to insure that treatment does not go on indefinitely. "One effect of the time-limited contract is to establish a 'set' which promotes rapid identification of problem areas and requires patients to begin quickly developing new modes of dealing with these problems." The patient is seen each day by several staff members who are usually nurses or aides in order to discharge dependence on the godlike figure of the doctor. To expose patients to different tactics, a fixed style of approach is deliberately not used. Team members also interact with patients in daily group therapy and family therapy. Self-reliance is stressed by focusing on the patient's responsibility, especially in making plans after discharge. While concern and interest are shown, "the staff avoids doing things for the patient which he can be encouraged to do himself." Psychotropic drugs are used to diminish target symptoms. There is early family involvement, and the entire hospital day is structured with activities. As for results, at the end of brief hospitalization of the first 100 patients, 18 percent were transferred for longer inpatient care after the 3-day intensive experience since they required longer term hospitalization. Another 19 percent were rehospitalized within 1 year of discharge. At the 1-year follow-up routine almost two-thirds of all patients had not been rehospitalized or transferred after the 3-day intensive hospital treatment. This compares favorably with rehospitalization rates with longer term therapy.

The function of the usual short-term hospitalization (i.e., 3 to 4 weeks) is, first, to bring about a rapid remission of symptoms and, second, to prepare the patient for, and to see that there is made available, an adequate aftercare program. The first objective is accomplished by drug therapy and ECT if necessary, individual family and group treatment, and milieu, occupational, and rehabilitative therapy, all tailored to the patient's needs. Because of the emphasis on the control of symptoms rather than alterations in the personality structure, crisis-oriented behavioral approaches along eclectic lines are most commonly practiced. Ideally, brief hospitalization should provide psychotherapy to prepare the patient for outpatient care (A. B. Lewis, 1973). The second objective, although most crucial to avoid the revolving door syndrome, is too often neglected. Unless the posthospital environment is regulated, ensuing stress will almost inevitably produce a relapse in symptoms. Among the measures necessary to prevent this are the adjustment of living arrangements so that the least strain is imposed on the patient's coping capacities, the use of halfway houses, facilities providing day and night care, supervised drug management, and rehabilitative, social, health, and recreational programs. The selective use of community outpatient psychotherapy of a not too intensive variety with an empathic therapist can be most helpful.

To safeguard against the fragmentation of an aftercare program, continuity of treatment with one professional person can help prevent treatment degenerating into management of a series of emergencies with inevitable rehospitalization. This person must have established a relationship with the patient and know the history of the latter's illness and something about the dynamics. What causes most patients to return to the hospital is poor aftercare planning with little or no provision for some kind of ongoing individual or group psychotherapy, improper monitoring of drug maintenance, failure to utilize emergency measures when needed (such as ECT), stressful living conditions, poor housing and inadequate provision of essential social and rehabilitative services. Where possible, the therapist who has worked with the patient in the hospital should be the one who continues seeing the patient and directing the aftercare program. Sometimes the hospital may provide some of the aftercare services, but the administrators should always strive to integrate the patient into the community as rapidly as possible. This is usually the best course. Where return to a family would be disturbing—for instance, where members are too hostile, demanding, and rejecting—placement in a halfway house and later in a foster home may be advisable.

Short-term hospitalization does not eliminate intermediate-term intensive treatment in a hospital, that is, 130 to 180 days, or for longer periods where the aim is a personality change. However, custodial care in patients who require continuing management can usually be achieved outside of a hospital facility. Wayne (1976) has appropriately pointed out that what determines the *duration* of hospitalization is not the diagnosis but the persistence of a habitual disruptive life-style, severe family, social, and occupational difficulties, and the presence of a serious physical disability or hypochondriasis. Where the proper environment is made available and aftercare supervision promoted, even chronic psychotic persons can make an adjustment outside of an institution.

There is evidence that short-term family therapy can cut down the need for hospitalization in acute cases of decompensation. To compare the outcome of outpatient family crisis therapy with hospitalization, Flomenhaft et al (1969) treated with the former modality 186 patients in need of admission to a mental hospital. A control group of 150 patients received hospitalization. The outpatients received an average of five office visits, one home visit, and three telephone contacts. The results of outpatient therapy were at least as good as hospitalization, in addition to being more economical and less stigmatizing. In a study by Langsley et al (1969) 75 acute decompensated psychiatric patients were given an average of six sessions of family crisis therapy organized along directive and supportive lines. A control group of 75 received hospitalization and inpatient treatment. In the family therapy group 61 patients were able to avoid hospitalization and only 14 patients required hospitalization within a 6-month period. In the hospitalization group 16 patients required rehospitalization after discharge within a 6-month period. Only an average of 8.1 days were required for improvement in the experimental group as compared to 24.3 days in the hospitalized group. Two years later a similar study was repeated with a larger group of patients. It confirmed that most patients with short-term family therapy could avoid hospitalization (Langsley et al, 1971). At the Eastern Pennsylvania Psychiatric Institute these studies were replicated, indicating the efficiency of short-term family therapy (Rubenstein, 1972). Focal therapy in a day hospital may also be employed as an alternative treatment (Frances et al, 1979).

Short-term Child and Adolescent Therapy

The question is often asked as to whether it is possible to do child therapy on a short-term basis since it is generally accepted that a long period of treatment of the child patient and parents is customary. There are some studies however, that indicate that good results may be obtained with short-term approaches (Cramer, 1974; Kerns, 1970; Martin, 1967; Negele, 1976; Nicol, 1979; Phillips & Johnston, 1954; Rosenthal & Levine, 1970, 1971; Shaw et al, 1968; Skynner, 1974). Other studies verify the utility of short-term group training for parents in managing problems in their children (G. R. Patterson et al, 1973a; Walter & Gilmore, 1973; Wiltz & Patterson, 1974). Many therapists believe that where the child is under 7 years of age the main therapeutic work is with the parents. From ages 7 to 11 the child and parents are seen separately. From 12 on family sessions seem best. Preadolescent children with acute problems have been materially helped by parent groups focused on discussions of child management, power ploys of children, and alternate approaches to problem solving. The children themselves are encouraged to experiment with more mature behavior through better ways of coping with people and situations (Epstein, 1976).

Utilizing a so-called "health" model, Weinberger (1971) describes a form of brief therapy for children "which sees clients basically coping and adapting but experiencing problems caused by ignorance, inappropriate expectations, social surroundings, or other factors which do not implicate the parents as malevolent and pathologically motivated." This is seen as a preferred therapy for the majority of children in contrast to the prevailing model of short-term treatment, which is either a compression of long-term treatment methods or an elongated diagnostic procedure that is appropriate for only 5 to 10 percent of all chidren sent for help.

As part of the therapeutic process, Weinberger states that it is important to try to ascertain how parents view the child's problem and what their expectations are of the therapist. This leads to the drawing up of a verbal "contract" of what the parents and therapist expect of each other. Usually the goal is the elimination of undesired behavior. The time limit set is 6 weeks during which a maximum of 12 sessions are arranged for the child and other family members. The child generally is ignorant of why he is actually seeing the therapist, has little real notion of his underlying problem, and no motivation to do anything about it. Should the child be aware that he is seeing a "doctor," he may regard this as punishment for his crimes while believing that the "doctor" expects him to change in accord with the wishes of his parents. If, on the other hand, the child is cognizant of his problem, he may rationalize it as a justified consequence of unfair demands and acts by his parents and others. It may be essential in order to secure cooperation with the treatment plan to work with the child until he verbalizes a problem on which he would like to concentrate.

One way of focusing on the problem in the event the child seems ignorant of it is to confront the child with what others say about him and to handle his reactions to the confrontation. Why does he believe he is seeing the therapist? Once the child admits to a behavioral deviation, other ways of reacting are suggested to him. Any distorted way the child conducts himself with the therapist may be an important means of bringing to his attention how he behaves, how other people may be affected by his behavior, and how he himself suffers the consequences of their reactions. These comments are made without anger, disgust, accusation, or threats of recrimination, providing the child with a different experience in relation to an authority figure. Concurrently, the therapist may work with the parents or see the patient together with other members of the family in family therapy. In conference with the parents it is important to alleviate their guilt, to try to clarify what is happening in their relation to the child, to explain unreasonable expectations and developmental norms, and to suggest alternative ways of dealing with the child's behavior. The extent of directiveness of the therapist will vary with the willingness and ability of the parents to make proper decisions on their own.

The plan of action and how it is carried out by the child and parents is monitored by the therapist in the remaining sessions, the plan itself being modified or discarded and a new one substituted depending on the progress that is being made. "A major part of this working through is to help the parents not only recognize and accept their own and their child's limitations, but to set more realistic goals for themselves as parents, and their child as a child with a unique life style of his own which must be understood, respected, and not enmeshed in their own needs and problems" (Weinberger, 1971). Based on 5 years' experience in the clinic with about 3,000 cases, Weinberger estimates that 50 percent of all children can be handled in brief therapy. More extensive therapy is required by 30 percent, and help other than psychotherapy (special classes, residential placement, etc.) is required by 20 percent.

Short-term Group Approaches

Manpower shortages reinforced by the factor of cost/benefit have accelerated the use of short-term group therapy, both for hospitalized persons and outpatients. Many group programs have accordingly been introduced, utilizing techniques that draw their substance from psychoanalysis, behavior therapy, cognitive therapy, guided imagery or any other theoretical school to which the therapists are dedicated.

1. *Crisis intervention groups* (Berlin, 1970; Crary, 1968; Donovan et al, 1979; Morley & Brown, 1969; Strickler & Allgeyer, 1967; Trakas & Lloyd, 1971).
2. *Experiential groups* (Back, 1972; Burton, 1969; Elmore & Saunders, 1972; Lewis & Mider, 1973; Perls, 1969; Rabin, 1971).
3. *Educational groups* (Druck, 1978).
4. *Behavioral groups* (Aronson, 1974; Fensterheim, 1971; Lazarus, 1968; Liberman, 1970; Meachem & Wiesen, 1969; Suinn et al, 1970; Wolpe, 1964).
5. *Inspirational groups* (Dean, 1970–1971; Greenblatt, 1975; Herschelman & Freundlich, 1972).
6. *Psychodramatic groups* (Corsini, 1966; Moreno, 1966).
7. *Transactional groups* (Berne, 1964; T. Harris, 1967; Karpman, 1972).
8. *Accelerated short-term groups* (Wolf, 1965).

Between 1947 and 1962 over a hundred papers were published on just the last category, (A. Wolf, 1965) and since then more have accumulated.

Short-term groups are usually open-ended and frequently conducted by cotherapists (Goolishian, 1962; Sadock et al, 1968; Shrader et al, 1969; Trakas & Lloyd, 1971. Outcome studies on groups report highly successful results, in some instances being considered as more effective than individual therapy (Trakas & Lloyd, 1971). The uses and abuses of groups are described by Imber et al (1979).

Short-term groups with children have been gaining popularity (Graham, 1976; Rosenthal & Levine 1970), some reports claiming successes equal to that in long-term therapy (Rosenthal & Levine, 1971). An example is the study by Burdon and Neely (1966) who treated 55 boys with repeated school failures. A 5-year follow-up showed increased school attendance with 98 percent passing and 73 percent earning promotions. Some useful methods for working with children in groups have been outlined by Rhodes (1973), Epstein (1976), and Levin & Rivelis (1970). Short-term group treatment may also be helpful for maladjusted adolescents (Eisenberg, 1975; Rivera & Battaggia, 1967), during brief inpatient care for adolescents (Chiles & Sanger, 1977; Moser, 1975), for delinquent adolescents (Danner & Gamson, 1968), adolescent drug users (Deeths, 1970), and youthful offenders in a detention unit (Would & Reed, 1974). The need to distinguish between adolescents whose problems are the product of entanglements related to the developmental process and those whose encounter with adolescence stirs up unresolved conflicts of earlier stages of growth will influence techniques and objectives (Sprince, 1968).

Group work with parents of problem children has also proven rewarding (Epstein, 1970; Maizlish & Hurley, 1963; Tracey, 1970), the training of parents in behavioral methods being especially popular as an effective intervention method (Bijou & Redd, 1975; Ferber et al, 1974; Patterson, 1973a, 1973b, 1974; Walter & Gilmore, 1973). One of the most difficult situations for the therapist is the unmotivated family of children with aggressive behavior disorders. A pilot study at the University of Chicago School of Medicine by Safer (1966) describes work with 29 such parents whose children ranged in age from 4 to 16. Family, conjoint and individual sessions produced improvement in most children, and this was maintained in follow-up evaluations after 4 to 16 months. The areas of change brought about by therapy in families with delinquent adolescents has exposed some interesting findings. For example, Parsons and Alexander (1973) discovered that one could utilize in studies four interaction measures that were not a function of extraneous variables.

Marital therapy is also often conducted on a short-term basis both in groups (Leiblum & Rosen, 1979; Wells, 1975) and with individual couples (Bellville et al, 1969; Fitzgerald, 1969; Kalina, 1974; P. A. Martin & Bird, 1963; P. A. Martin & Lief, 1973; Sager et al, 1968; Satir, 1965; Simon, 1978; Watzlawick et al, 1967).

An interesting model is described by Verhulst (1975). He has evolved an intensive 3-week approach resembling cognitive learning (Bakker & Bakker-Rabdau, 1973) that emphasizes confrontation and problem solving with the help of active, enthusiastic, facilitative therapists. Other methods are outlined elsewhere (Wolberg, 1977, pp. 733–740).

A number of reports have indicated that short-term marital therapy is at least as effective in dealing with marital conflict as long-term therapy. Gurman (1975) reviewed available data and found that a 76 percent improvement rate was achieved with an average of about 16 sessions. Review studies by Barten (1969), Reid and Epstein (1972); and Reid and Shyne (1969) confirm these positive results. Ratings at termination and at an average of 2½ years later of 49 couples who were involved in conjoint marital therapy (a comparison of these with reported results of outcome studies on individual short-term psychotherapy as well as with another form of conjoint therapy and with psychoanalysis) indicate that the conjoint approach has some technical advantages over and compares favorably with these other types of treatment (Fitzgerald, 1969).

Short-term family therapy continues to grow in popularity. Its techniques are described by Bartoletti (1969a, 1969b), Bloch (1973), Deutsch (1966), Eisler and Herson (1973), Haley and Hoffman (1967), Langsley and Kaplan (1968), Pittman et al (1966), Satir (1964a), and Watzlawick (1963). The number of sessions that are optimal for family therapy is dealt with in experimental evaluations by Stuart and Tripodi (1973). They randomly assigned 73 families with predelinquent and delinquent adolescents to 15-, 45-, and 90-day behaviorally oriented treatments. Outcome measures showed no difference between the groups. Thus it was concluded that there is no reason to choose longer over shorter family treatments. The idea that brief family therapy yields superficial results is challenged by Haug (1971), who describes a case where ego alteration coincided closely with rapid and persisting alterations in the body image. However, where the adaptive flexibility of parents is blocked by rigid defenses or the conflict in the child is markedly internalized, traditional longer term psychotherapeutic methods are probably more suitable (Haug, 1971).

The combination of group and family therapy appears to possess some advantages, as Kimbro et al (1967) and Durell (1969) have pointed out in their report of a pilot study of time-limited multiple family therapy with disturbed adolescents and their families. Groups of three families met with a therapist for weekly meetings. This design is being utilized more and more and Laqueur (1968, 1972) has written extensively on the rationale and process of bringing problem families from the same background together as a way of expediting treatment.

Massing Therapy Sessions

Attempts have also been made to study the effect of massing therapy sessions by literally immersing the patient in treatment throughout the day. Thus Swenson and Martin (1976) treated patients on a full-time basis for 3 weeks with combinations of different modalities that they considered complemented each other. Assessing the program on 335 patients at the time of discharge revealed significant improvement in the presenting symptoms, work capacities, interpersonal relationships, and general level of comfort. A follow-up study showed that this improvement was retained.

"Massed time-limit" therapy sessions for as long as 10 hours consecutively have been given (Berenbaum et al, 1969). A form of this therapy—"multiple impact therapy"—that has proven successful is described by MacGregor (1962). Goolishian (1962) employed the technique with 60 families and their problem adolescents. A team consisting of a psychiatrist, a psychologist, and a social worker met three times with the families for all-day sessions. Group and individual therapy focused on major dynamics and self-rehabilitation. Results were considered at least comparable to conventional psychotherapy.

Marathon group sessions (Bach, 1966, 1967 a–d; Casriel & Deitch, 1968; Teicher et al, 1974; Vernallis et al, 1970, 1972) while not as popular as in previous years continue to have their advocates.

Conclusion

Somehow, short-term therapy has acquired the reputation of being a substandard approach in which quality of results is sacrificed on the altar of expediency. Superficiality of goals, uncertainty of results, substitution of symptoms, and a general glossing over of effects are said to be inevitable. These ideas have proven grossly inaccurate. There is ample evidence from the reported clinical experiences with short-term therapy that it has a utility not only as an economic expedient, but also as a preferred form of psychiatric treatment. Whatever controlled research studies exist, these substantiate its value in individual therapy with adults, adolescents and children, as well as in group, family and marital therapy. A number of models of short-term therapy have evolved from which techniques may selectively be adapted to the working styles of psychotherapists trained in the various theoretical orientations.

The actual models in use are usually conditioned by the experience and theoretical orientation of the practicing professionals and the policies of the agencies, if any, under whose supervision the work is being done. The shortcomings of some of these systems is that they tend to be monolithic, circumventing factors related to the specific complaint and to such elements as the stage of the patient's readiness for change and preferred learning patterns. Not all persons are capable of utilizing the techniques that are offered. This is not extraordinary since patients generally harmonize with some interventions and not with others. Some do well with a cognitive approach in which they can absorb abstract concepts and insights that help them to alter their singular thinking patterns. Others fail to benefit from such tactics. They do better with behavioral techniques, experimenting with different modes of action, solidifying successful ones though reinforcements. Still others learn by modeling themselves after an admired authority, generally the therapist, bestowing on him virtues he may or may not possess. An effective short-term therapist is one who discerns the needs and learning proclivities of each patient and is flexible enough to alter his methods as he goes along.

Rigid therapists doggedly follow a set agenda into which they wedge all patients with little room for eclectic maneuvering. Yet one hardly ever sees a patient who could not utilize some of the effective interventions of different systems at successive stages of their treatment. Thus a therapist may with the same patient be active at some times and passive at others; he may selectively employ confrontation, reassurance, or suggestive or persuasive techniques. If familiar with the methods, he may utilize role playing, psychodrama, relaxation, hypnosis, family therapy, group therapy, milieu therapy, systematic densensitization, assertive training, and other behavioral techniques when necessary. He may employ psychotropic drugs when symptoms block effective learning. He may utilize the lessons learned from psychoanalysis that help expose and resolve unconscious resistances, particularly transference and acting-out. Obviously for best results the therapist must be highly selective about the modalities he uses so that he does not swamp the patient with unnecessary activity. All therapists cannot be expert in, or even aware of, every available technique that exists. But sufficient flexibility should prevail to prevent a stalemate when the patient fails to respond to the method that the therapist is applying at the moment.

The fact that the various short-term therapies in the hands of competent therapists do bring about relief or cure indicates that the particular techniques and stratagems employed are not the only important elements responsible for improvement. The proposition is inviting that therapeutic maneuvers merely act as a means of communication through which the therapist encourages the emergence of positive, and the resolution of negative, healing elements (Marmor, 1966). If a therapist feels most comfortable with a more active approach than with a less active one, with hypnosis rather than formal interviewing, with behavior therapy rather than analytically oriented therapy, he will probably be able to help more patients than were he to force himself to use a procedure with which he is not at ease or about which he is not enthusiastic. This is not to depreciate the virtues of any of the existing models and techniques. However, we do tend to overemphasize technical virtuosity while minimizing the vital healing processes that emerge in the course of the helping relationship as a human experience.

CHAPTER 2

A Rationale for Dynamic Short-term Therapy

Short-term therapy generally has three goals: (1) modifying or removing the symptom complaint for which help is being sought, which is the immediate objective, (2) producing some corrective influence on the individual's general adjustment, and (3) initiating essential alterations in the personality structure. With properly conducted treatment we may anticipate substantial or complete symptom relief as well as some modification for the better of behavioral coping. However, we may scarcely have broken ground on the third goal of personality reconstruction. We may hope, nevertheless, that the experience of treatment will have set into motion a process following therapy that over a long-term period will result in true character permutations. That such changes do occur has been demonstrated in follow-up studies of patients who have received appropriate professional help over a brief span. Though not anticipated, significant and lasting changes in the self-image and the quality of interpersonal relationships have been noted.

When we review the many systems of short-term therapy that address themselves to the goal of personality reconstruction, we find that the majority acknowledge the operation of unconscious conflict, along with the conditioning of faulty habit responses, as a source of the neurotic process. In dynamic forms of therapy a prime objective is helping the patient acquire greater knowledge of oneself including one's hidden motives. A question is whether the kind of treatment being employed can lend itself to the achievement of this objective.

Categories of Short-term Therapy

Throughout the literature one finds a tendency to subdivide short-term therapy into three distinctive categories: (1) crisis intervention, (2) supportive-educational short-term therapy, and (3) dynamic short-term therapy. The goals of crisis intervention usually differ from those in the other brief methods. Here, after from 1 to 6 sessions, an attempt is made to restore habitual balances in the existing life situation. Supportive-educational approaches, such as behavior therapy, constitute forms of intervention that are undertaken, along with educational indoctrination, to relieve or remove symptoms, to alter family habit patterns, and to rectify behavioral deficits. To attain these objectives, a variety of eclectic techniques are implemented, depending on the idosyncratic needs of the patient and the skills and methodological preferences of the therapist. The number of sessions varies, ranging from 6 to 25. In dynamic short-term therapy the thrust is toward achieving or at least starting a process of personality reconstruction. Sessions here may extend to 40 or more.

Some forms of crisis intervention that are being practiced are indistinguishable from the kind of counseling commonly done in social agencies. The focus is on mobilizing positive forces in the individual to cope with the crisis situation, to resolve remediable environmental difficulties as rapidly as possible, utilizing if necessary appropriate resources in the community, and to take whatever steps are essential to forestall future crises of a similar or related nature. No attempt is made at diagnosis or psychodynamic formulation. Other kinds of crisis intervention attempt provisionally to detect underlying intrapsychic issues and past formative experiences and to relate these to current problems. More extensive goals than mere emotional stabilization are sought.

The "social-counseling" forms of crisis intervention are generally employed in walk-in clinics and crisis centers where large numbers of clients apply for help and where there is a need to avoid getting involved too intimately with clients who might get locked into a dependent relationship. Visits are as frequent as can be arranged and are necessary during the first 4 to 6 weeks. The family is often involved in some of the interviews, and home visits may have to be made. The interview focus is on the present situational difficulty and often is concerned with the most adaptive ways of coping with immediate pressing problems. Vigorous educational measures are sometimes exploited to activate the patient. The employment of supportive measures and the use of other helping individuals and agencies is encouraged. The second, more ambitious, goal-directed forms of crisis intervention are often seen operating in outpatient clinics and private practice. If the assigned number of sessions have been exhausted and the patient still requires more help, referral to a clinic or private therapist or continued treatment with the same therapist is considered.

Brief supportive-educational approaches have sponsored a variety of techniques, such as traditional interviewing, behavior therapy, relaxation, hypnosis, biofeedback, somatic therapy, Gestalt therapy, sex therapy, group therapy, etc., singly or in combination. The number of sessions will vary according to the individual therapist, who usually anchors his decision on how long it takes to control symptoms and enhance adaptation.

The philosophy that enjoins therapists to employ dynamic short-term treatment is the conviction that many of the derivatives of present behaviors are rooted in needs, conflicts, and defenses that reach into the past, often as far back as early childhood. Some of the most offensive of these components are unconscious, and while they obtrude themselves in officious and often destructive ways, they are usually rationalized and shielded with a tenacity that is frustrating both to the victim and to those around him. The only way, according to prevailing theories, that one can bring these mischief makers under control is to propel them into consciousness so that the patient realizes what he is up against. By studying how the patient utilizes the relationship with him, the therapist has an opportunity to detect how these buried aberrations operate, projected as they are into the treatment situation. Dreams, fantasies, verbal associations, nonverbal behavior, and transference manifestations are considered appropriate media for exploration because they embody unconscious needs and conflicts in a symbolic form. By his training, the therapist believes himself capable of decoding these symbols. Since important unconscious determinants shape one's everyday behavior, the therapist tries to establish a connection between the patient's present personality in operation, such as temperament, moods, morals and manners, with early past experiences and conditionings in order to help the patient acquire some insight into how problems originated.

Universality of Dynamic Principles

The subdivisions of short-term treatment that have been described—namely, crisis intervention, supportive-educational short-term therapy, and dynamic short-term therapy—are artificial. In practice their boundaries become diffuse. Because patients respond selectively to different techniques, effective therapists in all three categories of treatment will vary their interventions according to the immediate problems and needs of their patients. Moreover, because all operate within the matrix of a relationship that develops between patients and therapists, underlying personality problems and conflicts will surface during therapy and yield vitally significant dynamic material for examination. What the therapist does with the material the patient brings up during interviews can affect the outcome of treatment. *Indeed the techniques and interventions used by the therapist to influence the patient's symptoms may be less important than the fantasies and behavioral responses they evoke in the patient.* For example, some manifestations reflect projections of past fears and desires in relation to early authority figures. These, if undetected or disregarded, may effectively block therapeutic progress. Such transference resistances are extremely common and are probably the chief reason for failures in therapy. Frequently they are apparent only in nonverbal behavior, dreams, fantasies, and insidious acting-out away from the therapist's office. *This is why a dynamic approach, during which the reactions of patients to the therapist and to the pervailing techniques, constantly assessed and taken into consideration, can prove useful in all forms of short-term therapy.* While the interview focus may be on symptoms, environmental distortions, and other complaint factors, the real therapeutic work will be organized around personality reactions and conflicts mobilized by the maneuvers of the therapist.

A man with emphysema who came to therapy requesting hypnosis to eliminate his smoking habit was exposed to my usual induction method. A technique that I customarily employ is to ask the patient to lift his left index finger when he experiences certain things that I suggest to him, for example, a fantasying of certain scenes. At the suggestion that he picture himself walking along the street and that he lift his left finger (which I touched) as soon as the image came to him, the patient instead lifted his right finger. He also resisted suggestions that his left arm would become so stiff and heavy that he could not move it. On the contrary, he spontaneously waved his arm in the air. On termination of the induction, I humorously pointed out these facts and speculated that his negating of my suggestions was probably an expression of oppositional tendencies. Said I, smiling, "Could you be an oppositional character who won't allow himself to be pushed around?" His immediate response was to laugh heartily and to say that people considered him a "stubborn cuss." It required no great effort to connect his oppositional behavior with a childhood pattern of asserting himself with his parents and older siblings by displaying negativism and sometimes violence to avoid what he considered being dominated and crushed. I commented that I certainly was *not* his parent, but that he might react to me and to what I was doing for him as if I was somebody who wanted to dominate and crush him. He could easily block himself by such an attitude from benefiting from treatment. My statement seemed like a revelation to him. He speculated that this was probably why his previous psychotherapeutic effort with another therapist had failed. He never could understand why he would have flashes of anger toward the therapist and would sometimes mumble to himself after he left the therapist's office, "I won't let that son-of-a-bitch brainwash me." He felt so ashamed of these reactions that he had concealed them from his therapist, who failed to pick up the transference resistance. By anticipating his transference reaction, I was able to secure his cooperation and to achieve a good result in treatment.

Had I not utilized hypnosis but just an ordinary interviewing technique or behavior therapy, the patient would undoubtedly have revealed his oppositional tendencies *were I to look for them*—if not in his behavior, then in dreams and other representations. The principle that I am trying to illustrate is that the therapeutic tactics employed, while aimed at relieving the immediate crisis situation or symptomatic upset, will usually set into motion customary resistances and defensive operations that may then be closely examined and worked through, if possible, as a means of inculcating essential insights. In other words, even though the methods may be nonanalytic, the patient's reactions to them and to the therapist become an important exploratory focus, if no more than to deal with obstructive transference and other barriers to change. Personality modifications eventually may evolve from this as a serendipitous dividend, one that may continue in a propitious environment for an indefinite time and ultimately become a permanent change.

It would seem prudent, obviously, in view of the great demand for services from the relatively small cadre of available trained therapists, that, at the start, at least, short-term therapy should practically be geared toward goals of optimal functioning. Hopefully, however, even a brief exposure to therapy will uncover fundamental personality conflicts, which the therapist, if he deems the patient prepared to scrutinize them, may carefully bring to the patient's attention with the object of inviting reconstructive change should the patient truly desire to move ahead in his development.

We must not expect to accomplish miracles with dynamic short-term procedures, even when executed with perfection. At the end of the formal brief treatment period we usually observe some alteration of the patient's symptoms, an alleviation of suffering, and a certain degree of behavioral correction. If we have diligently searched for them, we will have recognized fundamental character problems that are likely to create difficulties in the future, and during the treatment we may have been able to start the patient on a productive path toward altering self-defeating personality patterns. Unfortunately, the latter objective is avoided by some therapists. In my opinion, in most cases, this is because the therapist writes it off as unattainable and hence does not apply himself to its accomplishment. To repeat, we cannot expect too radical a personality reorganization within the limited treatment period. The most to be hoped for is the initiation of sufficient self-understanding to challenge some values and defenses and to encourage experimentation with new and more constructive ways of relating to others and to the self. In this way a chain reaction may be set off, continuing for months and even years after the treatment period, that will hopefully lead ultimately to extensive personality change. That such far-reaching results are achievable in an impressive number of patients is the finding among many therapists who have applied themselves to a dynamic approach in a disciplined way. They attained success because they found and worked on a specific important focus during the treatment.

Dealing with Unconscious Determinants

In patients with intact personalities a few well-conducted sessions, however superficial they may seem, may suffice to bring about an amelioration of symptoms, and no further treatment will be needed. However, there are many patients whose problems are more deeply entrenched who will require *for even mere symptom relief* some resolution of personality conflicts that are incessantly generating trouble for them. Even learning better modes of problem solving requires some insight into internal forces that govern behavior.

It is precisely because the most disturbing sources of turmoil so often lie beyond awareness that efforts in many patients applied exclusively toward environmental manipulation, persuasion, suggestion, reassurance, reeducation, or reconditioning so often are only partially successful. This is not to depreciate the effectiveness of supportive and educational measures, for in suitable patients, apart from bringing about necessary relief from suffering, a certain degree of personality change may occur through their implementation. Unfortunately, lasting characterologic alterations are rare. The chances are that if we really hope to succeed in bringing about explicit personality change, assuming that this is our goal, we will have to clarify and manage inner conflicts that are beyond the periphery of awareness in an effort to promote greater self-understanding. The question in short-term therapy is whether this can be done briefly in a specific case and, if so, how best it can be done.

Traditionally, the method most often employed in dealing with unconscious conflict is long-term psychoanalysis. A good deal of misunderstanding, however, still exists about psychoanalysis, some of which stems from its misapplication to areas in which its competence as a therapeutic procedure may be challenged. Such misdirection has tended to shred its authenticity. Freud's enduring legacy lies in his penetrating insights into human behavior. These include the concept of the unconscious, the trenchant nature of behavior, the indelible imprint of childhood experience on character structure, the consanguinuity of abnormal mental symptoms and normal mental processes, the significance of anxiety, the structure of symbolism, the nature of dreams, and the importance of transference and resistance. These innovations have become firmly incorporated into psychiatric and psychological thinking and have inspired practically all current systems of psychotherapy. They are intrinsic to our contemporary ideas about dynamically based short-term psychotherapy.

Psychoanalysis in its long-term classical form has not proven itself to be a practical form of therapy in the majority of cases seeking help—not only because it is expensive and drags on for years, but also, even where finances and a willingness to participate in a prolonged therapeutic relationship are present, only a small number of patients are suitable candidates for the technique. Identifying who might satisfactorily respond is difficult. Roughly, persons who are not too sick and not too immature, a so-called "normal-neurotic" group, qualify. These constitute only a small fraction of the vast army of people who cluster around clinics and practitioners' offices seeking help for a wide variety of problems.

Attempts to find other means than classical analysis to expose underlying sources of problems continue to this very day. Blocking such attempts are obstructions to surfacing of the unconscious and the stranglehold that hidden needs and defenses have on one's values and behavior. Because such unconscious ingredients are frozen into the character structure, efforts to demonstrate their unreasonableness are resisted with a desperate tenacity.

Are we then doomed in helping people reach reconstructive personality transformations? It is fallacious to conclude that a seriously defective childhood imposes a life sentence on everyone. Growth is possible at all stages of an individual's life, corrective emotional experiences being sponsored by constructive life events, particularly meaningful interpersonal relationships. Where an individual has lived through a crisis and has resolved it successfully, he may also be rewarded with new and better personality responses that can serve him well in handling future stressful situations.

The idea that the unconscious is forever concealed unless uprooted by formal psychoanalytic therapy is no longer accepted by disciples of modern cognitive approaches who contend that an individual is not a helpless pawn of his unconscious. Rather the individual exercises a certain degree of command over inner conflicts, constantly striving to make them conscious so he can gain mastery over them. To an extent, he is even capable of exercising decisions about which aspects of his unconscious to reveal, titrating their exposure against his tolerance of anxiety. As he works through his anxiety, he becomes increasingly aware of segments of himself that have been concealed and hence have evaded detection and control. Countering this, of course, are resistances that may obstruct such attempts at self-healing.

The virtue of the cognitive approach is the philosophy it espouses to the effect that techniques other than formal analysis can be immensely helpful in resolving resistance to the opening up of crucial areas for exploration and ultimately lead to self-understanding. Left to one's own resources, the average individual may not have sufficient motivation, the fortitude to struggle with the anxiety inevitable to the handling of repudiated aspects of the psyche, and the willingness to abandon the material and subversive gains accruing to neurotic indulgence. On the other hand, the individual who turns to a carefully designed approach executed by a skilled empathic therapist will learn to deal with resistances to self-understanding and support experimentation with more reality-oriented patterns.

How self-understanding helps to bring deeper problems to the surface and to encourage healthier adaptation is not entirely clear. Roy Schafer (1973) expresses it this way: "It is impressive that, as these changes take place in the patient's conception of himself, often by dint of and with the accompaniment of much suffering, he begins to feel better and to function better. His symptoms diminish in scope and persistence; his mood improves; his social and sexual relationships are enhanced. It seems that it can be a gain just to be able to recognize one's neurotic misery." Whatever the involved mechanisms, the individual's sense of mastery is helped.

Since the goal of self-understanding requires the uncovering of at least some unconscious determinants, the manner of their exposure and the timing are especially important in short-term therapy. Generally, the first few sessions will reveal data from the historical material (and particularly the present behavioral patterns of the patient) that offer clues regarding the operative dynamics. Usually it is unwise to present the patient with such clues, no matter how significant they may seem, until he himself expresses awareness of what is going on. Even then any interpretations must be cautiously offered in the form of tentative presentations (Wolberg, 1977, pp. 589–590). The relationship of expressed conflictual material to the present complaint factor is vitally important if such a relationship can be demonstrated.

A mild-mannered, soft-spoken patient came to my office with the complaint of migraine headaches. As he walked into the room, he tipped over a chair and then profusely apologized while ashes from his cigarette spilled over the carpet. During the interview I got the impression from his posture, the set of his jaw, and slashing movements of his hands that his fawning, obsequious manner was a cover for an inner boiling pot of anger. In my mind I made a connection between his smoldering rage and his migraine. I also speculated that he was not aware of the extent of his anger and how he repressed it. To have confronted him with my hypothesis would probably have ended our relationship before it began. Instead, I bided my time until I had more evidence to confirm my impression while working on establishing a closer relationship.

At the fourth session the patient spoke of needing some extensive dental work because he ground his teeth during his sleep. This reinforced my idea that his anger, under control usually, was strong enough to break through in sleep. Repetitive use of such phrases as

"The man is all chewed up," "It kills me to think of how people take advantage of welfare," "I slaughtered him at tennis," and so on, enabled me to say, "I wonder if you hold back on your anger when you have a right to be upset?" I then repeated some incidents that he had revealed to me in which he had felt taken advantage of but had failed to assert his rights. This led to an expostulation of indignation at the state of the world and the nefariousness of people who needed to "Jew you down." His next association was that Freud was a Jew and Freud was a psychoanalyst who was currently being criticized in articles he had read. "Is there," I asked him, "anything I as a psychoanalytic psychotherapist am doing that upsets you or makes you angry?" "Why," he replied astonished, "should I be?" "Well," I retorted, "are you?" The patient then laughed and in an embarrassed way talked about his resentment at the fee I charged, at the punctiliousness of my appointment times, and at the fact that I had given him an ending date when he was sure he could not get well in so short a period. The trouble, he insisted, with most doctors was that they were too busy to devote themselves to any single patient. This was the case also with some parents, including his own parents, who had spent little time with him.

Without apologizing for my actions or acting indignant, I encouraged him to tell me more about how he felt, implying that I approved of his frankness and his right to feel what he felt. As I anticipated, he backtracked, apologizing for his boldness and rudeness. This reaction, I replied, was in service of his guilt, a habitual pattern to keep his anger under control. "But," he retorted, "I really do like doctors and Jews. And there is some Jewish blood in my family."

Opening up some transference feelings served to help our relationship; and to support his ability to criticize his family more frankly for some of the ways he was handled as a child. A noticeable change occurred in the frequency of his migraine attacks, and at our termination date he expressed great satisfaction with the benefits he had received from therapy both in relieving his headaches and giving him a greater sense of freedom.

Conclusion

All persons, irrespective of the degree of emotional illness have a potential for improvement and growth, both spontaneously through constructive life experiences and, more expeditiously, when treated with appropriate psychotherapy. For radical and enduring amendments in the personality structure some cognitive alteration is essential. Without such change, improved habit and behavioral patterns are apt to be short-lived. During therapy far-reaching improvements may be approached by exploring and working through basic conflicts, especially those revealed in the transference. Where transference is not apparent in the therapeutic situation, it may often be detected in distortions in the individual's relationship with other people as well as in the dreams, fantasies, and acting-out tendencies. Irrespective of the techniques that are being employed, (e.g., nondirective interviewing, active anxiety-provoking confrontation, analytic interpretation, behavior therapy, Gestalt approaches, etc.), the patient will respond to these techniques with a wide range of habitual characterologic reactions and resistances. These, utilized as a productive focus on which to concentrate during therapy, may help penetrate defenses and initiate new ways of thinking, feeling, and behaving. Apart from the fact that time in treatment is usually too short to permit the development of too intensive transference reactions that reach a point of a transference neurosis, it is actually not essential for the patient to evolve and work through a transference neurosis to achieve extensive reconstructive change. Indeed, the effect of too great an intensification of transference may be to increase resistance to therapy and to prolong treatment. Where a relationship is found between the patient's presenting symptoms and complaints, prevailing character patterns, and their origins in early life experiences, the process of reconstructive change is expedited. Such change may continue the remainder of the individual's life, particularly where the patient's environment supports the change and he continues self-observation and experimenting with productive new patterns.

CHAPTER 3

Criteria of Selection

While the best patients are undoubtedly those who are adequately motivated for therapy, intellectually capable of grasping immediate interpretations, proficient in working on an important focus in therapy, not too dependent, have had at least one good relationship in the past, and are immediately able to interact well with the therapist, they generally constitute only a small percentage of the population who apply to a clinic or private practitioner for treatment. The challenge is whether patients not so bountifully blessed with therapeutically positive qualities can be treated adequately on a short-term basis with some chance of improving their general modes of problem solving and perhaps of achieving a minor degree of personality reconstruction.

Patient Classification

In practice one may distinguish at least five classes of patients who seek help. We have categorized them as Class 1 through 5. In general, Classes 1 to 3 require only short-term therapy. Classes 4 and 5 will need management for a longer period after an initial short-term regimen of therapy.

Class 1 Patients

Until the onset of the current difficulty Class 1 patients have made a good or tolerable adjustment. The goal in therapy is to return them to their habitual level of functioning. Among such patients are those whose stability has been temporarily shattered by a catastrophic life event or crisis (death of a loved one, divorce, severe accident, serious physical illness, financial disaster, or other calamity). Some individuals may have been burdened with extensive conflicts as far back as childhood but up to the present illness have been able to marshall sufficient defenses to make a reasonable adaptation. The imposition of the crisis has destroyed their capacities for coping and has produced a temporary regression and eruption of neurotic mechanisms. The object in therapy for these patients is essentially supportive in the form of *crisis intervention* with the goal of reestablishing the previous equilibrium. Reconstructive effects while not expected are a welcome dividend. Generally, no more than six sessions are necessary.

An example of a Class 1 patient is a satisfactorily adjusted woman of 50 years of age who drove a friend's automobile with an expired license and in the process had a severe accident, killing the driver of the car with which she collided and severely injuring two passengers in her own car, which was damaged beyond repair. She herself sustained a concussion and an injured arm and was moved by ambulance to a hospital, where she remained for a week. Charged with driving violations, sued by the owner of the car she borrowed and by the two injured passengers, she developed a dazed, depressed reaction and then periods of severe dizziness. Therapy here consisted of a good deal of support, reassurance, and help in finding a good lawyer, who counseled her successfully through her entangled legal complications.

Sometimes a crisis opens up closed traumatic chapters in one's life. In such cases it may be possible to link past incidents, feelings, and conflicts with the present upsetting circumstances enabling the patient to clarify anxieties and hopefully to influence deeper strata of personality. In the case above, for example, the patient recalled an incident in her childhood when while wheeling her young brother in a carriage, she accidentally upset it, causing a gash in her sibling that required suturing. Shamed, scolded, and spanked, the frightened child harbored the event that powered fear and guilt within herself. The intensity of her feeling surprised her, and their discharge during therapy fostered an assumption of a more objective attitude toward both the past and the immediate crisis event. It may not be possible in all cases, but an astute and empathic therapist may be able to help the patient make important connections between the past and present.

Class 2 Patients

The chief problem for Class 2 patients is not a critical situation that has obtruded itself into their lives, but rather maladaptive patterns of behavior and/or disturbing symptoms. The object here is symptom cure or relief, modification of destructive habits, and evolvement of more adaptive behavioral configurations. Multiform techniques are employed for 8 to 20 sessions following eclectic *supportive-educational* models under the rubric of many terms, such as short-term behavioral therapy, short-term reeducative therapy, and so forth.

A phobia to air travel exemplifies the complaints of a class 2 patient. This was a great handicap for Miss J since job advancement necessitated visits to remote areas. The origin of the patient's anxiety lay in the last flight that she had taken 8 years previously. A disturbance in one of the engines reported to the passengers by the pilot necessitated a return to the point of origin. Since that time Miss J had not dared enter a plane. Therapy consisted of behavioral systematic desensitization, which in eight sessions resulted in a cure of the symptom.

In utilizing the various eclectic techniques the therapist alerts himself to past patterns that act as a paradigm for the present symptom complex, as well as to manifestations of resistance and transference. In a certain number of cases the patient may be helped to overcome resistances through resolution of provocative inner conflicts and in this way achieve results beyond the profits of symptom relief.

Class 3 Patients

Those in whom both symptoms and behavioral difficulties are connected with deep-seated intrapsychic problems that take the form of personality disturbances and inappropriate coping mechanisms make up the Class 3 classification. Such patients have functioned at least marginally up to the time of their breakdown, which was perhaps initiated by an immediate precipitating factor. Most of these patients seek help to alleviate their distress or to solve a crisis. Some come specifically to achieve greater personality development. On evaluation either they are deemed unsuitable for long-term treatment, or extensive therapy is believed to be unnecessary. They often possess the desire and capacity to work toward acquiring self-understanding.

The goal for Class 3 patients is personality reconstruction along with symptomatic and behavioral improvement. Techniques are usually psychoanalytically oriented, involving interviewing, confrontation, dream and transference interpretations, and occasionally the use of adjunctive techniques like hypnosis. Some therapists confine the term *dynamic short-term therapy* to this class of patients and often employ a careful selection process to eliminate patients whom they feel would not work too well with their techniques (Buda, 1972; Davanloo, 1978, Malan, 1963; Sifneos, 1972; Ursano & Dressler, 1974).

An example of a Class 3 patient is a young mother who brought her son in for consultation because he was getting such low marks in the final year of high school that the chances of his getting into college were minimal. Moreover, he firmly announced his unwillingness to go to college, insisting on finding a job after graduation so that he could buy an automobile and pursue his two hobbies: baseball and girls. During the interview with the boy it was obvious that he had motivation neither for further college education nor for any kind of therapeutic help. It was apparent too that his stubborn refusal to study and to go on to higher learning was a way of fighting off the domination of his mother and stepfather. Accordingly, the mother was advised to stop nagging the boy to continue his schooling. Instead she was urged to permit him to experiment with finding a job so that he could learn the value of a dollar and to discover for himself the kinds of positions he could get with so little education.

The next day the mother telephoned and reported that she had followed the doctor's instructions. However, she asked for an appointment for herself since she was overly tense and suffered from bad backaches that her orthopedist claimed were due to "nerves." What she wanted was to learn self-hypnosis, which her doctor claimed would help her relax. Abiding by her request, she was taught self-hypnosis—not only for relaxation purposes, but also to determine the sources of her tension. Through interviewing aided by induced imagery during hypnosis, she was able to recognize how angry she was at me for not satisfying her desire to force her son to go to college. Images of attacking her father, who frustrated and dominated her, soon brought out her violent rage. She realized then that her obsequious behavior toward her husband was a cover for her hostility. Acting on this insight, she was soon able to express her anger and to discuss her reactions with her husband and the reasons for her rages. This opened up channels of communication with a dramatic resolution of her symptoms and an improvement in her feelings about herself and her attitudes toward people, confirmed by a 5-year follow-up.

Class 4 Patients

Patients of the Class 4 category are those whose problems even an effective therapist may be unable to mediate in a brief span and who will require more prolonged management after the initial short-term period of formal therapy has disclosed what interventions would best be indicated. The word "management" should be stressed because not all long-term modalities need be, and often are not, best aimed at intrapsychic alterations. Among individuals who appear to require help over an extended span are those whose problems are so severe and deep-rooted that all therapy can do for them is to keep them in reasonable reality functioning, which they could not achieve without a prolonged therapeutic resource.

Class 4 patients include the following:

1. Individuals with chronic psychotic reactions and psychoses in remission who require some supervisory individual or group with whom contact is regularly made over sufficiently spaced intervals to provide some kind of human relationship, however tenuous this may be, to oversee essential psychotropic drug intake, to regulate the milieu, and to sudue the perils of psychotic processes when these are periodically released. Such patients do not usually require formal prolonged psychotherapy or regular sessions with a psychotherapist; they could do as well, or better, with a paraprofessional counselor. Milieu therapy, rehabilitation procedures, and social or group approaches may be helpful.

2. Persons with serious character problems with

tendencies toward alcoholism and drug addiction who require regular guidance, surveillance, group approaches, and rehabilitative services over an indefinite period.

3. Individuals with uncontrollable tendencies toward acting-out who need controls from without to restrain them from expressing impulses that will get them into difficulties. Examples are those who are occasionally dominated by dangerous perversions, desires for violence, lust for criminal activities, masochistic needs to hurt themselves, accident proneness, self-defeating gambling, and other corruptions. Many such persons recognize that they need curbs on their uncontrollable wayward desires.

4. Persons so traumatized and fixated in their development that they have never overcome infantile and childish needs and defenses that contravene a mature adaptation. For instance, there may be a constant entrapment in relationships with surrogate parental figures, which usually evolve for both subjects and hosts into a sado-masochistic purgatory. Yet such persons cannot function without a dependency prop, and the therapist offers himself as a more objective and nonpunitive parental agency. Some of these patients may need a dependency support the remainder of their lives.

Many of the patients in this category fall into devastating frustrating dependency relationships during therapy or alternatives to therapy from which they cannot or will not extricate themselves. Realizing the dangers of this contingency, we can, however, plan our strategy accordingly, for example, by providing supportive props outside of the treatment situation if support is needed. Nor need we abandon reconstructive objectives, once we make proper allowances for possible regressive interludes. In follow-up contacts, I was pleased to find, there had been change after 5, 10, and in some cases 15 years in patients who I believed had little chance to achieve personality change.

5. Persons with persistent and uncontrollable anxiety reactions powered (a) by unconscious conflicts of long standing with existing defenses so fragile that the patient is unable to cope with ordinary demands of life or (b) by a noxious and irremediable environment from which the patient cannot escape.

6. Borderline patients balanced precariously on a razor edge of rationality.

7. Intractable obsessive - compulsive persons whose reactions serve as defenses against psychosis.

8. Paranoidal personalities who require an incorruptible authority for reality testing.

9. Individuals with severe long-standing psychosomatic and hypochondrical conditions, such as ulcerative colitis, or chronic pain syndromes that have resisted ministrations from medical, psychological, and other helping resources. Often these symptoms are manifestations of defenses against psychotic disintegration.

10. People presenting with depressive disorders who are in danger of attempting suicide and require careful regulation of antidepressive medications or electroconvulsive therapy followed by psychotherapy until the risk of a relapse is over.

Class 5 Patients

In Class 5 we place those individuals who seek and require extensive reconstructive personality changes and have the finances, time, forbearance, and ego strength to tolerate long-term psychoanalysis or psychoanalytically oriented psychotherapy. In addition, they have had the good fortune of finding a well-trained, experienced, and mature analyst who is capable of dealing with dependent transference and other resistances as well as with one's personal countertransferences. Patients who can benefit more from long-term reconstructive therapy than from dynamically oriented short-term therapy are often burdened by interfering external conditions that may be so strong, or by the press of inner neurotic needs so intense, that they cannot proceed on their own toward treatment objectives after the short-term therapeutic period has ended. Continuing monitoring by a therapist is essential to prevent a relapse. In certain cases the characterologic detachment is so great that the patient is unable to establish close and trusting contact with a therapist in a brief period, and a considerable bulk of time during the short-term sessions may be occupied with establishing a work relationship.

A special group of patients requiring long-term therapy are highly disturbed children and adolescents who have been stunted in the process of personality development and who require a continuing relationship with a therapist who functions as a guiding, educational, benevolent parental figure.

Long-term patients in Classes 4 and 5 usually constitute less than one-quarter of the patient load carried by the average psychotherapist. The bulk of one's practice will generally be composed of patients who may adequately be managed by short-term methods.

Conclusion

If we are pragmatically disposed to treat as many patients as possible for economic or other reasons, we may say that all patients irrespective of diagnosis, and severity and chronicity of problems are potential candidates for short-term therapy. Should any patients fail to respond to abbreviated methods, we can always continue treatment, having acquired invaluable information during the short-term effort as to what interventions would best be indicated for their problems. Even where the yardstick of cost effectiveness is not paramount, the majority of individuals who seek help for emotional problems can with efficient short-term methods achieve satisfactory results and may even go on by themselves, with the learnings they have acquired, to attain some degree of personality growth. A few may require an additional visit or two from time to time to resolve some problems that they are unable to handle by themselves. They thus will have been able through a practical brief therapeutic approach to have been spared the expense, inconvenience, and in some cases the dangers of long-term therapy.

CHAPTER 4

A General Outline of Short-term Therapy

There obviously are differences among therapists in the way that short-term therapy is implemented—for example, the focal areas chosen for attention and exploration, the relative emphasis on current as compared to past issues, the attention paid to transference, the way resistance is handled, the depth of probing, the dealing with unconscious material that surfaces, the precise manner of interpretation, the degree of activity, the amount of advice giving, the kinds of interventions and adjunctive devices employed, and the prescribed number of sessions. Moreover, all therapists have to deal with their own personalities, prejudices, theoretical biases, and skills, all of which will influence the way they work. In spite of such differences, there are certain basic principles that have evolved from the experiences of a wide assortment of therapists working with diverse patient populations that have produced good results. The practitioner may find he can adapt at least some of these principles to his own style of operation even though he continues to employ methods that have proven themselves to be effective with his patients and are not exactly in accord with what other professionals do. In the pages that follow 20 techniques are suggested as a general guide for short-term therapy.

Establish as Rapidly as Possible a Positive Working Relationship (Therapeutic Alliance)

An atmosphere of warmth, understanding, and acceptance is basic to achieving as positive working relationship with a patient. Empathy particularly is an indispensible personality quality that helps to solidify a good therapeutic alliance.

Generally, at the initial interview, the patient is greeted courteously by name, the therapist introducing himself as in this excerpt:

Th. How do you do, Mr. Roberts, I am Dr. Wolberg. Won't you sit down over there (*pointing to a chair*), and we'll talk things over and I'll see what I can do to help you (*patient gets seated*).

Pt. Thank you, doctor. (*pause*)

A detached deadpan professional attitude is particularly fatal. It may, by eliciting powerful feelings of rejection, provoke protective defensive maneuvers that neutralize efforts toward establishing a working relationship.

It is difficult, of course, to delineate exact rules about how a therapeutic alliance may be established rapidly. Each therapist will utilize himself uniquely toward this end in terms of his own techniques and capacities for rapport. Some therapists possess an extraordinary ability even during the first session, as the patient describes his problem and associated feelings, of putting the patient at ease, of mobilizing his faith in the effectiveness of methods that will be utilized, and of subduing the patient's doubts and concerns. A confident enthusiastic manner and a conviction of one's ability to help somehow communicates itself nonverbally to the patient. Therapist enthusiasm is an important ingredient in treatment.

The following suggestions may prove helpful:

Verbalize what the patient may be feeling

Putting into words for the patient what he must be feeling but is unable to conceptualize is one of the most effective means of establishing contact. "Reading between the lines" of what the patient is talking about will yield interesting clues. Such simple statements as, "You must be very unhappy and upset about what has happened to you" or "I can understand how unhappy and upset you must be under the circumstances" present the therapist as an empathic person.

Encourage the patient that his situation is not hopeless

It is sometimes apparent that, despite presenting himself for help, the patient is convinced that he is hopeless and that little will actually be accomplished from therapy. Where the therapist suspects this, he may say. "You probably feel that your situation is hopeless because you have already tried various things that haven't been effective. But there *are* things that can be done, that *you can do* about your situation and I shall guide you toward making an effort." Empathizing with the patient may be important: "Putting myself in your position, I can see that you must be very unhappy and upset about what is happening to you."

Sometimes it is useful to define the patient's role in developing and sustaining his problem in a nonaccusing way: "You probably felt you had no other alternative than to do what you did." "What you are doing now seems reasonable to you, but there may be other ways that could create fewer problems for you."

While no promise is made of a cure, the therapist must convey an attitude of conviction and faith in what he is doing.

Pt. I feel hopeless about getting well. Do you think I can get over this trouble of mine?

Th. Do you really have a desire to get over this trouble? If you really do, this is nine-tenths of the battle. You will want to apply yourself to the job of getting well. I will point out some things you can do, and if you work at them yourself, I see no reason why you can't get better.

Where the patient becomes self-deprecatory and masochistic, the positive aspects of his reactions may be stressed. For example, should he say he is constantly furious, one might reply, "This indicates that you are capable of feeling strongly about things." If he says he detaches and does not feel anything, the answer may be, "This is a sign you are trying to protect yourself from hurting." Comments such as these are intended to be protective in order to preserve the relationship with the therapist. Later when it becomes apparent that the relationship is sufficiently solid, the therapist's comments may be more provocative and challenging. The patient's defenses being threatened, anxiety may be mobilized, but the patient will be sustained by the therapeutic alliance and he will begin to utilize it rather than run away from it.

Deal With Initial Resistances

Among the resistances commonly encountered at the first session are lack of motivation and disappointment that the therapist does not fulfill a stereotype. The therapist's age, race, nationality, sex, appearance, professional discipline, and religion may not correspond with the patient's ideas of someone in whom he wants to confide.

Th. I notice that it is difficult for you to tell me about your problem.

Pt. (*Obviously in discomfort*) I don't know what to say. I expected that I would see an older person. Have you had much experience with cases like me?

Th. What concerns you is a fear that I don't have as much experience as you believe is necessary and that an older person would do a better job. I can understand how you feel, and you *may* do better with an older person. However, supposing you tell me about your problem and then if you wish I will refer you to the best older therapist who can treat the kind of condition you have.

This tactic of accepting the resistance and inviting the patient to tell you more about himself can be applied to other stereotypes besides age. In a well-conducted interview the therapist will reveal himself or herself as an empathic understanding person, and the patient will want to continue with him or her in therapy.

Another common form of resistance occurs in the person with a psychosomatic problem who has been referred for psychotherapy and who is not at all convinced that a psychological problem exists. In such cases the therapist may proceed as in this excerpt.

Pt. Dr. Jones sent me here. I have a problem with stomachaches a long time and have been seeing doctors for it for a long time.

Th. As you know, I am a psychiatrist. What makes you feel your problem is psychological?

Pt. I don't think it is, but Dr. Jones says it might be, and he sent me here.

Th. Do you think it is?

Pt. No, I can't see how this pain comes from my head.

Th. Well, it might be organic, but with someone who has suffered as long as you have the pain will cause a good deal of tension and upset. [*To insist on the idea that the problem is psychological would be a poor tactic. First, the therapist may be wrong, and the condition may be organic though undetectable by present-day tests and examinations. Second, the patient may need to retain his notion of the symptom's organicity and even to be able to experience attenuated pain from time to time as a defense against overwhelming anxiety or, in certain serious conditions, psychosis.*]

Pt. It sure does.

Th. And the tension and depression prevent the stomach from healing. Tension interferes with healing of even true physical problems. Now when you reduce tension, it helps the healing. It might help you even if your problem is organic.

Pt. I hope so.

Th. So what we can do is try to figure out what problems you have that are causing tension, and also lift the tension. This should help your pain.

Pt. I would like that. I get tense in my job with the people I work. Some of them are crumbs. [*Patient goes on talking, opening up pockets of anxiety.*]

The object is to accept the physical condition as it is and not label it psychological for the time being. Actually, as has been indicated, it may be an essential adaptational symptom, the patient needing it to maintain an equilibrium. Dealing with areas of tension usually will help relieve the symptom, and as psychotherapy takes hold, it may make it unnecessary to use the symptom to preserve psychological homeostasis.

Motivational lack may obstruct therapy in other situations, as when a patient does not come to treatment on his own accord but is sent or brought by relatives or concerned parties. Additional examples are children or adolescents with behavior problems, people who are addicted (drug, alcohol, food, gambling), and people receiving pensions for physical disabilities. Case 1 in Chapter 6 illustrates the management of a nonmotivated adolescent. More on handling lack of motivation is detailed elsewhere (Wolberg, 1977, pp. 458–470).

Gather Historical Material and Other Data

Through "sympathetic listening" the patient is allowed to tell his story with as little interruption as possible, the therapist interpolating questions and comments that indicate a compassionate understanding of the patient's situation. The data gathered in the initial interview should hopefully permit a tentative diagnosis and a notion of the etiology and possibly the psychodynamics. Should the patient not bring the matter up, he may be asked what he considers his most important problem to be? Why has he come to treatment at this time? What has he done about the problem to date? Has he himself arrived at any idea as to what is causing his difficulty? What does he expect or what would he like to get from therapy?

It is often advantageous to follow an outline* in order to do as complete a history or behavioral analysis as possible during the first session or two. This may necessitate interrupting the patient after the therapist is convinced that he has obtained sufficient helpful data about any one topic.

Among the questions to be explored are the following:

1. Have there been previous upsets that resemble the present one?
2. Were the precipitating events of previous upsets in any way similar to the recent ones?
3. What measures aggravated the previous upsets and which alleviated the symptoms?
4. Apart from the most important problem for which help is sought, what other symptoms are being experienced (such as tension, anxiety, depression, physical symptoms, sexual problems, phobias, obsessions, insomnia, excessive drinking?
5. What tranquilizers, energizers, hypnotics, and other medications are being taken?

Statistical data are rapidly recorded (age, education, occupation, marital status, how long married, and children if any). What was (and is) the patient's mother like? The father? Any problems with brothers or sisters? Were there any problems experienced as a child (at home, at school, with health, in relationships with other children)? Any problems in sexual development, career choice, occupational adjustment? Can the patient remember any dreams, especially nightmarish and repetitive dreams? Were there previous psychological or psychiatric treatments?

To obtain further data, the patient may be exposed to the Rorschach cards, getting a few responses to these unstructured materials without scoring. This is optional, of course. The therapist does not have to be a clinical psychologist to do this, but he or she should have read some material on the Rorschach. The patient may also be given a sheet of paper and a pencil and be asked to draw a picture of a man and a woman. Some therapists prefer showing the patient rapidly the Thematic Apperception Cards. What distortions appear in the patient's responses and drawings? Can one correlate these with what is happening symptomatically? These tests are no substitutes for essential psychological tests where needed, which can best be done by an experienced clinical psychologist. But they can fulfill a useful purpose in picking up gross defects in the thinking process, borderline or schizophrenic potentialities, paranoidal tendencies, depressive manifestations, and so on. No more than 10 or 15 minutes should be utilized for this purpose.

An example of how Rorschach cards can help reveal underlying impulses not brought out by regular interviewing methods is illustrated in a severely depressed man with a controlled, obsessional character whose passivity and inability to express aggression resulted in others taking advantage of him at work and in his marriage. When questioned about feelings of hostility or aggression, he denied these with some pride. The following were his responses to the Rorschach Cards.

1. Two things flying at each other.
2. Something sailing into something.
3. Two figures pulling something apart; two adults pulling two infants apart.
4. Animals' fur spread out. X-ray (*drops card*)
5. Flying insect, surgical instrument, forceps.
6. Animal or insect split and flattened out.
7. X-ray fluoroscope of embryo; adolescents looking at each other with their hair whipping up in the wind.
8. Two animals climbing a tree, one on each side; female organs in all of these cards.
9. Fountain that goes up and spilling blood.
10. Underwater scene, fish swimming, crabs, Inside of a woman's body.

* Further details on history taking and convenient appropriate forms may be found in Wolberg, 1977, pp. 401–409, 1176–1178.

The conflicts related to aggression and being torn apart so apparent in the responses became a principal therapeutic focus and brought forth his repressed anger at his mother.

Select the Symptoms, Behavioral Difficulties, or Conflicts that You Feel are Most Amenable for Improvement

The selection with the patient of an important problem area or a disturbing symptom on which to work is for the purpose of avoiding excursions into regions that, while perhaps challenging, will dilute a meaningful effort. Thus, when you have decided on what to concentrate, inquire of the patient if in his opinion these are what he would like to eliminate or change. Agreement is important that this chosen area is significant to the patient and worthy of concentrated attention. If the patient complains that the selection is too limited, he is assured that it is best to move one step at a time. Controlling a simple situation or alleviating a symptom will help strengthen the personality, and permit more extensive progress.

Thus the focal difficulty around which therapy is organized may be depression, anxiety, tension, or somatic manifestations of tension. It may be a situational precipitating factor or a crisis that has imposed itself. It may be a disturbing pattern or some learned aberration. It may be a pervasive difficulty in relating or in functioning. Or it may be a conflict of which the patient is aware or only partially aware.

Once agreement is reached on the area of focus, the therapist may succinctly sum up what is to be done.

Th. Now that we have decided to focus on the problem [*designate*] that upsets you, what we will do is try to understand what it is all about, how it started, what it means, why it continues. Then we'll establish a plan to do something about it.

Example 1. A symptomatic focus

Th. I get the impression that what bothers you most is tension and anxiety that makes it hard for you to get along. Is it your feeling that we should work toward eliminating these?

Pt. Yes. Yes, if I could get rid of feeling so upset, I would be more happy. I'm so irritable and jumpy about everything.

Example 2. A focus on a precipitating event

Th. What you are complaining most about is a sense of hopelessness and depression. If we focused on these and worked toward eliminating them, would you agree?

Pt. I should say so, but I would also like to see how I could improve my marriage. It's been going downhill fast. The last fight I had with my husband was the limit.

Th. Well, suppose we take up the problems you are having with your husband and see how these are connected with your symptoms.

Pt. I would like that, doctor.

Example 3. A dynamic focus

Whenever possible the therapist should attempt to link the patient's symptoms and complaints to underlying factors, the connections with which the patient may be only dimly aware. Carefully phrased interpretations will be required. It may not be possible to detect basic conflicts in the first interview, only secondary or derivative conflicts being apparent. Moreover, the patient may not have given the therapist all the facts due to resistance, guilt, or anxiety. Or facts may be defensively distorted. It is often helpful (with the permission of the patient) to interview, if possible, the spouse or another individual with whom the patient is related after the first or second interview. The supplementary data obtained may completely change the initial hypothetical assumptions gleaned from the material exclusively revealed by the patient.

Nevertheless, some invaluable observations may be made from the historical data and interview material that will lend themselves to interpretation for defining a focus. Thus a patient presenting great inferiority problems and repetitive difficulties in work situations with supervisors, who as a child fought bitterly with an older sibling, was told the following: "It is possible that your present anxiety while related to how you get along with your boss touches off troubles you've carried around with you for a long time. You told me you always felt inferior to your brother. In many cases this sense of inferiority continues to bother a person in relation to all kinds of new older brothers. It wouldn't be mysterious if this were happening to you. What do you think?" This comment started off a productive series of reminiscences regarding his experiences with his brother, a focus on which resulted in considerable understanding and betterment of his current relationships.

As has been indicated, more fundamental nuclear conflicts may be revealed in later sessions (for example, in the above patient an almost classical oedipal conflict existed), especially when transference and resistance manifest themselves.

Define the Precipitating Events

It is essential that we identify clearly the precipitating factors that led to the patient's present upset or why the patient came to treatment at this time.

Th. It seems as if you were managing to get along without trouble until your daughter told you about the affair she is having with this married man. Do you believe this started you off on the downslide?

Pt. Doctor, I can't tell you the shock this was to me. Janie was such an ideal child and never was a bit of a problem. And then this thing happened. She's completely changed, and I can't understand it.

Sometimes the events are obscured or denied because the patient has an investment in sustaining situational irritants even while he seeks to escape from their effects. Involvement in an unsatisfactory relationship with a disturbed or rejecting person from which the patient cannot extricate himself is an example. It may be necessary to encourage continuing conversation about a suspected precipitant, asking pointed questions in the effort to help the patient see the relationship between his symptoms and what he may have considered unrelated noxious events. Should the patient fail to make the connections, the therapist may spell these out, asking pertinent questions that may help the patient grasp the association.

Evolve a Working Hypothesis

After the first session the therapist should have gathered enough data from the present and past history, from any dreams that are revealed, and from the general attitude and behavior of the patient to put together some formulation about what is going on. This is presented to the patient in simple language, employing concepts with which the patient has some familiarity. This formulation should never be couched in dismal terms to avoid alarming the patient. Rather a concise, restrained, optimistic picture may be painted making this contingent on the patient's cooperation with the therapeutic plan. Aspects of the hypothesis should ideally bracket the immediate precipitating agencies with what has gone on before in the life history and, if possible, how the patient's personality structure has influenced the way that he has reacted to the precipitating events.

A woman experiencing a severe anxiety attack revealed the precipitating incident of discovering her husband's marital infidelity. As she discussed this, she disclosed the painful episode of her father's abandoning her mother for another woman.

Th. Is it possible that you are afraid your husband will do to you what your father did to your mother?

Pt. (*breaking out in tears*) Oh, it's so terrible. I sometimes think I can't stand it.

Th. Stand his leaving you or the fact that he had an affair?

Pt. If it could end right now, I mean if he would stop, it (*pause*).

Th. You would forget what had happened?

Pt. (*pause*) Yes—Yes.

Th. How you handle yourself will determine what happens. You can see that your present upset is probably linked with what happened in your home when you were a child. Would you tell me about your love life with your husband?

The focus on therapy was thereafter concerned with the quality of her relationship with her husband. There were evidences that the patient herself promoted what inwardly she believed was an inevitable abandonment.

The therapist in making a tentative thrust at the dynamics of a problem should present it in simple terms that the patient can understand. The explanation should not be so dogmatic, however, as to preclude a revision of the hypothesis at a later date, should further elicited material demand this. The patient may be asked how he feels about what the therapist has said. If he is hazy about the content, his confusion is explored and clarification continued.

For example, a patient with migraine is presented with the hypothesis that anger is what is creating his symptom. The patient then makes a connection with past resentments and the denial defenses that he erected, which apparently are still operative in the present.

Th. Your headaches are a great problem obviously since they block you in your work. Our aim is to help reduce or eliminate them. From what you tell me, they started way back probably in your childhood. They are apparently connected with certain emotions. For example, upset feelings and tensions are often a basis for headaches, but there may be other things too, like resentments. What we will do is explore what goes on in your emotions to see what connections we can come up with. Often resentments one has in the present are the result of situations similar to troubles a person had in childhood.

Pt. I had great pains and trouble fighting for my rights when I was small—a bossy mother and father who didn't care. I guess I finally gave up.

Th. Did you give up trying to adjust at home or work?

Pt. Not exactly. But fighting never gets anywheres. People just don't listen.

Make a Tentative Diagnosis

Despite the fact that our current nosological systems leave much to be desired, it may be necessary to fit the patient into some diagnostic scheme if for no other reason than to satisfy institutional regulations and insurance requirements. There is a temptation, of course, to coordinate diagnosis with accepted labels for which reimbursement will be made. This is unfortunate since it tends to limit flexibility and to invalidate utilizing case records for purposes of statistical research. Even though clinical diagnosis bears little relationship to preferred therapeutic techniques in some syndromes, in other syndromes it may be helpful toward instituting a rational program (Wolberg, 1977, pp. 6, 62–63, 410–418).

Convey the Need for the Patient's Active Participation in the Therapeutic Process

Many patients, accustomed to dealing with medical doctors, expect the therapist to prescribe a formula or give advice that will operate automatically to palliate the problem. An explanation of what will be expected of the patient is in order.

Th. There is no magic about getting well. The way we can best accomplish our goals is to work together as a partnership team. I want you to tell me all the important things that are going on with you and I will try to help you understand them. What we want to do is to develop new, healthier patterns. *My* job is to see what is blocking you from achieving this objective by pointing out some things that have and are still blocking you. *Your* job is to *act* to put into practice new patterns we decide are necessary, you telling me about your experiences and feelings. Psychotherapy is like learning a new language. The learner is the one who must practice the language. If the teacher did all the talking, the student would never be able to carry on a conversation. So remember you are going to have to carry the ball, with my help of course.

Make a Verbal Contract With The Patient

There should be an agreement regarding the frequency of appointments, the number of sessions, and the termination date.

Example 1. Where Limitation of the Number of Sessions is Deemed Necessary in Advance

Th. We are going to have a total of 12 sessions. In that time we should have made an impact on your anxiety and depression. Now, let's consult the calendar. We will terminate therapy on October 9, and I'll mark it down here. Can you also make a note of it?

Pt. Will 12 sessions be enough?

Th. Yes. The least it could do is to get you on the road to really working out the problem.

Pt. What happens if I'm not better?

Th. You are an intelligent person and there is no reason why you shouldn't be better in that time.

Should the therapist dally and compromise his confidence in the patient's capacity to get well, the patient may in advance cancel the termination in his own mind in favor of an indeterminate future one.

Example 2. When the Termination Date is Left Open

Th. It is hard to estimate how many sessions we will require. I like to keep them below 20. So let us begin on the basis of twice a week.

Pt. Anything you say, doctor. If more are necessary, OK.

Th. It is really best to keep the number of sessions as low as possible to avoid getting dependent on them. So we'll play it by ear.

Pt. That's fine.

The appointment times may then be set and the fee discussed.

Utilize Whatever Techniques are Best Suited to Help the Patient with Immediate Problems

Following the initial interview, techniques that are acceptable to the patient, and that are within the training range and competence of the therapist, are implemented, bearing in mind the need for activity and flexibility. The techniques may include supportive, educational, and psychoanalytically oriented interventions and a host of adjunctive devices, such as psychotropic drugs, hypnosis, biofeedback, behavioral and group approaches, and so on, in whatever combinations are necessary to satisfy the patient's immediate and future needs. An explanation may be given the patient about what will be done.

Th. At the start, I believe it would be helpful to reduce your tension. This should be beneficial to you in many ways. One of the best ways of doing this is by teaching you some relaxing exercises. What I would like to do for you is to make a relaxing casette tape. Do you have a casette tape recorder?

Pt. No, I haven't.

Th. You can buy one quite inexpensively. How do you feel about this?

Pt. It sounds great.

Th. OK. Of course, there are other things we will do, but this should help us get off to a good start.

Many therapists practicing dynamic short-term therapy ask their patients to reveal any dreams that occur during therapy. Some patients insist that they rarely or never dream or if they do, that they do not remember their dreams.

Th. It is important to mention any dreams that come to you.
Pt. I can't get hold of them. They slip away.
Th. One thing you can do is, when you retire, tell yourself you will remember your dreams.
Pt. What if I can't remember.
Th. Keep a pad of paper and a pencil near the head of your bed. When you awaken ask yourself if you dreamt. Then write the dream down. Also, if you wake up during the night.

Study the Patient's Reaction and Defense Patterns

The utilization of any technique or strategem will set into motion reactions and defenses that are grist for the therapeutic mill. The patient will display a range of patterns that you can study. This will permit a dramatic demonstration of the patient's defenses and resistances in actual operation rather than as theories. The patient's dreams and fantasies will often reveal more than his actions or verbalizations, and he should continually be encouraged to talk about these. The skill of the therapist in working with and interpreting the patient's singular patterns will determine whether these will be integrated or will generate further resistance. Generally, a compassionate, tentative type of interpretation is best, sprinkling it if possible with a casual light humorous attitude. A patient who wanted hypnosis to control smoking appeared restless during induction:

Th. I noticed that when I asked you to lean back in the chair and try relaxing to my suggestions, you were quite uneasy and kept on opening your eyes. What were you thinking about?
Pt. (*emotionally*) My heart started beating. I was afraid I couldn't do it. What you'd think of me. That I'd fail. I guess I'm afraid of doctors. My husband is trying to get me to see a gynecologist.
Th. But you kept opening your eyes.
Pt. (*pause*) You know, doctor, I'm afraid of losing control, of what might come out. I guess I don't trust anybody.
Th. Afraid of what would happen here, of what I might do if you shut your eyes? (*smiling*)
Pt. (*laughing*) I guess so. Silly. But the thought came to me about something sexual.

While the Focus at all Times is on the Present, be Sensitive to How Present Patterns Have Roots in the Past

Examining how the patient was reared and the relationship with parents and siblings is particularly revealing. An attempt is made to establish patterns that have operated throughout the patient's life of which the current stress situation is an immediate manifestation. This data is for the therapist's own consumption and should not be too exhaustive, since the patient if encouraged to explore the past may go on endlessly, and there is no time for this. At a propitious moment, when the patient appears to have some awareness of connections of his past with his present, a proper interpretation may be made. At that time a relationship may be cited between genetic determinants, the existing personality patterns, and the symptoms and complaints for which therapy was originally sought.

Watch for Transference Reactions

The immediate reaching for help encourages projection onto the therapist of positive feelings and attitudes related to an idealized authority figure. These should not be interpreted or in any way discouraged since they act in the interest of alleviating tension and supporting the placebo element. On the other hand, a *negative* transference reaction should be dealt with rapidly and sympathetically since it will interfere with the therapeutic alliance.

Th. [*noting the patient's hesitant speech*] You seem to be upset about something.

Pt. Why, *should* I be upset?

Th. You might be if I did something you didn't like.

Pt. (*pause*) No—I'm afraid, just afraid I'm not doing what I should. I've been here six times and I still have that panicky feeling from time to time. Do other patients do better?

Th. You seem to be comparing yourself to my other patients.

Pt. I—I—I guess so. The young man that came before me. He seems so self-confident and cheerful. I guess I felt inferior, that you would find fault with me.

Th. Do you think I like him better than I do you?

Pt. Well, wouldn't you, if he was doing better than I was?

Th. That's interesting. Tell me more.

Pt. I've been that way. My parents, I felt, preferred my older brother. He always came in on top. They were proud of his accomplishments in school.

Th. So in a way you feel I should be acting like your parents.

Pt. I can't help feeling that way.

Th. Don't you think this is a pattern that is really self-defeating? We ought to explore this more.

Pt. (*emotionally*) Well, I really thought today you were going to send me to another doctor because you were sick of me.

Th. Actually, the thought never occurred to me to do that. But I'm glad you brought this matter out because we will be able to explore some of your innermost fears about how people feel about you.

Examine Possible Countertransference Feelings

If you notice persistent irritability, boredom, anger, extraordinary interest in or attraction to any patient, ask yourself whether such feelings and attitudes do not call for self-examination. Their continuance will almost certainly lead to interference with a good working relationship. For example, a therapist is treating an unstable middle-aged female patient whom he regards as a plumpish, sloppy biddy who sticks her nose into other people's affairs. He tries to maintain an impartial therapeutic stance, but periodically he finds himself scolding her and feeling annoyed and enraged. He is always relieved as the session hour comes to an end. He recognizes that his reactions are countertherapeutic, and he asks himself if they are really justified. The image of his own mother then comes to his mind, and he realizes that he had many of the same feelings of exasperation, displeasure, and disgust with his own parent. Recognizing that he may be transferring in part some of these attitudes to his patient whose physical appearance and manner remind him of his mother, he is better able to maintain objectivity. Should self analysis, however, fail to halt his animosity, he may decide to send the patient to another therapist.

Constantly Look for Resistances That Threaten to Block Progress

Obstructions to successful therapeutic sessions are nurtured by misconceptions about therapy, lack of motivation, needs to maintain certain benefits that accrue from one's illness, and a host of other sources, conscious and unconscious. Where resistances are too stubborn to budge readily or where they operate with little awareness that they exist, the few sessions assigned to short-term therapy may not suffice to resolve them. One way of dealing with resistances once they are recognized is to bring them out openly in a noncondemning manner. This can be done by stating that the patient may if he desires hold on to them as defenses, but if this is so, he must suffer the consequences. A frank discussion of why the resistances have value for the patient and their effects on his treatment is in order. Another technique is to anticipate resistances from the patient's past modes of adaptation, dreams, and the like, presenting the patient with the possibility of their appearance and what could be done about them should they appear. The therapist should watch for minimum appearances of resistance, however minor they may be, that will serve as psychological obstructions. Merely bringing these to the attention of the patient may rapidly dissipate them.

Pt. I didn't want to come here. Last time I had a terribly severe headache. I felt dizzy in the head. (*pause*)

Th. I wonder why. Did anything happen here that upset you; did I do anything to upset you?

Pt. No, it's funny but it's something I can't understand. I want to come here, and I don't. It's like I'm afraid.

Th. Afraid?

Pt. (*Pause; patient flushes.*) I can't understand it. People are always trying to change me. As far back as I can remember, at home, at school.

Th. And you resent their trying to change you.

Pt. Yes. I feel they can't leave me alone.

Th. Perhaps you feel I'm trying to change you.

Pt. (*angrily*) Aren't you?

Th. Only if *you* want to change. In what way do you want to change, if at all?

Pt. I want to get rid of my headaches, and stomachaches, and all the rest of my aches.

Th. But you don't want to change to do this.

Pt. Well, doctor, this isn't true. I want to change the way *I* want to.

Th. Are you sure the way *you* want to change will help you get rid of your symptoms?

Pt. But that's why I'm coming here so you will tell me.

Th. But you resent my making suggestions to you because somehow you put me in the class of everybody else who you believe wants to take your independence away. And then you show resistance to what I am trying to do.

Pt. (*laughs*) Isn't that silly, I really do trust you.

Th. Then supposing when you begin to feel you are being dominated you tell me, so we can talk it out. I really want to help you and not dominate you.

Pt. Thank you, doctor, I do feel better.

Give the Patient Homework

Involve the patient with an assignment to work on how his symptoms are related to happenings in his environment, to attitudes, to fallacies in thinking, to disturbed interpersonal relationships, or to conflicts within himself. Even a bit of insight may be a saving grace. As soon as feasible, moreover, ask the patient to review his idea of the evolution of his problem and what he can do to control or regulate the circumstances that reinforce the problem or alleviate his symptoms. Practice schedules may be agreed on toward opposing the situations or tendencies that require control. The patient may be enjoined to keep a log regarding incidents that exaggerate his difficulties and what the patient has done to avoid or resolve such incidents. The patient may also be given some cues regarding how he may work on himself to reverse some basic destructive personality patterns through such measures as acquiring more understanding and insight, rewarding himself for positive actions, self-hypnosis, and so on. These tactics may be pursued both during therapy and following therapy by oneself.

For example, the following suggestion was made to a patient who came to therapy for help to abate migraine attacks:

Th. What may help you is understanding what triggers off your headaches and makes them worse. Supposing you keep a diary and jot down the frequency of your headaches. Everytime you get a headache write down the day and time. Even more important, write down the events that immediately preceded the onset of the headache or the feelings or thoughts you had that brought it on. If a headache is stopped by anything that has happened, or by anything you think about or figure out, write that down, and bring your diary when you come here so we can talk about what has happened.

Keep Accenting the Termination Date if One was Given the Patient

In preparing the patient for termination of therapy, the calendar may be referred to prior to the last three sessions and the patient reminded of the date. In some patients this will activate separation anxiety and negative transference. Such responses will necessitate active interpretation of the patient's past dependency and fears of autonomy. Evidences of past reactions to separation may help the patient acquire an understanding of the underpinnings of present reactions. The therapist should expect a recrudescence of the patient's symptoms as a defense against being on his own and as an appeal for continuing treatment. These manifestations are dealt with by further interpretation. *Do not promise* to continue therapy even if the patient predicts failure.

Pt. I know we're supposed to have only one more session. But I get scared not having you around.

Th. One of our aims is to make you stronger so you won't need a crutch. You know enough about yourself now to take some steps on your own. This is part of getting well. So I want you to give yourself a chance.

Many patients will resent termination of therapy after the designated number of sessions have ended. At the middle point of therapy, therefore, the therapist may bring up this possibility. The therapist should search for incidents in the past where separations have created untoward reactions in the patient. Individuals who were separated from their parents at an early age, who had school phobias produced by inability to break ties with the mother, and who are excessively dependent are particularly vulnerable and apt to respond to termination with anxiety, fear, anger, and depression. The termination process here may constitute a prime focus in therapy and a means of enhancing individuation.

Th. We have five more sessions, as you know, and then we will terminate.

Pt. I realize it, but I always have trouble breaking away. My wife calls me a holder-oner.

Th. Yes, that's exactly what we want to avoid, the dependency. You are likely to resent ending treatment for that reason. What do you think?

Pt. (*laughing*) I'll try not to.

Th. Well, keep thinking about it and if you have any bad reactions let's talk about it. It's important not to make treatment a way of life. By the end of the five sessions, you should be able to carry on.

Pt. But supposing I don't make it?

Th. There you go, see, anticipating failure. This is a gesture to hold on.

Pt. Well, doctor, I know you are right. I'll keep working on it.

Terminate Therapy on the Agreed-upon Date

While some therapists do not consider it wise to invite the patient who has progressed satisfactorily to return, others find it a helpful and reassuring aid for most patients to do so at the final session. I generally tell the patient to write to me sometime to let me know things are coming along. In the event problems develop that one cannot manage by oneself, the patient should call for an appointment. Rarely is this invitation abused and if the patient does return (which is not too common in my experience) the difficulty can be rapidly handled, eventuating in reinforcement of one's understanding.

Th. This is, as you know, our last session. I want you now to try things out on your own. Keep practicing the things I taught you—the relaxation exercises [*where these have been used*], the figuring out what brings on your symptoms and takes them away, and so forth. You should continue to get better. But setbacks may occur from time to time. Don't let that upset you. That's normal and you'll get over the setback. In fact, it may help you figure out better what your symptoms are all about. Now, if in the future you find you need a little more help, don't hesitate to call me and I'll try to arrange an appointment.

Actually relatively few patients will take advantage of this invitation, but they will feel reassured to go out on their own knowing they will not be abandoned. Should they return for an appointment, only a few sessions will be needed to bring the patient to an equilibrium and to help learn about what produced the relapse.

Stress the Need for Continuing Work on Oneself

The matter of continuing work on oneself after termination is very much underestimated. Patients will usually return to an environment that continues to sponsor maladaptive reactions. The patient will need some constant reminder that old neurotic patterns latently await revival and that he must alert himself to signals of their awakening. In my practice I have found that making a relaxing tape (a technique detailed in Chapter 15) sprinkled with positive suggestions of an ego-building nature serves the interest of continued growth. In the event the patient has done well with homework during the active therapy period, the same processes may continue. Institution of a proper philosophical outlook may also be in order prior to discharge. Such attitudes may be encouraged as the need to isolate the past from the present, the realization that a certain amount of tension and anxiety are normal, the need to adjust to handicaps and realistic irremediable conditions, the urgency to work at correcting remediable elements in one's environment, the recognition of the forces that trigger off one's problems and the importance of rectifying these, and the wisdom of stopping regretting the past and of avoiding anticipating disaster in the future. It must be recognized that while the immediate accomplishments of short-term therapy may be modest, the continued application of the methods the patient has learned during his therapy will help bring about more substantial changes.

Arrange for Further Treatment if Necessary

The question may be asked regarding what to do with the patient who at termination shows little or no improvement. Certain patients will require long-term therapy. In this reference there are some patients who will need help for a prolonged period of time; some require only an occasional contact the remainder of their lives. The contact does not have to be intensive or frequent. Persons with an extreme dependency character disorder, borderline cases, and schizophrenics often do well with short visits (15 to 20 minutes) every 2 weeks or longer. The idea that a supportive person is available may be all that the patient demands to keep him in homeostasis. Introducing the patient into a group may also be helpful, multiple transferences diluting the hostile transference that so often occurs in individual therapy. A social group may even suffice to provide the patient with some means of a human relationship. Some patients will need referral to another therapist who specializes in a different technique, for example, to someone who does biofeedback, or behavioral therapy, or another modality.

Th. Now, we have completed the number of sessions we agreed on. How do you feel about matters now?

Pt. Better, doctor, but not well. I still have my insomnia and feel discouraged and depressed.

Th. That should get better as time goes on. I should like to have you continue with me in a group.

Pt. You mean with other people? I've heard of it. It scares me, but I'd like to do it.

Where the patient is to be referred to another therapist, he may be told:

Th. You have gotten a certain amount of help in coming here, but the kind of problems you have will be helped more by a specialist who deals with such problems. I have someone in mind for you who I believe will be able to help you. If you agree, I shall telephone him to make sure he has time for you.

Pt. I'd like that. Who is the doctor?

Th. Dr.______. If he hasn't time, I'll get someone else.

Conclusion

Twenty operations are recommended for an effective dynamically oriented short-term therapy program. They consist of (1) establishing a rapid positive working relationship (therapeutic alliance), (2) dealing with initial resistances, (3) gathering historical data, (4) selecting a focus for therapy, (5) defining precipitating events, (6) evolving a working hypothesis, (7) making a tentative diagnosis, (8) conveying the need for the patient's active participation in the therapeutic process, (9) making a verbal contract, (10) utilizing appropriate techniques in an active and flexible manner, (11) studying the reactions and defenses of the patient to the techniques being employed, (12) relating present-day patterns to patterns that have operated throughout the patient's life, (13) watching for transference reactions, (14) examining possible countertransference feelings, (15) alerting oneself to resistances, (16) assigning homework, (17) accenting the termination date, (18) terminating therapy, (19) assigning continuing self-help activities, and (20) arranging for further treatment if necessary.

These operations may be utilized in toto or in part by therapists who can adapt them to their styles of working. Irrespective of theoretical persuasion, there are a number of areas of general agreement among different professionals practicing short-term therapy:

1. *Time.* The most frequently designated number of sessions range from 3 to 6 for crisis intervention, from 6 to 12 for supportive-educational approaches, and from 12 to 20 for more extensive psychotherapy along dynamic lines. These may be crowded into a span of a few weeks, or they may be distributed over a number of months. Some therapists prefer to see their patients on a once-a-week basis; others find twice a week the optimal frequency. In some cases 40 to 50 sessions are still considered acceptable for short-term coverage. Time limits are often set in advance with the patient.

2. *Selection of cases.* All types of problems of acute and chronic duration are considered suitable. Even patients with serious psychopathology are candidates. Some therapists who confine themselves to dynamic short-term therapy believe selection of appropriate patients is mandatory.

3. *Goals.* Reconstructive changes are deemed not only desirable but also obtainable in suitable patients, especially with the use of dynamic approaches, provided there exists proper motivation and concurrence of reconstructive objectives on the parts of patient and therapist.

4. *Degree of therapist activity.* A relatively high degree of activity is generally preferred.

5. *Focus of therapy.* A restriction of focus to a zone agreed on by patient and therapist is important, if not essential. If a nuclear conflict is identifiable and the patient does not defensively avoid it too much, its consideration as a focus is desirable in dynamically oriented approaches. Considered significant are transference phenomena, which in some systems may occupy a position of central importance.

6. *Techniques.* The full range of eclectic supportive, educational, and reconstructive techniques are used including, in dynamic approaches, traditional analytic techniques of transference analysis, interpretation of resistance, dream and fantasy exploration, and the relating of transference to genetic determinants.

CHAPTER 5

The Initial Interview

A. Common Questions

The initial interview is perhaps the most vital of all sessions since in its conduct rests the fate of the therapeutic alliance and, even more importantly, the eventuality of whether or not the patient will return for further treatment. How much time should ideally be spent on history taking? Should the interview be largely diagnostic or therapeutic? What degree of confrontation can safely be employed? These and many other questions challenge the interviewer. In the present chapter some of the points mentioned in the last chapter will be expounded by presenting relevant questions (and answers) brought up in teaching and supervisory sessions with therapists of different theoretical persuasions.

Would you consider the first session therapeutic or diagnostic?

While the initial interview is conducted for the purpose of assessing the presenting problem and planning treatment strategy, it should be managed so that it registers a constructive impact on the patient. It must be stressed that a sizable number of patients, especially those that come to outpatient clinics, do not return for a second interview. Follow-up studies show that the initial interview can have a definite therapeutic effect and may even start the patient on the road to recovery. The therapist, therefore, should assume that the first interview will be the only opportunity to work with the patient and thus that enough work must be done so that the patient can leave the session with something positive to grapple onto. The initial interview should be conducted in such a way as to give the patient a better idea about his underlying problem and an assay of what he can do to help himself. Naturally, most patients will return for more sessions unless the therapist has failed to incite their confidence or has committed serious errors in approach (detachment, belittling attitudes, frightening the patient with depth interpretations, hostility, etc.).

How thorough should history taking be in the initial interview?

During the initial interview exhaustive, ritualistic taking of a history is unnecessary. All that is required is the gathering of sufficient information to allow for treatment planning and perhaps for the making of a tentative diagnosis. In later sessions one may fill in this skeletal outline of history. More information will be revealed as the patient gains confidence in the therapist.

In appraising the degree of the patient's maladjustment at the initial interview, are there any criteria that can be applied?

There are a number of adjustment scales that are in use, none of which is perfect. It is helpful to view the present difficulty against the backdrop of previous maladaptations, particularly those during childhood. The data here is not entirely definitive since the patient could, in spite of a disorganized early life history, still make a reasonable adult adjustment under propitious circumstances. The second item one may consider is the quality of the present personal relationships, the adjustment to one's marital partner and children, the extent of creativity, and the values that mold behavior. Third, one may estimate the degree of anxiety that is manifest or that expresses itself in terms of such symptoms as depression and psychosomatic manifestations.

A fourth possibility is to examine the nature of defenses against anxiety, for instance, their ability to contain the anxiety and the effect that they have on the total functioning. Fifth, we ponder the extent of adaptational collapse. Here even though the patient seems to be making a good adjustment, we must ask at what expense. Thus, a detached person may show on the surface a fairly good adjustment. Consequently, it is essential to estimate how truly adequate this is in terms of what is happening to the individual as a whole. He may be escaping anxiety and working adequately only by the tactic of isolating himself from people. Or a dependent person may be functioning solely by attaching himself to a parental figure. The kind of adaptation helps us to determine the degree of support that will be required at the start of treatment, the amount of participation one may expect from the patient and how active the therapist should be in the relationship.

Is it advisable to spend more time on the initial interview than on other sessions?

If possible, yes. So much has to be done during the first interview that the usual 45 or 50 minutes of time allotted for a session may be insufficient. Extending the time, however, may not be practically possible. Hence, two sessions may be necessary in some cases to accomplish all essential tasks. An experienced interviewer, however, may require no more than one session.

Is it impossible to work with an unmotivated patient, and if so, can you give some examples of how this can be done?

It is not at all impossible provided one deals with what is behind the lack of motivation. To do this the therapist may try to retrieve unexpressed or unconscious emotions that are acting, or will act, as resistances to therapy. Such emotions underlie the patient's manifest behavior. Very frequently these emotions cannot be expressed in words, and the therapist will have to make assumptions through observation of the patient's behavior. For instance, in the event that a delinquent boy is referred for therapy, the boy may sulk in his chair, fidget, be evasive, answer in a disarming manner, express disinterest, or show negativism. The therapist may gain the impression from observing the attitudes of the boy that the boy resents being at the interview. He, therefore, might say to the boy, "You probably resent coming here," or "Probably you feel that you ought not to have come here," or "I can understand that you feel kind of mad about this situation." Such a remark cuts into the emotion of the boy and may enable him to perceive that his feelings are understood.

Another example is that of a woman referred by a social agency on the basis that the agency believes she is suffering from an emotional problem for which she should get help. Even if she is not yet prepared to receive this help, she may still appear for therapy in order to appease the caseworker or as a means through which she can gain further aid from the agency. Her motivation, consequently, would be to give as little information as possible about herself or to be as evasive as she can without offending. Under these circumstances, once the therapist realizes what is going on, he might say the following:

Th. I can very well see that you would feel resentful or uncomfortable about coming here. You probably do not feel that it is necessary and might believe that you could very easily do without therapy. I do not blame you for feeling this way inasmuch as you did not really come to the agency in order to seek help for an emotional problem.

This explanation probably would relax the woman considerably, since she would sense in the therapist a sympathetic person. She might then begin to express her feelings about the agency and at the end be willing to talk about herself and her problems.

A common problem is provided by the patient who views psychotherapy in the same light as consulting an internist. The patient tells the doctor about disturbing symptoms, and the doctor prescribes a remedy. The patient, consequently, will bombard the therapist with a flood of symptoms and complaints with the hope that everything will then be taken care of in some mysterious way. The patient really has no means of understanding what is supposed to go on in therapy other than through experiences with previous health vendors. The disadvantage with such an attitude is that once the patient has elaborated the problem, responsibility for it is transfered to the therapist and a cure will be expected. Should the therapist become aware of this attitude, he may offer this interpretation:

Th. It is understandable that you have suffered so long that you feel it is impossible for you to do anything about your problem yourself. It is natural for you to want somebody to step in and do for you what you haven't been able to do for yourself. But you and I have to work together as a team. I shall help you to understand what is happening to you, and you will find that you can do many constructive things for yourself. Together we should make progress.

The patient with a psychosomatic problem is often unconvinced that his physical symptom is or can be emotionally determined. The best way of losing such a patient is to insist that his problem is psychological. Since the patient may, at least temporarily, need his symptom, the therapist is wise at the start of therapy to allow the patient to retain the idea of its organicity. He may inform the patient that any symptom, even an organic symptom, creates tension because of discomfort or pain. The tension delays healing. What needs to be done is to reduce tension, and this can stimulate the healing process. Teaching the patient simple relaxing methods and allowing the patient to verbalize freely should soon establish a therapeutic alliance, and through this the patient may be helped to come to grips with his worries and conflicts.

A final example is provided by the host of patients who are sheparded into therapy against their free will, such as court cases, spouses of complaining mates, persons collecting disability payments, and individuals deriving strong secondary gains from their symptoms through avoiding hard work, supporting dependency needs, and getting attention and sympathy. Such patients cannot be forced to change. The primary task here, as in the case of the psychosomatic patient, is to first establish a therapeutic alliance. No hard-and-fast rules can be given since each patient will require innovative strategems designed for their special situations. Patients receiving disability checks are particularly difficult to convince that anything psychological keeps them from returning to work. One tactic is never to imply that the patient is in any way psychologically manufacturing his symptoms because this will obstruct the establishing of a working relationship. The approach at first may, as in the psychosomatic patient, be organized around tension reduction to help the patient assuage suffering. As tension is lessened, the patient will begin talking more about himself and perhaps about some family adjustment problems. The therapist may soon be able to inquire about the hopes, ambitions, and goals of the patient. Questions may be asked such as "What would you like to do?" "How would *you* like to feel?" "What do you enjoy most?" Very often when the patient realizes that the therapist does not expect conformity to standards that others set for the patient, a therapeutic alliance will begin. Reflecting the patient's anger without condemning it helps convince the patient that he is not bad for feeling the way he does. How the patient can go about fulfilling his own goals is then planned. An interesting article on techniques of dealing with such unmotivated patients has been written by Swanson and Woolson (1973).

If a patient is referred who is unprepared for treatment, how does a counselor prepare the person to accept referral to a therapist when there is no incentive to receive help?

An example may illustrate the situation. A college student is referred to a counselor by her school advisor because she was becoming more and more of a recluse, avoiding social activities and even staying away from classes. On interview she is manifestly depressed. However, she has no desire for therapy and no idea that there is anything wrong with the way she is behaving. She insists indignantly that there is nothing wrong with her mind. Because she refused to go out does not mean she needs a psychiatrist. The question is how to get this girl to accept psychotherapy.

In handling this type of problem, the first thing the counselor would want to do is establish some sort of an incentive for therapy. Without this incentive, it would be useless to refer the patient to a therapist. How to create an incentive is the case in point. One way is to ask if she is completely satisfied with her present-day life and adjustment. If she says that everything is going along well, the therapist may say: "It is very gratifying to feel that you are completely satisfied, and understandably under those circumstances, you will want to do very little about yourself. There may, however, be certain areas that are not as pleasant for you as you might want. Are you satisfied the way everything is going in every area?" Should the adamant reply be that things now are perfect, the therapist may have no alternative than to bring out the prevailing adjustment difficulties, such as staying away from classes. At the end of the session the still unconvinced student is invited to return at any time she feels she wants to talk things over.

On the other hand, the student may admit that while things are not too bad, there is the problem that she does not seem to have the energy to go out with boys though she likes boys. The counselor retorts: "If you really *have* a desire to get more energy, it may be possible for you to rectify this. Perhaps there isn't any desire to go out because there are fears of exposing yourself to some sort of contact." The patient may then deny this vehemently.

If the counselor has gotten the student to talk about herself, the chances are she will ask for another conference with the counselor. At the next visit she will perhaps say that she has thought the matter over and she does feel that perhaps she might be concealing from herself reasons why she does not want to go out. Under these circumstances the counselor may inform her that there are certain persons who specialize in handling problems of this type. In the past psychotherapists were looked upon as people who ministered to only severe emotional difficulties, but in recent years they have been handling both minor and major problems of normal people; people who could be much more happy within themselves and more efficient in their work or studies with some psychotherapeutic help.

Before referring a prospective patient to a therapist it would be important for the counselor (1) to establish the existence of a definite problem for which help is needed, (2) to deal with or to clarify whatever resistance there may exist that makes the person reluctant to consult a therapist, and (3) to correct any existing misconceptions about psychotherapy. How truly motivated for treatment the patient will be when a therapist is consulted will depend on how good a job the counselor has done. But, getting the patient to a therapist is the first step.

Since the presence of empathy is usually mentioned as the keynote to a therapeutic alliance, what happens if you simply cannot empathize with a particular patient? Does this mean you cannot treat that patient?

It often happens that a therapist does not like the kind of human being the patient is at the time he presents himself for treatment, nor may the therapist be able to condone the life the patient has led, nor approve of his attitudes, morals, values, or objectives. This does not mean one cannot work with the patient. Problems develop where the therapist because of intolerance, is hostile or judgmental. Particularly destructive to establishing a working relationship is repetition by the therapist of the same kind of arbitrary and disapproving manner displayed by other authorities with whom the patient has come into contact. The patient has already set up defenses against these authorities that will block his developing confidence in a therapist whom he identifies with past authorities. If the therapist can exercise control over impulses to verbalize disapproval, and can avoid displaying criticism through facial expressions and gestures, aspects of the patient's personality will sooner or later come through that may kindle warm feelings in the therapist. Many patients at the start often try to test a therapist by displaying anger or by presenting the most shocking or disagreeable aspects of themselves. If the therapist does not fall into this trap, the working relationship may very well develop even in the first session.

How can you communicate empathy?

One may show interest in what the patient is saying by listening carefully, by asking proper questions, and by displaying appropriate facial expressions. Sometimes communicating what must be on the patient's mind from clues given, verbally and nonverbally, can be helpful. The therapist may ask himself, "What goes on in the patient's mind as he sits there talking?" If one can penetrate beyond the facade of the patient's manifest verbalizations and get to the core of what he may actually be feeling, what fears, and anxieties exist, one may make a strong impression on the patient. When the patient first comes to therapy, he is usually quite upset, fearful, angry, or frustrated and he may anticipate counterhostility or disapproval. Typical ideas that occupy the patient's mind are these: (1) This is my last resort. If this doesn't work, I might as well commit suicide. (2) I feel degraded that I have finally had to resort to psychiatric help. (3) If anybody finds out about the real me, it will be too bad for me. (4) I will probably be blamed, rejected or hated. (5) I feel foolish to come here. It is silly for me to think I need help for my mind. (6) This must mean I am going insane.

The therapist should also countenance what may be going on in the therapist's own mind. These thoughts are very rarely acknowledged, let alone faced. They involve all sorts of formulations such as the following: (1) I wonder if I'm going to like this patient? (2) I wonder if he is going to like me? (3) I wonder if I'm able to help this patient or whether his kind of problem is the sort that I can treat? (4) I wonder if he can pay my fee and how am I going to handle the situation in the event that he is unable to afford treatment with me?

Assuming one can handle one's own feelings, the therapist may diplomatically ask the patient questions such as "I wonder if you are upset about coming here?" "Do you have questions about what I might be thinking about you?" "You may feel this is the last resort!" Other questions and comments will be suggested by observing the patient's reactions and reading between the lines of what the patient is saying.

Is there any way one can expedite empathy toward a person who comes from a socioeconomic group with which a therapist has little affinity?

In listening to a patient who belongs to a stratum of society with which one is not too familiar, one may try to understand the expressions and idioms the patient employs and to utilize the same language forms so that one can communicate on the same wave length. One may also try to find out if the destructive patterns the patient indulges are those common to or condoned by the patient's subcultural group, for example alcoholic excesses, dangerous drug usage, or delinquency. It is necessary to make sure at the start that one does not convey disapproval or disgust at indulgences the patient may consider normal. Later on, when a working relationship exists with the patient, it may be possible to point out destructive patterns that support the problems for which help is being sought. The therapist may also keep asking himself, especially when the patient comes from a disadvantaged group, how the therapist would feel and what he would do if he had to endure the intolerances and abuses the patient went through in the patient's past life. Would he be any different? The therapist may then better be able to empathize with the patient.

What do you do if a patient turns on you and attacks you verbally during the initial interview?

Many patients are inwardly very hostile when they come to the initial interview. The reasons for this vary. The patient may rightfully resent waiting for an appointment, the routine of a clinic, the fee to be payed, and other facts of life. Or hostility will stem from inner sources not at all related to reality. The therapist must accept this hostility and not act threatened by it nor respond in any adverse way. Hostility should be handled by bringing it out in the open during the interview, clarifying the reason for the disturbing reality situation if one exists. Or where hostility is not explicable, a casual statement may be made such as the following:

Th. It is understandable that you have suffered a great deal from your problem. People who suffer a great deal often are resentful of the suffering they have experienced and the ineffectiveness of the measures they have adopted to gain help. You may be angry at the fact that you are ill, or because of what has happened to you. Most people do feel resentful of what has happened to them. This is understandable. It is natural not to want to talk about one's feelings of resentment, too. The reason I am telling you this is that it is possible you may even feel angry at me or at the clinic as a result. If you do, do not feel guilty if you talk about it.

In spite of all the efforts you make to be tolerant, what do you do if you still find yourself being unsympathetic, even actually disliking the patient?

If your feelings interfere with your doing therapy, simply transfer the patient to another therapist. But, in all probability the patient will leave you first.

How would you show a patient you are tolerant of behavior about which the patient personally is ashamed and cannot or will not do much about?

Some patients will expect you, perhaps even want you to disapprove of their behavior. If you comply with this wish, it may temporarily be stabilizing by furnishing the patient with an outside control. The improvement, however, will be short-lived as long as the patient has a stake in destructively acting out patterns. The patient will then defy you or deceive you by perpetuating the patterns secretly at the same time that anger and guilt accumulate. The therapeutic alliance will, therefore, suffer. The best way to manage any revelation of conduct about which the patient seems guilty is to remark that the patient appears to be guilty and ashamed of what he or she is doing. The following excerpts illustrate how I handled two such cases:

Pt. I want you to know that I am homosexual.
Th. So what?
Pt. (*pause*) Well?
Th. Well what? Is that what you came to see me about?
Pt. No, but how do you feel about it?
Th. You must feel that I disapprove or should disapprove.
Pt. Don't you?
Th. Why should I if it's something you want to do. You told me that you were depressed and anxious a good deal of the time. Isn't that what you came to see me about?
Pt. Yes, it is.
Th. So let's work at that. Now, if your choice of a sexual partner has something to do with these symptoms we'll talk about that.

Pt. [*obviously relieved*] Fine, I knew you were liberal about these things.

A patient in her middle 60s came for help to relieve pain following a breast amputation for cancer.

Pt. I have to tell you, doctor (*laughs*) that I have a little habit that I am ashamed to tell you about.
Th. Are you afraid of what my reaction will be?
Pt. No, I guess I don't like it myself. It's that whenever I go into a store, I lift-sneak a little thing in my purse or bag.
Th. How do you feel about it?
Pt. I guess I do it for the excitement. I usually don't need the trinket. I guess you'd call it kleptomania. I read about it.
Th. You must disapprove of it, or doesn't it bother you?
Pt. My heart trembles for hours afterward. What if I'm caught? The disgrace.
Th. If it does bother you enough, we ought to take it up in our talks here.
Pt. Do you think I can get over this habit? It started shortly after my husband died.
Th. Perhaps you felt deprived. But if you really want to get over it, that's nine-tenths of the battle.

Are reasons for seeking help at the time of coming for help a good thing to focus on?

Harris et al (1964) describe a 3-year project at the Langley Porter Neuropsychiatric Institute in San Francisco where a method of up to seven sessions was designed around the focus of the factors that enjoined the patient to come to the clinic. The questions explored were why the patient was seeking help *at this time* and what he or she expected out of the contact with the clinic. This approach served not only as a satisfactory intake method, but also produced a return to adequate functioning in a significant number of patients. For the remaining patients the brief experience helped delineate the problem, clarified the extent of motivation, and acted as preparation for continuing help or intensive treatment. Focusing on the help-seeking factors is nothing new. Social-work agencies have for many years employed it in casework on a short-term basis. Similarly some counseling approaches have operated around a similar exposure of the immediate complaint factor. Both casework and counseling have often substantiated improvement beyond the mere alteration of the environmental disturbances or symptomic upsets that initiated the consultations.

How does a therapist know whether his appraisal of a chosen focus is the correct one?

A therapist's judgment concerning existing core problems involves speculations that are not always consistent with what another therapist may hypothesize. Given the same data, different therapists will vary in what they consider is the most significant area on which to focus. In a small experiment that I conducted three experienced therapists trained in the same analytic school witnessed the first two sessions conducted by a fourth colleague through a one-way mirror. Each therapist had a somewhat different idea of what meaningful topic was best on which to focus. In my opinion, such differences are not significant because multiple problems can exist and these are usually interrelated. Even where one strikes the patient's core difficulties tangentially, one may still register an impact and spur the patient on toward a better adaptation. After all, a reasonably intelligent patient is capable of making connections and even of correcting the misperceptions of a therapist where a good working relationship exists and the therapist does not respond to being criticized too drastically with a display of wounded narcissism. From a pragmatic standpoint, the focus is an accurate one if the patient responds positively to it.

Can a person get well without needing to work on basic nuclear conflicts?

Getting well embraces many degrees of improvement. Most people make a fairly good adaptation while retaining some aspects of their deepest conflicts. In short-term therapy we usually deal with secondary derivative conflicts because of the lack of time for depth probing and the working-through of resistance. However, personality changes can result over a period following therapy if the patient consistently works on himself and his problems. Apparently nuclear conflicts may sometimes be influenced through resolution of their manifestations in secondary conflicts. Hitchcock and Mooney (1969), for example, have written how in mental health consultion dealing with the consultee's work-ego function alone can have a more than superficial effect. D. Beck (1968) has also written an interesting article accenting the value of working on derivative conflicts. In many types of short-term therapy opening up a "bag of worms" through blunt interpretation of a nuclear conflict may create more problems than it solves. The therapist must judge how ready the patient is for an interpretation—that is, how conscious the patient is of an existing conflict—before exploring it. Where the patient has such an awareness and wishes to deal with his conflict, there is no reason to avoid it.

Suppose, in evolving a working hypothesis of the problem, that the therapist happens to be wrong. Would it not be better to wait until more facts are available before speculating about what is going on?

While the therapist will want to develop a working hypothesis of the problem, he must consider it tentative at best. Not all of the facts may be available during the first few interviews. Even if the therapist is wrong or partially wrong in the initial analysis, he will be able to correct or modify his ideas later on. If a connection with personality factors or inner conflicts is not apparent at the beginning, or if the patient is not ready to countenance the implications of such connections, interpretations may be confined to the immediate environmental precipitants while waiting for more data before linking these to underlying inner difficulties or more obscure external events.

How would you account for the fact that even though few or no psychodynamics may be apparent during the first interview, the patient still may experience a good deal of relief?

There are many reasons for this. First, the empathic understanding of the therapist enables the patient to unburden himself or herself in an atmosphere shorn of blame and authoratative pressure. Simply relieving oneself of painful thoughts reduces tension. But more importantly, putting into words feelings that float around in a nebulous way tends to identify them and helps the patient gain control over them. Moreover, revealing ideas and experiences to an authority who does not respond the way other past authorities have acted, or the way the patient imagined they would act or should act, softens the introjected parental image and relieves guilt. Faith and trust are kindled. The placebo element to the effect that something is available that can help and that matters are not hopeless, and the impact of direct or indirect suggestions made by the therapist may inspire the patient toward taking a corrective path of thinking and behaving. Of course, the extent of the patient's taking advantage of these positive elements will depend on his readiness for change. Where a readiness for change exists in good measure, the impact of the first interview can be dramatic even though basic nuclear conflicts are not touched. And the patient may be able to achieve an emotional equilibrium at least equivalent to that which prevailed prior to the onset of the present illness.

Can one prognosticate from the severity of symptoms or the sickness of a patient the possibility of improvement or cure?

No. Sometimes the sickest patients, even hallucinating psychotics, recover rapidly, while what seems like a mild depression, anxiety, or character problem will scarcely budge. Many variables obviously exist other than the current symptoms, which are related to the patient's latent ego strength, flexibility of defenses, readiness for change, secondary gain, selective response to techniques, capacity for developing a therapeutic alliance, skill and personality of the therapist, and many other factors. These will all influence the outcome. The effect of these variables cannot be anticipated in advance since they display themselves only after therapy has started.

Is there one factor you would consider the most important of all in insuring good results in therapy?

There are many factors that are operative, but I would consider the quality of the relationship between the therapist and patient the most important of all factors.

How much confrontation can be utilized during the initial interview?

There are varying opinions. Where the first interview is employed as a screening device to determine the suitability of a patient for an anxiety-provoking type of therapy, such as practiced by Sifneos, confrontation is part of a selection procedure. As a general rule, however, with the average patient, confrontation is best delayed until a good therapeutic alliance has been established to sustain the patient's hostility and anxiety. Otherwise the patient is apt to drop out of treatment prematurely, either because he mistakes the therapist's manner as an attack or because he is unable to handle the emotions stirred up in himself as a result of the pointed challenges. In some cases, however, the therapist is capable of setting up a working relationship rapidly in the first session, under which circumstance careful empathic confrontation may be gainfully employed.

Should not the therapist choose as a preferred focus the relationship between himself and the patient?

Effective learning can proceed only in the medium of a good interpersonal relationship. The latter serves as the matrix for whatever theoretical and methodological structures fashion the treatment maneuvers of the therapist. One usually assumes that the patient comes to therapy with some basic trust in the therapist as a professional who can help. Naturally, there are always latent some elements of fear and distrust, the degree dependent on previous experiences with irrational authority and with incompetant professionals. It is usually not necessary to focus on the relationship unless there are evidences, from the behavior and verbalizations of the patient, that the relationship is not going well or that transference exists that is acting as a resistence to treatment. As long as the relationship appears to be good, there is no reason to probe or challenge it.

Does not the relationship itself sponsor reconstructive change where the therapist is accepting and tolerant?

An assumption is often made that everyone has within oneself the capacity to achieve therapeutic change, provided there is a nonjudgmental, nonpunitive atmosphere in which to express feelings without fear of retaliation or censure. Growth is said to be contingent on the constructive relearning that comes about as a by-product of a nontraumatic relationship. The individual has an opportunity here to revise inherent concepts of authority out of a new experience with the therapist who operates as a different kind of parental symbol. In practice this happy result does not often follow because the individual, even in a completely noncensorious environment, will usually perpetuate personal problems by clinging to unjustified and unjustifiable assumptions. Even though the therapist does not repeat the parental attitudes or display their intolerance, the patient may react as if the original authorities were still present. This is because the problem has been internalized and forces the patient to operate with a sense of values that, merciless as it is, is uncorrected by reality. Indeed, the patient may even become indignant toward the therapist's tolerant standards and behavior as offering temptations for which one will later pay dearly. This serves as resistance against altering one's values. We, nevertheless, try to promote change by detection of negative attitudes and transference feelings and by their interpretation and working-through.

How important are optimism and enthusiasm on the part of the therapist?

Very important. Optimism and enthusiasm inspire faith and trust and tend to neutralize despair and hopelessness. The therapist's belief in himself and in his techniques must, of course, be real, since simulated optimism will easily be detected and will damage the relationship.

There is some controversy about the role of positive expectation on the part of the patient in promoting change. Does expectation influence short-term therapy?

As is usual in some questions, the answer is yes and no. Expectation that one will change acts as a placebo enhancing the patient's faith in the therapist and in the operative techniques. The therapeutic situation itself is a suggestive arena that promotes expectations of change. On the other hand, expectation may be bridled to certain assumptions about the therapist's power and invincibility that can be unrealistic. When the patient learns that the therapist has no magic and that the patient himself must work to achieve change, his expectations may dwindle to nothing and may even act as a negative placebo.

Is your immediate impression of whether you like a person or not a good gauge of how the relationship will develop?

That depends on whether the therapist is able to analyze his own countertransference and prejudices. Initial impressions are often the products of past experiences with a person or person whom the patient resembles or of intolerance related to the patient's race, religion, sex, age, facial expression, manner, speech, and the like. Misconceptions can abound, but a mature therapist keeps analyzing his own reactions to see whether they are the result of countertransference or prejudice, and he accordingly tries to correct attitudes that will interfere with establishing a therapeutic alliance.

Should the therapist prepare the patient for termination of treatment at the first interview?

Proper preparation of the patient for termination is an extremely important, yet the most grossly neglected, aspect of treatment. The therapist should be alerted for signs, even in the first interview, of impending problems with termination since the ending of treatment can be extremely difficult and disturbing for some patients. Moreover, the therapist will need to be aware of his own guilt at discharging some patients, particularly those who have become dependent on him. The therapist may consider the termination of treatment a form of abandonment. On the patient's part, termination may kindle previous upsetting reactions with experiences of separation or loss even as far back as childhood. The patient may interpret termination as a sign of the therapist's irresponsibility or lack of concern and this will activate a devalued self-image. If at the first interview the therapist discusses with the patient that some patients respond to termination of treatment with resentment and feelings of loss, this may ease, though not entirely dissipate, the patient's eventual reaction of anger and disappointment.

Where the history reveals an early loss of, separation from, or abandonment by a parent, the therapist must be triply mindful of the need to prepare the patient for termination and to watch for early signs of anger, depression, and grief. The patient, as part of treatment, should be encouraged to talk about developing separation reactions as well as past separation experiences. Among the emerging separation reactions will be a return of old complaints and the development of new symptoms such as anxiety, depression, and psychosomatic complaints. Some patients respond to termination by denial; where there are signs of this, the therapist must actively interpret the response. Vastly important is the need for the therapist not to consider the patient's hostility as a personal affront.

Are psychological tests necessary in short-term therapy?

Generally, no, A rapid exposure of the patient to the Rorschach cards and to a man-woman drawing, though they are strictly speaking not tests in the formal sense, are sometimes helpful diagnostically and toward spotting a dynamic focus. The same can be said for the Thematic Apperception Cards.

What about the Minnesota Multiphasic Test?

A great deal of information can be gotton from the MMT, although a good interviewer can get sufficient material to work on through ordinary history taking. Most therapists do not give their patients routine tests like the MMT, intelligence tests, and the like, unless there are special reasons for testing.

Is it advisable to make an initial diagnosis on every case?

Yes, for many reasons. The initial diagnosis, however, may have to be changed as more information is obtained during therapy.

Are past dreams important to explore in the initial interview?

Very much so. Dreams often reveal the operative dynamics not obtainable through usual interview techniques. Repetitive dreams and nightmares are especially important. Asking for dreams that the patient can remember from childhood may also be valuable.

It has been stated that patients who were interviewed and put on a waiting list did almost as well on their own as those who were accepted for formal treatment. If this is true, is not therapy superfluous?

Some skeptics downgrade psychotherapy by pointing out that there is no advantage in formal treatment to simply being placed on a waiting list after an initial interview. For example, in one study (Sloane et al., 1975) 94 patients were seen initially by experienced therapists and then randomly assigned to (1) a waiting list, (2) short-term behavior therapy, and (3) short-term psychoanalytically oriented psychotherapy for 13 or 14 sessions. Follow-up after 4 months by assessors showed that target symptoms in all three groups improved, but somewhat more so in the treated groups. Work and social adjustment showed no differences. *All three groups* 1 year and 2 years after the initial interview had improved significantly "regardless of whether or not further treatment was received during this period." We might conclude from this that with the no-treatment group doing almost as well as the treated groups after 4 months and fully as well after 1 and 2 years, formal psychotherapy was dispensable.

The fallacy of this assumption is that we fail to credit the initial interview with the therapeutic impact that it can score by itself even where no further professional help is secured. Nor is it true that a patient on a waiting list languishes without exploiting other helping resources. Often after a good initial interview the patient will have obtained sufficient support, reassurance, awareness, and hope to muster latent coping capacities or to find suitable helping aids outside of formal treatment. We should, therefore, consider even a single intake interview a form of short-term therapy.

That even one or two sessions have on follow-up registered themselves therapeutically on patients has been reported by a number of observers, such as Malan et al (1975). Not only had symptomatic improvement occurred, but in some cases the solitary interview appears to have released forces producing noticeable, and in some cases significant and lasting dynamic, changes. At the Beth Israel Hospital in Boston a sizable group of patients were given a diagnostic interview in the form of a two-session evaluation. No other therapy was administered. A follow-up interview 1 month later revealed a subgroup who improved with no other therapy. The results "confirm the conception of the diagnostic interview as a dynamic interpersonal process and adds support to the evidence that brief psychiatric contact during times of stress can produce significant changes in affect and behavior." Whether patients who improve will sustain or continue their improvement will probably depend on the nature of their transformation, their prevailing motivation to change, their ability to release themselves from their maladaptive coping patterns, and whether or not their environment reinforces or discourages the developing alterations.

CHAPTER 6

The Initial Interview

B. Case Histories

Although every initial interview will be conducted somewhat differently depending on the presenting problem, the capacity for verbalization, the personality of the patient, the initial resistances, countertransference arousal, and so on, certain basic techniques are manifest. This chapter consists of three transcribed initial interviews that bring out some salient features commonly encountered in first, a developmental personality problem, second, an obsessive neurosis, and, third, a schizoid personality disorder, who is not deemed suitable for short-term therapy.

Case 1

The patient is a 16-year-old boy whose parents called for an appointment, saying that he was failing at school, defying his parents, fighting with some of his classmates and generally being obnoxious. What concerned them most, however, was his going steady with a girl. They did not approve on the basis that he was too young for a serious relationship. They were desperate for some direction as to what to do. The boy had resisted going to see a therapist until they cut off his allowance, and then he consented to one appointment. The parents accompanied him and sat in the waiting room. The session brings out how to deal with a defiant adolescent so that he may continue in therapy as well as how to select a dynamic focus.

At the appointed time the patient entered my office, slouched into a chair, and looked about the room in a noncommittal way. The tactic I have found useful in dealing with such reactions is not to engage in criticisms or accusations, and not even to question the patient about his difficulties, but to confront the patient. Confronting this boy with his resistance and verbalizing his right to be angry may act as a shock stimulus starting him off toward enlisting the therapist as an ally to manipulate the parents to abide with his own desires. In this way a relationship gets started that may have therapeutic potentialities.

Th. So they finally captured you and brought you here, huh? (*Therapist smiles and the patient looks up, obviously surprised. He pauses, then breaks out in an embarrassed laugh.*)

Pt. Yes sir.

Th. Aren't you sore about it?

Pt. No, I guess not.

Th. I'd be furious, if I were in your position.

Pt. No, I'm not.

Th. After all, why would you come to see me, except that they inveigled you into this? (*smiling as if joking*)

Pt. I forgot about this until last night.

Th. How did they spring it on you?

Pt. We had an appointment at 10:30, they said.

Th. Wham, just like that—for what reason did they give you?

Pt. I don't know—they think I'm sick I guess.

Th. You mean they think you're mentally sick?

Pt. I don't know—they think something is wrong I guess.

Th. What do they think—in what area? I haven't spoken to them except briefly. So I don't know what the real problem is.

Pt. I don't know. I think they think I'm mixed up—something is wrong.

Th. Do *you* feel you are mixed up?

Pt. No.

Th. How would they get that conception; what's the story on that?

Pt. I don't know—it's just the way I get along with them—our relations.

Th. Your relationships. (*pause*) Well, maybe we can talk about that. Are they giving you a hard time? [*Here I am trying to verbalize what the patient may be feeling.*]

Pt. I don't know. I guess it's two ways.

Th. Are *you* giving them a hard time? Are you really? What are you doing?

Pt. I don't know, I don't go out of my way, but I have a little grudge against them. I don't know. (*pause*)

Th. Well, what have they done—do they deserve the grudge?

Pt. I don't know.

Th. They mentioned something on the telephone. You're at school now, away from home—and you've got a girlfriend—is that the story? (*pause*) So? [*I note that the patient seems angry and fidgetty. I decide to show him that in contrast to his parents I believe he has the right to choose his own company.*] Why do you think they stick their nose into that thing?

Pt. I don't know.

Th. Don't you resent it? Do you tell them everything?

Pt. I tell them to a degree. They find out anyhow.

Th. How would they find out if you kept it to yourself?

Pt. I don't know. Sometimes I see her, then I'll come home, and then they seem to find out.

Th. How would they know that you see her?

Pt. If someone sees me with Jane, then they tell them.

Th. You mean they report on you?

Pt. Well, someone must because I know I once went over to her house. Next time when I was nome, they said, "You saw her, didn't you?"

Th. What do they object to about her?

Pt. They say her parents are too forward, they don't like her, and so forth. Because her parents they invited me over to her house on her birthday for dinner once.

Th. So, what's the big deal about that?

Pt. I don't know, and there was a camp reunion and her mother let her go on the bus with me. We were going to have a camp reunion, and my mother felt she shouldn't have called up, I guess. I should have just gone there and met her. I don't know what it was.

Th. In other words, what they are trying to do is to break this thing up?

Pt. Yes.

Th. Ahhh, is that what the whole story is about?

Pt. Yes.

Th. Anything else? Any other beefs that you have with your parents?

Pt. Well, just sometimes they're different, I don't know, they have different views about kids and that. That's the biggest gripe, with that girl.

Th. Who do you get along with better, your mother or your father?

Pt. Neither.

Th. Neither one of them. They're both difficult right at this time? And they both harp on the same thing? (*pause*) Do you think that if you gave up this girl they'd be any different?

Pt. I doubt it.

Th. They'd pick on something else?

Pt. I don't know, you know my sister and I are very close. (*pause*)

Th. Your sister and you are very close.

Pt. And you know, she's up at college right now. We write. She wrote me a letter that it's so disappointing to come home because that anytime that she finds a boyfriend, or anytime I find someone—well, this is really the first girl I've been pretty serious over—I don't know, they find excuses and they're the worst excuses. I mean they're really bad. They have their reasons. They say you can't do this, you can't do that. Well, Dotty said—like when she came home last time—she said it was a disappointment to her. Her vacation started when she went back to school. She said she was more hurt when she came home like, she said, when you're away, everything is progressing and when you come home, it's just as stagnant as it's always been, and, I don't know, it looks pretty bad. They won't change.

Th. And you must know, they have their own ideas

and they come from a different world than you come from. I mean, your friends and your associations and your philosophy are different these days than in their day. So you must feel they are trying to impose old-fashioned ideas on you.

Pt. I don't know, pretty much trying to put their ideas on me. Like if they say you can't see her, I don't know, It's always the same excuse. Usually when they say, "You can't see her," you're all set to fight the next line.

Th. In other words, the minute they say you can't see her, inwardly you start rebelling.

Pt. I know. Right now my parents notice it, and that's very upsetting, but anytime they start to talk to me, I don't know, I get set for a fight or something.

Th. Because you feel they're critical of you. What would be the worst thing that could happen if you could see this girl all you wanted?

Pt. Nothing, but they feel that. Well, it started off—I was always seeing one girl. It was her. This was after last summer, and then they said I couldn't go out with one girl, and yet I had been out with her only three times. I had been over her house and stuff like that.

Th. Have you been over since you've been home only three times? Do you give them an accounting of everything that goes on?

Pt. I don't tell them anything.

Th. You feel that's your business, right? Have you thought you should go out with other girls too just to please them?

Pt. I can, but I made the mistake then, you know. I kind of understand it, but then they said I had to date one girl, then another, then another. If I wanted I could date this girl, then another and another, see. And I didn't follow up, and then they finally said, "You can't go out with her."

Th. At all?

Pt. At all, this is a long time ago, and then I continued to see her a little bit, and then we, I don't know, last Thanksgiving, we had a pretty bad weekend.

Th. Oh, you mean the last time you were home? The fur was flying?

Pt. Yes, then they said, finally, "You can never see her again. We'll call her if we think it's necessary. We'll speak to her parents and tell them that they're bringing up their child wrong." Maybe it's not for me to say, but who are they to say they're not bringing up their child right?

Th. Is she your steady girlfriend now?

Pt. I don't consider it; my parents say so.

Th. I mean are you going steady?

Pt. No.

Th. Would you marry a girl like this?

Pt. I don't see why not.

Th. Eventually?

Pt. I mean I'm not going to stay with her for the rest of my life until I get married. I'm bound to go with other girls, I mean, but at the beginning they said she had nothing in common with me. I'm not saying she's not in common with me, but I'm saying (*pause*).

Th. Well, she does have something in common with you; you went to camp together.

Pt. Yeah, there's a lot of that stuff and she's not athletic in the muscular sense, but she's an active girl, I don't know, She's smart my parents say.

Th. Is she a good-looking girl? Sexy? So-so?

Pt. She's not sex starved, but she's all right.

Th. And she's easy to talk to?

Pt. Yeah, we sit around and talk, and with her parents. We all get along real good, her parents and her brother.

Th. Do you like her parents better than yours?

Pt. I guess everyone does.

Th. Everybody's own parents are no good, you mean?

Pt. Yeah.

Th. She has a mother and father.

Pt. I think her father died.

Th. But her present stepfather is a nice guy?

Pt. We get along good like when I go over there. He and I will start talking for a while.

Th. Can't you talk that way with your own dad?

Pt. I don't know, I clam up when I'm around him. I don't know why.

Th. Do you feel he's looking down on you, or he's condemning you? Or what?

Pt. I don't know what it is, but he bothers me and I wish he didn't.

Th. You'd like to get him off your back? I'd like to help you get him off your back, really, if that is what you want, but how? [*Here I am joining the patient's feelings. This is in line with the desire to form an alliance with the patient.*]

Pt. I hope you can.

Th. I don't know if I can, but I'll try, if you give me an idea what I can do. What I could tell him is that the tactics they are using are not the right tactics. All they do is antagonize you. After all, this girl isn't going to do anything terrible to you. [*I am not sure whether or not the patient is giving me the right data about the problem. He sounds reasonable in resenting, at his age, the interference of his parents in what seems to be an average boy–girl relationship. If what he says is correct, it is the parents who need some counseling about adolescent needs and problems and the proper way to manage themselves.*]

Pt. I don't know, she's kind of cultured in a way.

Th. She's cultured.

Pt. Yeah, I don't know what they got against her. She knows how to behave at different times. You know she knows just how to act.

Th. She sounds very nice.

Pt. Thank you, that's what she is, but do you know about Fairview where we live. This new elite and then the village?

Th. (*smiling*) You mean that's where all the kids that have parents who have problems live. The parents have problems not the kids? (*laughing*)

Pt. Oh (*laughing*). Well, my father said the reason they didn't like her, she was using me as a bait to climb socially.

Th. Does your girl's family come from a lower economic status class?

Pt. I don't think so. They used to live in Queens, which isn't good, and they moved to where they are now. A nice house, but then my father said some of her best friends are kids that my father likes. So I told him I thought this would make him like her or something, and he said what she is doing is she is climbing, she is using these friends to climb up the ladder. All she wants is her friends in our area for the money, etc.

Th. How does he know that, he doesn't even know her?

Pt. I think he's seen her.

Th. How can he analyze what she is doing without talking to her. [*I am deliberately siding with the patient to firm up our relationship.*]

Pt. I don't know, but this is what he says. She's trying to climb socially, and she's just going to drop me. This is what he says.

Th. That's what he says, but that doesn't mean it's so, is it? [*again, siding with the patient to promote an identification*]

Pt. I know, but how can I argue with him? I don't know, the way I figure it is I won't be home that long and there will be a couple of arguments or so, and then I'll go away.

Th. Go away to college you mean? What are you going to do this summer?

Pt. I don't know yet.

Th. Well listen, between you and me, why can't you go around with other girls and then do what you want anyways?

Pt. (*laughing*)

Th. You know you can have a running battle going on with them all the time the way things are. There's no sense to it, because they'll get very upset and start busting your relationships up. Apparently, you don't want them busted up. You've got to be smart about these things. I'm not trying to give you any advice on how to conduct yourself, but I know that these things can get very, very sticky. You can get yourself into a jam with them, and you are economically dependent on them for a while anyways. So why can't you give them an idea that you're going out with other girls too? Maybe bring one or two around—you know. What's the big deal, you could go out with other girls if you wanted to, can't you? [*In giving the patient this advice, I am testing my own capacity to influence him at this point. I am not sure he will take my advice to defuse the situation.*]

Pt. I can.

Th. I mean, you don't even have to tell this gal anything about it if you don't want to.

Pt. Well, you see like last night, I was supposed to go to a party. Well, I told my parents it was going to be a party. It was kinda my fault. I said it was Christmas Eve, and if she was going to be at this party and if she was going, I was going with my best friend and some girl he knew. And I was going to go, and I asked my mother, and she said I could go providing—and that's only one thing we ask you to do and that's not to see this girl—just like that. And she said, "You'll have to give your father all the details, etc., how the party is going to be, he wants to know more about it." So I told my friend to go ahead and see his girl last night. And what we were going to do? We were going to plan a good one—there would be invitations.

Th. You're letting somebody else do the inviting, and you're just being invited to a party?

Pt. I don't know. They usually find out about that stuff anyhow.

Th. Well, look, whatever they find out, that's it. You don't have to tell them everything you do at your age, do you?

Pt. No, I don't intend to.

Th. All right, if you want me to I'll try to tell them that they are making a big fuss over nothing. [*I get the impression the patient needs an ally, and I am proposing an advocacy role on my part.*]

Pt. See, if you tell them that—I don't know. Sometimes they always have good stories, like something will go on in the house—you know between my mother and I—and then when my father comes home and I listen to her telling him what goes on. You know, it never went on.

Th. So that makes you very furious.

Pt. I mean they can twist a story so that they're the white knights. I mean when they're here—it's not us—and he goes out—I do go out for arguments I mean, when they make me angry.

Th. Well, it must make you furious and you probably feel you'll split a gut unless you come out with your feelings. You see what they object to, I think, they don't like to have you lie. They don't like to have you put one over on them. They say you're not supposed to do it, and they expect that you won't do it. Now, obviously, it would be silly to expect you to give up something that is very valuable to you, but yet they still have a feeling you're still just this big (*indicating a small size with fingers*). And some parents never get over that feeling about their kids. They want to be protective, and they come through as controlling. They don't realize that you have your own needs, and your own life, and everything else. And they won't get off your back on that account. What you have to do is reassure them—say to them what is true. I think the best way you can reassure them is to convince them that there's nothing too serious about this business—there's nothing too serious about your seeing this girl and that you're not going to marry her. [*more advice giving to test our relationship*]

Pt. Do you think they feel I am? (*The patient acts surprised.*)

Th. They may feel you're going to be so serious that you may even get her pregnant or something. You'll be in a jam then.

Pt. Well, if they do this with every girl, I mean, if they feel we're going to have these great times and everything, it's going to happen every time. They have to admit it.

Th. Admit what?

Pt. You, I mean that I'm not going to go out and screw every girl I see.

Th. Well, what you do is your own business, that's the point. What you do is your own business—you can screw the girls you want if that's what you want. [*supporting the patient's right to autonomy*]

Pt. What I mean is if they're going to act like—if those are their motives for breaking this up—then they'll do it with the next girl and the next girl.

Th. They might, they might, it's possible, but the facts are if you water that situation down, you'll probably get them off your back. What you do privately is your own business, and if you screw anybody, I guess you have enough sense to use a rubber and don't take any chances. You know what I mean? But that's your own business and nobody ever need know about it—you never need tell them or anybody else. [*again, backing the patient's right of autonomy*]

Pt. One day, for some reason or other, my mother suddenly said, "Give me your wallet," and she went through it and I had a rubber stuck in the inside of it.

Th. Did she find it?

Pt. Yes, and she took it. She didn't say much and I figured it was forgotten. And then my father—we were going to get pizza or something—and he starts asking me did you ever use it, when did you use it, and so on. And I said, "What am I supposed to say?" Then I'm not supposed to say "Jane and I did this" or "Sue and I," and "It was on the third night of May" or something.

Th. This is your own private affair, as long as you are careful and you don't get yourself too deeply messed up and involved. That's your own business and you're right in resenting her taking your pocket book and going through it, anyways.

Pt. That's true, and oh, the other thing, they found *Playboys* in my room, so ohhhhhhhh, no smut in the house, and they start yelling and at the same time, I know, I don't see anything wrong with it.

Th. There isn't anything wrong with it, but what they apparently feel is that they would like to have a son the ideal, moral, studious kind of a guy. I think most parents would like to picture their children as that. I mean from an ideal standpoint, anything that goes below that ideal and they start blaming themselves, start feeling guilty, feel you may be heading for a lot of trouble. I would think their anxieties are not to hurt you—their anxieties are motivated by a concern about you. Their motives are probably honorable ones, you know what I mean? At least they have a desire to see that you don't get into problems, that you don't get caught by any girl, that you don't get any girl pregnant, that you don't get a venereal disease. These are probably what their motives are. They may be living in the last generation and not in this one. They may not know what goes on these days. I suppose they felt you were all mixed up and needed advice and that I should evaluate what your problem is. Is that why they brought you here? [*I am defending the parents to see if I can give him another meaning for their behavior than their purely seeking to dominate and control him.*]

Pt. I don't know—I was going to ask you.

Th. I don't think you're mixed up in so far as what you have told me is concerned. [*I get the impression that we are developing a relationship. The patient tries to move his chair closer to me.*] So far you haven't told me a thing that is abnormal. [*At this point I introduce questions about other symptoms and complaints.*]

Th. I want to ask you a few questions about any symptoms you may have. How about tension? Do you feel tense?

Pt. Sometimes—I mean, yes. Not always.

Th. Under what circumstances?

Pt. When I get upset at things.

Th. Any anxiety, a feeling you're falling apart?

Pt. Why no.

Th. Depression?

Pt. Not too bad.

Th. Physical complaints or symptoms, like headaches, stomach trouble, bowel trouble, and so on?

Pt. I don't think so.

Th. How about sexual problems?

Pt. Nothing like that.

Th. Phobias or fears or thoughts that crop up that frighten you?

Pt. No.

Th. How do you sleep? Any insomnia?

Pt. Sleep OK.

Th. Do you dream a little or a lot?

Pt. A lot, but I don't remember any dreams.

Th. Remember any childhood dreams?

Pt. Like of falling, scary.

Th. Nightmares?

Pt. I don't remember.

Th. How about drugs? Taking any pills or things?

Pt. No, nothing. Some of the kids take grass. I don't like it.

Th. Now tell me a little about your mother.

Pt. What could I tell. She bosses my father around. Keeps telling me what to do.

Th. Scared of her?

Pt. No.

Th. How about your father?

Pt. I told you. I can't get to him. He doesn't understand.

Th. How about your sister, she's a few years older. How do you get along?

Pt. We get along fine. I can talk to her. We used to fight when I was small. We like each other now.

Th. How did you get along when you were a kid, at home, at school?

Pt. OK, I guess.

Th. No problems?

Pt. No, none I can think of.

Th. Have many friends?

Pt. Oh, yes.

Th. Any previous treatment with a psychiatrist or psychologist?

Pt. No.

[*I decide to show the patient the Rorschach cards to see if I can pick up any underlying dynamics. From the data he has given me I cannot yet discern problems other than parents and adolescent in conflict over behavior that is not too unusual. His story may conceal other aspects that he deliberately or unconsciously is holding back. It is possible that something will come through in his responses to the Rorschach cards or in drawings.*]

Th. I'm going to show you some cards, and I want you to tell me what you see. This really is not a test—just an idea of your impressions. (*I show him the first card*)

Pt. OK. Are those the pictures you look at and I'm supposed to say what it looks like?

Th. That's right—ever seen them?

Pt. I've heard about them.

Th. What does that look like? (*first card*)

Pt. I don't know, an insect. Can I turn this any way I want?

Th. Any way you want.

Pt. Or a mask.

Th. Anything else?

Pt. No.

Th. OK. What does that look like? (*second card*) Anything that comes to your mind. So far you are doing very well.
Pt. I don't know, it looks like a footprint or something. I don't know, a face or something.
Th. Where's a face?
Pt. That.
Th. Show me.
Pt. There, the lower part—the eyes—the nose—the eyes.
Th. Here's the third one.
Pt. It looks like two people dancing—it looks like two people dancing back to back the other way.
Th. Anything else? What kind of people are they?
Pt. Do you mean race-wise?
Th. No, no, are they men, women?
Pt. I don't know they look like both men and women.
Th. What makes them look like men?
Pt. There. (*points to projection*)
Th. You mean this is a penis?
Pt. Right.
Th. And what makes them look like women?
Pt. They look like they have breasts right here.
Th. Now, this is the fourth one.
Pt. Ugh, it looks like a dead rabbit. Also looks like a bat or some animal that got hit with a steam roller.
Th. All right, here's the fifth one.
Pt. That looks like a bat, that really does.
Th. Anything else?
Pt. No.
Th. All right, here's the next one. (*sixth card*)
Pt. It looks like a cat that kind of got hit.
Th. Pussy cat?
Pt. I don't know, some sort of cat, nothing else.
Th. OK, this is the seventh one.
Pt. Are these any special patterns?
Th. No, everybody has different associations.
Pt. Ummmmm—nothing.
Th. Well, look at it closely.
Pt. Oh, oh, it looks like two people dancing again—they're wearing a skirt or dresses or whatever. Have long hairdo's. That's all.
Th. OK, here's the next one. (*eighth card*)
Pt. Two men hanging onto something. This way it looks like a face. I guess that looks like a bomb. (*ninth card*) I don't know maybe some muscular guy or something sitting in the back. You know the back angle.
Th. OK, here's the last one.
Pt. It looks like the anatomy of some body—I don't know. (*hands card back*)
Th. All right. Now I'm going to ask you to draw me a picture of a person.
Pt. A person?
Th. Yes, anything you want. This is no drawing contest.
Pt. Boy or girl?
Th. Anything—just a picture—anything you want.
Pt. I'll draw about lifting weights. Did I say anything wrong with those pictures?
Th. No. You did pretty good. I could testify that you're not nuts if that's what you're afraid of. I can say there's nothing seriously wrong with your mind.
Pt. What's the purpose of having me draw this?
Th. I'll tell you when you get through—OK, now draw me a picture of a person.
Pt. A woman? (*Patient draws an ugly woman with large breasts holding a stick.*)
Th. Now a man.
Pt. You don't mind if it's inside? (*He draws a muscle man lifting weights.*)
Th. It doesn't matter. [*I get the impression from his responses to the Rorschach cards that he is immersed in incomplete separation-individuation, feels crushed (fourth and sixth cards) with a problem in identity (third card). I conjecture that the woman with a stick in his first drawing is his strong, punitive mother and the man, his compensating masculine self.*] Now, you see I gave you a test, and the test would seem to indicate that your basic defenses are pretty good and that you've got a lot of oomph, spark, a lot of fire [*an attempt at reassurance*]. But you do withdraw and you do inhibit when things get too tough for you [*sparse responses on cards*]. You pull back and you just don't let yourself come out of yourself. It also indicates that you are working out your feelings of masculinity, that somehow you're not too confident about your feelings of masculinity at the present time. Why do you smile?
Pt. I forget. [*I get the feeling from the nonverbal responses to the interpretations I have made that the interpretations are correct assumptions. His remark "I forget" indicates to me an active desire to deny. The dynamic focus to be worked on, if I am correct, would then be his separation-individuation and identity problems.*]
Th. All right, now where would these problems come from? From your relations with your

mother and your father? Do they have a lot of trouble together?

Pt. Yeah—a little bit—a lot.

Th. You see a person is brought up in a family and you see how the mother and father get along together—and you begin to pick up ideas about how males function with females. Does she kick him around? dominate him?

Pt. Sometimes—most of the times.

Th. That makes a woman a strong person in the conceptual thinking of a boy. He would like to identify with a strong father—who is able to stand up to his wife, to keep her from being too controlling, and stop her. Where the woman is too strong in the family, it's apt to reflect on the boy's feelings that women are the strong people. Now, this has an impact on the boy's developing sense of masculinity. And this is the one problem—it doesn't make you daffy or anything like that, but it is something that you have to work out—you have to begin to develop a different conceptualization of yourself as a strong masculine person. [*This is a strong interpretation, but I believe I am right. I wonder how the patient will handle the interpretation. If he denies it or bypasses it, a great deal of work will be necessary on his defenses. Where a person's identity problems are too strong and where they are responsible for many adjustment difficulties, long-term therapy may be needed.*]

Pt. Well, I know when I was in elementary school—I don't know why—but it used to be if the boys wanted to show off before the girls, they'd jump me. I used to be smaller and everything—and they'd say let's jump on the fag or something like that.

Th. Who would say that?

Pt. Oh, some of the kids.

Th. The kids would say to whom?

Pt. To me. They'd jump on me—and they'd say this to the other kids—that's I kinda—I've been doing weights—that's probably the reason I drew that. Then the other day, I went downtown just looking for a fight—I don't know, maybe to prove myself—who knows. [*The patient's admission that he had concern about others considering him homosexual, his realization that his drawing refers to himself, his insight about practicing with weights and looking for fights to compensate for his fear of lack of masculinity are good signs.*]

Th. Look, you'll never prove it that way. It's better to keep away from fights because all it will do is create problems for you. [*I am pushing advice—hoping that I have established sufficient credibility for him to follow this advice since he could get into serious trouble trying to prove his masculinity through violence and fighting.*]

Pt. Yeah, I know, like the last time I was home. Like one kid said, "How's school?" and I said, "It's not bad," and he said, "It must be a pansy school" or something like that. And I said, "Look it's kinda hard," and he said, "Well, then it must be a good school," and then he said, "If you're going there, the kids must be a bunch of JO's." And going on like this. This is one kid I hate. And it was just yesterday and I went to town just looking for him. And then before I left for school—the last time—I just went all over town looking for one kid.

Th. To beat the hell out of him?

Pt. If I could just find him. Because something happened between me and a girl—or something like that—and he was the cause of it. It wasn't this girl Jane—another girl. I was really mad then, and I told the girl, "Tell him if I see him again, I'll look for him tomorrow." Then some kid called me up, one of his friends, who must be a senior now, and he said, "If you lay a hand on him, I'll knock the shit out of you, and I got a marine friend who is going to do this to you." You know the whole marines, the army, like that. And I said, "Well, this is just between me and him, you know; if he's so tough let him be there." I don't know I spent the whole day in town, he never came around.

Th. You can have beefs with kids, and maybe you should be able to defend yourself. There's no reason why you shouldn't learn how to defend yourself, but to look for fights is another matter.

Pt. I think jujitsu is kind of for the birds. I mean if you get into a fight, you know. I used to think Judo is pretty good until last year. I saw a kid, and he said, "I take judo," and the other kid started laughing like anything, and then he just stood there laughing, and then the kid starts the fancy advances, and then the next thing you know the judo expert was on the ground, and he started bleeding.

Th. Do they have tough kids in that place you're in?

Pt. Not where I live, but downtown, yes.

Th. Well, listen, I think that you are concerned about defending yourself because of your own doubts of your own capacity to defend yourself and your own feelings of low masculinity. But that's a problem you won't work out by fighting. You work it out by talking about it, and if you want to come and see me and talk about these things, I'll be glad to see you. Because you can do a lot better by verbalizing than you can by fighting. [*I'm testing my effectiveness in the interview here. Have I established a relationship and does he have sufficient confidence in me to start therapy with me? His response to my invitation will tell.*]

Pt. That's what Jim said, you know Jim Sloan, my friend. I told him yesterday. He wanted to go out and I told him I gotta stay home, and I told him I was going to see a psychiatrist. And he said, you're really lucky 'cause they can do a lot of good for you. He said when you walk in there, trust him, he said, sometimes it may take a few times, to trust him eough to talk to him, but once you can, you're lucky. I didn't believe him. I didn't want to come, but I'm glad I came.

Th. Well, if you can clarify some things for yourself, you are lucky. Believe me, insight and understanding can be the greatest savior of your life. If you have an idea of what's cooking with you and where it originated, you can take a stand against it. But if you haven't the faintest idea of what's going on, all you feel are emotions and bad feelings, and then you've got to get rid of these feelings. And before you know it, you're in a mess. You don't solve anything. A lot of the feelings you've been having with your parents are these bad feelings that are coming up because you can't communicate with them. Now, maybe it's impossible to communicate. I don't know what you're up against with them because I don't know both of them. But I do believe they must have your welfare at heart. Their motives at least are good, but the way they express themselves may be bad.

Pt. Do you really feel that or are you just saying that?

Th. Why should I say that to you if I didn't mean it?

Pt. I don't know, to give me a certain feeling or something.

Th. But I think you can be much smarter than you've been, because what you have been doing is joining in on a battle with them. You are the low man on the totem pole. You haven't got a chance with them unless you use another kind of tactic.

Pt. How?

Th. You have to be kind of smart in communicating with them. Let them know your feelings, but don't tell them everything about what you do, about these girls. You can tell them what is true. Why not say about your girl, "This isn't serious." If they say, "Are you going to see her?" you could say, "Look I have certain things that I have to keep to myself, and I'm going to keep them to myself. I'm not going to do anything that will embarrass you, or hurt you. I'm not going to marry anybody, I'm not going to get anybody pregnant."

Pt. I told them often. We had a big argument one night. I said something like, "I don't know what you're so concerned about right now. I'm not going to latch onto one girl until I marry her." I said. "Don't worry. I'm not stupid; I'm not going to get into trouble." They get upset if a girl isn't our religion. It's a big thing. They just want to know, I don't know, but there's a whole bunch of these arguments, and I say, "Don't worry about this, this isn't going to happen," and they say, "Are you going to see Jane," and so forth and so forth. Because the other night I came home and my mother had gone to sleep and it was about 11:00 o'clock I came in, and he starts to talk to me. I had this feeling he wanted to hit on something, and I said, "Get to the point, Dad; what is it?" And he said, "I'm not hitting on anything. I just like you to go out with other girls," and so forth.

Th. Whereabouts is the place that you're going to school?

Pt. Haverstown.

Th. I wonder if I could find a person for you to talk to like you're talking to me. Would you want to see someone to talk things over. [*Since Haverstown is far from New York, I am contemplating referring the patient to another therapist who lives in the neighborhood of the school.*]

Pt. That would be pretty good.

Th. You haven't got communication with your parents. You need communication with somebody. Because you're getting too bottled up within yourself. These kids at school, you can't talk to kids the way you would talk to a therapist. They don't know what it's all about.

Pt. My sister is pretty smart.

Th. She's fine. You can talk to her, but she's not around.

Pt. That's true.

Th. I'll be glad to see you whenever you can come into town, but it would be better if you had somebody nearby. That would be great. How would you feel about that?

Pt. That would be pretty good.

Th. But there may not be anybody around there in Haverstown.

Pt. It's a hicktown; it's right near nothing. But I have a friend in one of the teachers. Every so often he'll tell me to drop into his room, his apartment, and maybe we'll have a talk or something like that.

Th. You need somebody who has more training, really more expert in this type of thing. You need somebody who knows about dynamics, about emotional problems, about relationships with and between parents, the involvement with one's own sense of self. This is a highly specialized and complicated business. An educator usually doesn't have this type of training. (*pause*) If there's nobody trained near Haverstown, I'll suggest that you come and see me as often as you can. How often can you come into the city?

Pt. Pretty often.

Th. Can you? I'll be glad to see you whenever you can get away. You know it will also make your parents feel as if you're not going to get yourself into trouble. You know, you have a lot on the ball, and you have a lot of very good stuff in you. I wouldn't say that you are abnormal, but you can get involved in trouble with all these feelings to act out, this fear of not being a man. You have to work it out on another level.

Pt. I don't mean to be untactful, but how much does one visit cost?

Th. I have a sliding scale. In other words, depending upon what a person can pay; in other words, if a person is able to pay a high fee, it's going to cost more. If he can't pay a high fee, I scale it down.

Pt. Suppose I was to be paying for this. [*This is a good sign and indicates that the patient wants to assume responsibility for his own treatment. In my mind I already have decided that I will see the parents also, who will make up for the small fee the boy can afford to pay. They will know too that the boy is carrying his own treatment costs.*]

Th. Yourself, depends on how much you could afford to pay—what could you afford to pay?

Pt. It depends if I could send you my allowance from school.

Th. I wouldn't want to take away your allowance, I'd work out something. Whatever you could afford to pay. I'll work that out with you next time. Well, let's leave it this way—that whenever you can come into town, let me know a couple days in advance. This will be just between you and me. They won't have any—I'm not going to tell them anything about what we talk about. It's the only way I can work with a person. If I were to reveal anything you told me, it would destroy our relationship, and it wouldn't be helpful particularly. The only thing I can tell them about my talk with you today is that, in my opinion, you don't have anything seriously wrong with you, that you're evolving and developing in a normal way, and that they have to establish better communication with you. And they have to stop going through your pockets. That would be great if I could put that across to them, wouldn't it?

Pt. That would be fine, but sometimes, I may be wrong, but sometimes I feel they think they can get through to me by giving me something of a talk. I don't know, they say, "You've had it too easy, we've given you everything." They say why we don't trust you is because you were there anyway, meaning about seeing Jane. They don't expect me to say I'm not going to go there, and if she means anything to me, they don't expect me to say I'm not going to go. And they are trying to corner me into saying I'll never go and give my word that I won't go.

Th. Well, I'll do my best. I'm trying to figure out what I can tell them to try to help the situation. I'll tell them that we talked things over and that I think that it would be better for you to talk to somebody else than to talk to them, and that I told you I'd be very happy to see you. If any problems come up, you would be able to discuss them with me. How far from New York City is Haverstown?

Pt. All I know is that it's about 75 miles.

Th. How would you get here?

Pt. Oh, I could take a train in.

Th. You could come in once in two weeks, once in three weeks, once a month. You know that isn't bad.

Pt. Once a month I could come in.

Th. Do you really want to come and see me and talk to me, no kidding about it?

Pt. I'm serious.

Th. You tell them then that you would very much like to come and talk things over with me and that if any problems come up, you will want to discuss them with me. I'll tell them that I've seen you, and I think it would be very helpful if I could have some talks with you. I'll tell them that you have no serious intention of getting yourself so completely immersed and involved with anybody that's going to interfere with your freedom. You know, give them some kind of assurance so that they will stop bugging you about this thing. You know what I mean? That's if you agree, I should tell them that.

Pt. I mean I agree with you about what you're going to tell them, but how am I supposed to act? Sure we can sit here and talk, but I have to live with them.

Th. You have to live with them, I know. Why can't you just say, "Look, Mom and Dad, I don't want to fight with you. I don't want to go behind your back and do things that are bad. I can assure you that I'm going to go out with other people, but I also probably want to see Jane."

Pt. I couldn't say that to them; they would start an argument. Anytime that name is mentioned, there is going to be an argument. Anytime it has been mentioned in the past, there's an argument. And I know it's a very sensitive subject. What could I say?

Th. Why not say simply: "Look, I'm going to talk things over with Dr. Wolberg. Get the idea?"

Pt. OK.

Th. I better see them for a couple of minutes. (*Patient walks out–parents come in and sit down.*)

Fa. We've been taking it.

Th. You've been really taking it? Surviving? What's been happening?

Fa. It's been tough, the son, he's been belligerent, and he's been walking with a chip on his shoulder (*separates hands widely*) this big. Knock it off, you know. There's no talking to him. I know I can't get through to him. I try to talk to him. There's no rapport, there's nothing.

Th. (*Addressing the mother*) Can you get through to him?

Mo. I can't.

Fa. I just can't get through. I don't like what's developing, developing in him.

Th. I don't like what's developing in him either, between you and me, because he can get himself into a hell of a lot of trouble the way he feels.

Mo. Well, he's—he doesn't want to do anything. He just likes to do nothing. It's very hard to sit and watch this for hours, I guess. I feel, I almost feel I don't give a damn.

Th. I can understand your emotions. I know you take it on the chin. He's a very handsome boy with a lot of stuff on the ball, but he is not living up to his own potential. He's acting out and so on. I gave him some tests to see what's what. He's got a lot on the ball, but he's just full of emotion. He's an extremely emotional kid, ready to explode any time, but his defenses are pretty good. I mean he's able to hold on to his emotions. The only basic problem that comes up is one common at his age, a fear of his own capacities as a growing boy, a need to prove his own masculinity. Proving himself with exercises and weight lifting is OK, but wanting to get into fights—this is a serious problem that I took up with him. He needs therapy. Now, it's going to be very difficult to find anybody around Haverstown. There's nobody in that area we can call on. I believe I was able to get to him, to communicate to him, to relate with him. I think he trusts me, and he opened up with me. He came in very defensively as you know. I was able to cut through, but you can judge that better when you talk to him. I think the worst thing you can do is keep putting injunctions on him—rules. He will break them down; you will not be able to stop him at this point. With some therapy he should be able to control himself. At the present time he is focusing everything on a battle with you, which isn't so unusual at this age when he is breaking his dependency on you.

Mo. What kind of rules, excuse me, what kind of rules? [*Apparently, she is quite defensive.*]

Th. He won't pay attention to rules.

Mo. There aren't any rules.

Th. You tell him not to see this girl. I would advise you—I don't know if you can do it—to lay off that situation for the time being. Don't countenance it and don't condone it, but don't quiz him about it. We talked about it, and he agreed it would be better for him to see other people. I told him it would be only sensible for him not to restrict himself to this girl. It isn't as serious as you think. He agreed it would be a good thing if he did not restrict himself to one person. The basic thing is he needs somebody to talk to. He needs to communicate with somebody, to open up with somebody, because he's a volcano inside, ready to bust wide open. And if he verbalizes, he's not so likely to act out. I told him, "I can see you anytime you come, if you call me in advance."

Fa. We were talking about that outside.

Th. And he said to me, "What do you charge?" I said, "I charge a sliding scale, what a person could afford to pay." He said, "I'd like to pay for this myself out of my allowance." so I said, "All right, we'll work out something. We'll work out something between the two of us, whatever you can afford to pay, because after all you can't afford a high fee and I do see some people here at a low fee scale." It would be better for him to feel he can handle it by himself, so he can send me five bucks or whatever it is.

Mo. That's his allowance.

Th. Then I'll talk to him; someday he can pay me.

Mo. He wants to come then?

Th. I think he very much wants to come. He was telling me that he was talking to a friend last night and said they (meaning you) want me to see a psychiatrist. This other kid said, "You know you're very lucky, you're very lucky you can see somebody to talk to."

Fa. He told us about it. The interesting thing is the fellow he says said it, his mother and father, can't get along with him.

(The patient came for a session the next week, again accompanied by his parents. At that time I convinced the parents to continue in therapy with me, both singly and together, during which I counseled them on the developmental requirements of adolescents and the need to encourage their son's independent strivings. It became apparent that the chief problem in the family neurosis was the mother's need to control and dominate both her husband and her children to a point that they had to obey without question to avoid her hysterical displays. The father was introduced to a group who challenged his passive yielding to his wife and encouraged his standing up to her and taking her son's side. The mother received about 40 sessions of psychoanalytically oriented therapy along with about 10 sessions of group therapy. The boy himself benefited sufficiently from 5 more sessions to discontinue therapy greatly improved. On follow-up the entire family structure and relationship between members of the family had changed remarkedly for the better.)

Case 2

The following illustrates the active, supportive first-session management of an acute exacerbation of anxiety in a chronic obsessive-compulsive patient. In deciding to terminate therapy after a few sessions, I toyed with the alternative possibility of engaging in a long-term process, but felt that the risks of enhancing the patient's dependency on me might be too great. Actually, the patient herself expressed an inability to continue in prolonged therapy. My objective then was to bring her rapidly to an anxiety-free equilibrium, offering her, if possible, some insight into her dynamics, which hopefully could in time, if she utilized it, have some reconstructive effect. There was no illusion that this brief treatment interlude would forestall future attacks. However, it was felt that if the patient could be tided over her immediate crisis, she might be helped to a better adjustment. Since tension was the motor that released her obsessional symptoms, helping her to learn to control tension by relaxation was the tactic I decided to utilize.

Pt. I called the Consultation Service and I spoke to Dr. G. and told him what I needed and he recommended you. He said that you were the person to tell me yes or no. [*The patient speaks rapidly and seems upset and perturbed. I get the impression that she needs a good deal of reassurance which may or may not be of help to her.*]

Th. You mean, whether my kind of therapy would be of value to you?

Pt. That's right.

Th. Well, supposing you give me an idea of your problem, and then I will tell you whether I can be of any possible help to you.

Pt. Can you treat me? I have obsessions that crowd into my mind and upset me.

Th. If you have the desire for help, that is usually nine-tenths of the battle. [*Because she is so upset, I decide to reassure her rather than to explore what she means by "obsessions."*]

Pt. Well, that's what I am. I am really obsessive, very badly.

Th. Tell me about it. How bad is it?

Pt. Well I will tell you the story. I get very upset over it. (*The patient pauses and is manifestly anxious.*)

Th. Take your time [*more reassurance*].

Pt. When I was 15, this first came out and it really bothered me. A word came to my mind, and I felt forced to repeat it. (*pause*) It is the repeating of the word (*pause*).

Th. The repeating of the word.

Pt. Yes, you see I come from a very religious family. I, myself, am not religious or anything like that. I don't know if you know what I am talking about. In the family that I came from there were constant prayers. Well, as a child, when I was about 15, I remember my father having a lot of financial trouble. There was a lot of worry and high tension in the house. I suppose I took this more or less to heart, whereas my sister and brother didn't really believe in all the complaints, the usual kinds of things that go on. One time I was up in my bedroom and I was just sort of like praying to God that everything would work out and it would be all right. I know I was feeling defiance and I know how this works, but I said to myself, "Well, if I can't pray to God to make everything all right, maybe if I say 'Jesus Christ' over and over again it will." Well, I started to repeat that in my mind and it seemed repulsive.

Th. Jesus Christ?

Pt. That's it.

Th. The repetition of Jesus Christ, was it sort of a defiant gesture?

Pt. I suppose it was. I don't quite understand it. Well, I couldn't stop repeating this thing in my mind. It would just go on and on and on, which never happened actually before. I didn't know what to do. Finally, I told my mother about it, and we went to our family doctor. I was 15 at the time. I am 21 now. He sent me to a psychiatrist. This guy was a psychiatrist and neurologist. Now, when I went to him, it was for a short time. A matter of a few months. He did absolutely nothing for me, as far as that goes. I told him the same story which I will tell you now that there is something that happened to me when I was 8 years old. I can remember when this thing first came out. I am positive about it. I am telling the same rotten story. I hate myself for this because it was just a waste of everything. Well, finally, after about 5 months I recall that it started to let down—this repeating of the words—and I got back to being myself. Just being myself. Period. [*The outcropping of the obsessional symptom is a derivative of many anxieties, some perhaps unconscious, dating back to her childhood. The patient recognizes the connection.*]

Th. During this period that you were seeing the psychiatrist what happened?

Pt. Yes. I went to him on and off, and then eventually he just told me that he really specialized in neurology and there was not a darn thing he could do for me. And if I could, I would have rather avoided this. I was a junior in high school at the time that I was 15. Toward the end of that year it more or less went away and I would forget about it. I would rather think that it had nothing to do with me and that I could stand it. I was all right in my senior year in high school. I was all right in my freshman year in college. Maybe it would start coming up, but I could sort of fight it down. When I was a sophomore in college, I went away to school.

Th. You were all right as a freshman in college?

Pt. Yes. Then I wanted to go away to school and live in a dorm. It was a new experience. Getting away and, of course, the change of environment suddenly. Everything was going along well, although it was new and I had never been away from home. But before I could get better, this thing got hold of me. You know what I mean?

Th. You mean the obsessions started again? When was that? How long ago?

Pt. This was when I was 18. It's not so much the repeating of the word, actually, although that occurred.

Th. The same word, Jesus Christ?

Pt. Yes, but it changed to all kinds of symptoms actually. I started just with saying, "Jesus Christ," but I know where all this came from. I will go back, but I just wanted to take it from here. Finally, when I was a sophomore, at the end of my sophomore year, I got home and everything was fine. It didn't bother me that much either that year as much as it did the first time. Then I became engaged. I was fine and I thought it wouldn't even bother me anymore. I got married. My husband and I have a very nice marriage—a successful marriage. [*Up to this point the patient does not present too coherent a story. She seems so concerned and upset with her obsessional symptom that she bypasses important details that I shall explore later.*]

Th. How old were you when you got married?

Pt. Nineteen. I'm 21 now.

Th. You have been married almost 2 years?

Pt. A year and 3 months. I was married for 10 months—this is why I am here now—this past April I was humming in bed, and, you see actually when I am out and active and everything, and if this starts to bother me, I can just get involved in other things and sort of keep it depressed, keep it down. When it came to the surface again, that really bothered me.

Th. It must have upset you a good deal.

Pt. It did, this past April.

Th. That's 5 months ago.

Pt. I have spoken to some people since then because my husband and I want a large family naturally. My husband and I want to plan on a family, and I don't want to have children because I will be suffering worse then. Because, if it is an anxiety, or whatever you call it, when I get it, really get it, I am miserable. You can't remove it sometimes lying there; you just don't know what it is. It's like your scared of something, but you don't know what you are scared of. It is very hard to say. I had spoken to some people about the thing that happened to me in April. I got petrified. I avoided everything and everybody. To me if I am not feeling guilty and it is not bothering me, I am fine. I realize now that it is something that will be recurring until I find out what it is that is needed, or destroy it, or put it down. I spoke to a few doctors, but nothing steady.

Th. Any other tries at psychotherapy?

Pt. Just the one time that I told you about. I had a girl friend talking to me once. I never told anybody about it because I am deathly ashamed of it, and deathly ashamed that anyone should know. Anyway, that bothers me an awful lot. She was telling me about when she was away one time. She stutters. She had gone to a person, who I believe is a psychiatrist, who taught hypnosis to other doctors or something of that sort, and she was telling me the story of how she was regressed to earlier times of her life. She was regressed to the time where she first started to stutter. Her mother took a knife to one of her brothers when she was 2 years old, when it happened that she stuttered. After she found out about that, then she began to talk. [*This conventional notion of the pathogenicity of "buried memories," and their need to disgorge them for cure, sends some patients in quest of therapists who can surgically dissect into the unconscious.*] After she found out about that, then she began to talk. Well, from what I had read about hypnosis and things like that, I thought that maybe, maybe this is one way of going back and finding out why I had this trouble. What is it covering up? I know this much at least. When I was 8 years old, I have three brothers, and an older brother, who is 6 years older than I—there was a lot of sex play between the two of us. I was brought up in a very strict home. Sex was something that was never talked about, and so forth. The way I feel about it, I have not a bad adjustment. I have had a very good adjustment in marriage. I can't understand how one has anything to do with the other. This is the only thing I can remember from my young childhood life. This thing is bothering me. There was no actual intercourse that took place at all, but there was like masturbation. He would touch me, and I would touch him, and so forth. [*What the patient wants is hypnosis to uproot important memories. This, in my opinion, is not what will help her. Naturally, she is not told this since it may discourage her to learn that the technique that she believes will save her cannot do so. Later, when I have a working relationship with her, I will be in a better position to apprise her of what I believe can help her.*]

Th. You remember the incident today quite acutely? You were only 8 years of age then. It still bothers you?

Pt. I remember every single thing that happened.

Th. Do you remember if you felt sexual excitement at the time?

Pt. Not me.

Th. Not you?

Pt. Well, it is a funny thing. If I were to be truthful, I'd say that I knew that I liked it. But here is the story. You see, when we first started—this went on for a very short time, but it wasn't just one time that it took place between the two of us—when it first started, I knew nothing about sex. I was just about 8 years old. I didn't even know what it was. During the time that this was going on, all the girls were getting together and starting to talk about sex. Then I realized what I was doing and that what I was doing was wrong. That made me feel different. (*pause*)

Th. It made you feel guilty?

Pt. Now, I was only 8, but I remember one time. Maybe it was extra nice or something like that. It was the summertime in my house. I wanted to tell my mother. I had to get this thing out of me. I can remember going to my room and crying about it. Always deathly afraid that I was pregnant. Even though, as I say, I knew I couldn't be, but I was scared that I was. I was scared all of my teenage life that someday I would be pregnant from this thing. I remember my mother came upstairs to my room, but she came in with my aunt, and I was going to tell her, but she was with my aunt and I couldn't. I looked at her and said, "Mommy, I am pregnant." Of course, my aunt burst out laughing. I would burst out laughing if it was anybody else. They just shut it off. It was just nothing. Some kind of silly business and that was the end of it. Well, to this day nobody knows anything about it except this doctor that I spoke to.

Th. Your brother was 14 at the time?

Pt. Yes. When this was going on, he would send me out of the room, and I never knew why. It was when he would reach an orgasm and the sperm would be coming out. One time I asked him why, and he let me stay, and I saw the sperm coming out, and he told me, "That's what makes you pregnant." I became, as a child of 9 and 10, I became very afraid of sperm. Things that my brother would touch I was afraid to touch for fear I would get pregnant. Sometimes I was scared in my married life. I can understand it rationally, but I do not want to have a pregnancy, and I am more scared of becoming pregnant just from sperm than I think a normal person would be. I am quite sure of that.

Th. Do you use contraceptives?

Pt. Yes. I became very afraid to touch anything that my brother touched. If I would, then I would run and wash my hands, wash my hands, and wash my hands. It was getting ridiculous, but I had to do it. If that is compulsion, well, then that is compulsion. I don't know what it is. Then, of course, I think that from that maybe you would determine that I was touchy. That doesn't bother me much. When I was younger, I would pick up the prayer book and start to read. When I would come to the end of the sentence, or something like that, I would have to say, "Jesus Christ" over and over to myself. It got to the point where I couldn't read with anybody, although I didn't say anything. Then this would come to my mind. As I grew up, I guess it subsided and didn't bother me, with the hand washing and things like that, although all through my teenage life I always was afraid I was going to become pregnant. Even as a child. It only went on for a short period, a matter of months. I don't really remember how long. Well, it was during this time that I started to repeat "Jesus Christ" to myself. And ever since that time, this thing has just been growing and growing and growing. Now it stops, now it flares up, now it doesn't. The last time was in April. It hasn't bothered me for quite a while. Although I could fight it down, I am purposely not fighting it down for the simple reason that I want to get rid of it because naturally we want to have a family. I know that I cannot make a decent mother with this sort of attack coming upon me. One other thing that bothers me—I guess this is because I am oversensitive to the problem—it is that when we told our family doctor, I was afraid, I am now scared that everybody knows. I am so afraid that people will find me out. The people around Connecticut, where I live, are nosy. I believe, I think it now.

Th. Find out about your obsession?

Pt. When it doesn't bother me and I think that someone knows, I just laugh it off. I think, "So what, what can I do about it. I can't help it. It is over and done with. It is a silly thing." In fact, I can remember actually laughing at myself in-between times to think that I would do something like that. Although that bothers me a lot, swallowing sometimes is a symptom.

Th. Swallowing? Tell me about that.

Pt. It is just nothing. All of a sudden I just can't swallow. It doesn't bother me a lot. It is all of a sudden. I am not doing it now. I am just talking about this whole thing, particularly the word repeating.

Th. Tell me about this. What other word besides Jesus Christ comes out?

Pt. I don't always say "Jesus Christ." I change the word around so that I don't have to say that particular word. I would say "cockadoodle" or something like that.

Th. Cockadoodle?

Pt. I don't know. Just anything in order to avoid saying the word that I am thinking of. But sometimes I will just be doing anything and it will come out just like that.

Th. When it comes out, it gives you anxiety?

Pt. Oh, yes.

Th. A great deal of anxiety?

Pt. Not always. But when I am feeling fine, and all of a sudden it comes out, I just pray that it isn't going to come to the surface, I don't pray. I didn't mean it that way. I just get scared and try to avoid it. Because I know how I can get so involved and engulfed in this thing.

Th. All right. Now, apart from this, do any other words come up in the same context as Jesus Christ?

Pt. Only if I try to cover it up with a swear word, but it doesn't bother me in the least actually.

Th. Tell me a little bit more about other symptoms. Do you get tension during the day?

Pt. Do you mean when I am upset or just a regular day?

Th. Regular day.

Pt. I know I have a lot of inferiorities. I can tell you that much. Here is a curious thing. I don't know if this means that your ego does strengthen up through time or not. At one time I felt like I was the ugliest thing in the world. I would walk down the halls—this my prejudice coming up—and if the colored girls would walk by me, I would think, "You know you are just the ugliest thing in the world." And yet, it doesn't bother me at all now, and hasn't bothered me since. I have had the other two attacks more or less which have been just as bad. And yet, when I was a senior in high school, I couldn't compete in my sorority, which must have been a shock to my ego. Now it really doesn't bother me anymore. I have two sisters, one is a year older than I. I know I was held in her shadow.

Th. I see. Did you have any other kinds of problems as a child? Did you have any tics or speech problems of any kind, instances of bedwetting or walking in your sleep? [*I could have focused more on the competitiveness with her sister, but I wanted to get as much information as possible in this interview to help me in designing a treatment plan.*]

Pt. I never walked in my sleep, never wet my bed. I don't know if this has anything to do with it, but I once asked my mother, although I certainly don't remember back that far myself. Of course, my sister has a baby now, and I like the way she is bringing her up. She lets her do things as she comes of age and that's how she controls herself. I supposedly never wet my pants, and by a year or something like it I never bed wet. I can never remember any one time in my life where I did bed-wetting. As far as tics are concerned, which means swallowing or some such funny thing, I don't know how old I was, but you know how you can click your throat or something. I used to do that, but not a lot. Not that it bothered me. I never got worried about it. Maybe yesterday or something it might have happened.

Th. How about depressions? Do you get depressed?

Pt. The only time I get depressed is when I get the attack. Right now I'm not depressed. If my husband wanted to go to a party and have a good time, I'd go. When I feel all right in between attacks, I am just like any other person. Sometimes I feel blue one day, but certainly not depressed. If somebody calls and wants to go someplace, okay. But I do get very, very downhearted when this thing gets me. Because, what can I do? Right now I am all right in that sense. What am I going to do? I can't break out. What's the use of going on from here. It is just ridiculous. (*pause*)

Th. Do you get any headaches?

Pt. Yes. I know when I get a headache and when I don't. I know this means it's a neurotic symptom, pressing on the sides. I get all this stuff. I have gotten this pressing feeling ever since the attacks started, from the time this started when I was a child.

Th. This depressing feeling?

Pt. Pressing not depressing. I had to go to the doctor to get a physical checkup because I was getting so excited and so scared inside that I would actually work a fever up inside myself. I can't explain it. I get so scared and so petrified that I don't know what to do. Well, I know when I get a fever. When I get a real fever, I know that I am sick, but when I get this kind of a "hotness" or something . . . now I can relate that to something when I refer back. When I was 8 years old, I can remember during the sex play between my brother and I, I could never understand why the air always felt so warm or so hot. Now I don't know if there is any direct correlation between these. I don't even know if it is that which is causing it. Maybe it is completely subconscious. But for some reason I always relate it to that. But it may have nothing to do with it.

Th. Do you relate the fever to that incident with your brother?

Pt. No, it was from my brother seeming to get excited or stimulated, of course. Warmth was just part of the sexual stimulation. I remember wondering about it especially when I handled his penis.

Th. When you handled his penis, did you have any feelings about that?

Pt. Me? Sexually?

Th. Did it excite you or scare you?

Pt. In the beginning, it didn't scare me. I was very curious about the whole thing and when we were little telling jokes. At the time I was just curious.

Th. Your sexual adjustment now, would you say it is a good one?

Pt. Yes.

Th. With a climax?

Pt. All the time. Yes. When we first got married, the only thing I couldn't get over the idea of having complete freedom in sex. But after a few months, it was fine.

Th. So that you are uninhibited more or less sexually?

Pt. My husband and I have come to an agreement. We both enjoy what we do, and that's how we feel about it.

Th. How about when you have a few drinks? During the times when you have anxiety does alcohol help?

Pt. I don't drink.

Th. How about tranquilizers? Have you taken any medication?

Pt. I once went to a doctor who gave me a pill. The first psychiatrist whom I went to when I was 15 gave me some pills, but he told me right to my face, he said, "You know your cure is not in the bottle." Which, of course, I know. This last time, I spoke to this one doctor—I just went to him once—and he gave me a prescription which he said would calm me down and I would forget about it, something like that. I took the pill, and it didn't do a thing, and I know myself that a pill is not going to cure me.

Th. Do you know which pill he gave you?

Pt. It was a green and black one.

Th. Sounds like Librium.

Pt. Yes, it was Librium.

Th. It didn't help?

Pt. It didn't do a thing. It's all up here (*points to head*). [*I get a better feeling about her basic strengths. She has made a good sexual adjustment and has some understanding of her problem.*]

Th. How about dreams? Do you dream a great deal or do you dream very little?

Pt. In fact, I had a dream this morning. I have been a little anxious about coming here. I have dreams. Certain ones have stood out, because I knew someday I would be telling somebody my story and I should remember these dreams. They are about things, and I will place my older sister doing them, and then I will probably want to do the same thing. This morning I had a dream about my sister and I. Now when we were little, we used to fight, at least I'd call it that, because I'd retreat. Georgette, my sister, who is a year older than I am, had an accident when she was a small child, and so she was always coddled and everything when she was about 3 years old. She broke one leg, she broke an arm, and things like that. If we hit her, she was going to fall apart. Anyway, it is the truth. I remember that we used to fight and I would never let myself go to really hit her back. In other words, I was always the one that was blamed for things and always got hit and all this other stuff. This morning I dreamt that the two of us were fighting and she was hitting me and really hurting me, and yet I couldn't really hit her back. But I was holding back all my strength, which is something that always happened when we were children. [*The patient continues to refer to her relationship with her sister as a source of keeping her down and crushing her. Actually, her sibling rivalry, never resolved, in later sessions turned out to be a core problem.*]

Th. And you have always held back? [*I would have liked to have gone into her relationship with her sister at this point, but I realized this would have consumed the remaining minutes of the session.*]

Pt. Yes.

Th. What about your mother and father? What kind of people are they?

Pt. My mother is a peculiar person. My family is the high-strung type.

Th. How did you relate to your mother when you were a child?

Pt. Mother and I were not close. The reason that I did what my brother wanted me to do—I know this—is because I got a lot of love from my brother. I would say my grandmother, who did not live with us, when I would see her, I would feel real true love. Now there is something wrong with my relationship with my mother and father. I could never talk to my mother. My older sister was always safer. This I know. I have always felt that way. I am close to my sister now. It wasn't until I got married that I could actually go over and look my mother straight in the face, and just sit there and talk and have a regular conversation as a mother and daughter should. As a teenager, I was very, very hurt when I was about 11 or 12 or 13. You see, my sister was a year older than me, and she would go in and start talking to my mother about her boyfriends and things like that. Once or twice when I tried to go into the kitchen, and just get together, the two of us, and speak and try to talk to her, it was always as if "Oh, you are just a kid; your boyfriends are nothing; just little playmates. I don't want to hear about your silly little things." So I kept everything to myself.

Th. How about your dad? What sort of man is he? How did you relate to him?

Pt. I always liked my father. I always liked my mother, too, but I could never get close to her.

Th. You couldn't talk to your father either?

Pt. No. Well that is something to think about for a second. I felt that I was "in" with my father, so to speak, and that was all right. My father is where all the religion comes to our family. He is a very religious person, pseudo-religious person. It depends on how you look at it. He is very well educated, in culture, background, and things like that.

[*At this point the patient is shown the Rorschach cards.*]

Th. Now I'm going to show you some cards and I want to ask you to tell me what you see in these cards. What does this one look like?

Pt. A butterfly, a crab. (*pause*)

Th. All right. How about this second one?

Pt. It looks like two elephants with their noses up and together.

Th. Anything else?

Pt. No.

Th. This is the third card.

Pt. Two people bending over and touching something together. Nothing else.

Th. And now the fourth card.

Pt. A bear rug. (*pause*) That's all.

Th. The next card.

Pt. I'm thinking of a great big bumblebee we had in the car the other day with a big furry coat on it.

Th. A furry bumblebee.

Pt. Yes, gigantic with big wings. It also looks like a butterfly.

Th. I believe this is the sixth card.

Pt. That looks like a scared cat. (*pause*)

Th. This is the seventh.

Pt. It just reminds me of cherubs inside of a church or something.

Th. Anything else here?

Pt. After looking at it, I can see where there may be two children or something like that.

Th. This is the eighth card.

Pt. This looks like a skeleton I once saw in a biology laboratory. (Patient tentatively tilts the card.)

Th. You can hold it upside down if you wish.

Pt. I see nothing else.

Th. This is the ninth card.

Pt. This one sort of looks like a volcano.

Th. Hold it any way you wish. (*pause*) This is the last card.

Pt. This in a way reminds me of the waves on the water where the water goes through. This looks like two crabs. There are other undersea fishes.

Th. Now we can talk a bit about your problem. I get the impression that the sexual experiences with your brother at the age of 8 initiated a good deal of guilt in you. Not that you might not have felt guilty about your feelings before, especially toward your mother and sister. [*In appraising her dynamics, it would appear that the patient has an overwhelming, punitive superego that punishes her for hostile feelings, probably toward her sister and mother. She had to repress aggression toward her sister because her sister was "weak." Her obsession of defiantly repeating "Jesus Christ" serves as an outlet for aggression and as a way of restraining her aggression. Anxiety results as even minimal hostility comes through.*] Now sex play between brothers and sisters is not too uncommon even though you rarely hear about it. [*This is an attempt at reassurance.*]

Pt. I know, I learned about that as I grew up.

Th. A child has to develop some ideas about sexuality before he or she grows up. Sexuality is like walking. You have to learn it. Our culture is prohibitive. Sex is regarded as hideous, terrible until one gets married. But like any other bodily function sex has a beginning early in life. Obviously, your experiences didn't do too much damage to you because you tell me you function well sexually now. [*More reassurance is given her, plus the attempt to get her to focus away from an event she considers irreparable, thereby establishing the hopelessness of her condition.*]

Pt. But isn't it wrong?

Th. You consider it wrong. Children in early life explore the sexual area. Often there is sex play that goes on among children within the family or outside of the family. You did nothing that is particularly different or bad. But your reaction to these incidents was abnormal. Perhaps the reason why you interpreted this as such a horrible and terrible thing was that, prior to the sex-play incident, you were already sensitized to "being bad." A terrible thing, a bad person, a horrible person.(*pause*). [*I am making active educational efforts that, though aimed at reassurance are probably not going to influence her underlying guilt feelings. Yet I believe this is what she wants to hear from me.*]

Pt. I want to say one thing. When I was a kid, I was always told that I am bad and rotten and no good, and when I was told that, I almost couldn't take it. If they would say, "You are pretty or nice or a good girl," I was always the bad, rotten, good for nothing. [*The patient is very emotional here. Her face is flushed, her fists are clenched. There are tears in her eyes.*]

Th. This is exactly the sort of thing that I am talking about. That sexual experience may have been merely grist for the mill. Then you went along with the religious exercises and prayers. You did this probably with a great burden on your soul.

Pt. I did, I did. I felt I didn't deserve to pray, that I was a hypocrite.

Th. You went along trying to absolve your guilt for many things. But the experience proved to you that you did a bad thing. That made you, in your thoughts, a bad person. Now why do you think you prayed?

Pt. I wanted to be forgiven. I wanted God to forgive me.

Th. When you made these pronouncements, these religious pronouncements, they may have been a sign of purity. But then you may have thought, "How could I pray and act holy when I know that I am such a horrible, awful and terrible person." The phrase Jesus Christ seems to symbolize something for you.

Pt. Yes, but when I'd say it, I felt hypocritical; then I'd get defiant and spit.

Th. It is probable that religion has many meanings for you. What you may have felt was that only a terrible person like yourself acts defiant in prayer. But there is a sort of healthy core to defiance too. You were fighting back. [*What I am trying to do with these tentative interpretations is to give her some explanation for her symptoms to show her that they have a mean-*

ing and function. This may get her to concentrate in later sessions on possible sources of her conflict rather than on her symptoms, on her devalued self-image and the notion that she is hopelessly ill and "bad" because she committed a sexual crime.]

Pt. (*excitedly*) You are right. I'd say, "I'll show them. Who do they think they are." [*I decide to utilize the patient's emotion to offer her more active interpretations, realizing that insight at this stage has largely a placebo effect. But I am striving for a rapid relationship.*]

Th. And why shouldn't you be aggressive and angry when you feel put into such a terrible position? Negated as a human being; a person who can't act in her own right. You may have felt you weren't supposed to be angry, forced to be namby-pamby, told that you were no good. And then the defiance came that somehow got involved with the word Jesus Christ. Perhaps you felt that Jesus Christ must know what an awful person you felt yourself to be. Therefore you should defy him.

Pt. Oh, yes, yes. [*The patient is quite moved, wiping tears from her eyes.*]

Th. It comes out of your depths, out of your deep emotions, which indicated to you what a horrible, terrible, evil, ugly person you were. But you couldn't countenance this. It went against your own ideas of the kind of person you wanted to be. A fear developed that people would find out that you were really a terrible person.

Pt. What frightens me more than anything else is that everybody will know I am bad and horrible. (*cries*) But sometimes I don't feel this way.

Th. What I'd like to have you do is to begin noticing situations where you feel yourself to be a terrible person. Does this have anything to do with people or situations, or does this all come up from the inside at times when you feel undermined. [*I am assigning the patient a task to keep herself alerted for sources of her symptoms.*]

Pt. But why am I this way?

Th. The mechanism is probably an extremely complex one. It takes many, many forms. I recently had a girl just about your age who would come up with expostulations of four-letter swear words that frightened her. This to her was horrible because the "dirty" words were not spoken in her family, indeed were forbidden. Her outbursts were an indication to her that she was a horrible person. Exactly the same thing you have, but using a different kind of symbol. The words used don't mean a thing in themselves. It's what's behind them. [*Sometimes the use of an example of a case with problems similar to the patient's problems reinforces an interpretation.*]

Pt. Doctor, you know something, I'm beginning to feel better, a lot better. Do you think we'll use hypnosis to find out things? [*The patient is obviously not going to give up easily in her quest to dig up and exterminate determining repressed memories.*]

Th. Now, I don't think that you are going to find any deep remarkable discoveries or secrets in your past. I really do not, I believe that hypnosis may bring you back to your childhood and help you experience some of the original fears and anxieties. But a good many of your mechanisms seem to be on the surface. Once you absorb what has frightened you, all these things, and realize how inconsequential these things really are, you may find yourself living in the present, not fearful of the past or terrified by the future. Once you firm up your ideas about what is going on in you, the next step is utilizing this insight in the direction of change. Here hypnosis may be of help to you. It may also be able to help you control your tension and anxiety whenever these pop up again. [*I will often utilize hypnosis in obsessional patients to help them control and "turn off" their tortured ruminations.*]

Pt. Dr. Wolberg, I was scared of coming here for the simple reason that I thought that I would leave this office as I have left too many or not hear anything but what I wanted to hear. I mean it. You just can't imagine how I feel inside.

Th. How do you feel inside?

Pt. Oh, If I could get rid of this thing, it would be the greatest thing in the world. I so much want to have a family and be able to be a mother and a good wife to my husband, and not the way I was where I couldn't even cook dinner. I was just too scared to move. I have always had depressions, and any doctor I went to, especially one I went to when I was 15, I would sit here, and he would sit over at the desk and I will tell him a story. He would practically fall asleep on me. I know it is funny and everything, but it would hurt me so much. I would walk out of there being the same hopeless person. No help, no change nothing. I didn't know what is going on inside of me. When it first came on, I just really thought I was going out of my mind. You don't know what is happening to you.

Th. What I said, does it make sense to you?

Pt. Oh, yes. You see, you are the first person who has ever explained it to me, in words like this. I always thought I was rotten, miserable, hated by everybody else, always. I always did have terrible inferiorities when I was a girl among girls. I was the worst one there. [*This can offer fertile fields for exploration later on involving her desire to be a tomboy and her inferiority feelings about her femininity.*]

Th. Apparently, you felt undermined when you were little. You never seem to have had a warm close relationship with your mother. And you had a father you couldn't communicate with too well. And you felt you had no right to complain. You couldn't act normal with your sister either. The healthy thing would have been to fight back, to beat the devil out of her when she beat you, then kiss and make up later. You were apparently frustrated and hamstrung. You couldn't express yourself, and, to boot, when you wanted to pitch into her, you were considered to be an evil, bad, horrible person who did terrible things to a sister who was so frail and weak. [*Active interpretations are made repeating the things the patient already knows, but with the focus on her need to repress her frustration and aggression.*]

Pt. I was always the one who got hit even if we got into fights, and afterward my sister would tell my mother even if it wasn't my fault. I was the one who got hit and punished and had to say, "I'm sorry."

Th. So, there again, the normal impulse would have been to express aggression to get it out of your system, to scream at your mother, if necessary to fight back with your sister. So far as sexual curiosity in childhood, there is nothing so unusual about this. But to you these were indices of how terrible you were. An awful person. You must have carted this image of yourself around all your life, and you have had to run away from this image because in your opinion it was such a horrible thing to look at.

Pt. Can I get over this?

Th. You are still young, and if you have the desire to do so, you should be able to get over this. The test I gave you seems to indicate that you really are not too badly off, that you have fairly good potentials. [*Employing her exposure to the Rorschach cards as a reassuring tool and as prop to her to working at her problem*]

Pt. How long will I have to come? You see it's hard for me to travel here, and besides I can't afford it.

Th. It is hard to say how long. Sometimes it takes time to integrate things you learn. You have toted this thing around for years and years and years. How long will it be before you completely discard it, I don't know. But if you have the right formula to work on, and if you apply yourself, you will gradually undermine this misconception of yourself. Perhaps what we can do is to have a few more sessions together. I'll teach you self-relaxation so you can control your tension and help your understanding better. And then we will see what happens.

Pt. Can I ask another question? I told you that I have a horrible fear of people knowing things about me. We told our family doctor. The only thing the family doctor was told, what my mother probably said was, "My daughter has 'Jesus Christ' running around her mind, and so on." He sent me to somebody else. Now, when I was waiting in this psychiatrist's office one time, I met my girlfriend. She just said hello and that was the end of it. She said, "What are you doing here?" and I said, "I was just going to talk to him." I felt awful that she knew I was there. When this thing bothers me, I become petrified, and I really mean petrified, when I think people you know know about it.

Th. This is part of the problem, the constant concern with "people will know." They will know what a "horrible" person you are. Again this is probably your guilt feeling showing in the form of a fear that people will see the terrible image you see in yourself. Remember you are the one who is designing this image. [*Again, active, strong, authoritative interpretations to bolster her against anxiety. I feel I have a* *working relationship with her.*] I'm afraid our time is up. Would you like to see me again?

Pt. Oh, yes.

Th. When would you like to see me?

Pt. I have two more years of school before I finish. I have decided maybe not to go to school this coming year and maybe work this semester.

Th. Well, then, supposing I see you a few more times, and then we'll discuss what to do thereafter. Perhaps after a few times you'll be able to go on by yourself. Then you can come back if necessary for an occasional session.

Pt. I know my husband wants to talk to you. There are certain things that my husband does not know. He should know. He wants to know if I really need it because he doesn't think there is anything bad about me.

Th. Of course, I'll be glad to see him if this is necessary.

Pt. And doctor, another thing, you know, the name I used is not my real name.

Th. (*laughing*) I guess you felt so ashamed of your identity that you decided to conceal yourself under an assumed name. Which is part of the problem, isn't it?

Pt. Yes (*smiling*). When shall I come back?

Th. Next week at the same time.

Pt. Very good (*arises*). Goodbye.

Th. Goodbye, see you next week.

The patient returned for three more sessions, during which we made a relaxing tape* for purposes of relaxing with her tensions, pushing obsessive thoughts out of attention, and reinforcing her insights. Our focus soon concentrated on her undermined conception of herself and on her relationship with her older sister. Her guilt feelings for her resentment toward her mother and sister, and toward transferential figures in her present life, gradually lifted. Momentary upsurges of anxiety were relieved both by her relaxing exercises and by her relating the upsurge of symptoms to provocative competitive incidents in her present environment. A 5-year follow-up indicated a significant change in her self-image. A dream she sent me reflected this different conception of herself.

Last night I had two dreams. In one I dreamt that I was in a fashion salon looking at a full-length oyster-white beaver coat being shown to me on a live model. The coat was a duplicate of one I had seen yesterday on the TV show. In the other dream I was in a very large private home about 10 miles from where I live. The home belonged to a lady psychiatrist, my psychiatrist. She had given me a partial physical examination (I listened to my heart) although I remember holding the end of the stethoscope to myself. The house was full of many people, all wanting to see her, but they were in a party-like mood, talking, walking around, eating in the kitchen, etc. She and I were talking about my having a baby, which was fine with her. She asked me to please bring the baby to her so that she may have a peek at it after it was born. (I think I felt the baby would be a girl.)

Shortly after this the patient became pregnant. A temporary upsurge of anxiety brought her in for two more sessions. Following the birth of her child, a brief period of anxiety was controlled also with a limited number of sessions.

* The technique of making a relaxing tape will be found in Chapter 15.

Case 3

Some patients are not suited for short-term therapy and require a long-term supportive approach until sufficient motivation is developed for a more productive type of treatment. Often such patients seek a parental type of relationship with the therapist that eventually, if the therapist is not aware of what is happening nor knows how to deal with the evolving situtation, becomes an interminable sadomasochistic encounter traumatic to both patient and therapist. These patients frequently refuse to accept a referral to a clinic or a therapist experienced in dealing with their type of problem since therapy is not what they want. This is illustrated in the next initial interview. The patient is a young single woman who asked for an interview through a letter in which she complained of tension and of having troubled dreams. A tall attractive woman entered my office at the appointment time, somewhat aggressively seating herself in the chair after we introduced ourselves.

Th. Would you like to tell me about your problem?
Pt. Exactly what is it you need to know so that you know what I'm doing? So you ask questions and I'll try to answer.
Th. You would rather have me ask questions.
Pt. It doesn't matter, except that I think you need to know what you need to know, and since I don't know you, I don't know what information you wish. [*Her initial responses to the interview are certainly unusual and strange.*]
Th. All right. Suppose you give me a general idea of the problem, and then we will decide the best thing that can be done for your problem.
Pt. The problem is this. I have found that belief, just belief, raises a tremendous role in the lives of human beings. What they believe in and how they believe; and I don't have to tell you quote miracle cures unquote, and things of this nature. I'd like very much to know how this operates—and how we can turn this to good use. I'd like to know very importantly how the subconscious mind functions because in my experience this is a perfect mechanism. It always tells the person exactly what is right for the individual. Now is this common? [*Again, her queries are strange, and I get the impression that she is quite a sick person.*]
Th. Have you in your experience found that this works for you?
Pt. Works consistently for me.
Th. Give me an example of that.
Pt. Yes, I can give you a very clear example of that. It's really a very funny one, too. I was going with a young man that I liked very much and I was trying to make up my mind, do I like him enough to sleep with him or don't I. And I seemed to need his affection and warmth, and in the middle of the decision I had a dream and the dream told me that I would feel like a prostitute if I slept with him. Now this is important to me, so the next day I asked Hans. We got to talking about it, and his first experiences. I might add he was from Chile, a German who lived in Chile. All of the women he had slept with were prostitutes. My subconscious mind picked it up. And because I was very willing to listen to my unconscious, I found it very accurate.
Th. Well, we may be able to talk about this specific quality, whether it's unique to yourself or whether it's a more general quality.
Pt. More general.
Th. Then we can discuss it in terms of whether it can be put to some constructive use, as you say.
Pt. Well, for me individually, I put it to use all the time. (*pause*)
Th. Is that so?
Pt. Oh yes, always.
Th. How? Do you ask yourself questions? How do you do this?
Pt. A problem is there, for example. You are in the middle attempting to find a solution. I find the best way is to lie down and relax completely. And I use a very funny expression, "I will to will the will of God," which makes me relax. Which is very, very good for me. And in this kind of state of suspended animation, which I suspect is a form of hypnosis, the answer to the problem will come to me.
Th. It will come to you almost like inspiration?
Pt. Not like an inspiration, but like a feeling.
Th. A kind of feeling. Do you get the impression that it comes from the outside world?
Pt. No, I do not. Sometimes when I don't like what's coming out, I stop it you see.
Th. What comes out?
Pt. Oh, I don't know, maybe I kind of have a propensity of making one choice, and another one is poking it's nose in. I have the impression of a double layer in my mind, of a thought coming up through. This may be an associating issue with Freud, however. I've had this sensation long before I ever knew Freud and his theories or anything about him. It's a physical feeling.
Th. I see. Now I'd like to have you tell me something about your problems, the things that really bother you and upset you. [*Now that the patient is beginning to talk more freely, I*

believe I can be more demanding of her to tell me about her real problems.]

Pt. You mean as an individual?

Th. As a person, yes.

Pt. That is what I want to do, I believe two main problems. I am unfortunately afflicted with very bad feet, which throws my spine out of balance—completely—which keeps me a little tired all of the time. I deeply resent this. It also makes me a little nervous and always gives me a consciousness of being tied to my body, which in my case is a very bad thing because I'm very tall. And so I become conscious about being tall and have a sense of being different. Two, I find it very difficult to believe that I'm an acceptable individual to other people. Now, there is no basis for this, except that I sometimes do very foolish and clumsy things. But these are derived from the feeling itself and not from anything inherent in me.

Th. I see.

Pt. This is a block that I would like very much to get over.

Th. What about your self-confidence? Do you feel confident?

Pt. No, I don't.

Th. No confidence at all?

Pt. No. I won't say exactly no confidence. It's a very funny thing. When I'm alone, and when I'm working, and when I'm doing something I like to do, I have a very basic self-confidence. I think so more than most people. I know I'm right. I've actually made very few mistakes in my life in terms of judgment and in terms of what I wanted to do. It always seems to somehow work out, but that doesn't mean that other people will accept my personality. And you see I want to be accepted.

Th. I see. Now to get back to the business about your belief, that is, your feeling that you are not acceptable.

Pt. I think I can give you the reasons for this. One, my father is a paranoiac. This problem I think managed to solve, but you can imagine his possessive love, and my rejection of this overdomination and of his heavy-handed way of handling people and supersensitivity. So you reject it, and consequently it isn't nice to reject father, so you don't like yourself. Two, I didn't like my sister arriving at the time she arrived. Three, my first experiences with young playmates were very unfortunate. Now, I don't remember this, but my mother tells me, I remember later when I had a reaction similar to that. The first girl I played with—I think was about 2—and mother said if she didn't watch, I would come running into the house just black and blue because if I wanted something and we were sharing something or it was my turn or something and Mary didn't like the idea, she just simply beat me up. I still can't be put against a wall. Now, these are things I'm pretty well adjusted to.

Th. And in your life situation have you adjusted? Have you gotten along fairly well all through childhood?

Pt. No, no.

Th. Tell me something about that.

Pt. My whole history as an individual, and in contact with other people, has been one of strain, tension, of shyness and maladjustment. Now I'm reaching the point where this is no longer true. As a matter of fact, a few years ago I went through pretty thorough therapy and got quite an understanding of it.

Th. Oh, is that so?

Pt. But it doesn't relieve the shyness, you see.

Th. Who were you treated by?

Pt. He was a doctor and they provided this service for students, and I went through the whole business with the Rorschachs and the IQ tests and things like that.

Th. And did you get any therapy?

Pt. It was therapy.

Th. How many times a week did you go?

Pt. I went twice a week for 6 months.

Th. Did you find out much about yourself?

Pt. Nothing I didn't know before.

Th. I see, but it did help you?

Pt. It helped because I liked the doctor, and I had the sense that he liked me, and that someone who is intelligent as well as likable would like me is something I needed very badly.

Th. I see, you went through college, and what do you do now?

Pt. I'm a secretary. This is a long sad story, this business of my occupation. I don't really work very well for other people.

Th. Is that so? What are your goals?

Pt. This is the whole point. I began in theater as an actress, and I might add I was a very good actress.

Th. Oh, is that so?

Pt. But I am too tall and consequently I didn't get

the parts I wanted. I couldn't get them. There were no leading men for me. They didn't explain this to me. No one helped; no one took the time to say, "Look, you're just too tall, don't try." They just didn't say anything, and let me go on and my basic lack of confidence increased, you see, so that I had nothing left. I turned to writing, and I'm very good at this.

Th. I see.

Pt. But I have a terrific block against writing. I can tell you this too. I know these things—and this is the irritating point. As a child—I was 9—I wrote a story about a dog and a little boy who found the dog, and he loved the dog, and he couldn't keep the dog. He had run away from home. And I remember he went down to the railroad tracks or something. It was a very complicated and ridiculous childish story. And my father who thought he could write, and probably could have at one time, tore it to shreds. I never got over it quite.

Th. Is that so?

Pt. It's this rejection you see. Now I understand his ego couldn't let him say it was all right to a 9-year-old child. He had to prove himself as being stronger and criticizing. It doesn't help the reaction.

Th. Now, I'm going to ask you a few questions rather rapidly. How old are you?

Pt. Twenty-nine.

Th. Ever married?

Pt. No.

Th. How about tension, do you feel tense?

Pt. Very much.

Th. A good deal of tension?

Th. What about depression?

Pt. A week before my period every month. This is chemical. I feel this coming on.

Th. Yes. What about physical symptoms?

Pt. My back, spondylitis.

Th. Any fatigue or exhaustion?

Pt. Mild anemia also.

Th. Any headaches?

Pt. Very seldom.

Th. Dizziness?

Pt. No.

Th. Stomach trouble?

Pt. No.

Th. Would you say you had any sexual problem?

Pt. Some inhibition, unless I know the man extremely well. I'm just not a casual person.

Th. Yes.

Pt. I just have to know people a long time. Then there is no problem. When I feel accepted, I have no difficulty.

Th. What about phobias?

Pt. None that I can think of.

Th. Any thoughts that come into your mind that torture you or bother you?

Pt. One, and this is the story of the "cat-mouses."

Th. Tell me about the cat-mouses.

Pt. The cat-mouses. Well, I tried to do something, and it didn't work very well. I'm paying off a rather large-sized penality for it. The cat-mouses are distorted children. They are, as you notice, part mouse and part cat. And so the first time I had the dream I sensed what it was and I didn't like it, so I turned it into a whimsical thing I could like.

Th. In the dream?

Pt. No, no after, and so later my subconscious kept telling me, apparently I disliked what happened. The story is a very badly handled abortion I had, and I mean badly handled, it was just awful.

Th. Is that so?

Pt. And so you see the relationship, and this is the story, and this thing occasionally pops up, under certain temperature conditions, and sometimes just before my period when there are cramps and I feel tight. It is the same physical feeling as during the operation.

Th. I see. Was the operation done by a person who is competent at all?

Pt. By an excellent doctor. The thing that went wrong was that I had had several shots before then in order to avoid the operation itself. So the fetus had shifted, and the doctor who did the operation thought it was a polyp and didn't touch it so consequently two days later on a train going home, I went into violent labor pains. And that was when it actually occurred—and that was just a messy mess.

Th. Did you see the fetus?

Pt. Yes, which is the unfortunate part you see. If I had not, I think it would have been better.

Th. It looked like a cat-mouse?

Pt. It did not. It looked like a chicken heart.

Th. Like a chicken heart.

Pt. Uh-huh, exactly.

Th. How many months pregnant were you?

Pt. I'd say 6 weeks, a little over.

Th. Well, that isn't too long.

Pt. Oh, no.

Th. Well, let's talk about those cat-mouses a little more. Give me an idea of what the dreams were.

Pt. The dreams all have three things in common—heat—the sensation of bodily heat. That's why I have them more often in summer. It's very hot, water, a thing of being in water or near water, or surrounded by water, and distorted animals, peculiar animals, I mean. Some of them are very charming and very whimsical. And in one I remember I had absolutely to get rid of the animals. I had to kill them, and it woke me up because I couldn't.

Th. You couldn't?

Pt. I just couldn't. I just absolutely couldn't touch the animals.

Th. These cat-mouses, are there many in the dream or just one?

Pt. Oh, they change; they're not always a cat-mouse. This is just the name I've given to the creature that evolved through this. They can be anything, but they are always combinations.

Th. But the cat-mouses symbol itself?

Pt. Call it a cat-mouse symbol.

Th. Cat-mouse symbol, can you describe it? How big is it?

Pt. Tiny, they're always very small, they're always little.

Th. The body what does it look like?

Pt. Like a mouse.

Th. And the cat?

Pt. The original one was like a cat—a cat's head and a mouse's body.

Th. And they would shift?

Pt. Well, to a dog-fish now.

Th. A dog-fish now?

Pt. Well, the cat-mouses are people with whimsy and who can understand whimsy and who have a sense of humor, and dog-fishes are just dull people.

Th. I see.

Pt. This I've done, and written some very charming little pieces which I wish I could turn into some money if I could.

Th. How do you feel? Do you think about these cat-mouse symbols a good deal?

Pt. No, as a matter of fact I don't.

Th. They don't bother you?

Pt. No.

Th. You seem to be rather preoccupied about that in the letter you sent me.

Pt. I did that because of—it's kind of a trick. I shouldn't have done it. Among other things I write advertising copy. It's my business to interest people, so I use tricks because people are attracted by this sort of whimsical thing.

Th. I see, it isn't really a problem then.

Pt. It isn't really a problem.

Th. All right, fine, now?

Pt. It's a little unpleasant. It isn't a problem; they'll go away.

Th. You have anxiety in your dreams with this symbol?

Pt. I don't know if it's anxiety or not. It's just a form of tension and a form of anxiety of being forced to do something I don't want to do. A very obvious reason. The abortion, it was very painful and very unpleasant.

Th. This symbol only occurred after the abortion?

Pt. I've never had it before. Never.

Th. And you feel very well satisfied that this is the basis of this?

Pt. It clicked over, if you understand this expression. It felt right.

Th. Now, do you have any insomnia?

Pt. No, I can put myself to sleep instantly.

Th. Good, What about nightmares?

Pt. Only this. However, I never have this except when I'm taking a nap. I don't have this at night.

Th. Only during the day.

Pt. But it's likely to be warm, and I'll be dressed and lying down.

Th. OK. Now, tell me a little bit about your mother and your father. Are they living?

Pt. They are. It would be such a story.

Th. What sort of people are they?

Pt. My father is a very intelligent man. As a child I remember him being a very wonderful man—and he adored children. He still does, but he is a paranoiac. I don't mean a paranoia personality, I mean a psychosis paranoiac. He is also an alcoholic.

Th. How did he relate to you? Was he close?

Pt. As a child, very close. We were very, very close.

Th. Did you really love him?

Pt. Deeply, I still do. This presents a problem. I've been unable to solve it because his whole personality structure is so obnoxious to me that I have had to split it off. And to love the man, the individual, the things underneath, and what I know is there and avoid the personality as if it were the plague. To watch the degeneration of a mind and a human being is not a pleasant thing for a child.

Th. I should say not, even as a child he was degenerating then.

Pt. I began to pick it up about 9. That's when he started to drink. That's when a lot of the trouble began, and we were never happy since.

Th. How about your mother? What sort of person is she?

Pt. My mother is also two people. She is the person she was 10 years ago, and the person she is now; she is—was a very stable person—a beautiful woman.

Th. How did you get along with her?

Pt. Wonderfully, just wonderfully. Oh, we scrapped a little bit, but with that kind of a family if we get mad, we say something. I mean mother threw plates and I stomped out of the house, but it never meant anything. I mean there was never any grudges held—overshadowing, long tension periods.

Th. Do you have any brothers and sisters?

Pt. I have a younger brother and younger sister.

Th. How young?

Pt. My younger sister is 2 years younger—she is married and has two children. Married a man just like my father who is also an alcoholic. So she refuses to stay married, and as long as they're divorced and live together, life is fine. She attempted to commit suicide. This probably is due to a brain injury. She has been sick all of her life. My brother is 19, is sensitive and intelligent, terribly depressed and inhibited. I should say basically just a fine boy.

Th. As a child did you have any emotional upsets that you remember?

Pt. I didn't remember a day when I didn't have any.

Th. What form did those emotional upsets take? By emotional upsets do you mean tantrums or outbreaks?

Pt. Outbreaks or nervousness. It was a repression. I always felt pushed into a corner and forced off, and my only freedom was when I was by myself and living in daydreams essentially.

Th. And your previous treatment, any sort of treatment prior to seeing the college doctor?

Pt. None.

Th. Taking any medicines or tranquilizers?

Pt. None.

Th. Now, I'm going to show you the Rorschach cards rather rapidly.

Pt. Oh, I've had that (*laughing*).

Th. I know. Just to give me an idea.

Pt. The last time it took me 3 hours.

Th. It will take just about 5 minutes with me. (*I hand her the first card.*)

Pt. Mountains, crab, sea crabs, woman praying, these are the most pronounced.

Th. All right. This is the second one.

Pt. Bears, two little bears, teddy bears, I always have to think this is a temple, the white part in the center. And I associate, the orange part with menstruation—blood.

Th. All right. This is the third card.

Pt. Oh, I remember these, these are my little cannibal women. They are cooking, the little guy who sits in the two corners here. (*fourth card*) Two tired birds sitting back to back. They are very tired. (*fifth card*) I associate that with the beer belly, a vegetable, and I cannot trace it. The top is a soldier's helmet. Women chiefly women, probably nursing or able to nurse and somehow associated with children in this case.

Th. This is the sixth one.

Pt. Navaho rugs, bear rugs, I have a sensation of wings.

Th. Where do you see the wings there?

Pt. The whole outside, the feathers, and the shape of it. (*seventh card*) These are the children. I'm remembering, by the way, some reactions from before. Little children, facing one another, in kind of a ballet dancers' pose, this way. (*eighth card*) This is the most, I can take it apart more. This one I remember liking. It's the colors; it's a weird combination here, it has a kind of offbeat like jazz music, the orange and the pink. It has a watery feeling to me. These are the polar bears over here, very strongly shaped. Animals of sorts around a wheel, sort of distorted pattern. I noticed something. I'm sort of attracted to the animal world.

Th. Uh-huh. This is the ninth one.

Pt. This is the one I didn't like. Because it's messy, very messy, because it reminds me of violence and insects, and this is something I dislike.

Th. Violence, insects.

Pt. When people are rough and vicious in a way.

Th. Do you see anything else there? . . . You can hold it anyway you wish. . . . All right, this is the last one.

Pt. Children that are like sea horses, and again slightly hysterical modern art. I like this one. Now I get an Eiffel Tower impression from this immediately, which I automatically switch over into a preferred symbol. And this is the feeling I have. This one is good, somehow, even though it seems discordant and disconnected. It has a coherence of warmth and good feeling that comes sometimes with good things. [*The disorganization of thought and the intensity of feeling in the last three cards point to a schizophreniform-like tendency.*]

Th. A good feeling?

Pt. Playful is the word I want.

Th. Now, I have a little better idea of the problem than I did before. So very rapidly I'm just going to give you my ideas, but I may not be absolutely accurate and I want you then to tell me your impressions. [*In presenting interpretations to the patient or in giving her a hypothesis of the problem, I must be careful that she does not regard what I say as an attack, or as being critical of her. She has already told me that what she seeks from me is approval and support.*]

Th. Now, you are an extremely sensitive and creative person. You have a great many talents and the ability to perceive nuances and to arrive very rapidly to intuitive feelings. That's because you live very close to your unconscious. You have a remarkable facility in that direction. There are people who do and people who don't. You just seem to have this facility. For that reason many of the phenomena that are ordinarily repressed and are not ordinarily perceived are available to you. So, you can become aware of many symbols the average person overlooks. You can also be influenced by your unconscious. You then can pose questions to your unconscious and get the answers. Now this is not average. I'd say most people cannot do this.

Pt. Then you see my interest in this field because I'm aware of this. I'll tell you something else that might interest you. If I talk to someone for 2 hours and let them talk to me, I can tell you which parent has caused the trouble in the person—just instinctively.

Th. Is that so. You would also be very good in analyzing dreams, analyzing the unconscious.

Pt. So it's unbelievable. Aside from myself, as long as I don't think about it.

Th. So you do have this facility, but this very facility can create problems for you.

Pt. Yes, it does.

Th. You're extremely sensitive, too sensitive. You feel slights, you get very tense, you are just like a weather vane. You just swing with the wind, and because of that, you may need some sort of help. Now, I would think that you could do very well with therapy—maybe not too intensive therapy but seeing someone about once weekly.

Pt. Just to study it out.

Th. Somebody that would stabilize you and would enable you to get some stability because you're too much like a weather vane.

Pt. I know, it would drive me wild, you see, and that's part of this whole thing. I've gotten track of this idea of using hypnosis as a form of research; now, I'm not adverse to working on myself. I don't mean to use it as an easy way out. I work awfully hard for everything I've ever had, and I don't mind. I even enjoy it, I have a feeling now of getting something that's going to mean enough to steady me down.

Th. I'm sure that you could utilize hypnosis very effectively.

Pt. I'm very good at it, by the way.

Th. Are you?

Pt. I've done a little bit of it, just enough, and if I use my eyes it works like a charm. I just go right out.

Th. You can certainly utilitze your facility in a very appropriate way. As far as you're concerned, I don't think hypnosis is absolutely necessary. It wouldn't make too much difference as far as your getting something beneficial out of therapy.

Pt. That wasn't the point. (*laughing*)

Th. You understand what I mean?

Pt. Yes, I know what you mean.

Th. So we're talking in two different frames of references: hypnosis is one thing and also you as a person in terms of your capacity to get something meaningful out of other kinds of therapy. As a matter of fact, I don't think hypnosis would be the best thing for you. You are too immersed in your unconscious now, and it would be much better for you to stabilize and build up a little more repression so that you are not being bombarded all the time by your unconscious. [*My feeling is that the patient would utilize hypnosis to stir up too many fantasies and in this way would frighten herself.*]

Pt. Well, you know that was part of the idea.

Th. Now, I think that you probably would do well in therapy with somebody to whom you could come on a once-a-week basis to talk things over. You'll feel an anchorage there. And in that reference I may be able to refer you to somebody who may be able to help you.

Pt. Because this costs money and this I don't have and you see I'm really in a corner on this financial business.

Th. That's one of the things I might be able to help you with by arranging for therapy in terms of your budget and in terms of your own ability to pay whatever you can. There are places in the city where you can receive some good help.

Pt. I don't need that kind of help. I need a father, Dr. Wolberg. No, this is true, I need somebody that is very strong, and very stable and won't laugh at me when I get off on one of my tangents. [*The patient is obviously seeking a prolonged supportive relationship, which is probably all she can use at this time. She is quite close to a schizophrenic break, in my opinion, but she still has good defenses, and might, if she is motivated, benefit from the proper type of treatment and perhaps some mild neuroleptic. I have in mind referring her to a hospital clinic where she could receive good therapy.*]

Th. Well, give me an idea of what you can afford, approximately.

Pt. Gee, it's so awfully tight that even something as little as $10 a week would be too much. That I could make, I could manage this.

Th. All right, I think I can find somebody for you at one of the clinics. I shall telephone him this afternoon and let you know.

Pt. All right.

The patient was referred to the head of a clinic in the neighborhood, whom I telephoned and informed about her problem. The clinic was willing to take her, but the patient never accepted the referral. A telephone call from me to her was never returned.

CHAPTER 7

Choosing an Immediate Focus

Many patients come to therapy convinced that their problems were brought about by some precipitating factor in their environment. An alcoholic husband, a disastrous investment, a broken love affair, a serious accident, these and many other real or exaggerated calamities may be blamed. What people usually want from treatment is help in getting rid of painful or disabling symptoms that are often ascribed to such offensive events. The symptoms include anxiety, depression, phobias, insomnia, sexual difficulties, obsessions, physical problems for which no organic cause can be found, and a great many other complaints and afflictions.

Even though we may be correct in our assumption that the basic troubles reside elsewhere than in environmental or symptomatic complaints, to bypass the patient's immediate concerns is a serious mistake. Later when there is firm evidence of the underlying causes, for example, faulty personality operations or unconscious conflict, a good interviewer should be able to make connections between the precipitating events or existing symptoms and the less apparent dynamic sources of difficulty. There will then occur a change in focus. This shift, however desirable it may seem, is not always necessary because we may find that our objectives are reached, and that the patient achieves stabilization, without delving into corrosive conflicts or stirring up ghosts of the past. It is only where goals go beyond symptom relief or behavioral improvement that we will, in the hope of initiating some deeper personality alterations, delve into dynamic problem areas. Even where the objective is mere symptom relief or behavioral improvement, resistance to simple supportive and reeducative tactics may necessitate a serious look at underlying personality factors that are stirring up obstructive transference and other interferences to change.

In practically all patients some immediate stress situation, usually one with which the individual is unable to cope, sparks the decision to get help. Usually the patient considers himself to be the victim rather than perpetrator of his identified troubles. This, in some cases, may be true; in most cases it is false. It is necessary, therefore, in all patients to appraise the degree of personal participation in their difficulties.

Since we are actually dealing with situations that generate tension and anxiety, it is essential to view environmental incidents through the lens of their special meaning for the individual. What may for one person constitute an insurmountable difficulty may for another be a boon to adjustment. During World War II, for instance, the London bombings for some citizens were shattering assaults on emotional well-being; for others they brought forth latent promptings of cooperation, brotherliness, and self-sacrifice that lent a new and more constructive meaning to the individual's existence. Indeed, wartime with its threat to life marshalled an interest in survival and subdued neurotic maladjustment, which returned in peacetime to plague the individual.

The understanding of stress necessitates acknowledging that there is no objective measure of it. One cannot say that such and such an environment is, for the average adult, 70 percent stressful and 30 percent nurturant. No matter how benevolent or stressful the environment, the individual will impart to it a special meaning as it is filtered through his conceptual network. This shades his world with a significance that is largely subjective. Conceptual distortions particularly twist feelings toward other human beings and especially toward the self. A self-image that is hateful or inadequate may plague the individual the remainder of his life and causes him to interpret most happenings in relation to his feelings that he does not have much value. Most of what happens to him in life will be viewed as confirming his own conviction that he is not much good and that nothing that he does will amount to anything. Such a pervasive belief, of course, makes nearly any occurrence productive of considerable stress.

With this as an introduction, it may be asserted that there *is* such a thing as realistic environmental stress:

1. *The environment may expose the individual to grave threats* in the form of genuine dangers to life and to security. Examples are exposure to disasters such as war, floods, storms, and accidents as well as severe deprivation of fundamental needs for food, shelter, love, recognition, and other biological and social urges engendered by a cruel or barren environment.
2. *The environment may be partially inimical,* the individual not having the resources to rectify it. The environment may be beneficent enough, but the individual, perhaps through early formative experiences, never developed the ability to use those resources that were potentially available.
3. *The environment may contain all elements essential for a good adjustment,* yet the individual may, as has been cited, be unable to take advantage of it because of a personality structure that makes him experience essential needs as provocative of danger. *Such defects may cause him to project out into the environment his inner dissatisfactions, and he may actually create circumstances that bring upon himself the very hazards from which he seeks escape.*

Some persons invariably regard their environment as one in which their assertiveness brings punishment. They are commonly referred to as "losers." A patient of mine constantly would involve himself with financial investments that almost inevitably would turn out to be less than profitable. He would then react with depression, rage, and shattered self-esteem. Yet no sooner would he accumulate any surplus of funds, then he would again plunge into fanciful schemes that ended in disaster. It was only after we had exposed his inner need to fail that he would recognize how he brought his troubles on himself. For a while it was with the greatest effort that he restrained himself from indulging in wildcat gambles. I felt that had he not needed to answer to me, he still would have taken impossible risks.

Character distortions engendered by defects in development, such as extreme dependency, detachment, aggression, masochism, perfectionism, or compulsive ambitiousness, are what usually prevent the individual from fulfilling himself and taking advantage of environmental opportunities. They make for the creation of abnormal goals and values that may seriously interfere with adjustment and that act as sources of stress irrespective of the environment.

It is rare then that environmental stress alone is the sole culprit in any emotional problem. Inimical, frightening, and desperate situations do arise in the lives of people, but the *reactions* of the individual to happenings are what determine their pathological potential. Under these circumstances minor environmental stress can tax coping capacities and break down defenses so that an eventuating anxiety will promote regressive devices like protective phobias. It is, therefore, essential that any precipitating incident that brings a patient into therapy be regarded as merely one element in an assembly of etiological factors, the most important variable being the degree of flexibility and integrity of the personality structure. It is this variable that determines a harmonious interaction of forces that power intrapsychic mechanisms when security and self-esteem are threatened by adversity from the outside and by common developmental crises that impose themselves from within. By focusing on what is regarded as a precipitating incident we may be able not only to initiate remediable environmental corrections but also to open a window into hidden personality resources.

From a practical viewpoint therefore, any environmental stress warrants close examination for its influence, good or bad, on the patient. An understanding of the how and why of its impact may prove invaluable. Sometimes the initiating factor may seem like a trivial spark to the therapist, but an exploration of the patient's past history, his attitudes, and his values may reveal the emotional explosive mixture that awaits detonation.

Focusing on Symptoms

Because symptoms are frequently a byproduct of stress, tension, and anxiety, it may be helpful to examine their development and meaning within the matrix of adaptation. As long as a person is capable of coping with his current life situation, as long as he can gratify his most important needs and dispose of others that he is unable to satisfy, as long as he can sustain a sense of security and self-esteem, and as long as he is able to mediate troubles that vex him, he will not experience stress beyond the point of adaptive balance. When, however, this is not possible, the threat is registered as a state of tension, with altered homeostasis affecting the viscera, the skeletal muscles, and the psychic apparatus. The person mobilizes himself to cope with the stress and if he is successful, homeostasis is restored. When attempts at adaptation keep failing, the continuing presence of tension in turn sabotages the development of more effective coping patterns.

Overstimulation resulting from *continued* stress is bound to register its effect on the bodily integrity ("exhaustion reaction"). Bombardment of the viscera with stimuli will tend after a while organically to disturb the functions of the various organs and systems. To such ensuing disturbances Selye (1950) has given the name "disease of adaptation." As insidious as are the physical effects of tension, the development of a castastrophic sense of helplessness produces the more disturbing phenomenon of anxiety. And it is often anxiety that brings the patient to therapy.

Anxiety and Its Defenses

A vast amount of human psychopathology is covered by the generic term anxiety. It is characterized by a violent biochemical and neurophysiological reaction that disrupts the physical, intellectual, emotional, and behavioral functions of the individual. It is indicative of a collapse of a person's habitual security structure and his successful means of adaptation. So uncomfortable are its effects that the individual attempts to escape from it through various maneuvers. These are usually self-defeating because those very maneuvers are often regressive in nature—that is, they revive outmoded childish ways of dealing with discomfort. They only further interefere with assertive and productive coordinations.

Where anxiety is uncontrolled, an actual return to infantile helplessness with complete loss of mastery may threaten. Reality testing may totally disintegrate, ending in confusion, depersonalization, an inability to locate the limbs in space, incoordination, and loss of capacity to differentiate the "me" from the "not me." This threat to integrity may initiate "parent-invoking" tactics ranging from quiet searching for support to screaming, tantrums, bewildered cries for help, and fainting. Such complete relapse to infancy is rare, occurring only in individuals with fragile personality structures.

Anxiety does not always have to be harmful. As a matter of fact, some anxiety is an adaptive necessity; its release acts as a signal to alert the individual and to prepare him for emergency action. Small amounts of anxiety sponsor somatic and visceral reactions that lead to attack or flight. Anxiety even facilitates information processing in the forebrain. The physiological and biochemical patterns of anxiety are innate in the organism. Its psychological ingredients are unique to the experiences and conditioning of the individual. These, constituting the security apparatus, are organized to reduce and to remove threats to the integrity and safety of the individual.

The signal of anxiety, therefore, activates adaptive reserves stimulating somatic and psychological mechanisms to prepare for an emergency. The individual learns to react to minimal cues of anxiety with a constructive defensive reaction that dispels the anxiety and perhaps eliminates its source. *But where the defenses fail to operate, anxiety can reach a pitch where it cannot be dispelled.* Somatic reactions of a diffuse, undifferentiated, and destructive nature then flood the body. Psychological responses become disorganized. Regressed, childish kinds of behavior, which solve little toward handling an adult anxiety situation, may then emerge. Because the individual cannot cope with intense anxiety, he may want someone to take over for him.

What generally shatters the defenses of the person so that he responds with global anxiety? The provocative agent may be any external danger or internal conflict, recognized or unrecognized, that disorganizes the individual's reality sense, crushes his security and self-esteem beyond mediation, and fills him with a catastrophic sense of helplessness to a point where he cannot stabilize himself. It is the *meaning* to the individual of an experience or a conflict that is the fundamental criterion as to whether he will respond with uncontrollable anxiety.

Let us proceed with examination of the physiological and psychological manifestations of the individual suffering from extreme anxiety since these may be chosen as a focus in therapy.

First, there is a vast undifferentiated, explosive discharge of tension which disorganizes the physiological rhythm of every organ and tissue in the body, including muscular, glandular, cardiovascular, gastrointestinal, genitourinary, and special senses. Long continued excitations may produce psychosomatic disorders and ultimately even irreversible organic changes. Thus, what starts out as a gastric disorder may turn into a stomach ulcer; bowel irritability may become a colitis; hypertension may result in cardiac illness, and so on.

Second, there is a precipitation of catastrophic feelings of helplessness, insecurity, and devaluated self-esteem. The victim often voices fears of fatal physical illness, like cancer or heart disease or brain tumor, as interpretations of the peculiar somatic sensations or symptoms that are being released by anxiety.

Third, there is a wearing down of repressions to the point where they become paper thin in certain areas. Consequently, a breakthrough of repudiated thoughts, feelings, and impulses, ordinarily controllable, now may occur at random. These outbursts further undermine security and produce a fear of being out of control, of not knowing what to expect.

Fourth, various defenses are mobilized, their variety and adaptiveness depending upon the flexibility and maturity of the individual. If these strategies fail to control or dissipate the sense of terror, then a further set of maneuvers is initiated.

Solutions for anxiety will depend on the source of the anxiety as well as the singular personality configurations of the individual.

The specific types of defense are chosen by the individual for reasons that are not, at our present state of knowledge, fully known. The following factors are probable. (1) The individual's unique experiences and conditionings focus emphasis on problems and coping mechanisms developed during certain periods in his life. For instance, as a child the individual's dependency needs may not have been satisfactorily resolved, causing him to measure his self-esteem chiefly in terms of how well loved he was by his parents (and later their internalized images in his conscience). He will be insecure when confronted with circumstances where he must take an independent stand. (2) Certain defenses appear in childhood that net the child a special gain. Such defenses, if successful, establish a pattern of behavior that may be pursued later on. Thus where violent and aggressive displays intimidate parents into yielding to the child's demands, he may tend to have outbursts of anger and to intimidate others as a preferred way of dealing with opposition. (3) Unresolved childish fears, needs, and strivings, with persistence of archaic concepts of reality, will influence the patterns adopted in the face of stress. Fears of the dark or of being alone may return whenever stress is excessive, where these were manifest in childhood. (4) Defensive reactions are often conditioned by parental neurotic attitudes and illnesses, which the individual may take over through the process of imitation. A mother's terror of lightning storms or recourse to headaches when difficulties come up may be adopted by her child.

The neurotic individual thus revives early techniques of adaptation that originally helped solve the difficulties in his childhood. Since these techniques have long outlived their usefulness, they create many more problems than they solve. Nevertheless, the individual is apt to implement them in a reflex manner, almost as if they were the most natural of devices to employ under the circumstances.

Many defensive responses to anxiety that are directed toward the reduction of anxiety may lead to a crippling of a person's flexibility and adaptiveness. The defensive technique of the phobia illustrates the destructive influence that a mechanism of defense may yield. The inhibition of function characteristic of phobic states is calculated to isolate the individual from certain sources of danger onto which he has projected his inner anxieties. For instance, a woman fearful of yielding to unrestrained sexual impulses may develop strong anxieties while walking outdoors. She may shield herself from such anxiety attacks through the symptom of agoraphobia, that is, by avoiding leaving her home, except perhaps in the presence of her mother. The phobia ultimately results in her incapacitation, interfering with her livelihood and her capacity to establish normal relationships with people. She may, as a result, undergo a shattering of self-esteem, and her feelings of inferiority may stimulate a further attempt to isolate herself from others. Her hostility, which is usually directed at her parent on whom she is so helplessly dependent, may become extreme, and she may have difficulty in expressing or even acknowledging her hateful feelings because they threaten her standing with her mother. Thus, while she has employed a defense to shield her from anxiety, she has suffered from gross difficulties in her functional relationships with life and people. The defense against the original anxiety plunged her into difficulties as great or greater than the stress that initially inspired her reaction.

Because defenses so often are sources of difficulty for which psychotherapeutic help is sought and because they frequently are an immediate focus in treatment, it may be productive to elaborate on how and why they evolve.

In general, four levels of defense are employed as outlined in Table 7–1: (1) conscious efforts at maintaining control by manipulation of the environment, (2) characterologic defenses aimed at manipulating interpersonal relations, (3) repressive defenses that manipulate the intrapsychic forces, and (4) regressive defenses that regulate physiological mechanisms. The individual may stabilize at any level, while retaining symptoms and defenses characteristic of previous levels. At different times, as stress is alleviated or exaggerated or as ego strengthening or weakening occurs, there may be shifts in the lines of defense, either up or down. The manner in which these four levels of defense are employed in adaptation is as follows:

First-level defenses: Control mechanisms

When tensions and anxiety are experienced, the first maneuver on the part of an individual is to manipulate the environment to fashion it

TABLE 7-1. Mechanisms of Defense

	MANIFESTATIONS and SYMPTOMS	SYNDROMES
Threats to Adaptation ADAPTATION SYNDROME	tension anxiety physiological reactions	Anxiety states Physical conditions arising from mental factors (psychosomatic illness)
1st Line of Defense CONTROL MECHANISMS	Removing self from sources of stress Escape into bodily satisfactions & extroversion Wish-fulfilling phantasies Suppression, rationalization, philosophical credos, self-control, emotional outbursts, impulsive behavior, "thinking things through" Alcoholic indulgence—excessive alcohol intake Sedation, narcotics—drug overindulgence	Substance use disorders (alcoholism, drug dependence)
2nd Line of Defense CHARACTEROLOGIC DEFENSES	STRIVINGS of an INTERPERSONAL NATURE 1. Exaggerated dependency (*religious fanaticism,* etc.) 2. Submissive technics (*passivity*) 3. Expiatory technics (*masochism, asceticism*) 4. Dominating technics 5. Technics of aggression (*sadism*) 6. Technics of withdrawal (*detachment*) STRIVINGS DIRECTED AT SELF-IMAGE 1. Narcissistic strivings (*grandiosity, perfectionism*) 2. Power impulses (*compulsive ambition*)	Educational disorders, habit disorders, work problems, marital problems, adjustment disorders, conduct disorders, sexual disorders and perversions, delinquency, criminality, personality disorders
3rd Line of Defense REPRESSIVE DEFENSES	A. EFFORTS DIRECTED at REINFORCING REPRESSION 1. *General:* (a) reaction formations, (b) accentuation of intellectual controls with compensations and sublimations. 2. *Inhibition of function:* a. Disturbed apperception, attention, & thinking b. Disturbed consciousness (*fainting, increased sleep, stupor*) c. Disturbed memory (*antegrade* and *retrograde amnesia*) d. Emotional dulling, indifference, or apathy (emotional inhibitions) e. Sensory defects (*hypoesthesia, anaesthesia, amaurosis, ageusia,* etc.) f. Motor paralysis (paresis, aphonia) g. Visceral inhibitions (*impotence, frigidity,* etc.) 3. DISPLACEMENT & PHOBIC AVOIDANCE (*phobias*) 4. UNDOING & ISOLATION (*compulsive acts & rituals*)	Posttraumatic stress disorders Conversion disorders Dissociative disorders Phobic disorders Compulsive disorders
	B. RELEASE of REPRESSED MATERIAL (direct or symbolic) 1. Impulsive break through with "acting-out" (*excited episodes*) 2. Obsessions, (*excessive revery & dreamlike states*) 3. Dissociative states (*somnambulism, fugues, multiple personality*) 4. Psychosomatic disorders (sensory, somatic, visceral; *tics, spasms, convulsions*) 5. *Sexual perversions* (*fetishism, scoptophilia,* etc.) 6. Internalization of hostility (*depression*) 7. Projection	Obsessive-compulsive disorders Conversion disorders Neurotic depression Paranoidal reactions
4th Line of Defense REGRESSIVE DEFENSES	A. Return to helpless dependency B. Repudiation of and withdrawal from reality 1. Dereistic thinking; disorders of perception (*illusions, hallucinations*); disorders of mental content (*ideas of reference, delusions*); disorders of apperception and comprehension; disorders of stream of mental activity (increased or diminished speech productivity, *irrelevance, incoherence, scattering, verbigeration, neologisms*) 2. Defects in memory, personal identification, orientation, retention, recall, thinking capacity, attention, insight, judgement C. Excited "acting-out" (hostile, sexual, and other impulses) D. Internalization of hostility (*depression, suicide*)	Psychotic episodes Schizophrenic disorders Paranoid disorders Manic-depressive disorders Involutional psychoses

to his needs, to escape from it, or to change his mode of thinking about it. Thus he may avoid certain activities or places or people. He will try to manage in some different way whatever he feels to be the source of stress. He may change his job, his wife, his haircut, his nose shape, or his domicile. Or he may try to change existing attitudes, attempting to think things through and to arrive at some new intellectual formulations about what his life is all about. In this regard he may try to suppress certain thoughts, to keep his mind on more positive channels, to exercise self-control, or to read self-help books that stimulate him to think through a new philosophy of life. He may develop different leisure-time activities in quest of satisfactions in a new hobby, a new social activity, or different friends. He may try to "get outside himself," or, just the opposite, he may become more absorbed in bodily satisfactions such as eating or drinking. He may deaden his feelings with sedatives, stimulate them with energizers, or drown them in alcohol. Daydreaming of a wish-fulfilling nature may help in escaping the painful realities of his daily troubles.

His emotional equilibrium may also shift, so that he permits himself emotional outbursts, fits of crying or laughing, and impulsive outbreaks designed to release tension.

All these, and other maneuvers like them, are the first attempts to be made when a person feels the uncomfortable tension that indicates a breakdown in homeostatis. Every person alive at various times employs some of these environment-manipulating devices. Pathological exploitation of certain first-line defenses, however—namely, alcohol and drugs—can cause addictive disorders such as alcoholism and drug addiction. Other first-line defenses, such as attempts at intellectual understanding regarding the basic nature of one's conflicts and anxieties, may help provide some degree of relief. On the other hand, a hit-or-miss application of self-help measures, without awareness of the nature of one's difficulties, may lead to nothing, necessitating the use of the next line of defense.

Second-level defenses: Characterologic defenses

In situations of increasing threat it is typical for a person to exploit in exaggerated form his normal characterologic drives. Aggression, withdrawal, and abnormal self-image restoration are examples.

Idiosyncratic adaptations to stress are developed early in life, primarily in coping with the parental figures who are the first source of a child's security. Certain character styles were promoted by the parents, and the child learns that there is a certain manner in relating to people and events that has the best chance of keeping him free of anxiety. Later in life, when anxiety is experienced, there is an unwitting return to the mode of life that worked most effectively in the past.

Thus these modes of defense may be termed "manipulating one's interpersonal relationships." If dependency is characteristic for a person, then in time of stress he may become abjectly dependent. If detachment is the way in which a person handles untoward experiences, then a serious tragedy will cause him pathologically to isolate and withdraw for long periods. It is the exaggeration of the usual mode that is the key to understanding this second level of defense.

It is typical of the exaggerated maneuvers of the second defense line that they get the individual into interpersonal difficulties. If a high school principal is accused by his teachers of being too controlling, the principal may become threatened. When threatened, he fears that he is losing control over his teachers and reacts perhaps by asking that they submit to him more complete lesson plans and that they sign out of the building when leaving for lunch. It is this very control that the teachers objected to in the first place, and the interpersonal conflict becomes exaggerated.

Examples of pathologically exaggerated character drives include many kinds of interpersonal, vocational, and educational difficulties. The following are typical. Educational and work disorders may be symptomatic of such excessive dependency that one is unable to pursue any independent, assertive line of thought or action. The writing of a term paper or the making of a business call may represent the exercise of personal responsibility; an individual with a devalued self-image may not be able to pursue such an activity on his own. Marital problems, so ubiquitous in our society, and parental mishandling of their children may represent the exaggeration of any or several character strivings.

Delinquency and criminality are syndromes representing the excess of hostile aggression. Sexual disorders often portray the nature of the interpersonal disorder. Hypochondriacal preoccupations may depict the fear of injury; psychopaths demonstrate the extravagant caricature of many interpersonal needs; immature, obsessive, schizoid persons have all, under the threat of anxiety, pressed their life-styles to extreme lengths. Usually, second-line defenses do not work effectively. Rather they plunge people into such interpersonal difficulties that conflict and stress are heightened rather than reduced. The chronic employment of dependency reactions, for example, is eventually resented by others on whom one leans, serving to alienate the person from his sources of support. Rather than have his needs gratified, he drives others away and is more alone. The emotionally poor get poorer if there is a blind repetition at the same pattern. Because of the ultimate ineffectiveness of the second line of defense, the individual usually goes on to the next level.

Third-level defenses: Repressive maneuvers

The third level of defense consists of the manipulation of one's *intrapsychic* structure. It is an attempt to gain peace by pushing troubles out of one's mind. In *repression* a barrier is set up to the motor discharge of needs, impulses, memories, ideas, or attitudes, awareness of which will set off anxiety. To avoid anxiety, selected ideational segments are sealed off along with any associational memories or links, the activation of which may challenge the repression. In this process there may be (1) a blocking in the perception, processing, storage, and retrieval of experiences; (2) an inhibition or distortion in the functions of intelligence, such as attention, learning, discrimination, judgment, reasoning, and imagination; (3) a blocking in the operations and expressions of emotions; and (4) a blocking in behavior.

The necessity of maintaining repression can absorb the energy resources of the individual. Constantly threatened are breakdowns in the repressive barriers, a filtering of the sealed-off components into consciousness, and a mobilization of anxiety. The individual may consequently be victimized by a ceaseless stress reaction, his physical system being in a perpetual uproar. Vulnerable organ systems may become disorganized with outbreaks of organic illness. At the same time a symbolic discharge (*displacement of affect*) may occur in attenuated or distorted forms, which will provide some gratification for the repudiated drives. At phases when repressed needs become particularly urgent, or for some reason or other are activated by physiological factors (such as a previously quiescent sexual drive stirring during adolescence) or experientially (as when an insult excites slumbering rage and aggression), a direct expression may occur followed by retributive reactions which will appease guilt feelings and serve to restore repressions.

The understanding of the repressive line of defense can best be seen in two groupings: those efforts aimed at reinforcing repression and the direct or symbolic release of repressed material.

First, *reaction formations* (such as chastity or heightened morality as a cover for perverse sexual or antisocial desire) may become pathologically exuberant in the urgent need to deny the existence of forbidden impulses.

Second, there is an *inhibition of function,* disturbed apperception, attention, concentration, and thinking occurring as one selectively inattends to certain upsetting aspects of one's inner or outer world. Disturbed consciousness may take the form of fainting, stupor, or excessive needs for sleep. Disturbed memory to the point of amnesia may develop. Emotional dulling can be seen in a person who exhibits indifference or apathy as a defense against being involved in a potentially threatening situation. Sensory defects, motor paralysis, and even visceral inhibitions may be *conversion reactions* that serve to block out the direct awareness of an anxiety-provoking thought or deed. Thus one may literally not be able to feel a frightening object, see a threatening event, or experience a sexually arousing stimulus—if such awareness would provoke undue anxiety.

Another effort at reinforcing repression is the development of a phobia. In *phobia formation* there is a displacement from a fearsome inner drive to an external object that symbolically comes to represent this drive. Thus a fear of snakes in a woman may conceal an exaggerated but repressed interest in the male sexual organ. A fear of heights may be a cover of a murderous impulse for which one may anticipate retributory punishment.

Further attempts to gain peace through repression are through *undoing* and *isolation*. By these maneuvers the individual, almost magically, robs a forbidden impulse of any vitality. When he thinks an angry thought, he quickly follows it with a thought that "undoes" the first thought. Or he does not "feel" the thought, and so he believes his sexual or hostile impulses have no real significance for him.

The release of repressed material through direct or symbolic means is the second form by which repressive maneuvers attempt to maintain a psychic equilibrium. As we have just noted, the first form of repressive maneuver reinforces the repression itself. This second form allows for an intermittent direct or symbolic discharge of the repressed material.

One such type of release is simply an impulsive breakthrough of some forbidden word or thought or impulse. Occasionally an excited episode of acting out some impulse can be noted in a person who otherwise relies heavily on repression as his typical form of defense. The fighting drunk may actually be a sober Casper Milquetoast whose repressions are temporarily deadened by alcohol, permitting a hostile release.

Obsession, that is the repetitive use of reveries and daydreams, is a second means that serves to drain away the repressed material. A symbolization of forbidden inner impulses through obsessional thinking drains off energy but promotes anxiety in their release. The individual may murder, rape, or torture special people in his fantasies or may explode the world with atom bombs to his own dismay and anxious discomfort. He may then neutralize his released impulses by engaging in *compulsive rituals,* which on the surface make no sense but which symbolically appease his guilt or divert his mind from his preoccupation. Thus "evil" thoughts may inspire repeated hand washing as a cleansing ritual.

A third measure for liberating repressed material is through *dissociative states,* such as somnambulism, fugues, and multiple personality. Acted out are the repressed impulses, too threatening to be integrated into one's conscious activities, but not remembered when the usual consciousness is restored.

Psychosomatic disorders may be a fourth evidence of the release of tensions that have not made their way into conscious awareness. Sensory, somatic and visceral changes may reflect the inner conflicts of an individual. Tics, spasms and convulsions are often symbolic revelations of inner psychic processes that cannot find direct expression.

The fifth means are the *sexual perversions,* such as fetishism, exhibitionism, and the like, that discharge erotic tension when these become uncontrollable.

The *use of the self as an object for aggression* is a sixth method by which unaccepted impulses gain some measure of expression. Angry impulses originally directed at others are repressed and then directed against the self. The resultant condition may be neurotic depression, a feeling that one is a miserable creature. The continuing self-recriminations that the depressed person indulges served to discharge his hostility—albeit in the wrong direction. There may also be dangerous abuses of the self, with accident proneness, mutilation tendencies, and even suicide.

Finally, a defense mechanism that allows for releasing repressed material is *projection.* Projection is a means of repudiating inner drives that are painful and anxiety provoking by attributing them to outside agencies and influences. Thus inner feelings of hate, too dangerous to accept and manage, are externalized in the conviction of being hated or victimized by an oppressor. Avarice may be concealed by a belief that one is being exploited. Homosexual drives may be credited to persons of the same sex toward whom the individual is sexually attracted. The projective mechanism serves the purpose of objectifying a forbidden and repressed danger that will justify certain measures, such as the expression of aggression without guilt. In this way punishment and self-blame are avoided. By projecting impulses and desires on to the outside world one may insidiously gain acceptance for his own forbidden drives. For example, insisting upon the fact that the world is sexually preoccupied, and finding prurient examples for this point of view, a sexually fearful individual may try to lessen the severity of his own conscience that punishes him for his sexual needs.

Fourth-level defenses: Regressive defenses

When all other measures are failing to restore emotional equilibrium, psychotic states are the last instrumentality with which to escape the painful demands of reality. There may be a return to completely helpless dependency, a repudiation of and withdrawal from reality, excited acting-out impulses without reference to reality demands, and depression that has reached delusional and suicidal proportions. In this fourth level of defense the individual shows evidence of psychotic functioning. There may be dereistic thinking, disorders of perception (*illusions, hallucinations*), disorders of mental content (*ideas of reference, delusions*), disorders of apperception and comprehension, disorders in stream of mental activity (increased or diminished speech productivity, irrelevance, incoherence, scattering, neologisms), and defects in memory, personal identification, orientation, retention, recall, thinking capacity, attention, insight, and judgment. There is evidence that special syndromes, such as *manic-depressive psychosis* and *schizophrenia,* have genetic components that bring out their peculiar characteristics in the face of stressful experiences.

These four levels of defense must not be regarded as arbitrary, static states. Each level never occurs in isolation. Each level is always mixed with manifestations of other defensive levels.

Conclusion

Once we have determined why at this time the patient has presented himself for therapy and explored with him his ideas about his situation including what he believes is behind his troubles, and what he wants to achieve from treatment, we may then select an immediate focus and organize our treatment strategies. A too early concentration on the patient's psychopathology and past conditionings that have created his conflicts and circumscribed his growth, however important these may be, will support regression and encourage long-term lingering in treatment. Rather, we should begin to focus on what is of *immediate* concern to the patient, such as incidents in life that have precipitated the symptoms for which he seeks help. In focusing on precipitating factors one must gauge the patient's vulnerability to stress as well as the virility of the stress factor itself. In focusing on symptoms the therapist should view them as an assembly of reactions to anxiety as well as consequences of mechanisms of defense.

During the explorations it is important to concentrate on problem solving, while examining, encouraging, and helping the release of whatever positive adaptive forces are present in the patient, focusing on the resistances that block their operation. In the course of doing this we may be confronted by the patient with his early formative experiences, but these are handled in the context of explaining obstructions to effective functioning in the present. Ample opportunities will be found later on to switch the focus to areas related to some central dynamic theme by establishing some connection between it and current problems and concerns should this be deemed desirable. Powerful resistance to treatment may make a focus on dynamics essential. Obviously, the therapist will deliberately have to select dynamic aspects that he can work with expediently, avoiding or dealing tangentially with even noticeable conflicts that do not seem offensive and would be difficult or impossible to handle in the brief period allotted to therapy.

CHAPTER 8

Choosing a Dynamic Focus

A. Probing into the Past

Little time is available in short-term therapy to explore the past. Much better use can be made of the treatment hour by dealing with pertinent elements in the here and now. However, where the therapist can determine important past events and contingencies that have molded the personality organization, this will facilitate a better understanding of the patient's illness and help select an appropriate dynamic focus. Enough data may be available from taking a good history to make assumptions of how the past has entered into the formation of personality distortions that burden present-day adaptations. More immediate clues may be gained from the transference that serves as a vital link to the kinds of early relationships that existed in actuality or fantasy that have been instrumental in laying down the foundations of the patient's character structure. Because behavior reflects to a greater or lesser degree conditionings set up in the past, it may be difficult to understand it fully without reference to what has gone on before. From a practical point of view in short-term therapy it is not possible to devote much effort in exploring the past beyond providing the patient with some guidelines to pursue on his own after the formal therapy period has ended.

This chapter constitutes a review of development from a psychodynamic perspective. It is included in this volume as an introduction to the more clinically important chapters that follow.

Transference

Of vital significance to psychotherapists of all persuasions was Freud's crucial perception that to a greater or lesser degree patients tend to project onto authority figures thoughts, wishes, and feelings identical to those formerly harbored toward important past personages (parents, parental substitutes, siblings). Reanimated during therapy are transference reactions, wholly inappropriate for the present, but reactions that recapitulate antecedent emotional situations. It is as if the patient seeks to relive the periods of infancy and childhood, recovering gratifications and resolving fears through the instrumentality of the therapist, who is endowed with power and attributes such as an infant harbors toward parental agencies. There may be exhibited also toward the therapist in transference a host of aberrant attitudes, such as rebelliousness, hostility, submissiveness, and sexual excitement. Such feelings may also develop outside of the therapeutic situation with any kind of an authority or sibling figure. Transference is diagnostically important, since it is a laboratory revival of much of what went on in the individual's childhood. It may explain a good deal of current behavior that on the surface seems illogical and maladaptive. It may also contain the key to why the patient is resisting the therapist and failing to respond to the therapeutic techniques that are being used. The detection and management of transference may, therefore, be crucial and decisive apart from helping to select a pivotal dynamic focus.

Synthesizing Factors of Personality Development

In order to understand how and why the past survives in the present and the mischief it invokes, it is necessary briefly to summarize some of the current findings on personality development that come from the biological and social fields. Attempts are constantly being made to bring objectivity to the data on development by studying material from a number of different sources. These include observations by trained workers of newborn babies at hospitals, institutions, and day-care centers; experiences of teachers with children at nursery schools, kindergartens, and grade schools; reports of parents describing the behavior of their offspring; studies or recordings of plays, art productions, dreams, fantasies, and spontaneous verbalizations of presumably normal children; psychological tests of children, especially projective tests; investigations by social workers, correctional workers, and psychologists of the socioeconomic environment, family relationships, and other areas of potential conflict among maladjusted, delinquent, and criminal youngsters and adults; scrutiny of case records of children with severe emotional problems who have been hospitalized in mental institutions; observations of psychotherapists treating children in their private practices or in outpatient clinics; exploration of memories, dreams, and transference phenomena that reflect childhood experiences of adult patients receiving psychoanalysis; field studies of anthropologists reporting on the customs, folkways, creative artistic expressions, modes of child rearing, and family structure of various cultural groups; demographic surveys by various social scientists of the incidence and prevalence of emotional problems in different parts of the world; analysis of reactions of individuals to psychotropic drugs; accounts by ethologists of animal behavior in a natural setting; and research findings of animal experimentors who have subjected higher mammals to artifacts in upbringing or to motivational conflicts.

Objective appraisal of this vast data requires a more a less precise application of the scientific method. Unfortunately, investigators in the field of personality research are handicapped by formidable methodological problems in attempting to subject their observations to clinical research. Moreover, current theories of human behavior are so complex, their inherent terms so operationally indefinable, their derivations so diffuse, their implications so global that we are unable to expose them readily to scientific experiment.

In spite of these seemingly insuperable obstacles, it has been possible to scrutinize many of the events associated with the development of personality and to examine and analyze this data, making appropriate connections, discerning combinations, and otherwise synthesizing the material in a constructive way. Out of this synthesis a number of propositions have emerged that may clarify pathological evolvements on which the therapist may wish to focus.

1. The task of human growth is to transform an amorphous creature, the infant, into a civilized adult capable of living adaptively in a complex

social framework. Toward this end the child cultivates restraints on his biological impulses, acquires skills in interpersonal relationships, evolves values that are consonant with the society in which he lives, and perfects techniques that allow him to fulfill himself creatively within the bounds of his potentials.

2. Growth is governed by a number of developmental laws—for instance, laws of maturation common to the entire species, laws peculiar to the cultural and subcultural group of which the individual is a part, and, finally, laws unique to himself, parcels of his personal experience that will make his development unlike that of any other individual.

3. While growth is broadly similar in all human infants and children, there is great difference in individual styles and the rate of growth.

4. Development may conveniently be divided into a number of stages of growth corresponding roughly with certain age levels. While there is some variation in timing and rate, the average individual appears to follow these stages with surprising sequential regularity.

5. The various stages are characterized by specific needs that must be propitiated, common stresses that must be resolved, and special skills that must be developed. A healthy personality structure develops on the basis of the adequacy with which these needs are supplied, stresses mastered, and skills learned at progressive age levels.

6. Difficulties may arise at each stage of growth that engender a partial or complete failure in the satisfaction of needs, the solution of current conflicts, and the learning of skills. Such failures handicap the individual in adapting to the more elaborate demands and requirements that constitute the succeeding stages of growth.

7. *Where essential personality qualities characteristic of maturity are not evolved, the individual will be burdened with residual childhood needs, attitudes, and ways of handling stress.* These anachronisms tend to clash with the demands of a healthy biological and social adjustment. Primitive strivings and conceptions of the world, early fears and guilt feelings, and defenses against these usually survive in their pristine form though they are not always manifest. They tend to contaminate an adult type of integration.

8. Personality, evolving as it does from a blend of heredity and experience, is not merely a repository of special abilities, attitudes, and beliefs. It is a broad fabric that covers every facet of man's internal and external adjustment. Through the medium of personality operations the individual satisfies even the most elemental of his needs.

9. Disturbed or neurotic behavior represents a collapse in the individual's capacities for adjustment. This collapse is sponsored by a personality structure that cannot sustain the individual in the face of his inner conflicts and the external demands. Inherent in every neurosis is an attempt at adaptation that strives to restore the person to some kind of homeostatic balance. Unfortunately, the expediences that are exploited are ultimately destructive to adjustment, crippling the individual in his dealings with the world.

10. The first few years of life are the most crucial in personality development, establishing thinking, feeling, and behavioral patterns that will influence the individual the remainder of the life. Where experiences with the parent and with the early environment are harmonious, the child is encouraged to evolve a system of security that regards the world as a bountiful place and to develop a self-esteem that promotes assertiveness and self-confidence. The child will be convinced of his capacities to love and to be loved, and this will form the foundation of a healthy personality. On the other hand, where the child has been deprived of proper stimulation and care, or where he has been rejected, overprotected, improperly disciplined, or unduly intimidated, the world will constitute for him a place of menace. A personality organization structured on the bedrock of such unwholesome conditionings is bound to be unsubstantial and shaky. *Incomplete separation-individuation, exaggerated dependency, intense resentment, guilt, sadomasochistic impulses, impaired independence, a damaged sense of identity and self-image, detachment, and a host of compensatory mechanisms interfere with a proper adaptation.*

Psychopathology becomes more understandable when viewed against the backdrop of personality development. Developmental studies, as has been indicated above, show that personality strength or weakness is more or less determined by the experiences during childhood. The child will tend to identify with the characteristics of those whom he admires, and to evolve an idealized image of himself (ego ideal) fashioned after the person or persons he venerates. If, in the first few years of life, the individual has developed a feeling of security, a sense of reality, a good measure of assertiveness, positive self-esteem, and capacities for self-control, he will probably be able to endure considerable environmental hardships thereafter and still evolve into a healthy adult. On the other hand, early unfavorable development handicaps the child in managing even the usual vicissitudes that are common to growing up. This does not mean that all children with a good personal substructure will inevitably emerge as healthy adults since an overly harsh environment can inhibit development at any phase in the growth process. Nor does it imply that a child with an inadequate personality structure may not in the face of favorable circumstances overcome severe early impediments in growth and mature to satisfactory adulthood. Were we to subscribe to the pessimistic philosophy that all early psychic damage is irreparably permanent, we would blind ourselves to the efficacy of psychotherapy that is predicated on the assumption that it is possible through the emotionally corrective experience provided by treatment to overcome many childhood personality distortions.

Personality traits in adult life, however, are never an exact reduplication of childhood strivings. Early conditionings are tempered by experiences in later life that tend to modify, neutralize, or reinforce them. Moreover, though behavior is influenced by patterns rooted in the past, responses vary widely in different situations in accordance with their symbolic significance and the prevailing social role played by the person at the time. The sundry variations of personality strivings in operation are infinite. Incorporated are attitudes, values, and patterns of behavior that issue out of a defective security system, distorted conceptions of reality, imperfect social control over bodily functions, vitiated sense of assertiveness, stunted independence, impaired self-esteem, inadequate frustration tolerance, improper mastery of sexual and hostile impulses, incomplete identification with members of one's own sex, deficient group identification, faulty integration of prevailing social values, and impaired acceptance of one's social role. Pressure of early unsatisfied needs, anticipation of the same kinds of turmoil that existed in childhood or the actual setting up of conditions that prevailed in one's early life, and survival of anachronistic defenses, symptoms, and their symbolic extensions, all are incorporated into the personality structure. Compulsive in nature, they permeate every phase of thought, feeling, and action; they govern the random and purposeful activities of the individual, forcing him to conform with them in a merciless way.

While the personality structure is tremendously complex and is understandably different in every human being by virtue of distinctive constitutional makeup and unique conditionings, certain common ingredients may be observed in all persons in our culture. Among these are (1) aspects of nuclear conflicts that accrue in the course of personality development, (2) interacting manifestations of unresolved childish promptings, and (3) reverberations of character drives, such as excessive dependency, aggression, compulsive independence, detachment, and manifestations of a devalued self-image. These are rich sources of problems that supply important areas of dynamic focus.

Possible Assumptions Based on the Past

An understanding of how the past life (see Table 8–1 on personality development) of a patient has influenced the existing psychopathology is thus of inestimable value in dynamic

(Cont'd, p. 108)

TABLE 8-1. Personality Development (See following chart* for corresponding numbers

(1) *Hereditary and constitutional elements are the building blocks of personality. Along with intrauterine influences they determine sensitivity and activity patterns and thus regulate the character of later conditionings. Under the promptings of maturation, needs emerge and skills evolve with surprising regularity. Environmental factors, nevertheless, may modify these prenatal forces and fashion the lines along which the personality structure is organized.*

(2) *Personality evolves out of the conditionings and experiences of the individual in his relationships with the world. Basic needs must be gratified and appropriate coping mechanisms evolved, the consummation of which, at any age level, if inadequate will retard and if satisfactory will expedite successive stages of growth. The social milieu, reflected in the disciplines and values sponsored by the family, designs the specific outlets for and modes of expression of the emerging needs.*

(3) *Personality maturation is contingent on execution of vital tasks that must be successfully fulfilled at the different age levels.*

(4) *What inhibits or distorts growth are depriving experiences that block the proper satisfaction of needs. An unwholesome milieu tends to foster destructive patterns that crush security, undermine self-esteem and interfere with the development of essential skills and values that are consonant with the requirements of adaptation.*

(5) *At any age level collapse in adaptation may be sponsored when basic needs are vitiated, and security and self-esteem are shattered with no hope of immediate reparation. If the reservoir of defenses is sufficiently flexible, considerable conflict may be endured. On the other hand, where the personality underpinnings are unstable, even minimal conflict may tax coping capacities. A combination of symptoms issue from the failure to solve conflicts, and include, in the main, the various manifestations of anxiety, defenses against anxiety, as well as technics of counteracting or solving the conflictual situation itself. While the elaborated symptoms are unique for every individual, being influenced by the specific experiences of the person, and by the singular mechanisms of defense he has found successful in past dealing with stress, definite groupings of symptoms appear with sufficient frequency to constitute familiar syndromes. Symptomatic evidences of a failing adjustment may persist from one age level to the next, accretions of succeeding difficulties being added to or substituting for problems existing at preceeding age levels.*

(6) *Residues of defective rearing contaminate adjustment by influencing disorganizing relationships with other individuals. Conflict is thus in constant generation. The specific deposits of defect display themselves in luxuriant forms, the cumulative product of pathological accruals from one age level to the next.*

(7) *Awareness of formative experiences and elaborated defenses may be dimmed by repression. Forgetting or repudiating them does not protect the individual against their forays into his conscious life in direct or derivative form. Early conflicts may be revived symbolically in dreams, through the use of psychotomimetic drugs, as a result of an overpowering emotional crisis, during an intense relationship with a personage who represents a parental or sibling figure, or by a transference neurosis inspired in the course of psychotherapeutic treatment.*

* *From* L. R. Wolberg, *Psychotherapy and the Behavioral Sciences* (New York, Grune & Stratton, 1966), pp. 62–63. Reprinted with permission.

TABLE 8-1, cont'd: Building Blocks of Personality

I. **HEREDITARY ELEMENTS** (neurophysiological biochemical,)

II. **INTRAUTERINE INFLUENCES** (Metabolic, postural, infectious)

↓

Sensitivity and Activity Potentials

↓

MATURATIONAL COMPONENTS AND EXPERIENTIAL CONDITIONINGS

YEAR	(2) NEEDS	(3) TASKS TO ACHIEVE	(4) BASIC TRAUMAS
1 (Infancy)	Intense and urgent demands for oral satisfaction (nutrition and sucking pleasure); sensory stimulation (optic, auditory, tactile, kinesthetic); love and approval.	Feelings of security and trust. Separation of self from nonself. Coordination; ambulation. Symbolization.	Interference with nutrition (acute or chronic illness, gastrointestinal upsets, allergies). Interference with sucking pleasure, sensory stimulation, love and approval (separation from, death of, or rejection by mother). Faulty weaning.
2–3 (Early Childhood)	Investigative and exploratory needs; genital manipulation. Beginning strivings for independence and mastery; aggressive assertiveness.	Feelings of autonomy; incorporation of disciplines; tolerance of frustration. Social outlets for aggression. Self-confidence.	Habit training (too lax or too severe disciplines, as in relation to toilet training). Interference with independence and mastery (overprotection). Faulty handling of rage and aggression (too severe restrictions or excessive permissiveness). Too great or too little emphasis by parent on rights of other members of family. Interference with investigative and exploratory activities. Interference with genital manipulation. Unconscious encouragement of rebellion by parent, alternating with excessive punishment.
3–5 (Childhood)	Need for extrafamilial group contacts and for cooperative play. Keen interest in sex, genital differences, and birth processes.	Sexual identification. Oedipal resolution.	Problems related to entry into nursery school and kindergarten. Interference with interest in sexuality; masturbatory intimidation. Precocious or excessive sexual stimulation. Seductive parent. Mother too dominant; father too passive or absent.
5–11 (Late Childhood)	Need for intellectual growth and understanding. Need for further social contacts and for organized team play. Need to belong to a group, club, or gang.	Group identification.	Problems related to entry into grade school (improper school and teachers: fear of relinquishing dependency). Neighborhood stresses. Exposure to racial and religious prejudices.
11–15 (Early Adolescence)	Intense sexual feelings and interests for which a social outlet is necessary (recreational programs, especially social dancing.) Need to practice skills for successful participation in groups.	Socialization of sex drives. Resolution of parental ambivalence.	Conflict between need for and defiance of parents. Conflict in relation to sexual demands and social restrictions; masturbatory conflicts. Too lax sexual environment. Poor supervision and discipline. Lack of cohesiveness in home.
15–21 (Late Adolescence)	Gradual emancipation from parents. Need to make a vocational choice. Growing sense of responsibility. Courtship; marriage.	Resolution of dependency. Assumption of heterosexual role.	Conflict between dependence and independence. Continuing sexual conflict. Severe economic problems.
21–40 (Adulthood)	Good sexual, marital, family, and work adjustment. Community participation.	Productive work role and economic independence. Marriage; parenthood. Community responsibilities. Creative self-fulfillment.	Extraordinary family stresses. Economic hardships. Natural disasters. Illness, and accidents. Racial and religious discriminations.
40–65 (Middle Age)	Acceptance of a slower life pace, physically and competitively. Need for new interests, hobbies, and community activities.	Mobilization of one's total resources toward achievement of personal happiness, family integration, and social welfare.	Menopausal and climacteric changes. Conflicts in relation to separation from children, unfulfilled ambitions, sexual declination, and, in women, cessation of child bearing.
65 on (Old Age)	Acceptance of physical, sexual, and memory recession. Need to engage in social activities, to cultivate new friends, to develop community interests and hobbies.	Continued work, interpersonal and social activities to the limit of one's physical capacities.	Conflicts in relation to loneliness, death of friends and mate, increased leisure time, retirement, failing work, physical and sexual activities. Illness. Fearful anticipation of death.

TABLE 8-1, cont'd: Building Blocks of Personality

I. **HEREDITARY ELEMENTS** (neurophysiological, biochemical,)

II. **INTRAUTERINE INFLUENCES** (metabolic, postural, infectious)

↓

Sensitivity and Activity Potentials

↓

MATURATIONAL COMPONENTS AND EXPERIENTIAL CONDITIONINGS

(5) SYMPTOMS OF ADAPTIVE BREAKDOWN	(6) SURVIVING PERSONALITY DISTORTIONS	(7) REPRESSION
1. Diffuse anxiety reactions. 2. Psychosomatic disorders: anorexia, vomiting, colic, diarrhea, breathing and circulatory disorders. 3. Rage reactions—screaming, crying. 4. Withdrawal reactions—dullness, apathy stupor.	Insecurity; mistrust; depressiveness. Preoccupation with oral activities. Search for an idealized parental figure or for nirvana. Propensity for addictions. Altered body image; austitic reactions; depersonalization.	4+
1. Anxiety, phobic and compulsive-like reactions. Psychophysiological reactions: (a) gastrointestinal disorders—feeding difficulties like anorexia; constipation, diarrhea. (b) speech disorders—stammering. (c) bowel and bladder disorders—soiling, enuresis. 2. Personality disorders: (a) rage reactions, (b) withdrawal reactions, (c) excessive dependency, (d) disturbed identity.	Lack of self-confidence. Stubbornness. Inability to control impulses and emotions. Frustration intolerance. Preoccupation with anal activities. Paranoidal ideas; fear of authority. Compulsiveness. Feelings of shame.	4+
1. Psychoneurotic reactions: (a) anxiety states, (b) phobic reactions, (c) psychophysiologic reactions: gastrointestinal disorders, speech disorders, bladder disorders, skin disorders, tics. 2. Personality disorders (as above). 3. Primary behavior disorders.	Persisting oedipal conflicts; inability to identify with persons of own sex.	2+ to 4+
1. Psychoneurotic reactions: (a) anxiety states and anxiety reactions, (b) phobic reactions, (c) conversion hysteria, (d) compulsion neurosis, (e) psychosomatic disorders: gastrointestinal, bladder, speech, skin, hearing and visual disorders, tics, muscle spasms, nail-biting, compulsive or absent masturbation. 2. Personality disorders (as above). 3. Primary behavior disorders—learning disabilities. 4. Juvenile schizophrenia.	Inability to accept a proper role. Disturbed relations with others. Problems in competitiveness and cooperation.	0 to 2+
as above, plus Schizophrenia	Sexual acting-out. Excessively hostile attitudes toward authority. Problems in identity. Isolation.	0 to 2+
as above	Excessive dependence. Devalued self-image. Confusion regarding social role. Sexual inhibitions.	0 to 2+
as above, plus Alcoholism Drug addiction Manic-depressive psychosis	Reinforcement of existent personality disturbances.	0 to 1+
as above, plus Involutional melancholia	as above	0 to 1+
as above, plus Arteriosclerotic and Senile psychoses	as above	0 to 2+

short-term therapy. While little time is available to explore the past, as has been mentioned, certain assumptions may be possible from the symptom picture, a good history, dreams, and particularly transference manifestations. The impact of the past may be summarized under seven headings.

Unpropitiated early needs constantly obtrude themselves on the individual, propelling him toward direct or symbolic actions to satisfy these needs. A man deprived during infancy of adequate sucking pleasure may constantly be obsessed with a need for mouth stimulation, over-indulging himself with food and alcohol to the point of obesity and alcoholism. A woman, restricted as a child in physical activity and assertive behavior on the basis that she was a girl, may continue to envy men and their possession of the emblem of masculinity, the penis. Accordingly, she will attempt to pattern her life along lines commonly pursued by males, masculinity being equated in her mind with freedom and assertiveness. With dogged persistence she will deny feminine interests, and she may even clothe herself in masculine-like attire, cropping her hair after the style of men.

Defenses evolved in childhood may carry over into adult life with an astonishing persistence. A boy, overprotected and sexually overstimulated by a doting mother, may vigorously detach himself from her. When he grows up, he may continue to avoid contact with women; any attempts at sexual play may result in incestuous guilt to a point where he is unable to function. A child rigorously and prematurely toilet trained may regard his bowel activities as disagreeable and filthy. Overcleanliness, overorderliness, overmeticulousness ensue and burden his adult adjustment. A younger sibling may carry over into adult life the conviction that he is small and ineffectual in relation to any person more or less unconsciously identified as his older sibling. This will promote withdrawal tendencies or provoke him to prove himself by fighting and pushing himself beyond his habitual capacities. An older sibling may continue to harbor hatred toward any competitor whom she equates with the preferred and privileged younger child in her family who displaced her as the favorite.

Mechanisms developed in early childhood that have insured a gratification of needs will continue to be indulged to a greater or lesser degree in adult life. Thus a child intimidated by his parents to avoid masturbatory activities responds with great hostility and, in a defiant manner, covertly continues his practice. Later the manifestation of hostility seems to be a condition prerequisite for any kind of sexual expression, sexual sadism being the ultimate outcome. Another youngster may have been enjoined by overscrupulous parents to perform meticulously on all occasions, on the threat of their condemnation or loss of love. Henceforth indulgence of the trait of perfectionism may become an essential factor in his experiencing any degree of positive self-esteem. A pampered child whose temper tantrums compelled his parents and siblings to give in to his whims, persists in self-oriented, selfish demands on the world to supply him with gratifications and satisfactions. Sensitive to the slightest rejection, he construes any casualness toward him as a designed personal injury. This mobilizes rage and releases coercive behavior to force people to yield to his demands.

The individual will repetitively set up and attempt to live through early destructive situations that he has failed to master as a child. A young woman repetitively involves herself in competitive relationships with older, more attractive, more gifted women in an attempt to subdue them. The feelings she experiences and the situations she creates parallel closely the rivalry experience with her older sister whom she could never vanquish. A child is severely rejected and physically maltreated by an alcoholic father. When she matures, she is passionately attracted to detached, sadistic, and psychopathic men, whose affection she desperately tries to win. A man in psychoanalysis develops paranoidal attitudes and feelings toward the analyst, imagining that the analyst wishes to humiliate and torture him. These are transference manifestations reflective of the same kinds of feelings he had toward his father during the oedipal period.

The individual often unwittingly exhibits the same kind of destructive attitudes and behavior patterns that he bitterly protests were manifested toward him by his parents. A woman reared by a petulant, argumentative mother may engage in the same kind of behavior with her own children, totally unaware of the compulsive nature of her pattern. A man victimized during his childhood by a hypochondriacal father may himself become obsessionally concerned with physical illness following marriage. Through insidious identification a son may become an alcoholic like his male parent, a daughter the victim of migraine like her mother; the examples of such identification are endless.

The individual may fail to develop certain mature personality features. A child severely neglected and rejected during infancy comes into adult life with pathological feelings of impending doom, a conceptualization of himself as inhuman and insignificant, tendencies to depersonalization, and an inability to love or respect others. A boy whose father is passive and detached identifies with a strong aggressive mother, emulating her manner and interests to the point of avoiding masculine attitudes and goals. A youngster who was discriminated against by his agemates because of his race may, from the beginning of his extrafamilial contacts, develop a contempt for his kinfolk and a fear of groups. A girl victimized by "proper" and "gentle" parents who cannot stand scenes is shamed into abandoning any demonstration of anger. She continues to display a bland, forgiving manner despite exploitation and intimidation.

The individual may tend to revive childhood symptoms in the face of stress. Vomiting, colic, and diarrhea, which were manifestations of stress during one's early infancy, may be mobilized by later episodes of tension to the embarrassment and dismay of the person. Fear of the dark and of animals, which terrorized the individual in early childhood, may overwhelm him in adult life when anxiety taxes his existent capacities.

Nuclear Conflicts

Table 8–2 summarizes the chief conflicts, which we call "nuclear conflicts," imbedded in the psyche of each person, products of the inevitable clash of maturing needs and reality restrictions, the mastery of which constitutes one of the primary tasks of psychosocial development. It must be emphasized that these conflicts are universal qualitatively, though quantitatively differing in all persons as a result of constitutional-conditioning variations and the integrity of the existing defenses.

The earliest nuclear conflicts are organized in relationship to the parents. For instance, the infant's association of the presence of mother with satisfaction of his needs (hunger, thirst, freedom from discomfort and pain, demand for stimulation) results in her becoming affiliated with gratification of these needs, with pleasure and the relief of tension. At the same time the absence of mother becomes linked to discomfort, distress, and pain. During the last part of the first year the child reacts with what is probably a primordial type of anxiety to separation from the mother, and with rage at her turning away from him toward anybody else, child or adult. This blended gratification-deprivation image of mother is probably the precurser of later ambivalencies, powering sibling rivalry and the rivalries during the oedipal period. It also gives rise to motivations to control, appease, and win favors from mother and mother figures, to vanquish, eliminate, or destroy competitors for her interest and attention, and to punish mother and mother figures for actual or fancied deprivations. The mother symbol becomes sym-

TABLE 8-2. Nuclear Conflicts*

Ages	Conflictual Elements	Legends	Residual Manifestations (repressed or suppressed)
0–3 mo.	Constant freedom from distress and pain *opposed* by realistic environmental restrictions.	"I must be everlastingly happy and comfortable; instead I suffer."	Search for nirvana. Demand for magic.
4 mo.–1 yr.	Need for oral, sensory, and affectionate gratification *opposed* by realistic deprivations.	"I want to be fed, loved, stimulated, and kept free from pain at all times; but mother denies me this gratification."	Ambivalence toward mother figures. Separation anxiety.
1–2 yrs.	Self-actualization *opposed* by essential restrictive disciplines.	"I want to do what I want to do when I want to do it, but I will be punished and told I am bad."	Impulsive aggressiveness. Guilt feelings.
3–5	Power impulses *opposed* by sense of helplessness. Oedipal desires *opposed* by retaliatory fears.	"I want to be big and strong, but I know I am weak and little." "I want to possess my mother (father) for myself, but I cannot compete with my father (mother)."	Inferiority feelings. Castration fears. Compulsive strivings for masculinity.
6–11	Demand for total group acceptance *opposed* by manifestations of aloofness and unfriendliness.	"I want everybody to like, admire, and accept me, but there are some people who are against me and reject me."	Fear of rejection by the group.
12–15	Sexual impulses *opposed* by guilt and fear of punishment.	"I feel a need for sexual stimulation, but this is wrong and not acceptable."	Fear of lack of "maleness" in men and "femaleness" in women.
16–21	Independence strivings *opposed* by dependency.	"I need to be a grown, independent person, but I don't want the responsibility. I would like to be a child, but this would make me feel like a nothing."	Continuing dependency.

* *From* L. R. Wolberg, and J. Kildahl, *The Dynamics of Personality* (New York, Grune & Stratton, 1970), p. 56. Reprinted by permission.

bolically linked to later sources of gratification or deprivation. Moreover, if a disruption of homeostatic equilibrium occurs at any time later on in life or if for any reason anxiety erupts with a shattering of the sense of mastery, the primordial anxiety imprints may be revived, activating separation fears and mother-invoking tendencies along lines pursued by the individual as an infant.

The gratification-deprivation, separation-anxiety constellations, laid down during phases of development early in the period of conceptualization, will tend to operate outside the zone of conscious awareness. Whenever habitual coping mechanisms fail the individual and he experiences anxiety, he may feel the helplessness and manifest the behavior of an infant, and he may seek out, against all logic, a mother figure or her symbolic substitute (such as food in compulsive eating activities). It is little wonder that mothers, and their later representatives (protectors, authorities), come to possess symbolic reward (pleasure) values along with symbolic abandonment (pain, anxiety) potentials. This conflict, deeply imbedded in the unconscious, acts as compost for the fertilization of a host of derivative attitudes, impulses, and drives that remain with the individual throughout his existence. Other conflicts develop in the child's relationships with the world, as noted in Table 8–2, that are superimposed on the conflicts associated with the demand for magic and for the constant presence of the mother figure.

The actual experiences of infants during the first years of life, the degree of need gratifications they achieve, the relative freedom from deprivation, their learning to tolerate some frustration and to accept temporary separation from their mothers provide them with coping devices to control their nuclear conflicts, which, nonetheless, irrespective of how satisfying and wholesome their upbringing may have been, are still operative (albeit successfully repressed), waiting to break out in later life should the psychological homeostasis collapse.

Nuclear conflicts, to repeat, are inherent in the growing-up process irrespective of the character of the environment. This is not to say that a depriving or destructive environment will not exaggerate the effect of conflict or keep it alive beyond the time when it should have subsided; a wholesome environment will tend to keep in check operations of conflict, helping to resolve it satisfactorily. *Nuclear conflicts are in part ordained by biological elements and in part are aspects of the culture. We should expect their appearance in minor or major degree in all persons. Their importance is contained in the fact that they give rise to reaction tendencies that, welded into the personality structure, may later interfere with a proper adaptation.* Of clinical consequence, too, is their tendency to stir from dormancy into open expression when anxiety breaks down the ramparts of the existent defensive fortifications.

The exposure of repressed nuclear conflicts that are creating problems constitutes a task of dynamically oriented therapy, the object being to determine the distortions they produce in the character structure, their affiliation with current conflicts, and the subversive role they play in symptom formation. It may be possible even in short-term therapy—especially in dreams, transference, acting-out behavior, and certain symptoms—to observe how an important nuclear conflict is continuing to disturb the present adjustment of the patient.

The operation of a nuclear conflict is exemplified in a person who habitually relies on alcohol as a means of escaping tension and anxiety. Feelings about deprivations in life are avoided through the tranquilizing effects of alcohol. At the same time the person reassures himself, at least as long as he drinks, that a nurturing agent is available to him that will keep him free of pain.

Another example of a nuclear conflict is evidenced in a teenager who establishes pseudoindependence through invariably doing the opposite of what his parents ask. A request to wear a green shirt immediately establishes in him an intensely felt desire to wear a red shirt. His own fears that he will succumb to his desire to be dependent on his parents drive him to exert his independence, little realizing that he is still not free because he is now imprisoned by his own needs to be oppositional. And much later in life, when a supervisor says "do it this way," he may still be bound up in his need to resist, irrespective of the merits of doing a task one way or another.

The current inability of many persons "to get involved" may be a manifestation of several nuclear conflicts. To remain one step removed from participation in a cause or to be a spectator rather than a player may be skillfully rationalized by saying that one does not have the time, or that the cause does not justify the effort, or that the candidate is all too human, or that the political platform is just so much window dressing. But behind these reasons that sound good, the real reason may be one's sense of helplessness and the subsequent despair about finding magical solutions. Or one may not become involved because of fear of not being totally accepted by any group or party that one joins; so it may be less painful not to expose oneself to such a possible rejection. The nuclear conflict is handled by avoidance.

Conclusion

Even though time does not permit an extensive probing of the past, an understanding of how the past has entered into and has produced personality vulnerabilities may be important for some patients in short-term therapy. Dreams and transference phenomena often yield data regarding past conditionings and may expose some nuclear conflicts that can serve as a focus in therapy. The object here is to determine the distortions they produce in the character structure, their affiliation with current conflicts, and the subversive role they play in initiating and sustaining symptoms. Having grasped the significance of how the past has entered into promoting adjustment problems in the present, many patients become motivated to explore these connections on their own after formal therapy has terminated. Such homework may facilitate a strengthening of defenses and ultimately act as a means of positively influencing personality growth.

CHAPTER 9

Choosing a Dynamic Focus

B. Some Common Dynamic Themes

By their effect on the personality structure the developmental vicissitudes set forth in the last chapter are responsible for a host of symptoms, coping mechanisms, and defenses that provide many dynamic themes on which we may focus. Because it is difficult for some patients to conceptualize these themes, it may be expedient to simplify personality operations and distortions by picturing them as products of the operation of five powerful motors: excessive dependency, resentment, reduced independence, devalued self-image, and detachment.

Dependency

Often at the core of problems is the first motor, *excessive dependency needs,* that had not been adequately resolved in childhood. A healthy balance between dependency and independence is essential for emotional well-being. Where it does not exist, problems ensue. Most likely the average person's childhood yearnings for nurture and affection were not optimally met, leaving a residue of unmet needs that tend to express themselves intensely when the pressures of life mount. Or dependency was pathologically encouraged by a mother who utilized the child as a vehicle for her own unfulfilled demands, hampering the child's growth and strivings for independence. *Unresolved dependency is a ubiquitous fountainhead of troubles. It stems from what is perhaps the most common conflict burdening human kind—inadequate separation-individuation.* And people are apt to blame their troubles on the world: the revolt of youth, governmental corruption, inflation, communism, capitalism, or the atom bomb. Most people, however, somehow muddle through, working out their troubles in one way or another. It is only where separation-individuation is too incomplete and dependency needs too intense that solutions will not be found.

People with powerful dependency needs will often cast about for individuals who demonstrate stronger qualities than they themselves possess. When a swimmer tires, he looks about for something or someone on whom to lean or with which to grapple. A dependent person can be likened to a tired swimmer, and he* wants to find someone or something who can do for him what he feels he cannot do for himself. What he generally looks for is a *perfect* parent, an ideal that exists only in his own fancy. Actually, there are no perfect parental figures who are able or willing to mother or father another adult. So our dependent person is continually being frustrated because his hopes and expectations are not met by someone else. A man who weds expecting an all-giving mother figure for a wife is bound to be disappointed. Further, if he does find a person who fits in with his design and who

* The generic "he" is employed to designate both males and females. There are, however, some distinctive roles played and effects scored for males and females, which will be differentiated as much as possible.

treats him like a helpless individual, he will begin to feel that he is being swallowed up, that he is losing his individuality, that he is trapped. Consequently, he will want to escape from the relationship. Also, as he senses his dependency, he will feel that he is being passive like a child. And this is frightening because he knows that he is not being manly; he may actually have homosexual doubts and fears since masculinity is associated with activity and independence.

We will call his first maneuver his *dependency motor,* which begins to operate especially at times when he is under pressure. As he searches for the element missing in his psychological diet, namely a parental figure, he will most assuredly be disillusioned. Women are no less victimized by dependency than are men. And their reactions are quite similar in that they are apt to regard both males and females on whom they get dependent as potential nurturing mother figures. They are also no less subject to the consequences of the other motors that we shall describe.

Resentment

A second motor that inevitably accompanies the first is the *resentment motor.* Resentment invariably fires off because either one must find a perfect parent who will take care of him or he feels trapped when someone does take care of him and he senses his own passivity and helplessness. Resentment breeds guilt because people just are not supposed to be hateful. Even guilt does not always keep the hostility hidden. Sometimes when our man has had too much to drink or when he is very frustrated about something, his hate feelings leak or pour out. That in itself can be terribly upsetting because he may fear he is getting out of control; or the mere awareness of his inner angry condition can make him despise himself. Sadism and sadistic behavior may be directed at the object of his dependency who he believes is trapping him or who fails to live up to expectations. It may be drained off on scapegoats: blacks, Chicanos, Jews, Communists, capitalists, and so on. Self-hate complicates his existence because it sponsors tension and depression. Hatred directed outward and then turned in results in masochism, in the form of major and minor self-punishments. These may range from fouling up a business deal to inability to accept success, to dangerous accident proneness, to physical illness, to foolish, outrageous, or embarrassing behavior.

Low Independence

Now our man has two motors going most of the time when under pressure: the dependency motor and the resentment motor, with accompanying kickbacks of guilt and masochism. The picture is not complete, however, without a third motor, *low independence,* which is an invariable counterpart of high dependence. Low independence is a feeling that one cannot gain, by his own reason or strength, the desirable prizes of our culture—whether they be love and justice or wine, women, and song. A spin-off of low independence is a feeling of inferiority, a lack of proficiency on achieving desirable goals. Part and parcel of inferiority feelings is the uncertainty about being manly and masculine. Self-doubts about one's sexual integrity are torturous; the usual sequel is to try to compensate by being the quintessence of everything masculine: overly aggressive, overly competitive, and overly dominating. Proving himself with women may lead to satyriasis and Don Juanism. Our man may have fantasies and images in his mind of strong men (often symbolized by their possessing large penises) and may be particularly attracted to them because of their strength. But his awareness of how much he thinks about men may cause him to wonder if he is homosexual and to fear the very things that he admires. He may actually on occasion be sexually attracted to idealized male figures, and he may fantasize incorporating their penises into himself.

Interestingly, low-independence feelings in women lead to the same self-doubt and compensations as in men. Such women will try to repair the fancied damage to themselves by acquiring and acting as if they have the symbols of masculinity (e.g., by swaggering and wearing male apparel) that in our culture are equated with independence. They will compete with and try to vanquish and even figuratively castrate males. In its exaggerated form, they will act toward other females as if they themselves are males, dominating and homosexually seducing them.

Devalued Self-image

By now in our illustration we have a fully operating fourth motor, a *devalued self-image.* With the constant reverberating of his first three motors, our man is now feeling spiteful toward himself. He feels he is miserably incompetent, undesirable, and unworthy. Everywhere he sees evidence of his insignificance: he is not tall enough, he has developed a paunch, women do not seem to pay attention to him, his hair is thinning, his job is not outstanding; his car, his house, his wife—nothing is perfect. He may even think his penis is of inadequate proportions. He feels like a damaged person. These feelings torment him, and he vows to prove that he is not as devalued as he feels. He commits himself to the task of being all-powerful, ambitious, perfect so as to repair his devalued self-image. Then he imagines he can surely respect himself. If he can live without a single misstep, all will be well. He tries to boost himself on his own to the point where others will have to approve of him. He may only daydream all this, or he may, if events are fortuitous, accomplish many of his overcompensatory goals.

If he climbs high, he will most likely resent those below who now lean on him and make demands on him. To those who exhibit weakness, he will show his anger. While he may be able to be giving on his own terms, an unexpected appeal from someone else will be regarded as a vulgar imposition. He actually wants for himself someone on whom to lean and be dependent. However, giving in to such a desire speeds up all his motors and makes him feel even worse. He pursues just the reverse course from his original dependency drive; he competes with any strong figure on whom he might want to lean. He shows the pseudoindependence reminiscent of the adolescent who disagrees on principle with whatever his parents say. And he may compensate for his devalued self-image by exploiting all the cultural symbols of being a worthy person, such as being perfectionistic, compulsively ambitious, and power driven. These compensatory drives may preoccupy him mercilessly, and he may organize his life around them. One failure means more to him than twenty successes, since it is an affirmation of his lowly status.

These difficulties are compounded by the way they interact with our man's sexual needs. When one's dependency needs are being gratified, there is often a pervasive feeling of well-being that floods one's whole body. Upon awakening following surgery, for example, the confident, smiling face of a nurse can suffuse a man with grateful, loving feelings, at least part of which may be sexual. The sexual feeling is not that of adult male to adult female but rather that of a helpless child toward a warm mother. Such a feeling is tantamount to an incestuous surge and may bring with it great conflict and guilt. Should this dependency be the nature of a husband's continuing relationship to his wife, he may be unable to function sexually with her since he is virtually involved in a mother–son relationship. On the other hand, if the nurturing figure is a man, homosexual fears and feelings may arise with equations of the host's penis with a nipple. For women the dependency situation does just the reverse. A nurturing mother figure calls up in her fears and feelings of homosexuality which may or may not be acted out in passive homosexuality with yearnings for the breast. Moreover, low feelings of independence may, as has been indicated, inspire ideas of defective masculinity in males with impulses to identify with muscle men. Fantasies of homosexuality or direct acting-out of homosexual impulses may follow. In women feelings of defective independence may inspire a rejection of the feminine role and fantasies of possessing a penis, the symbol in our culture of power and independence. Sadism and masochism may also be acted out in sexual activities in both men and women.

The reverberating of all these machines calls for strenuous efforts on the part of our subject. It all began with the dependency motor, which then activated the resentment motor (together with its components of aggression, guilt and masochism). This threw into gear the third motor of low independence, which in turn fueled the fourth motor of self-devaluation with its overcompensations and sexualizations.

Detachment

Where can a man turn next to gain some sense of composure? He often turns to the fifth motor, *detachment*. Detachment is an attempt at escaping from life's messy problems. Our man by now is fed up with the rat race and wants to get out. He says, "No more committees, no more parties, no more responsibilities, no more extras of any kind, no more involvement with people." He wants an island fortress, or at least a castle with a moat around it, and he would pull up the drawbridge and say no to everything and everyone. He is sure that this is the solution; he decides not to become rich and famous.

But it does not work. People need people. Life is not satisfying alone. Our man finds loneliness to be a worse state than what he was enduring before. He realizes that people constitute one of life's richest gratifications. So, he plunges in again. By now his first motor of dependency is really driving him. And if he is desperate enough, he may attach himself all over again to a figure who holds out some promise of being the perfect parent. Then the neurotic cycle is on its way again. The fifth motor of detachment has again revived the first, second, third, and fourth motors.

These drives, these five motors, are never entirely quiescent. In the average person there is invariably some fuel to keep them going. There is no one whose dependency needs were perfectly met early in life. This hunger lives on, and with this hunger, the mechanism of dependency is continually operative. In our culture, in this generation, the unmet dependency needs sets in motion the successive motors just described. As long as fuel is available and the speed of the motors can be controlled, the individual may manage to keep going, switching on one or the other motors and turning them off if they threaten to carry him away. To some extent all people are victims of the five motors described—to a minor degree at least.

Dependency inevitably breeds resentment in our culture. If outlets for the resentment are not available and if compensations for a devalued self-image cannot be pursued—in other words, if the individual cannot readily switch from one engine to another—then the conflict and stress reach proportions where one feels catastrophically overwhelmed. When the tension mounts excessively and there seems to be no way of escape, anxiety strikes—which is the feeling that one is overwhelmed and lost. Operations to defend against the anxiety will be instituted, but the defense is often ineffective or more burdensome than the condition it was designated to combat.

Case History

The patient, Roger, was a man in his mid 30s whose wife telephoned my secretary for an appointment. At the initial interview a well-groomed gentleman presented himself with an expression of depression and bewilderment. The problem, he said, started while discussing seemingly casual matters with his best friend and partner during a lunch hour. He was overwhelmed with a feeling of panic, with violent heart palpitations and choking sensations, which forced him to excuse himself on the basis of a sudden indisposition. Back at work, he recovered partly, but a sensation of danger enveloped him—a confounding agonizing sensation, the source of which eluded all attempts at understanding. Upon returning home, he poured himself two extra jiggers of whiskey. His fear slowly vanished so that at dinner time he had almost completely recovered his composure. The next morning, however, he approached his work with a sense of foreboding, a feeling that became stronger and stronger as the days and weeks passed.

Roger had obviously experienced an anxiety attack the source of which became somewhat clearer as he continued his story.

The most upsetting thing to Roger was the discovery that his symptoms became most violent while at work. He found himself constantly obsessed at the office with ways of returning home to his wife. Weekends brought temporary surcease; but even anticipating returning to his desk on Monday was enough to fill him with foreboding. He was unable to avoid coming late mornings, and, more and more often he excused himself from appearing at work on the basis of a current physical illness. Because he realized fully how his work was deteriorating, he was not surprised when his friend took him to task for his deficiency. Forcing himself to go to work became easier after Roger had consumed several drinks, but he found that he required more and more alcohol during the day to subdue his tension. At night he needed barbiturate sedation to insure even minimal sleep.

The surmise that I made at this point was that something in the work situation was triggering off his anxiety. I felt that Roger had attempted to gain surcease from anxiety by implementing mechanisms of control (first-line defenses, see p. 94) such as trying to avoid the stress situations of work and deadening his feelings with alcohol and sedatives. These gestures seemed not too successful since he was obliged to remain in the work situation no matter how much he wanted to avoid it.

Continuing his story, Roger said that wild, unprovoked feelings of panic were not confined to his work. Even at home, his habitual haven of comfort and safety, he experienced bouts of anxiety, which burst forth at irregular intervals. His sleep, too, was interrupted by nightmarish fears, which forced him to seek refuge in his wife's bed. A pervasive sense of helplessness soon complicated Roger's life. Fear of being alone and fear of the dark developed. Other fears then occurred, such as fear of heights, of open windows, of crowds, and of subways and buses. In the presence of his wife, however, these fears subsided or disappeared. Roger consequently arranged matters so that his wife was available as often as possible. For a while she seemed to relish this new closeness, for she had resented what she had complained about for a long time—his coldness and detachment from her.

What apparently had happened was that not being able to escape from the anxiety-provoking situation at work, and being unable to develop adequate first-line defenses to control or neutralize his anxiety, Roger was retreating to and sought safety in a dependent relationship with his wife (second-line defenses, see p. 96) that paralleled that of a small child with a mother. Various fears of the dark and of being alone were indicative of his childlike helplessness. This kind of adaptation obviously had to fail.

Not long after this, Roger continued, he developed fantasies of getting into accidents and having his body cut up and mutilated. When Roger confided to his wife that he was greatly upset by these occurring fantasies, she enjoined him to consult a doctor. He rejected this advice, contending that he was merely overworked, and he promised to take a winter vaction, which he was sure would restore his mental calm. Fearful thoughts continued to plague Roger. He became frightened whenever he heard stories of violence, and he avoided reading new accounts of suicides or murders. Soon he was obsessed with thoughts of pointed objects. Knives terrified him so that he insisted that his wife conceal them from him.

The return to a childish dependent position apparently mobilized fears that in too close association with a mother figure he would be subjected to multilation and destruction. Sexual feelings toward his wife were equated with forbidden incestuous feelings for which the penalty was bloody mutilation. Fantasies of accidents and bloodshed could be reflections of Roger's castration fears. The repetition of the oedipal drama thus could follow a shattering of Roger's repressive system. Attempting to reinforce repression by repressive (third-line defenses, see p. 76), Roger employed phobia formation striving to remove himself from symbols of mutilation such as knives and other cutting instruments.

When asked if he had other symptoms or fantasies, Roger, in an embarrassed way, confided that in the presence of forceful or strong men, he experienced a peculiar fear, which he tried to conceal. Sometimes he was aware of a desire to throw his arms around men and to kiss them in a filial way. This impulse disturbed Roger greatly, as did fantasies of nude men with huge genital organs. His sexual life continued to deteriorate. While he had never been an ardent lover, he had prided himself on his potency. His sexual powers now seemed to be disappearing, when he approached his wife, he was impotent or had premature ejaculations. This upset Roger and created fears that he never again would function well sexually. To disprove this, he forced himself compulsively to attempt intercourse, only to be rewarded by further failures. Anticipatory anxiety soon made sexual relations a source of pain, and when his wife suggested that they abstain, he agreed, but he was frightened that she would leave him for another man.

The fear Roger manifested of strong males, the desire to act in an affectionate way with them, the terror of homosexual assaults by nude men with huge genital organs were, if we follow our previous line of reasoning, the products of his fear of attack by father figures irate at his appropriation of the maternal object. A disintegration of Roger's sexual life was inevitable because he was relating to his wife not as a husband but as a child. Abandonment of a male role with his wife was, therefore, necessary to avoid anxiety. While serving as a spurious protective device, his sexual inhibition obviously further undermined his self-esteem.

In attempting to make a tentative diagnosis of Roger's condition at this point, I was confronted with the contemporary contradictions that plague our attempts at classification. All emotional difficulties spread themselves over a wide pathological area, involving every aspect of the person's functioning—intellectual, emotional, physical, and behavioral. Based as they are on presenting complaints and symptoms, systems of nosology often lose sight of the fact that the entire human being is embraced in any emotional upheaval. The particular classification into which a patient fits then may depend merely upon the relative emphasis the diagnostic agent (i.e., the therapist) or the patient puts upon selected symptoms.

This may be illustrated in the case of Roger. His complaints were those of tension, irritability, explosiveness, anxiety, depression, psychosomatic symptoms, phobias, and obsessive thoughts. In addition, he exhibited a character disturbance in such manifestations as excessive submissiveness and dependency. Were Roger chiefly concerned with his physical ailments—his headaches, dyspepsia, listlessness, fatigue, failing health, or impotence—we would be inclined to regard him as a person suffering from physical disorders of psychological origin, that is, a type of somatoform disorder. Should his anxiety attacks have caused him greatest concern and were he to have focused his attention on his anxiety, we might classify him as "anxiety disorder." In the event his depression was of prime interest, a diagnosis of "psychoneurotic or reactive depression" might be entertained. If emphasis had been put on his obsessive concern with bloody amputations, death, and pointed objects, he might be called an "obsessive disorder." His fear of heights, subways, buses, and crowds and of solitude and the dark are those often found in "phobic disorders." Finally, had his submissiveness, passivity, and other character defects been considered his most significant problem, he might be labeled as a "personality disorder." The matter of diagnosis, then, would be essentially a matter of what seemed immediately important. Actually, we might say that Roger suffered from a mixed psychoneurotic disorder with anxiety, depressive, psychophysiologic, obsessive, phobic, and distorted personality elements. This diagnostic potpourri is not surprising when we consider that every individual whose homeostasis has broken down exploits dynamism characteristics of all levels of defense in addition to displaying manifestations, psychological and physiological, of homeostatic imbalance and adaptational collapse.

When Roger was asked what he believed had precipitated his anxiety originally, he was unsure, but he hazarded that it might have been related to a change in his position at work. Not long after his tenth wedding anniversary, at age 33, Roger was promoted to senior member of the firm. His elation at this was short-lived as he became conscious of a sudden depressed feeling, which progressively deepened. Inertia, boredom, and withdrawal from his ordinary sources of pleasure followed. Even his work, to which he had felt himself devoted, became a chore. Always eager to cooperate, he experienced, during work hours, a vague dread of something about to happen which he could not define. He could not understand why he would react to a promotion that he wanted by getting upset.

Should a therapist not be interested in pursuing the patient's symptoms further to determine their origin in early past experience or in unconscious conflict, in other words, avoiding a dynamic approach, an abbreviated approach aimed at symptom reduction might now be selected without further probing into history.

First, an effort may be made to treat his symptoms through medicaments, like sedatives or tranquilizers for anxiety and energizers for depression. Roger may be enjoined to slow down in his activities and to detach himself as much as possible. He might be requested to take a vacation, engage in hobbies and recreations in order to divert his mind off his difficulties.

Another way of handling the problem might be to assume the source of the difficulty to be Roger's work situation and to get him to change his job to one that did not impose too great responsibility on him. He would be encouraged to try to detach himself more from his wife and slowly to begin functioning again on the basis of the customary distances that he erected between himself and others. Active guidance and reassurance may make it possible for Roger to return to his own bedroom and to assume the reserve with his wife that would enable him to function without anxiety.

On another level, the therapist might utilize behavior modification methods to desensitize the patient to his anxieties as well as to institute assertive training to promote greater self-sufficiency and independence. Approaches such as these understandably would not correct any basic character problems that lay at the heart of Roger's distress. Yet they might make it possible for him to get along perhaps as well as he had ever done prior to the outbreak of his neurosis.

Since my approach was a dynamic form of short-term therapy aimed at some personality rectification, I proceeded to explore as completely as I could his past life through interviewing and to probe for more unconscious motivational elements through exploration of dreams and fantasies and through observation of the transference.

Roger was the younger of two brothers. He was reared by a domineering mother who was resentful of her role as housewife, which had halted a successful career as a fashion designer. Unhappy in her love life with her husband, she transferred her affection to her younger son, ministering to his every whim and smothering him with cloying adulation. Roger's brother, George, bitterly contested this situation, but getting nowhere, he subjected his sibling to cruel reprisal. Roger's father, recoiling from the not too well concealed hostility of his wife, removed himself from the family as much as he could manage and had very little contact with his sons.

The dynamics in Roger's case became apparent during therapy. Basic to his problem was a disturbed relationship with his parents, particularly his mother. The yielding of her unmarried professional status to assume the role of housewife apparently had created in the mother resentment toward her husband and rejection of her children. This inspired a "reaction formation" in the form of overprotection, particularly toward her younger child, Roger. Frustrated and unfulfilled, she used Roger as a target for her own needs and ambitions with the following effects: (a) in Roger, encouragement of overdependence and passivity, strangling of assertiveness and independence, and stimulation of excessive sexual feelings toward the mother and (b) in George, hostility displayed directly toward Roger as aggression, and (c) in her husband, detachment.

Overprotected by his maternal parent, neglected by his father, and abused by his brother, Roger took refuge in the relationship offered him by his mother. His dependency on her nurtured submissiveness and passivity, with alternative strivings of rebelliousness and fierce resentment which he repressed because they threatened the security he managed to derive through compliant behavior. Roger both cherished and loathed the crushing attentiveness of his mother. Toward his father and brother he felt a smothering fear, which he masked under a cloak of admiration and compliance.

The withdrawal of his father made it difficult for Roger to achieve the identification with a masculine object necessary for a virile conception of himself. Roger turned to his mother for protection. He revolted, however, against too great dependency on her, fearing that excessive closeness would rob him of assertiveness and that his aroused sexual feelings would bring on him disapproval from his mother as well as punishment from his father and brother. Repudiating competitiveness with the other male members of the family, he attempted to win their approval by a submissive, ingratiating attitude.

During adolescence Roger emerged as a quiet, detached lad, never permitting himself to be drawn into very intimate relationships. He was an excellent and conscientious student, and he was well liked for his fairness and amiability. At college he was retiring, but he had a number of friends who sought his companionship because he was so easy to get along with. His romantic attachments were superficial, and the young women he squired to parties admitted that he was attractive but complained that it was difficult to get to know him.

Adopting detachment as a defense against a dependent involvement, and compliance as a means of avoiding physical hurt, Roger evolved a character structure that enabled him to function at home and at school, although at the expense of completely gratifying relationships with people.

Upon leaving college, he entered a business firm, arrangements for this having been made by his father. He resisted for two years the exhortations of his mother to marry the daughter of one of her best friends; but finally he succumbed, and he seemed satisfied and happy in his choice. The young couple lived in harmony, and he was considered by his group to be an ideal example of an attentive husband and, after his son was born, of a devoted father. His steadfast application to his work soon elevated his position, until he became a junior member of the firm. His best friend and confidant was one of the senior members, toward whom Roger bore the greatest respect and admiration.

His work and marital life, which were more or less arranged for him by his parents, turned out to be successful since he was able to employ in them his compliance and detachment mechanisms. Toward his best friend and other senior firm members Roger related passively as he had related previously toward his father and brother. Toward his wife he expressed conventional devotion, keeping himself sufficiently distant to avoid the trap of a tempting dependent relationship that would threaten the independent assertive role he was struggling to maintain.

The only distressing element in Roger's life was his failing health. Constantly fatigued, he evidenced a pallor and listlessness that inspired many solicitous inquiries. Dyspeptic attacks and severe migrainous headaches incapacitated him from time to time. In addition to his physical symptoms was a pervasive tension, which could be relieved only by recreational and social distractions.

Inner conflict between dependency, submissiveness, compliance, detachment, and aggression, however, constantly compromised Roger's adjustment, producing a disruption of homeostasis with tension and psychosomatic symptoms. His failing health, fatigue, pallor, listlessness, dyspeptic attacks, and migrainous headaches were evidences of adaptive imbalance. What inspired this imbalance was an invasion of his capacity to detach, produced by the demands made on him by his wife and associates. In addition, his submissive and compliant behavior, while protecting him from imagined hurt, engendered in him overpowering hostility, which probably drained itself off through his automatic nervous system producing physical symptoms.

As might be expected, Roger's affability and needs to please won for him the praise of his superiors at work, and he was advanced and finally offered a senior position.

Had Roger at this point refused to accept senior membership in the firm, he might have escaped the catastrophe that finally struck him. His legitimate desires for advancement, however, enjoined him to accept. His conflict became more and more accentuated until finally he no longer was able to marshal further defenses. Collapse in adaptation with helplessness and expectations of injury announced themselves in an anxiety attack during luncheon with his friend.

As long as he had been able to satisfy to a reasonable degree his needs for security, assertion, satisfaction in work and play, and creative self-fulfillment, Roger was able to make a tolerable adjustment even with his psychosomatic symptoms. The precipating factor that had brought about the undermining of Roger's capacities for adaptation was his promotion to senior membership in the firm. While Roger had ardently desired this promotion, for reasons of both status and economics, actually being put in a position of parity with his friend violated his defense of passivity, compliance, and subordination and threatened him with the very hurt he had anticipated as a child in relationship to his father and brother. To accept the promotion meant that he would be challenging of and perhaps trimphant over father and brother figures. This touched off fears of injury and destruction at the hands of a powerful and punitive force he could neither control nor vanquish. Yet Roger's desire for advancement, inspired by realistic concerns, made it impossible for him to give up that which he considered his due. Since he was aware neither of how fearfully he regarded authority nor of how he was operating with childish attitudes, he was nonplussed by his reactions.

A dream revealed during one psychotherapy session will illustrate some of our patient's maneuvers that became operative and apparent in therapy.

Pt. I had a dream last night that upset me. I am in bed with this big woman, big wonderful breasts. She's my wife, but she changes into a negress. She strokes and touches me all over, and I feel completely loved and accepted. I awoke from the dream with a strong homosexual feeling that upset me. [*Here Roger symbolizes in dream structure his dependency impulses, his repulsion against his dependency, his incestuous desire, and the resultant homosexual residue.*]

Th. Yes, what do you make of this?

Pt. I don't know. The woman was comforting and seductive. I always like big-breasted women. Exciting. But my wife isn't as stacked as I'd like her, or as she was in the dream. (*pause*)

Th. How about the negress?

Pt. I never liked the idea of sleeping with a colored woman. Makes me feel creepy. Colored people make me feel creepy. I know I shouldn't feel that way. Last time I was here I noticed you had a tan like you had been in the sun. I said, "Maybe he's got negro blood." I know I shouldn't care if you did or not, but the idea scared me for some reason.

Th. Sounds like the woman in your dream was partly me. [*This interpretation was proffered in the hope of stirring up some tension to facilitate associations.*]

Pt. (*pause*) The idea scares me. Why should I want you to make love to me? (*pause*) By God, maybe I want you to mother me, be giving, kind.

Th. How *do* You feel about me?

Pt. I want you to be perfect like a God; to be accepting and loving; to be wise and strong. I realize I'm dependent [*motor one*]. I resent my need to be dependent on you [*motor two*]. When you show any weakness, I am furious. I feel guilty and upset about my feelings. I feel like killing anybody who controls me. I know I must face responsibility, but I feel too weak and unmasculine [*motor three*]. I feel like a shit [*motor four*] and hate myself. I am a nothing and I'd like to be a somebody, but I can't.

Th. Apparently it scares you to be a somebody. When you were promoted, you started getting upset.

Pt. Why should I? I suppose I feel like I'm stepping out of my depth. Like I'm not man enough. The whole thing puzzles and frightens me.

Th. So what do you do?

Pt. I am constantly running away [*motor five*]. I get so angry at people. I don't want to see anybody. I'm so upset about myself. I try not to feel. But I can't seem to make it on my own. [*The reinstituting of motor one*]

FIG. 9-1. Personality Mechanisms*

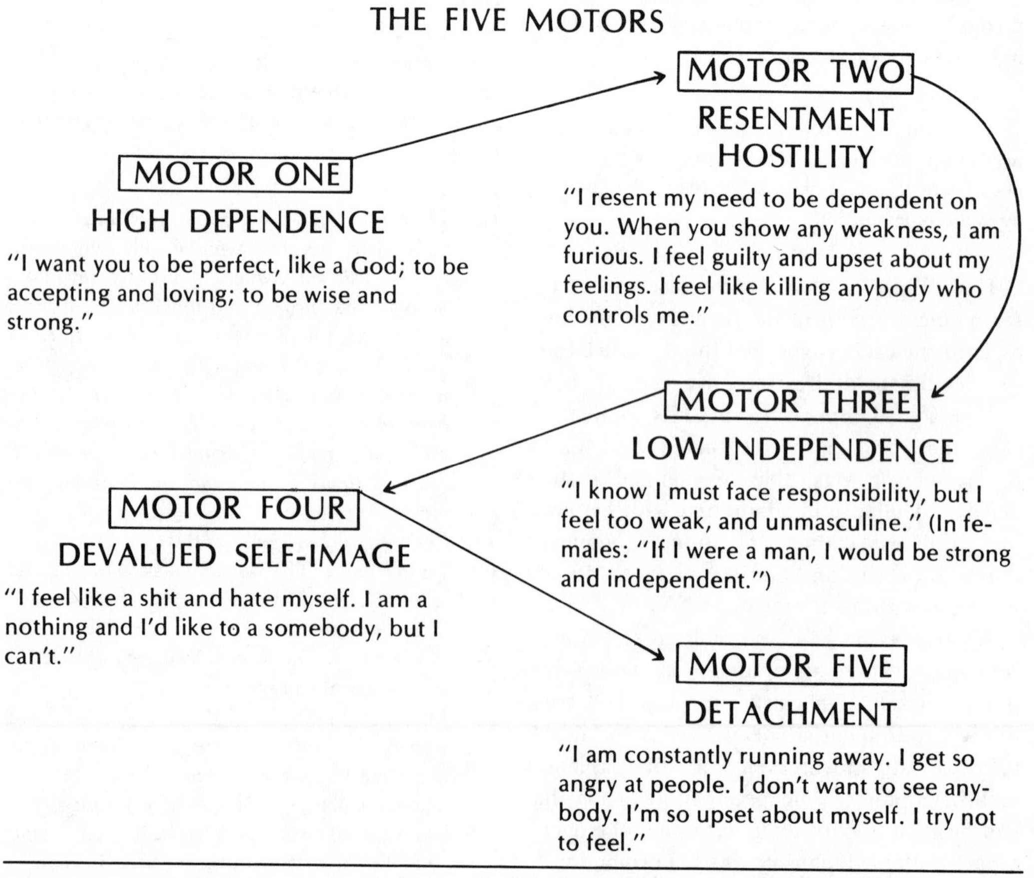

* From L. R. Wolberg and J. Kildahl, *The Dynamics of Personality* (New York, Grune & Stratton, 1970), p. 215. Reprinted by permission.

HOMEOSTATIC MECHANISMS

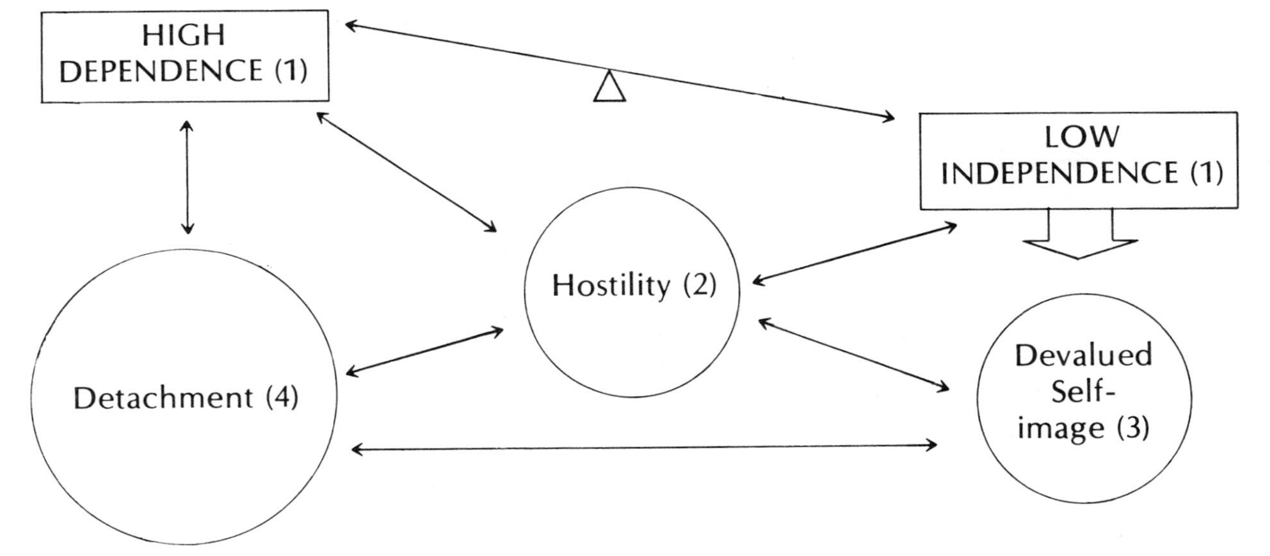

(The traits above in mild form are more or less universal. In exaggerated form, however, they serve as defense against anxiety (q.v. "Second Lines of Defense: Interpersonal Defenses") and therefore may be considered pathologic.)

(1) *Manifestations:* passivity, immaturity, childishness, neurotic feminine identifications in males.
Compensations: excessive aggressiveness and competitiveness, compulsive masculine strivings, neurotic masculine identification in females.

(2) *Manifestations:* aggression, cruelty, sadism
Compensations: exaggerated gentleness, self-punishment, masochism.

(3) *Manifestations:* self-depreciation, self-denial, compulsive modesty.
Compensations: excessive perfectionism and ambitiousness, power drives, grandiosity, arrogance.

(4) *Manifestations:* isolation, withdrawal
Compensations: compulsive gregariousness and sociability.

The patient in the session was manifestly groping with his passive-dependent strivings (*motor one*), his rage (*motor two*), his feelings of low independence (*motor three*), his devalued self-image (*motor four*), his detachment (*motor five*), together with concomitant unresolved incestuous drives and unexpressed homosexual impulses. Many aspects of Roger's personality problem were being projected onto his therapist in transference.

These patterns are delineated in Figure 9–1. Interpretation of the patient's reactions to me in terms of his habitual personality responses, connecting them with his experiences in growing up and relating them to the incidents leading to the collapse in his homeostasis, enabled Roger to approach a different relationship with me. This occurred about the twentieth session and acted as a nucleus for different feelings toward himself. Not only was homeostasis restored with cessation of his symptoms, but he also was able to accept his post as a senior member of the firm with subjective and objective strengthening of his ego.

Conclusion

Common psychodynamics are shared by people in our culture. They include the ravages of high dependency, resentment and hostility, low independence, a devaluated self-image, and detachment. It is the degree of intensity of these drives that determine their pathogenicity. Offshoots from resentment include aggression, perhaps to the point of sadism, and also guilt resulting from the hateful feelings, even eventuating in masochism.

High dependency is associated with passivity and a feminine identification. Feelings of hostility sponsor guilt, masochism, aggression, and sadism. Low independence prompts the overcompensatory strivings of compulsive aggressiveness and competitiveness, making for a neurotic masculine identification. A devalued self-image also leads to compensatory measures such as perfectionism, ambitiousness, and power drives. And detachment often provokes one to abandon one's isolation and plunge into compulsive gregariousness. Any and all of these drives may become sexualized, so that one's sexual impulses become linked to feelings of incestuous passivity or competitive domination with consequent fears of retaliation or with masochistic or sadistic impulses. When these drives fail to maintain homeostasis and conflict is unresolved, then anxiety results and various levels of defense mechanisms operate to cope with the anxiety. A great many dynamic themes eventuate (see Figure 9–2) and offer themselves as possible foci for exploration.

CHAPTER 10

Choosing a Dynamic Focus

C. Presenting Interpretations

The most effective focus is one that deals with a basic repetitive conflict, the manifest form of which is being expressed through the immediate complaint factor. As an example, consider a crisis situation involving a wife, the mother of two small children, who insists on a divorce because of continuing disenchantment with her marriage. The divorce decision appears to be the terminal eruption of years of disappointment in her husband's failure to live up to her ideal of what a man should be like. After we cut through endless complaints, it became apparent that the standard against which she measures her husband is her father, whom she worships as the epitome of success and masculinity. This idealization actually has little basis in fact, being the remnant of an unresolved oedipal conflict. Be this as it may, it has thwarted her ability to make a proper adjustment to her marriage, and now with the decision of a divorce the integrity of her family is being threatened. She comes to therapy at the urging of her lawyer who realizes that she is too upset at present to make reasonable decisions.

A therapist who minimizes the importance of dynamic conflicts may attempt to achieve the goal of crisis resolution by invoking logic or appeals to common sense. He may suggest ways of patching things up, insisting that for the sake of the children a father, however inadequate, is better than no father. He may, upon consulting with the husband, point out various compromises the husband can make, and after the wife has verbally disgorged a good deal of her hostility in the therapeutic session, she may be willing to cancel her divorce plans and settle for half a loaf rather than none. The reconciliation is executed through a suppression of her hostility, which finds an outlet through sexual frigidity and various physical symptoms. On the other hand, should the therapist recognize the core conflict that is motivating her idea of divorce, there is a chance that the patient may be helped to an awareness of her merciless involvement with her father and the destructive unreasonableness of her fantasies of what an ideal marriage is like. She may then allow herself to examine the real virtues of her husband and the true advantages of her existing marriage.

A dynamic focus should, therefore, be prospected in the course of exploring the immediate complaint factor. Such a focus is often arrived at intuitively (Binder, 1977). The more empathic, skilled, and experienced the therapist, the more likely he will be to explore the actual operative dynamics. However, no matter how firmly convinced he is in his immediate assumptions, he realizes that these are being predicated on incomplete data. He knows that his patient may deliberately withhold important information, or though the patient may recognize certain conflicts she is still oblivious to their significance or completely unaware of their existence. Whatever tentative theories come to the therapist's mind, he will continue to check and to revise them as further information unfolds. Interviews with relatives and friends are extremely valuable since they may open facets of problems not evident in the conversations with the patient. Moreover, once the patient during the first encounter has divulged data, later interviews will help uncover rationalizations, projections, and distortions that will force the therapist to revise his thesis and concentrate on a different focus from the one that originally seemed so obvious.

No matter how astute the therapist has been in exposing a truly momentous focus, the patient's reactions will determine whether the exposure turns out to be fruitful or not. For example, even though an underlying problem is causing havoc in a person's life and is responsible for the crisis that brings the person to therapy, this does not imply that the patient will elect to do anything about it. Its emotional meaning may be so important to the patient, the subversive pleasures and secondary gains so great, that suffering and misery are easily accepted as conditions for the indulgence of destructive drives even where the patient has full insight into the problem, recognizes its genetic roots, and realizes the complications that inevitably indemnify the indulgence. I recall one patient whose yearning for revenge on a younger sibling produced a repetitive series of competitive encounters with surrogate figures toward whom retaliatory hostilities and violence brought forth punishment by employees, colleagues, and friends. A series of abuses culminated in a disastrous incident in which a physical assault on a fellow employee resulted in the patient's discharge from a promising executive position. This happening was so widely publicized in the industry that the patient was unable to secure another job. During therapy the patient was confronted with the meaning of his behavior and particularly his revenge and masochistic motives; he readily recognized and accepted their validity. This did not in the least deter his acting out on any occasion when he could vent his rage on a sibling figure. At the end of our brief treatment period, it was recommended that he go into long-term therapy, which he bluntly refused to do. He seemed reconciled to pursue a damaging course for the momentary joy that followed an outburst of aggression.

Experience with the addictions provide ample evidence of the futility of focusing on the dynamics of a dangerous and what appears on the surface to be a disagreeable way of behaving. But, that some patients disregard logic does not nullify the need to persist in making careful interpretations in the hope of eventually eroding resistance to the voice of reason.

We may expect that a patient in need of help will communicate sufficiently to supply essential material from which a focus may be extrapolated. Understandably, there will be differences in emphasis among therapists, even among those who have received similar theoretical grounding. The available material is usually sufficiently rich to enable therapists to empathize with aspects that synchronize with their needs, intuitions, ideas, and biases.

Since all people share certain conflicts that are basic in our culture, some of these can constitute the dynamic focus around which interpretations are made. Thus manifestations of the struggle over separation-individuation following the ideas of Mann (1973), persistence of oedipal fantasies as exemplified in the work of Sifneos (1972), and residues of psychic masochism such as described by Lewin (1970) are some of the core conflicts that may be explored and interpreted. Sensitizing oneself to indications of such conflicts as they come through in the patient's communications, the therapist may repeatedly confront the patient with evidence of how he is being victimized by the operations of specific inner saboteurs. There is scarcely a person in whom one may not, if one searches assidiously enough, find indications of incomplete separation-individuation, fragments of the oedipal struggle, and surges of guilt and masochism. It is essential, however, to show how these are intimately connected with the anxieties, needs, and defenses of each patient and how they ultimately have brought about the symptoms and behavioral difficulties for which the patient seeks help.

Lest we overemphasize the power of insight in bringing about change, we must stress that to a large extent the choice of a focus will depend on the therapist's seeing the presenting problem of the patient through the lens of his theoretical convictions. A Freudian, Jungian, Adlerian, Kleinian, Horneyite, Sullivanian, Existentialist, or behavior therapist will focus on different aspects and will organize a treatment plan in accordance with personal ideologies. While the focus, because of this, will vary, there is considerable evidence that *how* the focus is implemented and the quality of the relationship with the patient are at least as important factors in the cure, if not more so, than the prescience of the therapist and the insightful bone of dynamic wisdom he gives the patient to chew on. That implantations of insight sometimes do alter the balance between the repressed and repressive forces cannot be disputed. How much the benefits are due to this factor and how much are the product of the placebo effect of insight, however, is difficult to say. Where a therapist is firmly convinced of the validity of the focus he has chosen and he convinces his patient that neurotic demons within can be controlled through accepting and acting upon the "insights" presented, tension and anxiety may be sufficiently lifted to relieve symptoms and to promote productive adaptation. Even spurious insights if accepted may in this way serve a useful purpose. Without question, nevertheless, the closer one comes in approximating some of the sources of the patient's current troubles, the greater the likelihood that significant benefits will follow.

In this respect for some years I have employed a scheme that I have found valuable in working with patients. This consists of studying what resistences arise during the implementation of the techniques that I happen to be employing at the time. The resistances will yield data on the existing dynamic conflicts, the most obstructive of which is then chosen as a focus.

Experience with large numbers of patients convinces that three common developmental problems initiate emotional difficulties and create resistance to psychotherapy—first, high levels of dependency (the product of inadequate separation-individuation), second, a hypertrophied sadistic conscience, and, third, devaluated self-esteem. Coexisting and reinforcing each other, they create needs to fasten onto and to distrust authority, to torment and punish oneself masochistically, and to wallow in a swamp of hopeless feelings of inferiority and ineffectuality. They frequently sabotage a therapist's most skilled treatment interventions, and, when they manifest themselves, unless dealt with deliberately and firmly, the treatment process will usually reach an unhappy end. Dedicated as he may be to their resolution, the most the therapist may be able to do is to point out evidences of operation of these saboteurs, to delineate their origin in early life experience, to indicate their destructive impact on the achievement of reasonable adaptive goals, to warn that they may make a shambles out of the present treatment effort, and to encourage the patient to recognize his personal responsibility in perpetuating their operation. The tenacious hold they can have on a patient is illustrated by this fragment of an interview.

The patient, a writer, 42 years of age, who made a skimpy living as an editor in a publishing house came to therapy for depression and for help in working on a novel that had defied completion for years. Anger, guilt, shame and a host of other emotions bubbled over whenever he compared himself with his more successful colleagues. He was in a customarily frustrated, despondent mood when he complained:

Pt. I just can't get my ass moving on anything. I sit down and my mind goes blank. Staring at a blank piece of paper for hours, I finally give up.

Th. This must be terribly frustrating to you.

Pt. (*angrily*) Frustrating is a mild word, doctor. I can kill myself for being such a shit.

Th. You really think you are a shit?

Pt. (*angrily*) Not only do I think I am a shit, I *am* a shit, and nobody can convince me that I'm not.

FIG. 10-1. Outline of Personality Operations*

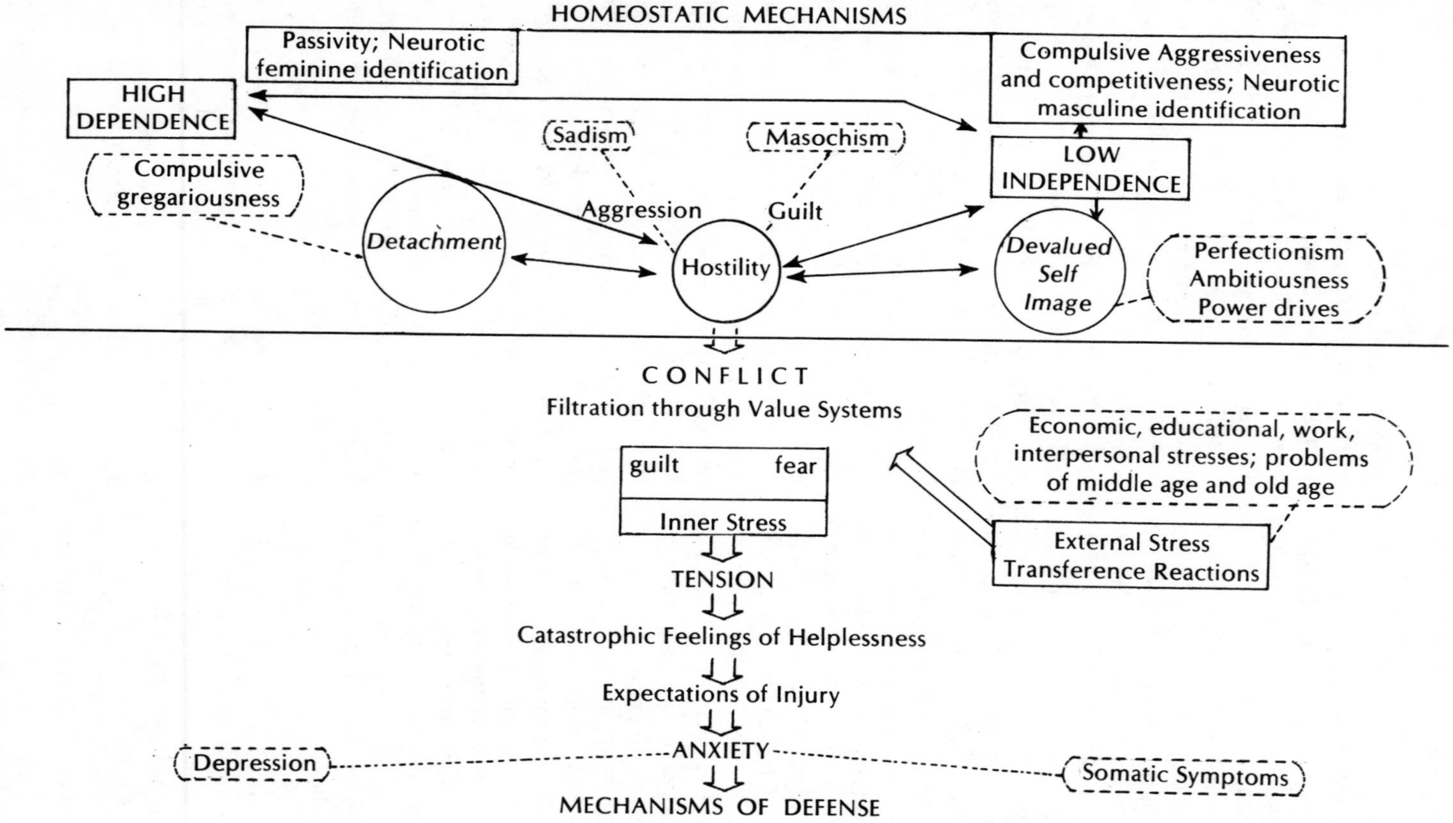

First Level: Environmental—Escape and Control Defenses (situational problems)
Second Level: Interpersonal—Characterological Defenses (personality and behavior disorders)
Third Level: Intrapsychic—Repressive Defenses (psychoneurotic disorders)
Fourth Level: Physiological—Regressive Defenses (psychotic disorders)

* From L. R. Wolberg and J. Kildahl, *The Dynamics of Personality* (New York, Grune & Stratton, 1970), p. 216. Reprinted by permission.

Th. Frankly, Fred, I'm not even going to try. But you must have had some hope for yourself, otherwise you never would have come here.

Pt. I figured you could get me out of this, but I know it's no use. I've always been a tail ender.

Th. (*confronting the patient*) You know, I get the impression that you've got an investment in holding on to the impression you are a shit. What do you think you get out of this?

Pt. Nothing, absolutely nothing. Why should I need this?

Th. You tell me. [*In his upbringing the patient was exposed to a rejecting father who demanded perfection from his son. The father was never satisfied with the even better than average marks his son obtained at school and compared him unfavorably with boys in the neighborhood who were prominent in athletics and received commendations for their school work. It seemed to me that the paternal introject was operating in the patient long after he left home, carrying on the same belittling activities that had plagued his existence when he was growing up.*]

Pt. (*pause*) There is no reason. (*pause*)

Th. You know I get the impression that you are doing the same job on yourself now that your father did on you when you were a boy. It's like you've got him in your head. [*In the first part of the session the patient had talked about the unreasonableness of his father and his own inability to please his father.*]

Pt. I am sure I do, but knowing this doesn't help.

Th. Could it be that if you make yourself helpless somebody will come along and help you out? [*I was convinced the patient was trying to foster a dependent relationship with me, one in which I would carry him to success that defied his own efforts.*]

Pt. You mean, you?

Th. Isn't that what you said at the beginning, that you came to me to get you out of this thing? You see if I let you get dependent on me it wouldn't really solve your problem. What I want to do is help you help yourself. This will strengthen you.

Pt. But if I can't help myself, what then?

Th. From what I see there isn't any reason why you can't get out of this thing—this self-sabotage. (*The patient responds with a dubious expression on his face and then quickly tries to change the subject.*)

In the conduct of brief treatment one may not have to deal with the underlying conflicts such as those above *as long as the patient is moving along and making progress. It is only when therapy is bogged down that sources of resistance must be uncovered.* These as has been indicated, are usually rooted in the immature needs and defenses of dependent, masochistic, self-devaluating promptings. At some point an explanation of where such promptings originated and how they are now operating will have to be given the patient. This explanation may at first fall on deaf ears, but as the therapist consistently demonstrates their existence from the patient's reactions and patterns, the patient may eventually grasp their significance. The desire to make oneself dependent and the destructiveness of this impulse, the connection of suffering and symptoms with a pervasive desire for punishment, the masochistic need to appease a sadistic conscience that derives from a bad parental introject, the operation of a devalued self-image, with the subversive gains that accrue from victimizing oneself, must be repeated at every opportunity, confronting the patient with questions as to why he needs to continue to sponsor such activities.

Sometimes a general outline of dynamics (such as are detailed in Chapter 9) may be offered the patient with the object of either stirring up some anxiety or resistance or of providing the patient with an interpretation that fosters a better understanding of himself. While the delineated drives and defenses are probably typical in our culture of both "normal" and neurotic individuals, the specific modes of operation and the kinds of symptoms and maladjustments that exist are unique for each individual. Every person has a thumb, but patterns of thumbprints are all different. The therapist, employing a blueprint such as Figure 10–1, may try to fit each patient's problems into it and then choose for focus whatever aspects are most important at the moment. For example, the patient may during a session complain of a severe headache and thereafter proceed to beat himself masochistically, blaming himself for being weak and ineffectual. The therapist should then search to see how this trend affiliates itself with guilt feelings and what immediate situation inspired such feelings. The therapist may discover that what is behind the guilt is anger in the patient at his wife for not living up to his expectations in executing her household duties. Further probing may reveal anger at the therapist for not doing more for the patient. Such transference manifestations may enable the therapist to make a connection with the patient's mother toward whom there has existed since childhood a good deal of anger for her neglect and rejection. This will open up a discussion of the patient's excessive dependency needs and the inescapable hostility, low independence, and devalued self-esteem that dependency brings about. An association may be established between the patient's hostility turned inward and the migraine headaches for which therapy was sought in the first place. The therapist should in this way take advantage of every opportunity to show the patient the interrelationship between his various drives, traits, and symptoms, keeping in mind that while a certain trend may encompass the patient's chief concern at the moment, it never occurs in isolation. It is related intimately to other intrapsychic forces even though the connection may not be immediately clear.

An individual can make a reasonable adjustment for a long time even with a vulnerable character structure. His personality motors, defective as they may have been, still operate harmoniously; various balances and counterbalances maintain the psychological equilibrium. Then because of the imposition of an external crisis situation or because of stresses associated with inner needs and external demands, anxiety, depression, phobias, and other symptoms appear. The patient may consider that his adjustment prior to the presence of some precipitating factor was satisfactory if not ideal, with no awareness of how his tenuous personality interactions have been sponsoring various symptoms and ultimately had produced his breakdown. He is very much like a man with back pain who credits his "sciatica" to one incident of lifting a weight that was too heavy, oblivious of the fact that for months or years he has, through faulty posture and lack of exercise, been accumulating weak and strained muscles.

Thus a patient whose self-image is being sustained by a defense of perfectionism, for as far back as he can remember, will have to perform flawlessly even in tiny and most inconsequential areas of achievement. To perform less than perfect is tantamount with failure and signals inferiority and a shattered identity. The merciless demands he makes on himself may actually be impossible of fulfillment. At a certain point when he cannot face up to demands in some truly important situation, his failure will act like a spark in an explosive mixture. The eventuating symptoms that finally bring him into treatment are depression and insomnia. It will require little acumen for a therapist to spot the perfectionistic trends around which the patient fashions his existence. But to argue him out of his perfectionism and to counter the barrage of rationalizations evolved over a lifetime are difficult, if not impossible, tasks. We may, nevertheless, attempt to work with cognitive therapy and select perfectionism as a focus, pointing out the distortions in logic that govern the patient's thinking process. Not all therapists have the skill and stamina to do this, nor do we yet have sufficient data to testify to the efficacy of this approach in most cases.

What would seem indicated is to review with the patient the full implications of his perfectionism, its relationship to his defective self-image, the sources of self-devaluation in incomplete separation-individuation, the operations of masochism, and so forth. Obviously, the therapist must have evidence to justify these connections, but even though he presents an outline to the patient of possibilities and stimulates the patient to make connections for himself, he may be able to penetrate some of the patient's defenses. Giving the patient some idea about personality development may, as I have indicated, be occasionally helpful, especially where insufficient time is available in therapy to pinpoint the precise pathology. Patients are usually enthusiastic at first at having received some clarification, and they may even acknowledge that segments of the presented outline relate to themselves. They then seem to lose the significance of what has been revealed to them. However, in my experience later on in follow-up, many have brought up pertinent details of the outline and have confided that it stimulated thinking about themselves. Thus in the case of Roger described in the last chapter, I gave him the following general interpretation:

Th. I believe I have a fair idea of what is going on with you, but I'd like to start from the beginning. I should like to give you a picture of what happens to the average person in the growing-up process. From this picture you may be able to understand where you fit and what has happened to you. You see, a child at birth comes into the world helpless and dependent. He needs a great deal of affection, care, and stimulation. He also needs to receive the proper discipline to protect him. In this medium of loving and understanding care and discipline, where he is given an opportunity to grow, to develop, to explore, and to express himself, his independence gradually increases and his dependence gradually decreases, so that at adulthood there is a healthy balance between factors of dependence and independence. Let us say they are equally balanced in the average adult; a certain amount of dependence being quite normal, but not so much that it cripples the person. Normally the dependence level may temporarily go up when a person gets sick or insecure, and his independence will temporarily recede. But this shift is only within a narrow range. However, as a result of bad or depriving experiences in childhood, and from your history, this seems to have happened to you to some extent [*the patient's father a salesman was away a good deal of the time and his older brother brutally intimidated him*], the dependence level never goes down sufficiently and the independence level stays low. Now what happens when a person in adult life has excessive dependency and a low level of independence? Mind you, you may not show all of the things that I shall point out to you, but try to figure out which of these do apply to you.

Now, most people with strong feelings of dependence will attempt to find persons who are stronger than they are, who can do for them what they feel they cannot do for themselves. It is almost as if they are searching for idealized parents, not the same kind of parents they had, but much better ones. What does this do to the individual? First, usually he becomes disappointed in the people he picks out as idealized parental figures because they never come up to his expectations. He feels cheated. For instance, if a man weds a woman who he expects will be a kind, giving, protective, mother figure, he will become infuriated when she fails him on any count. Second, he finds that when he does relate himself to a person onto whom he projects parental qualities, he begins to feel helpless within himself, he feels trapped, he has a desire to escape from the relationship. Third, the feeling of being dependent, makes him feel passive like a child. This is often associated in his mind with being nonmasculine; it creates fears of his becoming homosexual and relating himself passively to other men. This role, in our culture, is more acceptable to women, but they too fear excessive passivity, and they may, in relation to mother figures, feel as if they are breast-seeking and homosexual.

So here he has a dependency motor that is constantly operating, making him forage around for a parental image. Inevitably they disappoint him. (*At this point the patient interrupted and described how disappointed he was in his wife, how ineffective she was, how unable she proved herself to be in taking care of him. We discussed this for a minute and then I continued.*) In addition to the dependency motor, the person has a second motor running, a resentment motor, which operates constantly on the basis that he is either trapped in dependency, or cannot find an idealized parental figure, or because he feels or acts passive and helpless. This resentment promotes tremendous guilt feelings. After all, in our culture one is not supposed to hate. But the hate feelings sometimes do trickle out in spite of this, and on special occasions they gush out, like when the person drinks a little too much. (*The patient laughs here and says this is exactly what happens to him.*) If the hate feelings do come out, the person may get frightened on the basis that he is losing control. The very idea of hating may be so upsetting to him that he pushes this impulse out of his mind, with resulting tension, depression, physical symptoms of various kinds, and self-hate. The hate impulse having been blocked is turned back on the self. This is what we call masochism, the wearing of a hair shirt, the constant self-punishment as a result of feed-back of resentment. The resentment machine goes on a good deal of the time running alongside the dependency motor.

As if this weren't enough, a third motor gets going along with the other two. High dependence means low independence. A person with low feelings of independence suffers terribly because he does not feel sufficient unto himself; he does not feel competent. He feels nonmasculine, passive, helpless, dependent. It is hard to live with such feelings, so he may try to compensate by being overly aggressive, overly competitive, and overly masculine. This may create much trouble for the person because he may try too hard to make up for his feelings of loss of masculinity. He may have fantasies of becoming a strong, handsome, overly active sexual male, and, when he sees such a figure, he wants to identify with him. This may create in him desires for and fears of homosexuality, which may terrify some men who do not really want to be homosexual. Interestingly, in women a low-independence level is compensated for by her competing with men, wanting to be like a man, acting like a man, and resenting being a woman. Homosexual impulses and fears also may sometimes emerge as a result of repudiation of femininity.

A consequence of low feelings of independence is a devalued self-image, which starts the fourth motor going. The person begins to despise himself, to feel he is weak, ugly, and contemptible. He will pick out any personal evidence for this that he can find, like stature, complexion, physiognomy, and so on. If he happens to have a slight handicap, like a physical deformity or a small penis, he will focus on this as evidence that he is irretrievably damaged. Feelings of self-devaluation give rise to a host of compensatory drives, like being perfectionistic, overly ambitious, and power driven. As long as he can do things perfectly and operate without flaw, he will respect himself. Or, if he is bright enough and his environment favorable, he may boost himself into a successful position of power, operate like a strong authority and gather around himself a group of sycophants who will worship him as the idealized authority, whom in turn the individual may resent and envy while accepting their plaudits. He will feel exploited by those who elevate him to the position of a high priest. "Why," he may ask himself, "can't I find somebody strong whom *I* can depend on?" What he seeks actually is a dependent relationship, but this role entails such conflict for him that he goes into fierce competitiveness with any authority on whom he might want to be dependent.

So here we have our dependency operating first; second, resentment, aggression, guilt, and masochism; third, drives for independence; and fourth, self-devaluation and maneuvers to overcome this through such technics as perfectionism, overambitiousness, and power strivings, in fantasy or in reality.

To complicate matters, some of these drives get sexualized. In dependency, for instance, when one relates to a person the way a child or infant relates to a parent, there may be experienced a powerful suffusion of good feeling that may bubble over into sexual feeling. There is probably a great deal of sexuality in all infants in a very diffuse form, precursors of adult sexuality. And when a person reverts emotionally back to the dependency of infancy, he may reexperience diffuse sexual feelings toward the parental figure. If a man relates dependently to a woman, he may sustain toward her a kind of incestuous feeling. The sexuality will be not as an adult, but as an infant to a mother, and the feelings for her may be accompanied by tremendous guilt, fear and perhaps an inability to function sexually. If the parental figure happens to be a man instead of a woman, the person may still relate to him like toward a mother, and emerging sexual feelings will stimulate fears of homosexuality. [*If the patient is a woman with sexual problems, the parallel situation of a female child with a parental substitute may be brought up. A woman may repeat her emotions of childhood when she sought to be loved and protected by a mother. In body closeness she may experience a desire to fondle and be fondled, which will stir up sexual feelings and homosexual fears.*] In sexualizing drives for independence and aggressiveness, one may identify with and seek out powerful masculine figures with whom to fraternize and affiliate. This may again whip up homosexual impulses. Where aggressive-sadistic and self-punitive masochistic impulses exist, these may, for complicated reasons, also be fused with sexual impulses, masochism becoming a condition for sexual release. So here we have the dependence motor, and the resentment-aggression-guilt-masochism motor, and the independence motor, and the self-devaluation motor, with the various compensations and sexualizations. We have a very busy person on our hands. (*At this point the patient revealed that he had become impotent with his wife and had experienced homosexual feelings and fears that were upsetting him because they were so foreign to his morals. What I said was making sense to him.*)

In the face of all this trouble, how do some people gain peace? By a fifth motor, that of detachment. Detachment is a defense one may try to use as a way of escaping life's messy problems. Here one withdraws from relationships, isolates himself, runs away from things. By removing himself from people, the individual tries to heal himself. But this does not usually work because after a while a person gets terrified by his isolation and inability to feel. People cannot function without people. They may succeed for a short time, but then they realize they are drifting away from things; they are depriving themselves of life's prime satisfactions. Compulsively, then, the detached person may try to reenter the living atmosphere by becoming gregarious. He may, in desperation, push himself into a dependency situation with a parental figure as a way out of his dilemma. And this will start the whole neurotic cycle all over again.

You can see that the person keeps getting caught in a web from which there is no escape. As long as he has enough fuel available to feed his various motors and keep them running, he can go on for a period. But if opportunities are not available to him to satisfy his different drives and if he cannot readily switch from one to the other, he may become excessively tense and upset. If his tension builds up too much, or if he experiences great trouble in his life situation, or in the event self esteem is crushed for any reason, he may develop a catastrophic feeling of helplessness and expectations of being hurt. (*The patient here excitedly blurted out that he felt so shamed by his defeat at work that he wanted to atom bomb the world. He became angry and weak and frightened. He wanted to get away from everything and everyone. Yet he felt so helpless, he wanted to be taken care of like a child. He then felt hopeless and depressed. I commented that his motors had been thrown out of gear by the incident at work and this had precipitated excessive tension and anxiety.*)

When tension gets too great, and there seems to be no hope, anxiety may hit. And the person will build up defenses to cope with his anxiety, some of which may succeed and some may not. For instance, excessive drinking may be one way of managing anxiety. Fears, compulsions, physical symptoms are other ways. These defenses often do not work. Some, like phobias, may complicate the person's life and make it more difficult than before. Even though ways are sought to deal with anxiety these prove to be self-defeating.

Now, we are not sure yet how this general outline applies to you. I am sure some of it does, as you yourself have commented. Some of it may not. What I want you to do is to think about it, observe yourself in your actions and relations to people and see where you fit. While knowing where you fit will not stop the motors from running, at least we will have some idea as to with what we are dealing. Then we'll better be able to figure out a plan concerning what to do.

Sometimes I draw a sketch on a blank paper showing "high dependence," "low dependence," "devalued self-image," "resentment-guilt-masochism," and "detachment," and repeat the story of their interrelationship. I then ask the patient to figure out and study aspects that apply to him. If a general description of dynamics is given the patient, along the lines indicated above, a little insight may be inculcated that can serve as a fulcrum for greater self-understanding. The insight may be temporarily reassuring at first; then it seemingly is forgotten with a resurgence of symptoms. A review of what has occurred to stimulate an attack of anxiety may consolidate the insight and solidify better control. An important tool here is self-observation, which the therapist should try to encourage and which will help the "working-through" process, without which insight can have little effect.

Conclusion

In dynamic short-term therapy the most productive focus is often on some aspect of a nuclear conflict. Since the patient usually defends himself against revealing significant unconscious content, the therapist will have to arrive at it by observing its manifest derivatives. These may be highly disguised and symbolized. However, a sensitive and astute therapist will be able to detect vital undercurrent forces from the patient's verbal and nonverbal behavior, from periodic transference displays, and from dreams, fantasies and acting-out tendencies. These manifestations will be especially prominent during periods of resistance to techniques that the therapist is implementing. Accordingly, the therapist should alert himself to what lies behind the patient's inability or refusal to respond to treatment interventions. A general outline of dynamics presented to the patient with the object of stirring up some tension in the interview and hence expediting explorations, or of working toward fitting the patient's special problems and mechanisms into the outline, is sometimes helpful.

CHAPTER 11

Techniques in Short-term Therapy

Psychotherapy as it is practiced today is no longer a homogeneous operation. Entering its mainstream are tributaries from various branches of the biological and behavioral sciences. This is because behavior embraces every constituent of the human being from physiological makeup to spiritual promptings. In Table 11–1 the various links in the behavioral chain are delineated, as well as the fields of interest these embrace, and the therapeutic modalities related to each link to which certain syndromes are often assigned. Take as an example the syndrome of schizophrenia.

Schizophrenia is a disease that is variantly attributed to many causes. There are those who regard it as a biochemical affliction, the product of defects in the function of the neurotransmitter dopamine, which, operating in excess, affects the mesolimbic, infundibular, and nigral pathways. Under these circumstances pharmacotherapy would appear to be the preferred approach, neuroleptics, for example, being employed to block the action of dopamine. Others regard schizophrenia as a neurophysiological disorder, characterized by a lack of left cerebral dominance and defective cerebrolimbic functioning that sponsor abnormalities in linear cognitive ability. Adherents of this viewpoint might consider certain forms of somatic therapy suitable under some circumstances, ECT, for instance, as well as some forms of relaxation therapy. Some ascribe schizophrenia to faulty learning and conditioning, considering it a developmental problem, the consequence of severe family pathology with projective use of the child by parents who communicate conflictual "double-bind" themes. A behavioral approach, consequently, might be in order. Then there are those who prefer an intrapsychic explanation, seeing it as a thinking disorder that provokes "primary-process," primitive, irrational, wishful ideation, with excessive condensation, displacement, and the distorted use of symbols. The result is an interference with proper emotional modulation. This viewpoint sometimes sponsors a psychoanalytic approach. On the interpersonal level certain authorities credit the disease to the mischief of regressive, archaic defenses that encourage detachment, distrust, and extraordinary dependency. Family therapy, group therapy, and psychoanalytically oriented therapy would fit in here. Social forces are considered by some to be the prime culprits, inspiring the patient to assume anomalous social roles terminating in alienation and deviations in task performance. Millieu therapy, casework, counseling, social therapy, and rehabilitative therapy could be utilized with these factors in mind. Finally, there are professionals who prefer a more esoteric spiritual explanation, viewing schizophrenia as a unique and singular mode of perceiving and experiencing reality. Existential therapy and a crop of philosophical approaches, many deriving their substance from Eastern systems of thought, have their advocates who seek to influence this elusive dimension. Different approaches to treatment thus accord with multiple ways of regarding the disease. Actually, schizophrenia embraces all of the bodily systems, and no one etiological factor can be considered exclusively dominant. And any of the many modalities singly or in combination may in some cases register a beneficial effect.

TABLE 11-1. The Biological and Behavioral Links of Behavior*

THE BEHAVIOR CHAIN	FIELDS	RELATED THERAPEUTIC MODALITIES	SYNDROMES
Biochemical links	Biochemistry	Pharmacotherapy	Schizophrenia (neuroleptics) Mania (lithium) Major depressions (antidepressants) Anxiety states (anxiolytics) Hyperkinetic syndromes of childhood
Neurophysiological links	Neurophysiology	Biofeedback Somatic therapy Relaxation therapy (meditation, relaxing hypnosis) Emotive release	Tension states (relaxation, biofeedback, emotive release) Suicidal depressions (ECT) Physical conditions arising from mental factors (biofeedback)
Developmental-conditioning links	Developmental theory Learning theory	Behavior therapy Cognitive therapy Persuasion Suggestive hypnosis	Phobic reactions (behavior therapy) Habit disorders (hypnosis) Behavior disorders (behavior therapy) Obsessive-compulsive disorders (behavior therapy, persuasion, cognitive therapy) Adjustment reactions Developmental delays
Intrapsychic links	Psychoanalysis Cognitive theory	Psychoanalysis Hypnoanalysis Existential analysis Guided imagery	Personality disorders Neurotic disorders
Interpersonal links	Dynamic theory Role theory Group dynamics Social psychology	Psychoanalytically oriented therapy Group therapy Marital therapy Family therapy Psychodrama Experiential therapy Transactional analysis Cognitive learning	Personality disorders Neurotic Disorders Marital problems Family problems Borderline personality Drug abuse and dependence
Social links	Sociology Anthropology Economics Political science	Milieu therapy Social casework Counseling Social therapy Recreational therapy	Situational problems Psychoses in remission
Spiritual links	Theology Philosophy Metapsychiatry	Religious therapy Eastern philosophical systems Existential therapy	Reactive depression Anxiety states Addictions

* Behavior is a complex entity composed of a chain of interrelated biochemical, neurophysiological, developmental-conditioning, intrapsychic, interpersonal, social, and spiritual links. Difficulties in one link will by feedback influence all other links in the chain. Distinctive fields of interest and special theories related to each link inspire a number of therapeutic modalities that are preferred approaches in certain syndromes even though through feedback interventions bracketed to other links may also be effective.

By the same token, practically every neurotic or behavioral disorder may be causally associated with multiple links in the behavioral chain. They too may be approached with a variety of techniques that correspond to different links. This is the rationale of eclecticism, which in short-term therapy is a preferred mode of operation.

The fact that we have so many different approaches to the same emotional problem can in itself be confusing. Because there is so little time available in brief therapy, we will want to select the one method or combination of methods that is most applicable to the specific difficulty. In this respect we can console ourselves in a minor way. No matter what technique we employ, if we are skilled in its use, have faith in its validity, and communicate this faith to the patient, and if the patient accepts the technique and absorbs our faith, it will influence him in some positive way. In resolving a difficulty related to one disturbed link in his behavioral chain, this will influence by feedback other links. Thus, if we prescribe neuroleptics for a schizophrenic with a disturbing thinking disorder, the impact on his biochemistry will register itself positively in varying degrees on his neurophysiology, his general behavior, his intrapsychic mechanisms, his interpersonal relations, his social attitudes, and perhaps even his philosophical outlook. Applying behavior therapy to a phobic will in its correction influence other aspects from the biochemical factors to spiritual essences. Working with modalities that are directed at the intrapsychic structure in a personality disorder through psychoanalysis or cognitive therapy, we may find that all other links in the behavioral chain are affected in a gratifying way. This global response, however, does not in the least absolve us from trying to select the best method within our range of skills that is most attuned to the patient's unique learning aptitudes.

Be this as it may, there are some general principles that are applicable to most patients. First, we start therapy by allowing the patient to unburden himself verbally, to tell his story uninterruptedly, interpolating comments to indicate our understanding and empathy and to keep him focused on important content. Second, we help him arrive at some preliminary understandings of what his difficulty is all about. Third, we select a method that is targeted on that link that is creating greatest difficulty for that patient—biochemical, behavioral, intrapsychic, interpersonal, or social. Fourth, we try to show him how he himself is not an innocent bystander and that he, in a major or minor way, is involved in bringing his troubles on himself. Fifth, we deal with any resistances that he develops that block (a) an understanding of his problem, (b) his productive use of the techniques we employ, and (c) the application of his treatment toward behavioral correction. Sixth, we try to acquaint him with some of the personality distortions that he carries around with him that can create trouble for him in the future—how they developed, how they operate now, and how they may show up after he leaves therapy. And, seventh we give him some homework that is aimed at strengthening himself so that he may minimize or prevent problems from occurring later on. Within this broad framework there are, of course, wide differences on how therapists with varying theoretical orientations will operate. By and large, however, psychotherapists with adequate training should anticipate satisfactory results with the great majority of their patients.

Employing whatever techniques or group of techniques are indicated by the needs of the patient and that are within the scope of one's training and experience, the therapist may be able to achieve the goals agreed on in a rapid and effective way. Where the therapist has become aware of the underlying dynamics, it may be necessary to mention at least some salient aspects and to enjoin the patient to work on these by himself after therapy has ended. On the other hand, the therapist may not be able to achieve desired goals unless interfering dynamic influences that function as resistance are dealt with during the treatment period because the patient is blocked by the resistance against making progress.

In long-term therapy a dynamic theme that explains the patient's personality operations and resistances gradually reveals itself through a leisurely study of the patient's verbalizations, behavioral proclivities, dreams, fantasies, and transference projections. No such casual indulgence is possible in short-term treatment. Piecing together data from the patient's history, general demeanor, interpersonal exploits, associations, and the few fantasies and dreams that are available, and correlating these with reactions to therapy and to the therapist, as well as to any brief psychological tests that may have been given (e.g., man-woman drawings and exposure to Rorschach cards), the therapist will be able to make some assumptions about the patient's dynamics. These will be a guide in confrontations and interpretive work.

As has been amply illustrated in the past chapters, a number of dynamic themes, present in the great majority of people in our culture, have been repeatedly observed that can guide in bringing some basic problems to light during therapy, recognizing that many configurations exist that are unique for each individual. Among familiar themes that have been described are those related to incomplete separation-individuation, residual guilt feelings and needs for self-punishment, and devalued self-esteem. It is rare that one sees any patient in therapy who does not possess an abundant share of these leitmotifs, although the ways that they manifest themselves in the character structure and the kinds of symptoms they sponsor are distinctively idiosyncratic.

Working with the operative dynamics constitutes a valuable means of helping a patient to face and, if motivation is present, to alter his repetitive self-defeating behavior. Pointed interpretations of the dynamics underlying ego-syntonic symptoms, traits, and behavior only too frequently result in denial and anxiety, for maladaptive as they are, neurotic conflicts and needs are welded into the patient's habitual coping modes and yield florid gratifications compared to which the pleasures of healthy patterns pale. What is the best way of dealing with such obstructions? A pithy epigram in the Koran contends that "God is with those who persevere." This certainly applies to the undaunted therapist who in the face of obstinate resistance doggedly works against it. In long-term therapy the task of dealing with resistances to a recognition of one's dynamics and managing stubborn oppositional reactions to the relinquishing of destructive behavior consume a bulk of the time devoted to therapy and can tax the endurance of the most resolute therapist. In short-term therapy the task would seem tc be doubly complicated since there is only limited time to prosecute the search for conflictual themes and to resolve resistance to their disclosure and rectification. Understandably, one cannot duplicate in 10 sessions what could be achieved with skillfully conducted therapy in 100. Yet, experience bears out the value of bringing to the patient's attention a glimpse of his operative dynamics and demonstrating to him his responsibility in bringing about the disasters that he has hitherto credited to destiny and misfortune.

Confrontation

One technique that has been advocated by some short-term therapists to cut through resistance to understanding one's dynamics is that of confrontation. This is sometimes utilized to get at underlying trends by provoking anxiety or negative feelings. Usually the patient will respond to the therapist's challenges of his behavior with anger that may be promptly suppressed. What will appear instead are disavowal, protest, self-justification, and self-abasement, laying the blame for one's behavior on malevolent circumstances or the dereliction of others. Negative transference rapidly precipitates out. Opportunities are thus rich for interpretation of feelings about and reactions to the therapist. This technique is dramatic and often effective in patients with good ego strength. However, it can drastically hurt the therapeutic relationship in a good number of patients if implemented too early in therapy before proper rapport has been established. The patient is apt to regard the therapist's actions and manner as arbitrary, unjustifiable, recriminatory, malicious, and reflective of the therapist's inability to understand him or to empathize with his suffering and situation. It takes a great deal of skill to select those who are suited for confrontation and to titrate the degree of forcefulness of challenges to the patient's existing strengths. Experienced therapists are capable of doing this even in the first interview with some patients, but the average therapist will be compensated for his efforts with an extraordinary number of dropouts from treatment. In most patients who come for help a minimally provocative posture will be indicated at first; the therapist should work toward the establishing of a good working relationship before battering away at the patient's defenses through strong confrontations.

Selection of fruitful areas for confrontation when it is done is important. Since most patients possess an overly primitive and severe conscience (superego) that provokes guilt, feelings of wickedness, and masochistic behavior, these pathological zones provide a productive area for attack and discussion. Some therapists employ a technique that interprets the symptoms of the patient, no matter what they may be (for example, anxiety, depression, worry, outbursts of anger, conversion reactions, compulsions, phobias, insomnia, anorexia, etc.), as manifestations of self-punishment, the consequences of a guilty conscience (Lewin, 1970). Each symptom is delineated as serving both self-tormenting needs and provocative aims toward others. Even an individual's disturbed character patterns are reduced to the masochistic need to suffer and "drive people away so that he can torment himself with loneliness." The patient is helped "to see what he wants to do and what his conscience forces him to do" and how the disparity creates difficulties. The contrast between a healthy conscience that guides while inhibiting destructive actions and the patient's existing sadistic conscience that viciously torments and punishes is pointed out. It becomes essential for the patient to recognize that an intemperate and merciless conscience is the "*common enemy* against which the therapist is his ego's strong ally." No immediate interpretations are made of specific conflicts. "The initial confrontations are confined to the patient's need for self-punishment and his masochistic responses to anger."

This focalization, it seems to me, is used as an expedient to provide the patient with a single insight into which he can converge his energies. Since masochism is a common defense, the therapist may not be too far off if its existence is pointed out—that is, of course, if the patient presents even slight evidences of its operation. Obviously, masochism is not the only basis for symptoms, and the therapist should not be sidetracked by using the explanation of masochism as a strategy for breaking up the patient's resistance. The therapist will usually discover, if a search is made for them, additional reasons for some of the patient's symptoms.

Other explanations than masochism may be offered by therapists trained in specific schools of psychology or psychiatry. One universal basic cause is presented for all types of emotional illness, and this single etiological factor is tortured to fit in with *every* symptom and behavioral manifestation. Thus, the patient may be dazzled by brilliant explanations of the malfunctions of pregenital splitting, or of the Oedipus complex, or of the devalued self-image, or of subversive archetypes, or of conditioned anxiety, or of any of the countless theories around which current psychologically ideologies are organized. While such single explanations may not be accurate, they certainly are convenient and they may be temporarily effective, especially when dogmatically stated.

One of the advantages of dogma is that it makes critical thinking unnecessary. And some patients are only too eager to hand over their minds to the therapist who will do their thinking for them—that is, until the treatment ends, after which the patient will begin to reconstitute his own frame of reference and enthusiastically recreate the conditions that got him into trouble in the first place.

This does not mean that we should throw the baby out with the bath. Some of the theories and explanations may be helpful more than temporarily when applied to certain kinds of symptoms and personality problems. Accident proneness, obsessional self-torment, suicidal tendencies, and hypochondriacal preoccupations, for example, may be indications of a generalized masochism. An explanation such as the following may be offered: "You feel angry at what your parents did to you as a child. But you also feel guilty for your anger and thoughts. So you punish yourself for these thoughts and feelings. Your symptoms and your behavior seem to me to be the results of your punishing yourself. Now what are you going to do about what you are doing to yourself?" More direct suggestions may be: "Whenever you torture yourself with upsetting thoughts, or you get depressed, or you have symptoms (enumerate these) ask yourself, 'Why am I punishing myself?' Tell yourself, 'I've punished myself enough so just stop it!'" Should these explanations and injunctions fail to produce results, some therapists resort to stronger challenges and confrontations.

While aggressive confrontation under these circumstances may prove profitable in some patients with good ego strength, it may not be applicable to sicker patients unless the confrontations are toned down to a point where they are executed in an empathic reassuring way. Even then it may be necessary to wait until a good working relationship has been established, and then only after it becomes apparent that masochistic maneuvers are obviously being employed by the patient in the interests of resistance—"You seem to be punishing yourself by refusing to get well."

The phrasing of questions can be crucially important in helping a patient explore and come to grips with determining problems. For example, the patient states, "I wish I had a father who was like you." The therapist may reply variantly along the following lines: (1) "And I would like to have a daughter (son) like you." (2) "In what way did your own father disappoint you?" (3) "You must be very angry at your father." (4) "Reaching out for another father figure isn't going to help you much. You've got to learn to stand on your own feet." (5) "Your saying that is a manifestation of your continuing dependency." (6) "What is there about me that makes you say that?" (7) "You don't know me well enough to be sure of wanting me as a father." (8) What do you think would have happened to you if I had been your father?" Each of these responses will elicit certain important reactions in the patient and will influence the relationship.

Interpretive Activities

As therapy moves on during the first sessions, the patient's responses to interpretation will become apparent. If there is rejection of interpretations, lack of tension after a challenging interpretation is made, or bizarre responses, paranoid tendencies, or acting-out without insight occur following interpretations, the patient is probably not amenable to dynamic short-term therapy. In most cases, however, it will be possible to make interpretations and to help the patient acquire an understanding of problems and defenses.

The interpretation of resistance is indicated from the very start of its appearance, particularly where it takes the form of interfering with the working relationship. Should a negative transference appear either in dreams or in the patient's behavior, the therapist must immediately deal with it in as expedient a way as possible.

For example, the response of a patient after the second hypnotic session during which a relaxing cassette tape was made for her was irritation and anger at listening to the tape. Upon urging her to tell me her reactions to the tape, she stated the following.

Pt. When I tried listening to the tape, I found my mind wandering. When you say, "You are tired and drowsy," tired and drowsy are antonyms. Tired means not relaxed. When you say, "Even your leg muscles are relaxed," why "even"? When you say "the four S's (symptom relief, situational control, self-esteem, self-suggestions)" I say the four asses. I resented you. I want to apologize for my feelings. I am surprised at myself for liking you. When you said last time you might prescribe a drug for my depression, emotionally I felt you wanted to kill me, to immobilize me with medicine. In the tape you say, "You are filled with negative thoughts that we must neutralize," what thoughts? At the end you say "You will relax or fall asleep." They are incompatible. I said to myself about you, "He is so goddam impermeable, unreachable." I felt this way also about my mother and father. You say, "You will imagine a beautiful relaxed scene." I can't figure out if I should just see something or be in it personally—sitting, lying, or sleeping. The scene I settled on was the bank of a river with a boat—sunlight on the river reflected it on the water. Yesterday I populated the water with a swim. Also I thought this was all nonsense. I tried to open my eyes, but my lids were so heavy they wouldn't open. You say, "Even if you are conscious, the suggestions will be effective." I *am* conscious. The whole thing gives me a fear of emptiness. This is what I felt with my parents. I have guilt in relation to my parents. With my mother, I rejected her much of my life. I think I identified with my father. I took on his symptoms.

Her reaction provided the basis for our discussion of her transference to me and the possibility that she would reject the tape and its contents, even refusing to listen to it.

I felt I had a sufficiently good relationship to offer an immediate and repeated interpretation of resistance and negative transference. This did help consolidate the working relationship. The patient continued listening to the tape, and she derived a good deal of benefit from it.

Unless the patient is highly motivated and the therapist has been able to establish an early firm working relationship, provoking anxiety too soon by focusing on and interpreting defenses will tend to drive the patient out of therapy. Interpretations should be balanced against the state of the patient's willingness to explore problems and the quality of the patient–therapist relationship. Constant examination and use of the transference to point out habitual patterns of the patient and the origin in past relationships may be helpful. Unlike formal analysis, transference neurosis should be avoided, and deepest character problems remain unexplored since to manage them would require more time than is available in the short span devoted to treatment.

To interpret unconscious or partially conscious impulses prematurely is worse than useless. There are therapists who divining the conflicts of a patient at the first interview bombard him with interpretations that are presumed to put the patient expeditiously on the road to cure. Actually, an astute dynamically oriented interviewer may be able to induce a patient to disgorge a good deal of material related to early drives, including sexual and aggressive impulses and fantasies, to show the patient how these are affiliated with present drives and symptoms, and to demonstrate some transference manifestations that reflect a carryover of childish distortions into one's contemporary relationships. These disclosures, dramatic as they seem and perhaps are, have an effect in the great majority of cases that is diametrically opposite to that which is hoped for. The interpretations fall on deaf ears.

Not long ago I attended a conference on short-term therapy where, to my astonishment, some trained analysts in talking about what they did were naively practicing what Freud himself condemned in his 1910 paper on "Wild Psychoanalysis" (Standard Edition, Vol. 2, pp. 225–226) by confronting the patient with aspects of his unconscious during the first interview. If knowledge about the unconscious, wrote Freud, "were as important for the patient as people inexperienced in psychoanalysis imagine, listening to lectures or reading books would be enough to cure him. Such measures, however, have as much influence on the symptoms of nervous illness as a distribution of menu-cards in a time of famine has upon hunger." Many years ago in my pristine enthusiasm with deep hypnosis, I attempted to uncover in the trance some of the fundamental core conflicts of patients, enjoining them to remember the revelations that they themselves with great emotion divulged, only to discover that the effect on the patient's behavior was barren and bleak. I learned that a much better tactic was to safeguard the information for my own private enlightenment and not waste time convincing patients of my brilliance as a psychological detective. Once I had established a good working relationship with my patients (and it required more than one session), I could providently guide them with proper interviewing techniques toward coming upon the essential connections of their present topical behavior with fundamental intrapsychic determinants. They would then tell me what I had previously hoped I could smuggle into their minds in a flash. Essentially, I was doing what Freud in 1913 had recommended in his paper "On the Beginning of Treatment" (Standard Edition, Vol. 12, pp. 139–142), that is, to wait until the patient evinced some preconscious awareness of his conflicts.

There are, of course, ways a skillful and experienced therapist can in a roundabout, carefully phrased, and empathic way allude to the essential dynamics by projective techniques such as those described by Arlene Wolberg (1973) in her book *The Borderline Patient.* In this manner one may avoid an escalation of the patient's anxiety or a hardening of resistance, which so often in premature interpretations takes the form of animosity toward the therapist and abrupt termination of treatment. For example, a young woman of 28 came to therapy because of anxiety attacks and a dull paralyzing depression. One of her chief concerns was her 2-year-old child whom she feared she was neglecting so much that he would not survive. The disasters she envisioned ranged from accidental lethal poisoning to a fatal accident. A repetitive nightmare related to her child falling out of a window in spite of her efforts to save him. Her symptoms started shortly after the birth of her child and caused her to give up an excellent position in a firm for which she had worked since graduating from college. It does not require a great deal of imagination to construct a hypothesis of what was going on dynamically. A reckless therapist might reveal to the patient that part of her would like to see her child dead so that she can be liberated back to an independent life and that she undoubtedly resents her role as a woman, which resentment started in her early tomboy days and accounts for her present sexual frigidity. This intriguing explanation, however true it may be, would in all probability set off spasms of renewed anxiety and increase the patient's despair and hopelessness. On the other hand, should the therapist be assured that a therapeutic alliance has been started, he might instead employ a projective technique interpreting somewhat as follows:

Th. I can understand how upset you must be. Women do take a kind of a beating in our society. There are quite a number of intelligent educated women who when they get married resent giving up their careers. After all, there is little stimulating in washing dishes and pushing a mop. Some of these women fantasy an escape from this trap (smiling at this point as if joking) by imagining that their husbands will in one way or another drop dead, thus freeing them again. But they really don't want their husbands dead. They love their husbands. But this is the way the human brain works: it operates by peculiar symbols and fantasies that do not mean they will literally be carried out.

What the therapist is doing is employing an example roughly and tangentially related to the patient's problem, but using another person as the target. If she is ready to identify with the example, the patient will begin working on it as it applies to her and her relationship with her own husband and her child. If not, she will pass it by as irrelevant. In the former instance, when the patient opens up, the therapist may gradually be more and more direct in his interpretations, titrating these to the patient's level of tolerance of anxiety while being sure to preserve the working relationship. In the latter instance, that is, where the patient avoids the interpretation, the therapist will drop the subject and wait for a more strategic moment when the patient shows greater awareness before engaging in challenging interpretive work again. In the case of the young woman just cited, my interpretation was completely ignored, but two sessions later she brought up fantasies about the death of her husband, and we were able to discuss her feelings and to make good progress from that point on.

In presenting interpretations the therapist should search for areas where explanations will be most productive and where the most resistances to getting well reside. Among these are nuclear conflicts, derivative conflicts, negative transference; and sundry other resistances.

Nuclear conflicts frequently persist throughout the life of the person and are responsible for symptoms and behavioral difficulties. Example: A patient whose mother died during his infancy and who was raised by a succession of relatives has since childhood been in constant search for a loving, giving, maternal figure. He minimizes relationships with women who are accepting but seeks out liaisons with unstable, rejecting females with whom he acts out the theme of entering a perfect idealized union, only to experience rejection, humiliation, feelings of abandonment, and separation anxiety. A current crisis caused by discovery of infidelity on the part of the young woman with whom he has had a relationship for a year has brought him to therapy. Recognizing the depth of the problem and the impossibility of altering the dependency need in a brief therapeutic effort, the therapist focuses on alleviating the separation anxiety with ego supports. He brings the patient to an awareness of the origins and the destructive behavioral residues of his symbiotic needs and through cognitive approaches helps him to fight off the urge for future entanglements with rejecting women.

Derivative conflicts are closer to awareness than nuclear conflicts, and the patient has better control over them. Example: A patient who has been unable to achieve passing grades at college sees herself as a "loser." Her history reveals a series of failures in achievement and in interpersonal relationships. It becomes apparent that there is operative a fear of success which is equated with being aggressive and destructive toward others. The therapist predicts that this fear of success may sponsor a failure in therapy. Without probing the origins of her aversion toward aggression, the therapist focuses on the various manifestations of the need to fail and through desensitization and other behavioral techniques helps the patient to master anxieties related to a coming school examination. Utilizing the patient's successful passing as a fulcrum, the therapist helps the patient evolve ways of coping with future challenges.

Negative transference will block any productive therapeutic effort. This focus is perhaps the most important of all areas. When manifestations of negative transference appear, its resolution becomes a primary task. Example: A patient after the second session becomes highly defensive and argumentative challenging almost every interpretation the therapist makes. It is apparent that he wishes to avoid establishing a working relationship with the therapist. The therapist, recognizing that the patient is unresponsive and obstructive, confronts the patient with his behavior. A section of the interview follows:

Th. I notice that you constantly disagree with what I say.

Pt. No, should I take for granted everything, like gospel?

Th. It's interesting that you say gospel. Your father, you told me, is a minister.

Pt. Are you trying to tell me that I'm acting as if you are my father?

Th. Are you?

Pt. (*long pause*) I don't think so, but (*pause*) maybe you're right. I was an atheist ever since I was 6 years old.

Th. You mean fighting the gospel?

Pt. (*laughs*) What you are trying to do here is hardly religion.

Th. But you may be acting with me as if I'm a high priest.

Pt. (*laughing*) You're trying to tell me I'm misbehaving.

Th. This is how *you* must feel. I certainly don't believe you're misbehaving. You have a right to your own thoughts. What we're trying to do is to find out how you can get along better with people. Any maybe if you can work out a better relationship with me it will help you get along better with others. That doesn't mean I'm always right in what I say. But I think I can be more objective about what you do than you can. And if I point out things that seem like criticism, I'm not trying to be mean or arbitrary. Let's talk it out. It's important for *you* to decide if I'm right or wrong.

Pt. Doctor, I hope you can be tolerant with me. I know you are right in what you are saying. I'll try.

Th. This doesn't mean you have to take for granted everything I say. After all, I'm not a high priest.

Various other resistances interfere with progress in therapy. It may even be helpful to anticipate resistances if the historical data and initial workup point out areas of impending trouble. Example: An accident-prone patient with an obsessive-compulsive personality seeks therapy for anxiety and depression. From early childhood on he has been fearful of harboring a dreadful disease, the present form of which is cancer. At the fifth session when it becomes apparent that reassurance has failed to allay his fear of succumbing to a cancerous process of the brain akin to that of a colleague in his profession, the therapist confronts him with his masochistic need.

Th. I realize that, as you have told me, doctors make mistakes. But I get the impression that in your case, with so many medical and neurological checks, there is little chance you have cancer of the brain. More important than this is why you have to torture yourself with this idea or with other fears. Like all the other cancers you thought you would develop in the past and didn't.

Pt. Doctor, I tell you, I get so upset. I can't eat or rest. I get up in the middle of the night with a cold sweat.

Th. (*firmly*) Now listen to me. You are giving yourself a hard time. Now why in the devil do you *have* to wear a hair shirt all the time. One torturous idea after another. You've always had it. I really feel you've always had it. I really feel you've got a stake in punishing yourself. All the guilt feelings you have about your parents. You must feel that you are a terrible person for feeling the way you do.

Pt. I can't get the thoughts out of my mind about what will happen to me when they die.

Th. Like what?

Pt. (*pause*) I don't know. I'm afraid I can't get along without them. And yet I have these awful thoughts that something terrible will happen to them. [*Obviously the patient is caught in a conflict of dependently needing his parents, feeling trapped, resenting his helpless dependency, fearing that his anger will somehow bring about their death and turning this resentment back on himself. His guilt feeling enjoins him to punish and torture himself. This will probably prevent him from benefitting from therapy. To try to take away his masochistic need for self-punishment without dealing with the basis for his guilt would prove either futile or would only be temporarily successful.*]

Th. Now look. You have this need to punish yourself and all the torture you're putting yourself through, and all your symptoms and the messes you get into, accidents and all, are, I feel, directly related to this need for self-punishment. The reason I bring this up is that as long as you have this need, you will block yourself from getting well in our treatment.

What we are going to do is plan how you can break this vicious cycle.

A treatment plan then was evolved to help him break his dependency ties by getting him to take vacations away from home and then to find an apartment for himself away from his family. Having been enjoined to vent his anger, the patient became increasingly able to tolerate his hostility and to accept his parents for what they were. With support he was able to resist their insinuations that he was a disloyal son for leaving them and for living his own life. A dramatic change occurred in his symptoms, and a 2-year follow-up showed continued improvement and maturation.

Separation anxiety will emerge as the end of therapy approaches. Example: A patient who was making progress up to the seventh session began to experience a return of symptoms. His dreams revealed fears of abandonment, feelings of helplessness, and resentment toward the therapist. A frank discussion of how natural it was to experience fear of being unable to function on his own as therapy threatened to end, and how important in his growth process it was to tackle his fears and master them, brought out early anxieties about going to school, leaving home for college, and breaking up with former girlfriends. Putting his present reaction into the perspective of a pattern that was not so terribly abnormal enabled him to terminate at the set date with feelings that he had the strength to carry on by himself.

Special Applications of Technique

Short-term therapy embraces a heterogeneous group of interventions catalyzed by the therapist's enthusiasm, the patient's faith, and shared hope. While it is true that techniques serve to release important healing agencies, the choice of interventions and the skill with which they are implemented are crucial to success. It is to be expected that modifications in traditional psychotherapeutic techniques will be introduced by certain therapists who fashion their theories around methods that seem to work for them personally. This is all to the good, of course, except where the therapist attempts to incorporate all of psychopathology within his cherished theory and to insist that only *his* methods are valuable. We may forgive these narcissistic maneuvers should the methods presented have sufficient value to justify experimenting with them to see if they fit in with our unique ideologies and working styles. And we may be able to modify and shape some of them to our personal advantage. But, acceptance of the theoretical premises for these innovative procedures will require thorough experimental validation.

Sokol (1973), for example, has devised a short-term method for handling "simple" or "endogenous" depressions based on some principles of psychoanalytic theory. The hypothetical assumptions around which the treatment process is oriented contend that several factors must operate to produce a clinical depressive reaction. First, there must be a current loss of some kind, such as the death or removal of a person close to one. This acts as a spark, igniting the explosive mixture of an earlier loss in the child–parent relationship. Second, a primitive, punitive conscience (superego) must exist that will not permit the release of conflictual emotions, particularly hostility. Since hostility cannot be handled by the simple mechanism of repression, more primitive ego mechanisms are utilized, such as denial, introjection, and incorporation. Usually other emotions cannot also be tolerated, and both negative and positive feelings are blotted out. Third, "this leads to further shame and guilt and begins a regressive spiral." If we concede the validity of this hypothesis in order to cure a depression, hostility toward the lost object must be recognized, tolerated, and released. Since the patient cannot do this for himself, the therapist must do it for him. "I reasoned," said Sokol, "that, if the attack came from me, the pressure on the patient's superego would be diminished and the affectionate impulses could be expressed in defending the lost person from this external attacker." Using this tactic brought about a remission in the cases described by Sokol.

Lest one get too enthusiastic about Sokol's method, even though the dynamics may sound plausible, one must remember that only three cases were cited in this study. Moreover, in each case both antidepressants and tranquilizers were coordinately used. Other innovations claiming good results with depression exist and employ different techniques oriented around completely dissimilar theories, for instance, the cognitive therapeutic methods of A. T. Beck (1971, 1976).

In cognitive therapy an attempt is made to rectify conceptual distortions in order to correct the ways that reality is being experienced. Interviewing techniques analyze defects in a patient's views of the world (cognitive assumptions or "schema"), his methods of stimuli screening and differentiation, and the erroneous ideas that mediate destructive response patterns. Homework assignments reinforce the patient's ability to deal constructively and confidently with adaptive tasks. The treatment is short term, consisting of approximately 20 sessions on a twice-a-week basis. Cognitive therapy for depression is organized around a number of assumptions (Rush & Beck, 1978; Rush et al, 1977). As a consequence of early events, the patient retains a "schema" that makes him vulnerable to depression. Among such events is the death of a parent or other important person. What results is a "predepressive cognitive organization." Operative here is a global negative attitude on the part of the patient. Thus he misconstrues situations to a point where "he has tailored facts to fit preconceived negative conclusions" (Rush, 1978).

The patient regards himself as unworthy and assumes this is because he lacks essential attributes to merit worthiness. He assumes his difficulties will continue indefinitely in the future, that failure is his destiny. These characteristics constitute the "cognitive triad" in depression. In treatment the patient is enjoined to keep a record of aspects of his negative thinking whenever this occurs and to connect these episodes with any associated environmental events that trigger them off. The simple quantifying of any symptoms—in this instance negative thinking—tends to reduce them. The therapist, whenever the patient during a session brings up a negative thought, asks the patient to reality test it and then, away from therapy, to do this by himself. Through this means the patient is helped to see how he makes unjustified assumptions ("arbitrary inferences"), how he magnifies the significance of selected events ("magnification,") and how he uses insignificant situations to justify his point of view ("overgeneralization"). Other "cognitive errors" are identified, such as how offensive details are used out of context while ignoring more important constructive facts ("selective abstraction"), how circumstances and thoughts that do not fit in with negative "schemas" are bypassed ("minimization"); how unrelated events are unjustifiably appropriated to substantiate his ideas ("personalization"). The patient is encouraged to review his record of thoughts, to identify themes and assumptions, and to identify past events that support his faulty schemas. Point by point the therapist offers alternative interpretations of these past events. By so doing he hopes that sufficient doubt will develop in the patient so that he will engage in experimental behaviors, recognizing the fallaciousness of his hypotheses, and arrive at different, less destructive explanations for events. A marital partner or family may also be involved in cognitive therapy to reinforce correction of distorted negative meanings.

Step by step the patient is encouraged to undertake tasks that he hitherto had considered difficult ("graded task assignment") and to keep a record of his activities ("activity scheduling") and the degree of satisfaction and sense of mastery achieved ("recording a mood graph"). Discussions in therapy focus on the patient's reactions to his tasks and his tendencies at minimization of pleasure and success. Homework assignments are crucial. These range from behaviorally oriented tasks in severe depression to more abstract tasks in less severe cases oriented around correcting existing schemas. Should negative transference occur, it is handled in the manner of a biased cognition.

Employing a cognitive model of personality, Morrison and Cometa (1977) have evolved what they call "emotive-reconstructive" short-term therapy (ERT). The theory behind the technique is that unfortunate early childhood stress experiences lead to a "person's inadequate construction of self and others." This produces a playing of faulty roles and self-conceptualizations in later life. Thus some children, not being able to endure their parents as nonloving, distort reality by construing them as loving and themselves as bad. "Essentially locked into the role of bad child as a means of reducing the stress and confusion of paradoxical family communications, individuals' subsequent life experiences are but replays of early roles." What must occur to overcome this distortion then is a discovery of key conflicts and a correction of their interpretation. Instead of trying to force this by inappropriate search strategies, as is the case in traditional psychotherapy, a technique of direct experiencing is used by Morrison and Cometa. Patients are asked to shut their eyes and "to immerse themselves in past events by focusing on the contextual surroundings (colors, odors, noises, texture) of early experiences" describing these briefly. Periodically, when the therapist wishes to arouse the expression of a certain feeling, the patient is asked to hyperventilate "by breathing deeply and rapidly for 30- to 60-second time periods." Gestalt and role-playing techniques may coordinately be employed. Support is given and empathy shown when necessary to comfort the patient. Approximately 15 sessions often lead, it is reported, "to a reconstruing of self and significant others, which in turn facilitates the adoption of more productive life roles" toward rapid personality and behavior change. The similarity of many aspects of this ERT technique with Freud's early cathartic method will be recognized.

Another example of the use of a theoretical principle to fashion a clinical approach is provided by Suess (1972). He points out that dynamic short-term therapy is obstructed in the obsessive-compulsive individual by rigid tendencies to avoid feelings of excessive intellectualization, self-control, and attachment as well as by great fears of surrendering oneself to hurt and exploitation in any interpersonal relationship. An important objective in interviewing these patients, therefore, is to help them recognize their feelings by working on those that are aroused in the current interview situation. These, manifested in "verbalizations, voice tone, facial expression, body movement and other nonverbal cues," are dealt with by such phrases as "You sound angry," "You look angry," "You look disgusted," "You appear uncomfortable inside." Present meanings are more important than referral to past history and genetic origins. Whenever the patient attempts a diversion by theoretical, philosophical, or intellectual discussion, it is arrested and the focus redirected at feelings, such as being angry, guilty, affectional, depressed, and so on. The defensive nature of silences on the part of the patient should also be interpreted, for example, the incessant and paralyzing need to maintain control. Self-criticism powered by an excessively punitive superego is tempered by suggesting the possibility of less critical attitudes. Focusing on the emotions behind verbalizations rather than the content is important, especially when the patient keeps talking about his symptoms. Intellectualizations and doubts utilized as a way of guarding against recognition of feelings in one's present life may seduce the therapist into engaging in fruitless debates, thus falling into the patient's trap of avoiding feelings. The proper response to these maneuvers, claims Suess, is to expose them as resistances.

Some innovative attempts at prophylaxis of emotional illness have been made. Among these is the work of Stein et al (1969) on brief therapy with seriously physically ill patients. The development of an illness, particularly of an incurable and debilitating nature, imposes a severe strain on any individual. Where the patient is unable to accept the imposition of a temporary or permanent handicap, where his security is threatened and his self-image damaged by the realization of his vulnerability, pathological psychological reactions (particularly anxiety, depression, tendencies toward denial, anger, and a variety of neurotic and occasionally, in those with fragile ego strength, psychotic manifestations) will impose themselves. Because the patient may as a consequence become a psychiatric casualty, psychotherapeutic interventions instituted as soon as possible are urgent.

At the Central Psychiatric Clinic in Cincinnati an early-access brief treatment subdivision (Stein et al. 1969) accepts patients who preferably have severe physical problems of recent origin. Up to six sessions are given, each lasting from 15 to 50 minutes, spaced on the average of one visit each week. In the majority of these patients symptomatic improvement and restoration of satisfactory functioning has followed this brief treatment (Gottschalk et al., 1967). The treatment process is best organized by (1) handling the tendencies to denial, (2) managing a shattering of the sense of mastery, and (3) dealing with the conviction of impaired body integrity.

Handling of the tendencies to denial is crucial. Blank unbelief often operates as a primary defense to insulate the patient from the implications of his illness (Lindemann, 1944). Such denial, interfering with the true assessment of the reality situation, constitutes a great danger for the individual. In coronary illness, for example, the patient may engage in dangerous overactivity, neglect of his diet, and forgetting to take essential medications. It is, therefore, important to review with the patient his ideas of his illness and his attitudes toward it especially his hopelessness. By careful clarification coupled with reassurance we may be able to correct existing misconceptions and cognitive distortions. The relationship with the therapist can greatly help the patient to accept a factual assessment of his situation. The therapist here serves "in a role similar to the protecting parent who makes painful and threatening reality less intolerable to the child, thus enabling the child to accept and face reality, with its hazards, rather than having to deny and 'shut out' (Stein et al., 1969).

Managing a shattering of the sense of mastery is important, especially in those persons who habitually must maintain control. The fear that an illness can strike without warning and that it may be a harbinger of other unknown and perhaps more serious physical disasters destroys the individual's confidence in his own body. Reassurance that anticipated catastrophes are not inevitable and that preventive measures are a best means of helping to avoid unwelcome troubles may quiet the patient's fears. Encouraging the patient to ventilate fantasies associated with the illness, the therapist is then in a better position to offer advice concerning specific medical and neurological consultation resources.

Dealing with the conviction of impaired body integrity involves restoring faith in one's body. This is especially necessary in traumatic injuries and surgical procedures. To some extent a reaction of fatigue and a reaction of depression temporarily follow even relatively minor accidents and operations. But after serious operations, such as breast and limb amputations and effects of mutilating accidents, a prolonged period of upset can be expected. With the advent of open-heart surgery many untoward residual psychological sequelae have been reported. Severe anxiety and psychotic reactions are especially threatened in persons whose adaptive balance is precarious. It does not require intensive probing to recognize how angry a patient is at what has happened to him. Such anger may be displaced or projected onto family members and even on the patient's physician, and this may alienate the patient from essential sources of support and comfort. Opening up discussions around this dynamic can be most constructive.

Brief Group and Family Therapy

Brief group psychotherapy is an economical way of handling patients who have the motivation and capacity to interrelate in some way in a group. As a diagnostic and intake procedure it has been employed with success in certain clinics (Peck, 1953; Stone et al, 1954), particularly where there are waiting lists and an undesirable delay in assignment to a therapist. Here the group serves as more than a holding operation, some patients benefitting sufficiently from the group contact so that further individual treatment is not needed. At the Metropolitan Hospital Center in New York, Sadock and his colleagues (1968) have operated a short-term group therapy service for socially and economically deprived patients as part of a walk-in clinic. At the initial interview the 10 sessions' limit is explained by the social worker with the addendum that should this be insufficient, longer therapy might be arranged. One-hour sessions are held weekly, conducted by a cotherapist team of psychiatrist and social worker. No more than eight patients are in a group with new patients added as vacancies occur. The average number of sessions attended is five. The patient population is heterogeneous educationally, racially, and diagnostically. Where necessary, community agency contact is made for environmental alterations. The group discussions are pointed toward problem solving, each new member, after being introduced, being encouraged to give biographical data and to relate the problem that brought him or her to the clinic. Reactions of other members to the patient's account and suggestions for coping with problems are encouraged, and goals are formulated. Approximately two-thirds of the patients have been rated as improved at the end of their treatment.

A good deal of literature has accumulated on the subject of brief group therapy, and a number of different models having been described in the first chapter of this book. Some reports on the efficacy of short-term groups are especially enthusiastic. Trakas and Lloyd (1971) working with an open-ended group of patients for no more than six sessions reported twice as much improvement as was the case in patients receiving other kinds of help, including long-term group therapy. Waxer (1977) introduced motivated patients from a general hospital psychiatric ward into a group for no more than one month and was also very optimistic about the results. On the other hand, McGee and Meyer (1971) compared two groups of schizophrenics utilizing various rating materials and found that long-term groups were more effective.

The kinds of patients, their preparation for therapy, and the skill and personality of the group therapist are obviously crucial elements in determining the results in short-term groups. The therapist's attitude toward group therapy and his interest in working with a group are crucial for success.

A few pointers may be helpful. One way of approaching a patient to enter a group is suggested in this excerpt:

Th. I believe that your type of problem will be helped best in a group setting. We will have about six sessions.

Pt. Will that be enough to cure this condition?

Th. You should get enough out of therapy to have gotten started on the road to getting better. Whether you will be all cured is hard to say. Generally, after so short a time in treatment your symptoms should be improved, and you will have an idea of how you can go about continuing to get well and stay well.

Should the patient show resistance to entering a group, this is handled as in long-term group therapy (see Wolberg, 1977, p. 706).

At the first group session members are introduced by their first names and the confident nature of the meetings emphasized. The obligation to come to all sessions is stressed. patients are told that the number of sessions is so few that the sooner they open up and focus on their problems, the faster they will get better.

Th. You have an opportunity to talk about things here that you ordinarily keep secret. Just opening up and putting your feelings into words will help. What you want to do about upsetting matters will be your own decision, but you should be able to think more clearly about *what* to do as a result of your group experience and the help you get from the discussions. When you are ready, you will want to take action and that should set you on the road to getting well.

Pt. But what should I talk about?

Th. The best way to start is to talk about what brought you into therapy, how it began and what has happened up to the present.

Should the patient delve too much into past history, he should be discouraged, as should any too detailed theorizing about his condition. The focus should be on the *present,* and it is emphasized that no matter what has happened to a person in the past, one can change if one has the desire for change. As patients begin to talk, their reactions to the group and to the therapist will become manifest. Some patients will try to convert the group into a private session; they are then asked to address their remarks to the group rather than the therapist. The management of the group session as well as special problems that occur is described elsewhere in detail (Wolberg, 1977, pp. 708–719).

Most patients when they enter a group are highly intolerant of criticism, which they anticipate will happen should they reveal themselves. In a well-conducted group the patient becomes capable of distinguishing between destructive, hostile attacks and constructive criticism motivated by a desire to help. Moreover, he begins to realize that some critical comments are really not personal but are projections that are being falsely directed at him. Such exposures help many patients become less critical of themselves, less rigid and defensive, and more accessible to reasonable values. These learnings may generalize outside of the treatment session and influence relationships with others. Less hostile to themselves, they are more lenient with persons with whom they are related. Cooperative and tender impulses emerge.

A number of stratagems may be employed in the group to facilitate activity. One technique is to ask each member of the group to talk about any fears he or she had as an adolescent. Group members often are able to talk more easily about past fears and problems, especially those they have overcome, than present unresolved ones or about situations with an immediate stress potential. Patients can find comfort in listening to how other persons have had to cope with difficulties similar to their own. Once past fears are aerated, present concerns are taken up about some common problem. Should patients be on a hospital ward, they may be questioned as to how each feels about a routine that some have found distasteful. Once the ice is broken and communication is flowing, more personal immediate problems may be approached.

An interesting technique that may be used with patients who are not too sick, in a group that is inactive and bogged down, is asking for a volunteer to leave the room so that the rest of the group can talk about him, airing their impressions of the kind of a person he is. After a short period the patient is invited back into the room and asked to relate how he felt when he was out of the room, what thoughts came to him, and what he believes the group felt and said about him. Then another volunteer patient leaves the room, and the process is repeated. Later when the group is more integrated, the patients may compare how they originally felt about each other with changes in their perceptions. This technique can stir up a great deal of feeling and anxiety and should be restricted to patients with good ego structures. Individual sessions may coordinately be held to handle anxieties.

Role playing and psychodrama may also be utilized in some groups to help a patient act out what he feels about different people important to him as well as to rehearse new patterns and different ways of relating. Videotape recording and feedback may also be employed as a way of giving the patient insight into paradoxical and ambiguous behavior and communications.

Since groups are usually open-ended and patients enter therapy at various levels of psychological sophistication and readiness for change, the therapist will have to display a considerable degree of flexibility in the methods utilized at different times. Particularly difficult is work with actively psychotic patients. The conduct of such a group will call for methods of a special kind, such as those didactically oriented toward an educational goal (Druck, 1978; Klapman, 1950, 1952; Preston, 1954; Standish & Semrad, 1963). Here topics are chosen that deal only tangentially with the patient's affects and conflicts. Thus if patients wish to discuss hallucinations and delusions, a general discourse is given on hallucinations and delusions and not any individual's delusions as a personal problem.

In a brief group therapy with the socially and economically deprived there are advantages in having the group composed of peers who can identify with each other's experiences and tribulations. The therapist is often regarded as a representative of bureaucratic authority, and the presence of persons with similar socioeconomic backgrounds is desirable to lend support to the patient and to interpret what is being felt.

Because hospitalization is considered as sponsoring regressive patterns and destroying self-confidence and social relationships, alternatives to psychiatric hospitalization have suggested family group approaches on the basis that the family is actively involved in sponsoring and maintaining pathology in the presenting patient. At the Colorado Psychopathic Hospital a Family Treatment Unit set out to test the hypothesis that family-oriented crisis therapy has advantages over other methods (Pittman et al, 1966). The unit is manned by a team of psychiatrist, psychiatric social worker, and psychiatric public health nurse and operates 24 hours a day. All cases considered candidates for immediate hospitalization and who live not too far from the hospital are scrutinized for treatment by the Family Treatment Unit. Usually the crisis is brought on by a change in role demanded of one or more family members produced by some shift in the family situation.

At the unit, work is done with the family to bring the members to a realization that the designated patient is not the only cause of the crisis and that a solution will not appear with his removal to a hospital. Rather, the entire family is involved and, therefore, responsible for bringing about solutions. The behavior of the designated patient is interpreted as an attempt at communication. An interpretation is also made of the family role changes that led to the crisis, with firm but empathic confrontation of all members of the family as to their part in the patient's upset. Their responsibility is outlined, the around-the-clock availability of the therapist explained, and a home visit scheduled within 24 hours. Tasks are assigned to each family member. The patient and family are informed that any insistance on hospitalization is a way of escaping responsibility and that the crisis will be resolved only if family roles and rules are altered. In this way each family member is given something to do, such as cleaning the kitchen, writing a letter, taking medications, and so on. This is a way of testing the family's cooperation. A member of the team may actually participate in helping with one of the tasks. The patients and occasionally family members may be given psychotropic medications in adequate dosage if necessary.

The next step is the home visit to observe the family interactions and if necessary to renegotiate role assignments. At first the family as a unit is seen daily, at which time the behavior of the members is monitored. The therapist may apply direct or indirect pressure to encourage one or another person (patient or family member living within or outside the home) to change. The focus is on the firm and uncompromising need to accept responsibility. The patient may be instructed to communicate more clearly and not through his symptoms. This often dramatically produces improvement.

With this technique hospitalization was completely avoided in 42 of 50 cases, only an average of six home or office visits per family being needed. Ten of the 50 families called over a month following discharge about a subsequent crisis, which was usually handled over the telephone; several required one or two office visits.

Short-term family therapy has had increasing acceptance in clinics devoted to crisis intervention, the theoretical base being that behavior disturbance is a product of a continuing family system disorganization rather than rooted in individual pathology. Combining principles from group therapy and family-centered educational approaches, the practitioner functions as both therapist and educator (Guernsey et al, 1971; Wells, 1974).

In family therapy the therapist must utilize a much more challenging and confronting technique than in ordinary group therapy since the interlocking neurotic family mechanisms are extremely rigid and self-perpetuating. Yet, the degree of challenge must be titrated against the quality of the relationship that exists between the therapist and the family being treated. The therapist must also be ready to expose himself to challenge. Growth is not restricted to the participants of the group; it also involves the therapist.

Multiple family therapy especially has increased in popularity in recent years (Laqueur, 1968; 1972), and an excellent article on its literature, rationale, and some of its techniques has been written by Luber and Wells (1977). In multiple family therapy "the families and their members can become mutually supportive of each other in confronting stressful areas; intense family feelings are more diluted in the group context, and hence more approachable, and families can learn by observation and identification with other families" (Luber & Wells, 1977). Many families may be helped with a time-limited approach in this way, and for those who require a longer period of treatment the kinds of problems needing further help will have been identified.

Donner and Gamson (1968) have described their experience in dealing on a short-term basis (16 sessions) with groups of families experiencing problems with adolescents. The objectives were (1) to provide a setting conducive to exploration of family problems that contributed to difficulties of the adolescent members, (2) to help families acquire new and better solutions to quandaries confronting them, and (3) to employ insights gained as a means of recommending further therapy if needed. Evening sessions of 1½ hours once weekly were conducted, usually by a cotherapist team. Out of their experience a number of techniques are recommended. At the initial session the group is instructed that a problem in one family member involves not only the member but the entire family. One should not regard any member as "the bad one" or "sick one" because when trouble starts, there is something going on in the entire family. A family exploration of the problem enables them to deal with the cause. "All of us together will try to understand what is going on in the different families that contribute toward the young people's difficulties, and each can make contributions to the others." The group is told that since family members in one family live so closely, they may not be able to see the problem as clearly as when they see the same problem going on in another family. By observing how other families solve their problems each family may obtain valuable insights. Feelings should be ventilated freely with no restrictions, and there must be no punishment at home for what is said. Other ground rules are that all present members must attend each session (father, mother, adolescent, and, if possible, other siblings). Families during this treatment process are not to socialize outside the group since this will affect how they interact in the group.

As family members air their anger, despair, hurt, and indignation, new ways of dealing with problems generally emerge. "The families lose their feeling of having something wrong about them, which isolates them from others." The changes in one family group reinforce changes in the others; the families become active helpers of one another.

Common Questions about Techniques in Short-Term Therapy

There is a great deal of current interest in biochemical causes of emotional problems, and particularly chemical neurotransmitters, that may be influenced by pharmacotherapy. Do you believe that this minimizes the role of psychotherapy? Certainly it would be quicker and cheaper to give a person a drug rather than to spend session after session in interviewing.

What you are asking is whether drugs eventually will replace psychotherapy. A current article in a national magazine implies that we will in the not too distant future be able to control all behavior by injecting or extracting chemicals into and from the body. In my opinion, this frightening possibility is quite remote. In explicating neurotransmitters, or any other chemicals, as the ultimate ingredients in behavior, biochemical enthusiasts commit the same kind of error that the classical Freudians made in deifying the Oedipus complex as the fountainhead of all mortal blights. Both neurotransmitters and the Oedipus complex may come into play, but they are merely some of the agencies that are operative in the complex series of transactions that constitute human behavior. Biochemical, neurophysiological, developmental-conditioning, intrapsychic, interpersonal, social, and spiritual factors are all vital links in the behavioral chain, influencing each other by feedback. No one link is most important. Every thought, idea, wish, and fantasy has its biochemical correlates. Conversely, biochemical changes, including the influences of psychotropic drugs, resonate throughout the entire chain affecting other links. But while drugs may molify, it has been demonstrated that they will not solve the manifold social, interpersonal, and other distortions that are ubiquitous. Actually, more people are being funneled back into hospitals in spite of medications than ever before. So let us give biochemistry and pharmacotherapy their proper due without encouraging the public to seek cures for spiritual, social, interpersonal and emotional ills in their local drug stores. In short, it is foolish to anticipate that drugs will ever replace good psychotherapy.

Can you give examples of what you mean by eclectic therapy?

It is a rarity today to find a therapist who confines himself to one specific technique. There are several ways of alleviating psychological distress. Among the most recent entries into the therapeutic arena are the modern somatic therapies that aim at rectification of existing neurophysiological and biochemical distortions. An effective therapist may, from time to time, have to prescribe or refer his patient for prescription of neuroleptics for schizophrenic and other psychotic reactions, antidepressants (Tofranil, Elavil, Sinequan, Nardil, Parnate, etc.) for deep depressions, antimanic medications (Lithium for manic attacks), minor tranquilizers (Valium, Librium, Serax, etc.) for severe anxieties, sedatives and hypnotics for the temporary relief of insomnia, and electric convulsive therapy for suicidal depressions. So doing will result in correcting rapidly a host of symptoms that interfere with psychotherapy.

A second mode available to the therapist is diverting the patient and producing a calming effect through biofeedback or relaxing exercises, like meditation, hypnosis, and autogenic training. A third way is flooding the mind with philosophical, persuasive, or suggestive formulations, as in cognitive therapy. A fourth group of techniques attempts to divert the patient through externalization of interests, music therapy, dance and movement therapy, poetry therapy, social therapy, and occupational therapy. A fifth mode is alteration of the environment to reduce stresses being imposed on the patient and to surround him with constructive stimuli. Among the tactics employed here are guidance, milieu therapy, marital therapy, family therapy, therapeutic counseling and casework, and supportive group therapy. A sixth mode aims at rectifying faulty habits and developing new and more productive patterns through behavior therapy, role playing, and cognitive learning. A seventh mode explores unconscious conflict and releases latent creative potentials through dynamic psychotherapy, existential analysis, transactional therapy, experiential therapy, hypnoanalysis, narcoanalysis, exploratory art and play therapy, visual imagery, and analytic group therapy. As has been stressed, however, techniques in each of the modes do not confine their influence to one area. They will influence other parameters in cognitive, emotional, and behavioral areas.

Isn't the principle of eclecticism an invitation to confusion that ultimately defeats its purpose?

If you are referring to eclecticism as a mixing of various theories into one "grand stew," yes. It is foolish to attempt to apply theories related to one area of functioning, say the biochemical link, to another area, for example, the intrapsychic and interpersonal links or vice versa. All you will achieve is confusion. Even if one attempts to mix different theories that relate to a single link in the behavioral chain, the result can be a mess of scrambled ideas that explain nothing. On the other hand, if eclecticism refers to a technical blending of methods, each of which is suited for a different dimension of functioning, you can through such blending enhance the efficiency of your operations. For example, in a severe depression you may want to correct the pathology in the biochemical link by prescribing imipramine. You may also simultaneously decide to deal with the intrapsychic problem by utilizing psychoanalytic psychotherapy or cognitive therapy. Moreover, if a family problem exists, you will be wise to do some family therapy. These blended techniques enhance each other. After all, if a surgeon had only one technique at his disposal, like appendectomy, it would be silly to try to treat every stomachache or bowel cramp by taking out the appendix.

If a patient does not respond to the techniques you are using even though there appears to be a good therapeutic relationship, what do you do?

The first thing is to search for transference that may not be apparent on the surface. The patient's resistance to the therapist and to relinquishing his illness may be masked by a complaint and seemingly cooperative attitude. Often transference becomes apparent only by observing nonverbal behavior or by searching for acting-out tendencies away from therapy. It may be detected sometimes in the patient's dreams. Once transference is confirmed, confrontation, frank discussion, and interpretation are in order. Another reason why the patient may not be responding well to treatment is that the proper techniques are not being employed that accord with the patient's learning capacities. For example, some patients cannot seem to utilize the abstract concepts of interpretive techniques. They do better with role playing or assertive training. Other patients respond better to relaxation methods. One may fruitlessly work with an alcoholic and his family, yet will find that he improves immediately with an inspirational supportive group patterned after Alcoholics Anonymous. To do good short-term therapy, the therapist must be flexible and exploit a range of eclectic techniques. If certain techniques best suited for a patient are not within one's range of skills, one should refer the patient to a specialist. Whether the patient is to be transferred entirely or seen jointly will depend on the specific problem and on how advisable it is to maintain a therapeutic relationship with another professional as a cotherapist.

How important are the therapist's attitudes in short-term therapy?

Attitudes are important, for instance, enthusiasm and conviction about what one is doing. Beginning therapists, in their eagerness to help, often communicate enthusiasm that catalyzes therapy. Apparently experience for some reason dampens enthusiasm, therapists becoming more "scientific," cautious, and conservative about their healing powers. Such attitudes have a dampening influence. Somehow the therapist must get across to the patient conviction in the validity of his approach. This enhances both the placebo effect of therapy and consolidates the patient's faith in the therapist, thus strengthening the therapeutic alliance. A show of confidence on the part of the therapist will help carry the patient through the resistance phases of treatment. Where the therapist anticipates a long period of treatment, cues may be released that play into the patient's dependency and fears of separation, thus prolonging therapy.

When is countertransference most likely to appear?

Countertransference is likely to appear among therapists at any phase of treatment, selective characteristics in patients sponsoring aversive reactions that can interfere with progress. Serious psychiatric impairment in patients is an especially prominent stimulus that sparks off untoward responses in many professionals. This was borne out in a study of the reactions of nonpsychiatric physicians to medical patients (Goodwin et al., 1979). The most disliked patients were those who possessed strong psychopathological characteristics. The author of the article concluded that the emotion of dislike in physicians was a sensitive clue to psychiatric impairment in patients. Recognition of the inappropriativeness of one's negative feelings gives one an opportunity to examine those feelings and to control them, thus helping to avoid adverse effect on therapy.

Can countertransference ever be used in a therapeutic way?

Yes. Therapists recognizing that their own neurotic feelings are being activated may look not only into themselves, but also into what neurotic needs and drives in their patients are activating their personal reactions. They may then bring up these provocations as foci for exploration. They may ask, "is the patient aware of aberrant impulses and behaviors? What does the patient want to accomplish by them?" Confronting the patient with his behavior may have a therapeutic impact on him.

Are negative feelings in the therapist always evidence of countertransference?

Of course not. The patient may be acting in an offensive and destructive way, legitimately stirring up irritation and anger in the therapist. There is no reason why, when a working relationship exists, the therapist should not confront the patient with his behavior in a noncondemning but firm manner.

Can you describe what is meant by the "need for activity" in short-term therapy?

The need for activity on the part of the therapist is explicable on the basis of the limited time available for treatment. Passive waiting for the patient to work through his problem within a few sessions will bring meager results. It may be necessary to guide, support, exhort, and confront the patient as forcefully as is required at the moment, always mindful of the need to preserve a warm therapeutic climate. Activity in therapy may require ancillary services of physicians, lawyers, social workers, teachers, and other professionals as well as whatever community resources are needed at the moment. Especially in crisis intervention, assistance with economic, housing, and other situational problems may be necessary. By his activity the therapist communicates the expectations "that an early resolution of the presenting crisis is achievable. *Often it is exactly that expectation which serves as the primary therapeutic agent*" (Amada, 1977) Activity will require an abandonment of anonymity and the revealing of oneself as a genuine person rather than as a professional automaton. This does not mean a relinquishing of the proprieties of an ethical therapist–patient relationship, but rather a loosening of the straightjacket of rigid formality and detachment that are so destructive to good rapport. Activity may take the form of putting into words the nebulous feelings of the patient, and it may even be expressed in direct advice giving through presenting the patient with several options and helping him to make the proper choice.

How active should the therapist be? What if by nature the therapist is a passive person?

Activity is the keynote of short-term therapy. This does not mean the therapist should do all the talking. Even a therapist who is quite quiet and reserved can adopt a style of greater activity, avoiding sitting back and allowing the patient to ramble on with verbal inconsequentialities. By utilizing the principle of selective focusing (Wolberg, 1977, pp. 366–370), searching for evidences of transference and countertransference, immediately dealing with resistances when they arrive, changing from one technique to another when the former proves ineffective, and posing challenging questions and confrontations, a good degree of activity will come into play.

In focusing on a limited area, do we not stand the danger of neglecting important parameters of a person's life?

In short-term therapy it is pragmatically necessary to circumscribe the number of variables with which one deals during the interview. By concentrating on a limited area for focus and confining one's work to that area, some therapists feel they achieve the greatest impact. The patient reveals his problem through multiple channels: the way he walks, the way he sits, his bodily movements in talking, his facial expressions, revelations of his past life, his current entanglements, his dreams, the manner of his relationship to the therapist, and so on and so on. The therapist may decide to work with one constellation, let us say the individual's present relationships, perhaps focusing on his immediate family. The hope is that by altering the character of the family interactions a chain reaction will have been started to influence other relationships and ultimately the deepest patterns of one's thinking and feeling life. Memories of past difficulties may sometimes break through with a reappraisal of one's past existence. Indeed, a complete revolution may take place in the personality structure. Or we may focus on a specific symptom—exploring its history, the events or conflicts that initiate it, the circumstances that ameliorate it—and even start a regimen to control it. We may then find that with symptomatic improvement other dimensions of the personality are positively influenced.

Once a focus is chosen, should you ignore or direct the patient away from material brought up that has nothing to do with the focus?

Because there is so little time available, it is unproductive to deal with all of the random events and ideas the patient brings up during a session. Often these are advanced in the interests of resistance. Yet there will occur incidents of great concern to the patient that on the surface have little to do with the area of focus. To ignore these will indicate to the patient disinterest and lack of empathy, apart from it being bad therapy. For example, if a core problem is destructive competitiveness issuing out of rivalry with a parent or sibling and the patient has that morning found a lump on her breast, it would be foolish to bypass the patient's desire to talk about the incident. Even lesser areas of trouble preoccupying the patient should in commanding attention challenge the therapist to find a connection with a deeper focal problem. This can be done in most cases even though the route chosen may be devious. Thus a patient with a core problem of passivity and lack of assertiveness, a product of incomplete separation-individuation, is intent on talking about an art exhibit he had attended at a local museum. Underneath the great admiration for the artist is, it seems, a feeling of envy and despair at one's own lack of productiveness. The patient may then be brought back to the core problem with the statement, "How would you compare your own talents with those of the artist?" If a therapist cannot find any connections, a question like "What does that have to do with your own basic problem we have been exploring?" will usually help the patient resume dealing with more significant material.

How much advice giving should be used in short-term therapy?

Advice giving in psychotherapy should be handed out sparingly and selectively—and only when patients cannot seem to make an important decision by themselves or if their judgments are so faulty that they will get into difficulties should they pursue them. Even in the latter case it is best to present alternatives to the patients for their own choice and to continue questioning them as to why they find it difficult to pursue a constructive course of action without help.

Is telephoning the therapist permissible in short-term therapy?

In short-term therapy, and especially in crisis intervention, the availability of the therapist can be most reassuring. While the therapist does not encourage the patient to telephone as a routine, telling the patient to call if an emergency arises can allay anxiety and present the therapist as a caring person, thus bolstering the therapeutic alliance.

What is the conventional number of sessions that should be spent in short-term therapy?

A good deal of variation exists in the times alloted to short-term therapy. These range from 1 session to 40, the frequencies varying from once to three times weekly, the session lengths from 15 minutes to 2 hours. On the average, however, there are approximately 6 sessions over a 6-week period in crisis intervention, from 7 to 15 sessions over a 4-month span in supportive-educational short-term therapy, and as many as 40 sessions in dynamic short-term psychotherapy. Most sessions are for a 45-minute "hour." Some therapists establish a set number of sessions at the first interview and firmly adhere to a termination date. Other therapists are more flexible and determine the length of treatment according to the response of the patient to therapy.

How effective is the firm advanced setting of the number of sessions, and if effective, shouldn't this be a routine with all patients?

The firm setting of limits of time on therapy, originally described by Rank (1947) and Taft (1948), has been beneficially employed by many therapists (Haskell et al, 1969; S. Lipkin, 1966; Meyer et al, 1967; Muench 1965; Shlien, 1964; Shlien et al, 1962). An interesting finding is that a termination date accepted as an immediate reality will influence the process of therapy and stimulate greater patient activity than where an unlimited number of sessions seduces the patient into complacent torpor. The research done tends to support the advantages of restricting sessions in short-term therapy to a designated figure. Again, the therapist will have to exercise sufficient flexibility so as not to subvert his clinical judgment to a rigid rule. In certain cases he will want to keep his options open, merely mentioning to the patient that he will limit the number of sessions and that he will decide on the exact number soon after therapy has started. The therapist may quote the figure as soon as he has a better idea of the extent of the problem and the capacity of the patient to achieve projected goals.

How flexible should one be about appointment times, which usually are spaced at weekly intervals.

A certain flexibility of appointment times will be required, particularly in crisis intervention when double and triple sessions, several sessions on the same day, and the spacing of sessions are determined by the patient's rather than the therapist's needs. Also during the first week of therapy with patients who are extremely anxious three sessions will be needed for adequate support, reassurance, and the consolidation of a relationship. Weekly sessions thereafter usually suffice. Then there may be a tapering off to one session in 2 weeks and the next in a month, followed by termination. Should there be no improvement with weekly sessions, an additional weekly session in a group may be helpful, the group therapy also being conducted on a short-term basis.

What do you do about taking a vacation in the middle of a patient's therapy?

Preparing patients for vacations or other absences of the therapist is often overlooked. Sufficient notice should be given to allow at least two sessions before the therapist departs in order to observe and manage the patient's reactions. Naturally, if a verbal contract was made with the patient that included the time of termination and no notice had been given the patient that there would be an interruption of treatment, springing a vacation on the patient can have a bad effect on the relationship. In the absence of a definite contract involving the exact date of sessions or the date of termination no difficulty should be encountered where the patient has been forewarned at least two sessions in advance, except in the instance of prolonged vacations (a contingency that can occur particularly in older therapists by virtue of their having achieved sufficient levels of age, fatigue, or economic security).

What do you do if a patient keeps talking about how hopeless he feels about getting well and little else?

Patients often express hopelessness about getting well soon after they start therapy. To such lamentations the therapist may reply, "These are resistances fighting back as soon as you begin making efforts to get well. They will pass if you disregard them and go ahead with the plan of action we discussed." No matter how pessimistic the patient may seem about himself, the therapist should retain an optimistic stance: "No matter how bad and impossible things seem, if you keep working on your problems, you can get better." Naturally, an analysis of why the patient feels hopeless with proper interpretation of his masochism would be indicated. If the therapist knows how to do cognitive therapy, he might try to use this next. In the event the patient is severely depressed, and particularly where there is early morning awakening, loss of appetite, or retardation, an antidepressant should be prescribed along with any of the other measures recommended above. Should negative discouraging thoughts persist, the patient may be taught methods of behavioral aversive control (Wolberg, 1977, pp. 694–695).

How soon should you deal with angry, negative attitudes that a patient manifests toward you, expressed by criticizing your clothes, your office furniture, etc.

The maintenance of a positive warm working relationship is, of course, the best therapeutic climate. Whenever negative feelings threaten, unlike long-term therapy where they may be allowed to foster regression and then analyzed, they must immediately be explored and dissipated as rapidly as possible to restore the patient's confidence. By the same token, in personal dress and grooming the therapist should not appear so offbeat as to offend the sensibilities of his patient. On some level the therapist becomes a model for the patient. The arrangement and furnishings of one's office should also reflect orderliness and good taste.

Are there any risks in seeing another member of a patient's family, such as a husband or wife?

Yes. A hostile member may utilize the interview as a way of attacking the patient by misquoting for the patient's discomfort something the therapist has said that is detrimental to the patient. An example is the following letter received from a patient who did well in short-term therapy. I had an interview with the wife during which she vented her anger at her husband. She refused to consider marital therapy or individual treatment for herself even though I felt I had made some contact with her when I saw her.

Dear Dr. Wolberg:

For some time, I have been taunted by Mrs. G with derisions based on specific remarks she firmly states you made to her concerning me. These statements are that I am "hopeless," that I will "never get better," that I am "too old to get help," and worse than all, that I have "neither the desire nor the inclination to get better." These remarks have been repeatedly hissed at me, and although I have tried to discount and erase them as statements from you, they have been repeated and I am deeply hurt and humiliated that they may possibly have had you as their source.

As you will recall, I came to you in a desperate emotional state pleading for help. I had a severe anxiety and depression and the distressing symptoms of muscle spasm. I attributed these to the conflict at home, particularly the interactions between my son and his mother. How could I not have the desire nor the inclination to get better? I developed a very effective rapport with you and after a few months my symptoms left me. Some two months later, the situation at home sporadically erupted, and it soon developed that Mrs. G was the common denominator (not my son) as the provoking and disturbing influence at home, that her cruelty and constant agitation created the daily environment of hostility and chaos at home and these had their dire effects upon me and my son. This proved to be true because every symptom of anxiety, fear, and depression left me when Mrs. G left last June for Florida.

She returned home a few weeks ago and the turmoil, cruelties, and hostilities returned with her. I had reached a state of internal stability and equanimity while she was away, but now her daily tirades have resumed, opening up old wounds, and particularly referring to you as making the specific remarks I have already stated. I realize she is doing this with sadistic intent, and although I have every reason to discount and disbelieve such statements from you, I do feel deeply hurt and I do not want to go on thinking that you might, for some reason, have given her these terrible impressions. Except for what is understandably a personal hurt with the weapon she is using against me, I am otherwise feeling fine. I felt I should write you of this and give you an opportunity to let me know the truth of what you did or did not relate to Mrs. G Your reply will remain strictly between us, but I do owe it to myself to seek the truth.

Cordially,
Mr. G

Crediting certain remarks to the therapist is bound to affect the relationship with the patient. The best way to handle the misunderstanding is to arrange a joint session with the patient and other family member avoiding accusations about who said what about whom. The therapist may then in a noncondemnatory way help clarify what has been happening. This can be a sticky situation and will call for a great deal of tact. That incidents such as the one cited in the letter above can occasionally occur should not discourage the therapist from seeking interviews with other family members.

Can supportive therapy be anything more than palliative, and isn't dependency encouraged in this kind of treatment?

The supportive process may become more than palliative where, as a result of the relationship with the helping agency, the person gains strength and freedom from tension, and substitutes for maladaptive attitudes and patterns those that enable him to deal productively with environmental pressures and internal conflicts. This change, brought about most effectively through the instrumentality of a relationship either with a trained professional in individual therapy or with group members and the leader in group therapy, may come about also as a result of spontaneous relearning in any helping situation. Some dependency is, of course, inevitable in this kind of a therapeutic interaction, the adequate handling of which constitutes the difference between the success or failure of the therapeutic relationship in scoring a true psychotherapeutic effect. Dependency of this kind, however, can be managed therapeutically and constitutes a problem only in patients who feel within themselves a pathological sense of helplessness. The sicker and more immature the patient, the stronger his dependency is apt to be. It is essential that the helping agency be able to accept the patient's dependency without resentment, grading the degree of support that is extended and the responsibilities imposed on the patient in accordance with the strength of the patient's defenses. (See also the second and third questions that follow.)

Where the aim is the simple alleviation of symptoms and no personality alterations are deemed necessary, what tactic should be used?

The therapeutic tactics essential for the modest aim of symptom relief are uncomplicated, consisting essentially of developing a working relationship, encouraging emotional catharsis, giving proper support, guidance, and suggestions, employing techniques such as behavior therapy and relaxation procedures where these are indicated, and, if necessary, temporarily administering psychotropic medications.

Isn't symptom control a very superficial therapy, and doesn't it often result in a return of symptoms?

There are still a substantial number of therapists who believe methods aimed at symptom control, while rapidly palliating suffering and perhaps even reinstating the previous psychological equilibrium, operate like a two-edged sword. Justifiable as symptom control may seem, these skeptics insist that it fails to resolve the *underlying* problems and difficulties that nurture the current crisis. Irreconcilable unconscious needs and conflicts continue to press for fulfillment, and, therefore, they insist, we may anticipate a recrudescence or substitution of symptoms. These assumptions are based on an erroneous closed-symptom theory of personality dynamics. Symptoms once removed may actually result in productive feedback that may remove barriers to constructive shifts within the personality system itself. Even though these facts have been known for years (Alexander, 1944; Alexander & French, 1946; Avnet, 1962; Marmor, 1971; Wolberg, 1965) Marmor, 1971) and have been corroborated in the therapeutic results brought about by active psychotherapeutic methods, the time-honored credo branding symptom removal as worthless persists and feeds lack of enthusiasm for symptom-oriented techniques. (See also the second question above and the question that follows.)

Does therapy focused on helping or removing symptoms prevent a person from achieving deeper changes?

The evidence is overwhelming that symptom-oriented therapy does not necessarily circumscribe the goal. The active therapist still has a responsibility to work through much of the patient's residual personality difficulties as is possible within the confines of the available time, the existing motivations of the patient, and the basic ego strengths that may be relied on to sustain new and better defenses. It is true that most patients who apply for help only when a crisis cripples their adaptation are motivated merely to return to the dubiously happy days of their neurotic homeostasis. Motivation, however, can be changed if the therapist clearly demonstrates to the patient what really went on behind the scenes of the crisis that were responsible for his upset. (See also the preceding question and the third question above.)

What do you think of Gestalt therapy, and is it useful in short-term therapy?

Gestalt therapy is one of the many methods that if executed properly by a therapist who has faith in its efficacy can be extremely useful. Some of the techniques, like the empty chair technique, are especially valuable as a means of stimulating emotional catharsis, arriving at an understanding of suppressed and repressed feelings, and providing a platform for the practice of behaviors that the patient regards as awkward or forbidden. As with any other technique, resistances are apt to erupt that will require careful analysis and resolution.

What is "ego-oriented psychotherapy"?

Sarvis et al (1958) have written about the effectiveness of time-limited "ego-oriented psychotherapy" without setting up predetermined criteria for motivation or readiness. No arbitrary topic is set, but focus "is a *process* arising out of the interchange between the patient and therapist." The authors conceive of therapy as being open-ended, applicable at any point in the "adaptive-maladaptive integrations of existence." They regard it as a "limited" dynamically directed form of psychotherapy that is distinguished from psychoanalysis and psychoanalytically oriented psychotherapy in both process and goals. A crucial focus is what has brought the patient to therapy at the time he applies for help (why now?). Frequency of sessions is flexible, depending on the needs of the patient; the total time devoted to therapy is limited though not predetermined in advance. The therapist "tries actively to empathize with, conceptualize, and interpret the patient's material—particularly preconscious trends, the current therapeutic interaction, and the evidence of transference, in terms of ongoing integrative adaptations rather than toward regressiveness."

What are the objectives of cognitive approaches to therapy?

Recent cognitive approaches attempt to improve problem-solving operations as well as to enhance social adjustment. Where rudiments of adaptive skills are present and where anxiety is not too paralyzing, the individual in a relatively brief period with proper therapy along cognitive lines may be able to reorganize his thinking strategies and to find alternative solutions for problems in living that are much more attuned to a constructive adjustment. Intervention programs along cognitive lines have been described that are applicable in a variety of clinical and educational settings (Spivack et al., 1976). In my opinion, the techniques related to cognitive approaches can be implemented within a dynamic framework.

Is "cognitive therapy" of any value as a method in short-term therapy?

Preliminary studies are encouraging, but whether it is superior to other methods in certain conditions is difficult to say and will be judged by further research. The many factors that influence all psychotherapies for better or worse undoubtedly apply also to cognitive therapy. It has particularly been recommended in depression, but it is doubtful that it is a substitute for antidepressant pharmacotherapy, especially in endogenous depression. It may, as a psychotherapeutic adjunct, function here as a prophylactic retarding further attacks. Cognitive therapy is most helpful in patients with biased and faulty thinking problems, obsessional and phobic patients responding positively to a well-conducted and skillfully operated program. An important thing is *how* cognitive therapy is done and the faith of the therapist in its efficacy. To a therapist who believes in its value and who dedicates himself to the arduous task of altering established cognitive frames of reference, it may be a preferred approach. Other therapists may be more dedicated to and get better results with techniques with which they have a special personal affinity.

Are there any drawbacks to using behavior therapy in dynamic short-term therapy?

Not at all. It can be quite useful. Where the therapist is oriented toward behavior therapy, he will approach some of the patient's difficulties as manifestations of faulty learning. He will usually start therapy with a behavioral analysis. The symptom to be altered is analyzed to determine what benefits the patient derives from it. Explorations will deal with identification of factors that touch off and reinforcements that sustain the maladaptive behavior and of elements that reduce such behavior. Action rather than insight is accented. A method that helps to encourage motivation is the keeping of a daily diary that scores the frequencies of symptomatic occurrences. Simple score keeping has been found to reduce the number of symptomatic upsets. The patient's positive efforts to control, alter, and reverse his maladaptive behavior are rewarded by attention, praise, and enthusiasm. The patient's reactions to the techniques should be observed, the therapist being alerted to transference and resistance. There is no reason why dynamic principles cannot be applied to what is happening during behavior therapy or any kind of therapy. (See also the following question.)

Can behavior therapy be used for conditions other than phobias?

Yes, for various conditions like obsessions, hypochondrias, depression, and habit disorders where the symptoms are circumscribed and the events that produce the symptoms are identifiable. Behavior therapists utilize behavioral techniques along with other methods like pharmacotherapy and various kinds of psychotherapy. More and more therapists are seeing the advantage of utilizing behavior therapy within a dynamic framework. Increasing numbers of analytically trained therapists are finding desensitization, assertive training, and other forms of behavior therapy useful in their work. (See also the preceding question.)

What is the value of hypnosis in short-term therapy?

Hypnosis is chiefly employed as a catalyst in psychotherapy. It potentially facilitates the therapeutic process in a number of ways. First, hypnosis may exert a positive influence on the relationship with the therapist by mobilizing the essential hope, faith, and trust that are parcels of every helping process and by cutting through resistances that delay the essential establishing of rapport. This is especially important in detached and fearful individuals who put up defenses against any kind of closeness and hence impede the evolvement of a working relationship. Second, hypnosis, owing to its enhancement of suggestibility, will promote the absorption by the patient of positive pronouncements, verbal and nonverbal, that may alleviate, at least temporarily, symptoms that interfere with exploratory techniques. Third, hypnosis often expedites emotional catharsis by opening up founts of bottled-up emotion, thereby promoting temporary relief and signaling some sources of residual conflict. Fourth, impediments to verbalization are often readily lifted by even light hypnosis. Fifth, where motivation is lacking toward inquiry into sources of problems, hypnosis, through its tension-abating and suggestive symptom-relieving properties, may help convince the patient that he can derive benefits from treatment if he cooperates. Sixth, by its effect on resistances hypnosis may help expedite such insight techniques as imagery, dream recall, and the release of forgotten memories. Seventh, hypnosis may light up transference, rapidly bringing fundamental problems with authority to the surface. Eighth, by dealing directly with deterrences to change hypnosis may expedite the working-through process, particularly the conversion of insight into action. Toward this end, teaching the patient self-hypnosis may be of value. Finally, hypnosis may sometimes be helpful in the termination of therapy, enabling the patient who has been taught self-relaxation and self-hypnosis to carry on the therapeutic process by himself.

Is hypnosis ever used with a psychomimetic drug to speed up therapy?

Ludwig and Levine (1967) claim substantial therapeutic changes of a reconstructive nature through the use of a combination of hypnosis and LSD administration in a technique they term "hypnodelic therapy." Few other therapists use this combination.

What are the principle objectives of dynamic psychotherapy, and how are these objectives reached?

In dynamically oriented therapy the objective is to bring the individual to an awareness of prevailing emotional conflicts, the defenses employed in avoiding such awareness, the way such conflicts originally had developed in the past, the influence they have exerted on development, the insidious ways they pollute one's present existence, and their relevance in sponsoring existing symptoms and complaint factors. Such clarification is in the interest of helping to face anxieties and to develop new ways of relating to oneself and to people. Interpretations, the chief methodological tool, are targeted on defenses at the start, on any existing anxiety, and finally on the drives and impulses that are being warded off. Essential is the maintenance of sufficient tension in the interview to create an incentive for handling and working through of the initiating conflicts. A most fertile arena for exploration is the transference, which presents the patient with a living example of some of the core conflicts in action. Most vitally transference interpretation enables the linking of what is going on in the present with important determinants in the past. Transference may not be displayed exclusively toward the therapist. It may be projected toward others outside of the treatment situation.

In dynamic therapy shouldn't the chief aim be the developing of insight in the patient since without knowing the causes a cure is impossible?

Many therapists still believe that understanding the causes of a problem is tantamount to a cure. The search for sources then goes on relentlessly. Should improvement fail to occur, the patient is enjoined to dig deeper. Obviously, one task of therapy is to determine underlying causes; but we are still at a stage where our knowledge of *which* causes are paramount is not yet too clear. However, practically speaking, assigning to symptoms some reasonable etiology that the patient can accept serves to enhance self-confidence and to lower anxiety and tension levels. The patient may then be willing to experiment with more adaptive patterns. If no more than a placebo, then, insight can serve in the interests of expediting therapeutic goals.

Obviously, the more perceptive and well trained the therapist, the more likely will the patient be helped to arrive at underlying etiological factors. But, however, accurate these discoveries may be, a tremendous number of elements other than insight enter into the therapeutic Gestalt. Again, this is not to depreciate insight, but rather to assign to insight a significant but not exclusive importance.

How important is dream analysis as an adjunct to whatever techniques are being used?

Dream analysis constitutes a vital means of helping patients recognize some of their fundamental problems and their own participation in fostering neurotic maladjustment. Working with college students, Merrill and Cary (1975) found that focusing on dreams lowered resistance to self-experience in students struggling with the independence-dependence conflict. It also reduced acting-out by encouraging the acceptance of disowned feelings. A dream is best utilized in relation to current experience, though its roots in past conditionings are not neglected especially when transference elements are obvious in the dream. (Chapter 12 deals extensively with the use of dreams in short-term therapy).

Are psychoanalytic techniques, such as dream analysis, imagery evocation, interpretation of resistance and transference, and other modes of exploring the unconscious absolutely essential toward promoting depth changes in the personality? It is sometimes pointed out that a number of patients do achieve considerable personality growth when

treated by a therapist who utilizes supportive and educational methods exclusively, purposely avoiding probing for conflicts and dealing only with manifest symptoms and problems.

There are a few patients whose repressions are not too severe, whose defenses are not too rigid, and who possess a strong readiness for change. If the therapist is nonjudgmental and empathic, the therapeutic relationship itself can serve as a corrective emotional experience. The conception of punitive authority is altered, and softening of the superego results in strengthening of the self-image. This, however, is more likely in long-term than in short-term therapy. Most people do require some challenge in order to change, and a certain amount of anxiety needs to be tolerated to give up old habits and patterns exchanging them for unfamiliar ways of behaving. We see this during and after crises when people realize that their usual adaptations are ineffective and can only get them into more trouble. During short-term therapy confrontations and interpretations impose on the individual challenges with which he must come to grips. A purposeful focusing on unconscious material can be most helpful in promoting self-understanding, which may then act as an incentive for change.

Does one have to be a psychoanalyst to deal with resistance?

Of course not. But the therapist who has no understanding of psychoanalytic theory and method is at a disadvantage in dealing with resistance. In my supervisory work I have gotten the impression that it is resistance that principally accounts for failures in the active approaches like hypnosis and behavior therapy. Referrals to me of a sizable number of patients who were unable to achieve satisfactory results with nonanalytic therapies, revealed in practically every case that transference had interfered with positive responses to the therapist's methods. Such reactions occurred with me also, but I was soon able to detect them from the patient's associations and dreams. They then constituted the focus in our therapy. For example, in several cases referred to me for hypnosis by experienced hypnotherapists who were unable to induct a hypnotic state, I was able easily to detect the transference resistance that interfered with hypnotic induction. Without exception, once this impediment was brought to the surface and explored with the patient, he was able easily to achieve a satisfactory trance.

Some authorities insist that transference is not a problem in short-term therapy since the time element is too brief for its appearance. Other authorities base their entire strategy around the detection and exploration of transference. What is the discrepancy?

In dynamic short-term therapy transference is a key dimension and should always be looked for. It is often purposefully bypassed or overlooked when the therapist decides to act like a giving, helpful, active, benevolent authority, symptom relief being expedited by this kind of relationship. In nondynamic short-term therapy a benevolent type of transference thus may be desirable for results. We are not so much concerned with this form of transference. We are more vitally concerned with another type of transference that acts as resistance to treatment manifesting itself in distrust, hostility, excessive demands for love and attention, sexual impulses, and so forth. Progress will be interrupted unless this show of transference is resolved. Whether it can be resolved depends on the skill of the therapist and the patient's motivation and ability to work it through. Sicker patients may require an extended period of treatment to overcome such destructive transference. Where a therapist is trained to detect transference (e.g., by observing nonverbal behavior, slips of speech, acting-out, dreams, etc.) and deals with it by appropriate interpretation, it may serve as a means toward helping the patient to understand some of the deepest conflicts. In summary, while the therapist may not wish to interfere with a positive transference, indeed he may employ it as a prod toward symptom relief and positive corrective behavioral actions—a negative transference will definitely require attention and resolution. In some cases negative transference will appear toward the end of therapy as termination poses a threat. This is especially the case where separation-individuation has been impaired.

Would you utilize other techniques when the chief method employed is group therapy or family therapy?

Group therapy or family therapy does not restrict the use of any other techniques that might help any of the members. These include pharmacotherapy, individual therapy, milieu therapy, and so on.

Isn't electroconvulsive therapy passé?

By no means. It still is a most, if not *the* most, effective treatment measure in deep suicidal depressions. In excited manic and schizophrenic patients it also is occasionally used when lithium and neuroleptics fail to quiet the patient down.

Is drug therapy still warranted in depression, and if so, what is its rationale?

Definitely it is warranted. There are different kinds of depression, of course, for example, depression as a primary condition and as secondary to anxiety or hostility. There are certainly biological correlates in depression. The latest hypothesis is that in depression there is a deficiency of neurotransmitters, that is, of catecholamines at the adrenergic receptor sites in the brain, particularly a deficiency of norepinephrine, and also a deficiency of indoleamines (serotonin). Antidepressant drugs, namely the tricyclic antidepressants (Tofranil, Elavil, Sinequan), increase the concentration of neurotransmitters at the receptor site by blocking their reuptake from the synapse. When tricyclic antidepressants are used, they must be given in adequate dosage (individually regulated) and the effects may not be apparent for 3 to 4 weeks. After the depression lifts, the dosage is lowered to as small a maintenance dose as symptom control requires. Another way of increasing the concentration of neurotransmitters in the brain and lifting depression is by preventing their metabolism through inhibiting the enzyme monoamine oxidase (MAO). Usually the response to the MAO inhibitors (Nardil, Parnate) is also delayed. Psychostimulants like dextroamphetamines (Dexamyl), for example, are sometimes cautiously used in mild depressions. Where depression is secondary to anxiety, tranquilizers (Librium, Valium) occasionally help, but because of the danger of habituation, tricyclic antidepressants or low doses of neuroleptics (Mellaril) are preferred. In primary depression complicated by anxiety tricyclics (Elavil, Sinequan) are the drugs of choice. A patient taking antidepressants should be seen periodically by a physician, preferably a psychiatrist acquainted with drug therapy, where the therapist is a nonmedical person, since side effects are common.

Is lithium helpful in schizophrenia?

Neuroleptics are the preferred drug. A few studies do reveal that in some cases lithium may be useful, but the subgroups that respond have not as yet been identified.

How do neuroleptics operate?

Neuroleptics block the dopamine receptors in the brain interfering with dopamine transmission. Some of the symptoms of schizophrenia are believed to be the product of dopamine excesses.

Which neuroleptics are preferred in schizophrenia?

There are several classes of neuroleptics: first, the phenothiazines (Thorazine, Mellaril, and Prolixin); second, the dibenzoxazepines (Loxapine); third, the butyrophenones (Haldol); fourth, the thioxanthenes (Navane); and fifth, the dihydroindolones (Moban). Other classes will probably be introduced as well as additions to each class. There is little difference among the various drugs, but occasionally a patient may develop an intolerance to specific drugs and not to others. Some patients do well on drug therapy; some do not respond at all; and still others respond so badly that they have to be taken off medications.

Should neuroleptics be used with psychotherapy in schizophrenia?

It has been shown in schizophrenia that adequate dosages of neuroleptics coupled with family therapy are followed by the smallest number of relapses. Great flexibility is necessary on the part of the therapist, experimenting with other modalities also since special techniques will suit some patients and not others. Perhaps the most important therapeutic agency is a good relationship with the therapist. Psychotherapeutic techniques are valueless without this.

Should neuroleptics always be employed in schizophrenia?

By no means. Actually, they are being overemployed and in some cases used without proper supervision and follow-up. Young patients in their first attack, especially those going through an identity crisis, often do well without drugs. Where symptoms are too disruptive, however, neuroleptics should be used.

If neuroleptics are useful in schizophrenia, why shouldn't they be given indefinitely?

There are some disagreeable side effects and sequelae with neuroleptics, especially when given over a long period and in large dosage. Tardive dyskinesia is a neurological condition that affects as many as 40 percent of patients on prolonged drug therapy. Once tardive dyskinesia has become entrenched, it may plague the patient permanently even after the drug is withdrawn. Neuroleptics should, therefore, be lowered in dosage after the desired effect has been achieved, and periodically they should be withdrawn (drug-free holidays) to see how the patient reacts.

After an acute episode of schizophrenia and the patient is relatively symptom-free, should neuroleptics be continued?

Yes, for a while, if the patient has been on neuroleptics. The relapse rate is greater where drugs are not continued. Roughly after the first attack the patient should continue on medication for 1 to 1½ years. After a second attack they should be prescribed for 2 to 5 years. After a third attack they may have to be used indefinitely with occasional drug-free holidays. Supervision is essential to see that the medications are taken and to adjust the dosage to lessen side effects and sequelae.

When would you prescribe sleeping pills, and which would you recommend?

While benzodiazepines (Valium, Dalmane) are safer than barbiturates, they should very rarely if ever be given to new patients for insomnia for more than 2 to 4 weeks. Beyond that time consistent use causes them to lose their effectiveness. Occasional use of hypnotics, however, can prove helpful, as when a temporary stress situation interferes with sleep. Dalmane (flurazepam) in the 15-milligram dosage is generally as effective as the 30-milligram dosage. many persons also find 5 milligrams of Valium (diazepam) effective.

In matching patient and method how valuable is a developmental diagnosis, that is, knowledge of where in the patient's development the primary arrest occurred?

Matching patients and methods is still an unsolved problem. A number of attempts have been made to establish criteria for a patient-method alignment, for example, the symptomatic diagnosis (like behavior therapy for phobias, an inspirational group such as AA for alcoholism, etc); the characterologic diagnosis (like the personality typologies proposed by Horowitz, see p. 217); responses to hypnotic induction (Spiegel & Spiegel, 1978); and the developmental diagnosis (Burke et al., 1979). The latter authors believe that therapeutic methods may be selected to resolve conflicts which develop in different stages of development (Erikson, 1963). Thus Mann's technique (1973) of focusing on separation-individuation, in an empathic "feeling" atmosphere, would seem most useful with passive-dependent patients unsuccessful in resolving the adolescent's conflict of "identity vs. role confusion." Here the struggle over termination of therapy brings the early separation-individuation conflict to the fore and gives the patient an opportunity to resolve it in a favorable setting. The hypothesis is that if patients successfully master separation from the therapist, they will move on to greater individuation and overcome their dependency needs. Patients who in their development have moved beyond the crisis of identity toward the "First Adult Life Structure" (Levinson, 1977) and, in their efforts to establish intimate relations, have been blocked by resurgence of oedipal conflicts are well suited to the intellectual, interpretive, confrontation style of Sifneos and Malan. Problems of the latency period that emerge during the midlife transition brought about by challenges of "productivity, creativity, and the maturity to deal with new generations at home and at work" would be suited most for a "corrective action" approach such as that of Alexander and French, the maximum therapeutic effect coming "from transference manipulations and a managerial stance by the therapist." Under these circumstances. Burke et al (1979) contend, a careful developmental diagnosis will help identify patients who can benefit from psychotherapy; it can also help in the selection of an appropriate therapeutic method.

However, none of these selection schemes, involving symptom manifestations, character structure, or developmental conflicts, has been proven entirely reliable. This is because of the interference of numerous miscellaneous patient, therapist, environmental, transferential, countertransferential, and resistance variables. The very choice of a diagnosis and the identification of the prevailing developmental conflict around which the therapeutic plan is organized is subject to the therapist's bias as is the method to which the therapist is attuned. This bias will prejudice the patient's response. A therapist who applies himself to a favorable technique with enthusiasm and conviction will expedite the patient's progress, whereas the same technique used casually and unenthusiastically may have a minimal effect on the patient. The style of some therapists and their investment in their theories will support or militate against the effective use of any of the methods such as those proposed by Sifneos, Malan, Davanloo, Alexander and French, Lewin, Beck, and others. In summary, at the present stage of our knowledge we cannot be sure that a selected method exists for every patient we treat. Our options must remain open, and we must be willing to change our methods when a selected technique proves to be sterile.

Conclusion

A wide variety of techniques is available to a therapist, their selection being determined by the existing symptoms and complaints of the patient, the familiarity of the therapist with applicable methods, and the patient's willingness and ability to work with the chosen interventions.

Whether we attempt to influence the patient's biochemistry through pharmacotherapy, or his neurophysiology through other somatic therapies or relaxation procedures, or his habit patterns through behavior therapy, or his intrapsychic structure through psychoanalysis, or his interpersonal reactions through group or family therapy, or his social behavior through milieu therapy, or his philosophical outlook through existential therapy, the patient will react globally to our ministrations, every aspect of his being, from physiological makeup to higher psychic processes, being influenced through a feedback effect.

The proper use of techniques calls for a high degree of expertise. Required are qualities in the therapist that permit establishing rapidly a working relationship with the patient, a dealing with motivational deficiencies and other resistances as they develop, and a managing of those personal reactions that are prejudicial to maintaining an objective and empathic therapeutic climate. The atmosphere for the most effective operation of techniques may periodically call for support and reassurance tempered by sufficient maintenance of tension during the interviewing process to promote incentives for exploration and for experimentation with new patterns of behavior. Confrontation may periodically be required to break through resistances to change, but confrontation if used must be carefully titrated against the patient's tolerance of anxiety. Interpretive activites on some level are required, especially when resistance to the therapist, to the therapist's techniques, and to change paralyzes the therapeutic effort. The most effective detecting of and dealing with such resistances necessitates understanding of how to implement dynamic interventions such as the use of dreams and the analysis of transference.

Short-term therapy, even where the methods are supportive or reeducative, as has before been repeatedly emphasized, is much more effective where it is skillfully executed in a psychodynamic framework. No more than a few interviews conducted along dynamic lines may be needed to unbalance the shaky homeostasis that has ruled the patient's existence and to make possible beginning constructive changes in the way that the patient relates to himself and others. Where the individual has been brought to some recognition of the initiating factors precipitating the difficulties for which he sought help, where he becomes cognizant through interviewing of the presence of some pervasive personality problems that sabotage his happiness, where he relates aspects of such problems to his current illness, and where he gains a glimmer of awareness into early sources of difficulty in his relationship with his parents and other significant persons, he will have the best opportunity to proceed beyond the profits of symptom relief.

By pointed questioning the patient is encouraged to put the pieces together for himself, particularly to figure out the circumstances that have impaired his adjustment prior to coming to treatment. There is an exploration as to why the patient is now unable to work out his present difficulty by himself, coming hopefully to a realization of the resistances that prevent a resolution of problems. The patient, encouraged in self-observation, is taught how to relate symptoms to precipitating happenings in the present environment as well as to inner conflicts within himself. What we are trying to do is to mobilize some insight into the underlying difficulties. We must modestly admit that some of the insights we offer the patient are not always complete or even correct. Even though they are partially valid, however, they often serve to alleviate tensions by providing an explanation that may help the process of stabilization.

The nonspecific windfalls of insight do not invalidate the specific profits that can derive from a true understanding of the forces that are undermining security, vitiating self-esteem, and provoking actions inimical to the interests of the individual. In opening up areas for exploration, the short-term therapist must confine himself as closely as possible to observable facts, avoiding speculations as to theory so as to reduce the suggestive component. The more experienced the therapist, the more capable he will be of collating with minimal delay pertinent data—from the patient's verbal content and associations, gestures, facial expressions, hesitations, silences, emotional outbursts, dreams, and interpersonal reactions—toward assumptions that, interpreted to the patient, enable him to reflect on, accept, deny, or resist them. Dealing with the patient's hesitancies to the acceptance of interpretations and to the utilization of his expanded awareness toward actions that may lead to change, the therapist continues to examine his original assumptions and to revise them in terms of any new data that present themselves.

Even though a therapist may utilize a variety of techniques, their employment within a dynamic framework seems to catalyze the therapeutic process. The patient's unique response to the methods employed (interviewing, confrontation, behavior modification, hypnosis, etc.) will almost inevitably expose habitual characterologic styles and perhaps resistances that can become an important focus during treatment. Where the patient manifests a desire to examine his reactions, the results may be particularly gratifying. And where a transference situation can be detected and explored, and its genetic roots understood, an enduring imprint may be etched. The therapist should, therefore, be alerted to any behavior or attitudes that in any way reflect transference. Often such behavior is not manifest and is detected only in dreams and acting-out. Even though time in therapy is short, the therapist, if sufficiently perceptive, will detect some transferential behavior in the way the patient relates to the therapeutic situation, especially if the therapist is active and provocative. And yet in a considerable number of cases the patient may control or mask his transferential responses so that they are not at all apparent. Here, all is not lost; since with the other data available, one may still be able to establish a consociation between the patient's symptoms and complaints, character structure and the genetic roots of the prevailing neurotic needs and defenses. A hopeful prospect is that therapeutic change will not cease at the termination of the short-term contact but will continue the remainder of the individual's life.

CHAPTER 12

The Use of Dreams

The growth of ego psychology and the development of new concepts regarding energy and identity have encouraged minimization of the importance of dreams. Moreover, as we have gained greater understanding of ego dynamisms, we have tended to veer away from the traditional search for latent dream content. This diversion is unfortunate because the average dream embodies a mass of information that, sorted out and selected in relation to the problems being dealt with at the time and the particular goals with which we are immediately concerned, can be of inestimable value in short-term therapy.

Properly utilized, dreams illuminate the existing dynamics of emotional illness. They reveal conflicts, coping mechanisms, defenses, and character traits. Most importantly, they reflect what is going on in and the patient's responses to the therapeutic process. Thus, where therapy is not proceeding well, dreams may reveal more than any other form of communication what resistances are obstructing progress. Even if the therapist does not laboriously work out the meaning with the patient, as in supportive and reeducative therapy, dreams may still provide guidelines for circumventing roadblocks to the most effective use of techniques.

What are dreams? We may conceive of them as images or fantasies that are an intrinsic part of normal sleep. We know from human experiments that dream deprivation (interfering with dreaming by awakening the subject when he shows physiological—REMS—or electroencephalographic evidences of beginning to dream) can produce personality aberrations. We have learned a great deal about dreams from contemporary dream research. The REM periods during sleep that are accompanied by dreaming have been found to be associated with activity in the limbic system, the primitive portion of the brain associated with the emotional life of the individual. This lends emphasis to the theory that the dream is a regressive phenomenon. However, we are merely talking here of the neurophysiological activity that sponsors the formation of dream images, not of their specific content or significance, which may involve other dimensions than regressive emotional ones.

Relaxation of ego controls liberates needs and impulses that, lacking opportunities for motor release, find access in sensory discharge. The content of the dream draws from past impulses, memories, and experiences as far back as early childhood. The conversion of repudiated drives and desires into dream images sets into motion oppositional defenses and prohibitions that may appear in the dream in a direct or masked way. Immediate experiences and current conflicts participate in the structure of the dream. It is likely that a happening in daily life that the individual interprets as significant serves to stir up important needs, frustrations, memories, and drives from the past. The latter, constantly dormant, invest certain immediate experiences with special meaning, alerting the individual to signals that in other persons would go unnoticed.

Some years ago, I initiated a group of experiments in the hypnotic production of dreams. Dreams under hypnosis range from fleeting fantasy-like productions in light trance states to, in deeper stages of hypnosis, highly distorted symbolizations akin to regular dreaming during sleep. I found that hypnotic dreams could easily be triggered by immediate stimuli and that from the content of the dream one could not always identify the specific provocative stimuli that produced the dreams. Thus bringing an open bottle of perfume under the nose of a person in a trance, with no verbal suggestions to influence associations, would in some individuals inspire a dream that revived memories of previous experiences. At different times the same stimulus acted to provoke different kinds of dream content. For example, in one subject the perfume initially touched off a dream of being scolded by a maternal-like figure, the subject crouching in guilt. No other dreams or fantasies were recalled. On rehypnosis the subject was asked to redream the same dream and to reveal it in the trance. She brought up a pleasurable sexual dream, which was followed by a second punitive dream identical to the one previously described during the waking state. Apparently the subject had repressed the initial part in the first trance, denying the content and reprocessing it by elaborating the punishment scene. The punitive dream might be considered equivalent to the manifest content, those manifestations acceptable to the patient. The repressed portion could be regarded as the latent content that the patient could not accept. On another occasion the perfume stimulus created a dream of wandering through a botanical garden.

The mood of a dream also fashions the dream content. An upset patient during hypnosis utilized the sound of a bell that I rang to elaborate a dream of fire and fire engines with reactions of anxiety. At another session, during a quiescent period of this patient's therapy, the same sound produced a dream of worshipping in a church. A disturbed female patient at the beginning of therapy interpreted my touching her hand during hypnosis adversely by dreaming of a man choking her. Later in therapy the same stimulus produced a dream in which her father was embracing her tenderly.

The dream content is additionally subject to changes of attitude on the part of the dreamer. For example, a patient on being asked to bring in dreams responded with the following written comments to this suggestion:

> The doctor requests that I dream. He is interested in helping me, so I better dream. In dreaming I am pleasing his authority, so why should I dream just because he asks me to. He is trying to force me to do what *he* wants. But I want to do what *I* want to do. I may not want to dream. But if I don't bring in a dream, the doctor will be displeased. Should I defy him or should I please him? What will happen if I don't dream? What does he want me to tell him? If I dream and confirm what he has said about me, he will like me. If I dream opposing his ideas about me, he will not like me or he will punish me. If I don't dream or I dream something that opposes his ideas, this will make me feel strong and superior. I do want to find out about myself so I can get well, since my therapist tells me this is how I can help him help me. This is why I should dream. But I am guilty about some things and afraid of some things, and I am afraid of what I will find out about myself if I dream. So maybe I better not dream. Maybe I'll find out something about myself I don't like. It is normal to dream, and I want to be normal. But if I do dream, I have a better chance of getting well, but getting well will throw more responsibility on my shoulders. I'll have to be more independent, take responsibility. Maybe I better not get well so fast. Therefore, I shouldn't dream. Or maybe if I do dream, I can mention only those things that please him and that don't scare me and don't make me get well too fast.

Not all patients are so obsessively stimulated by a casual suggestion. But in all patients the act of dreaming does involve varying motivations that are incorporated in the dream work and fused into a complex kind of symbolism, distorting, repressing, displacing and otherwise disguising the content. What may come through is a compromise of part forgetting and part remembering, of primary and secondary process thinking, of present and past, of impulse and defense.

The Structure of Dreams

The traditional components of a dream are its (1) manifest content, (2) latent content, and (3) dream work. The manifest content is organized in the form of a cryptic language that requires translation before its true meaning can be comprehended. The latent content embodies conscious, preconscious, and unconscious elements reflective of both past and present impressions. The bricks and mortar of the dream are what Freud described as the "dream work," which defies the laws of rationality and logic. The chaotic upsurge of excitation characteristic of regressive primary process mental operations makes for a tumultuous and bizarre fusion of emotions, symbolic forms, and time sequences. Operative are mechanisms of condensation and displacement. In condensation, characteristics of multiple objects are combined into a composite symbolic entity. A single image may embrace so many complex formulations that a good deal of searching may be required to reveal the great variety of imbedded meanings. In displacement energy inherent in one idea is transferred over to another. This may take the form of projecting feelings and actions from significant objects or areas to seemingly innocuous ones, and from whole to partial areas. What results is considerable distortion, which is particularly prominent in the phenomenon of representation by opposites wherein there is a reversal of the true meaning of the dream. Thus action of a kindly and concerned nature in a dream may conceal murderous intent. The individual often employs disguised symbols of himself in dreams, clues to his identity becoming apparent only in his associations to the dreams. Symbolism contributes to the rich and often bizarre nature of dream structure. An understanding of the dreamer, his problems, and the way that he conceptualizes is usually mandatory for a translation of the symbols. The use of pictorial metaphors and the employment of secondary revision are modes employed by the ego to make unconscious and repudiated elements acceptable to the dreamer.

Symbolism is an unconscious process organized around association and similarity whereby one object comes to represent another object through some quality or aspect that the two have in common. In symbolism abstract and complex ideas are expressed in sensorial and concrete terms. Sometimes the dream symbols are recruited from the cultural and social world that envelops the dreamer. At other times the kinds of representations draw from primitive language forms in which oral, excretory, and phallic components are prominent. These symbols, actual or disguised, portray incorporation, power, punishment, and annihilation meanings. A fear of snakes or daggers may accordingly be a symbol for a wish for an intact penis or penal penetration. Terror of being bitten by animals may disguise in infantile impulse to devour the mother or her breast. Delusions, hallucinations, obsessions, compulsions, phobias, hysterical conversions, morbid affects, hypochondrias, and personalization of organs or organ systems are often explicable by considering their symbolic connotations. Similarly in dreams.

Because the dream is a condensation of a host of life experiences, past and present, because it contains unconscious components, defenses, character drives in operation, and approving and condemnatory attitudes of authority (superego), a selection of areas pertinent to the immediate goals of the therapist would seem to be in order. This does not mean that we are always able to track down the essential meaning of every dream, for many of them are so spottily remembered or so highly distorted that, with all of our analytic expertise, we may be unable to understand them.

Generally, we deal with the manifest content, which reflects the problem-solving activities of the ego or self system. A study of the manifest content will generally reveal a good deal about the defensive integrity of the ego, and specifically about the coping mechanisms the dreamer habitually employs or latently wishes to employ for purposes of problem solving in general and specifically for the problem prevalent at the time. Not only does the dream give insights into the defensive structure and unconscious needs of the dreamer, it also throws light on the contemporary social realities that precipitated the problem for which help is being sought. The individual may have rationalized social distortions by subtle psychological mechanisms of self-deception or philosophical camouflage. The scotoma that cloud perception of what is going on in the environment may lift somewhat during dreaming. This awareness may, however, be masked by converting social symbols into personal symbols. The latent content of the dream may in addition to unconscious conflicts refer to social conflicts that the individual may have been unable to process and resolve readily in his waking life. Proper interpretation can force on the individual clearer understanding of the social and environmental realities with which he must deal.

Techniques of Dream Interpretation

How dreams are used in therapy will vary among different therapists. It generally suffices to ask the patient to remember and bring in any dreams. Where the patient forgets his dreams, he may be enjoined to keep a pad of paper and a pencil near the head of the bed and to record the dream when awakening. Dreams are usually freshest in mind before the day's activities crowd out memories. If there are no dreams, resistance may be operating since it is normal to dream several times during sleep. Some therapists attempt to stimulate their dreamless patients through hypnosis during which it is suggested that the patient be able to recall important dreams. Fantasies and dreams may also be stimulated during the trance state itself and discussed if desired during or after the hypnotic session.

Because the dream embodies so much material, therapists generally select aspects for discussion that accord with what they are trying to emphasize at a specific session: inculcation of insight, confirmation of a hypothesis, probing of past traumatic events and memories, defensive operations, transference manifestations, resistances to the therapist and to the techniques, fears of utilizing insight in the direction of change, and so forth. Sometimes a therapist will merely listen to a dream for his own information; at other times interpretations are given the patient. In advance of this the patient is asked for associations to a dream and for formulation of impressions about it. Many patients rapidly become skilled at understanding the meaning of their dreams. To facilitate associations, some therapists summarize the dream events and ask the patient specific questions in relation to people and incidents in the dream. Dreaming about different people is occasionally a way of representing different aspects of oneself. The therapist, if the meaning of the dream is not clear, may ask about the setting of the dream. Does the patient recognize it? Is it in the past or present? Does it have any significance for the patient? Do the characters in the dream have any meaning for or relationship to the dreamer? Do any of the characters represent the patient's parents, or the therapist, or oneself? Are any underlying wishes or needs apparent? What personality traits are revealed in the characters? What mechanisms of defense are displayed—flight, aggression, masochism, hypochondriacal preoccupation? What conflicts are apparent? What is the movement in and the outcome of the dream incidents?

Therapists interpret dreams in line with their theoretical persuasions, some treating a dream like a Rorschach, projecting into it their own special fantasies. While this may be effective for highly skilled, experienced, and intuitive professionals, it is better for most therapists to work out the meaning together with the patient. It is a poor tactic to interpret dogmatically the latent content of the initial dreams revealed by a patient. First, the therapist does not know enough about the patient and the operative defenses. Second, to penetrate into the unconscious prematurely will merely promote greater repression of and distortion in later dreams as a way of avoiding anxiety. One may, however, productively search for current reality reactions (for example, resistances to the therapist or to the techniques; fears, or misinterpretations the patient may harbor about therapy) or for bizarre hopes and expectations that could result in a defeat of the therapeutic attempt. Or character drives may advantageously be explored as they exhibit themselves in the dream, provided that the patient is already aware of these.

Resistance is apt to occur as the treatment process proceeds. It may appear in relation to the setting up of the working relationship at the start of treatment, to the exploration of the dynamics of the inherent neurotic process, to the putting into action of insight, and, finally, to the termination of therapy. Manifestations of resistance may first appear in dream structure. The dream provides a great opportunity to deal with it before it becomes an irreparable obstacle to treatment. Of confounding concern, however, is the employment of dreaming itself as a form of resistance as the patient becomes aware of the importance of dreams. He may thus use dreaming as an outlet to frustrate or impede the therapist. The patient here may dream incessantly and try to flood the therapeutic hour with an avalanche of dreams, or he may unconsciously elaborate the symbolism of the dream as a way to confuse the therapist and to divert from central issues. Some patients bring in pages of written dreams, which may overwhelm the therapist, and this may be one way of avoiding dealing with reality problems. These resistances should be interpreted.

Of vital importance are the revelations in dreams of transference in which impulses, experiences, and defenses in relationship to important past personages are revived through the agency of the therapist. A wealth of information can be exposed in such dreams, and opportunities are afforded the patient and therapist for understanding of how early attitudes and patterns disturb the patient's present existence. This provides a means to work through transference distortions. In the process of interpreting transference, one must always search for reality provocations that are initiated by the therapist personally. The way transference in dreams is handled will depend on when it appears and its function as resistance. A demand for infantile gratification in terms of complete givingness, lovingness, and understandingness, an expectation of hurt and condemnation for the revelation or expression of impulses of which the patient is ashamed, can serve as blocks to therapeutic progress. Such demands and expectations will require careful interpretation. On the other hand, a delving into genetic foci, into important early formative experiences, if employed at all, may require tact and great patience. Premature or too forceful interpretations may do more harm than good.

One of the ways that the dream can help the therapeutic process is by revealing signals of anxiety before it becomes too intense and interferes with therapy. Where the dream brings out anxiety in relation to important incidents, past or present, it may be possible to help the patient endure it enough to avoid the upsurge of too great resistance.

Often the dream will reveal the nascent drives that marshall anxiety. These may be imbedded in a pregenital fusion of sexuality and aggression. Their emergence in symptoms and in acting-out tendencies may be responsible for the patient's current difficulties as well as for a pervasive inhibition of function and other ego defenses. The studied interpretation of dream elements will do much toward clarifying the punishing and masochistic reprisals of the superego. By ferreting out projective, denial, isolating, and repressive defenses, as they come out in the dream work, one may occasionally liberate early memories that concern themselves with the fantasies or actual experiences associated with the patient's sadistic and masochistic maneuvers. Obviously, the interpretations proferred must take into account the patient's readiness for change and the intensity of anxiety. Above all, the manner of interpretation serves as an important factor in helping or retarding the patient in accepting and integrating the significance of the dreams.

Case Illustrations

Case 1

Sometimes a patient will present a long complex dream that crystallizes an awareness in symbolic terms of feelings that are being shielded from oneself. Often, as is brought out in the session that follows, the repressing agent is guilt. Because the feelings are not being acknowledged, they may be converted into symptoms—physical symptoms as in conversion reactions, self-castigation and remorse as in reactive depressions, and fears as in phobic reactions. During therapy with empathic, encouraging, nonjudgmental therapists, patients may come to grips with their guilt and begin accepting their right to express feelings. Such was the case in my patient, a married woman of 40, sent to me by a general practitioner who could find no organic reason for the leg pains and difficulties in walking for which the patient had consulted him. After referring the patient to a neurologist and an orthopedic surgeon, who similarly could find no organic basis for her complaints, the practitioner advised the patient to receive psychological help. She accepted his advice readily and during the initial interview we decided on a short-term program.

A working alliance was readily achieved, and the patient spoke freely about her early relationship difficulties, but she could seem to find little wrong with her present situation except for a feeling of detachment from her husband, a man eight years younger than herself about whom she spoke little at first. She was, she admitted, not truly happy with her relationship, but it was tolerable and she did not believe she was too affected by it. It was better, she said, than her first marriage to an authoritative man who kept her down and minimized her abilities, criticizing her incessantly. She chose her present husband because he was gentle, noncompetitive, and easy to get along with. But, for some reason she was not happy. Her leg symptoms started after the marriage, but the patient could see no connection between the two. With the patient's permission, I interviewed her husband. He gave me some primitive, disorganized, contaminated responses to the Rorschach cards. Clinically, he impressed me as being at least borderline but probably schizophrenic.

My patient, an extremely capable and intelligent woman, rapidly caught on to what a dynamic approach was all about. There were, however, no dreams, even though I constantly reminded her of the need to report dreams to me. I kept focusing on her relationship with her husband and encouraged her to begin to come to grips with her disappointment in him. I insisted that she work on her leg symptoms, saying that they had something to do with the way she felt. Two sessions prior to the present one, she was finally able to articulate her anger at her husband and even some hatred toward him. She noticed that her awareness of her anger tended to relieve her leg symptom. The breakthrough of these emotions, I felt, inspired dreams that convinced her of the depths of her hostility toward her husband, the relationship of this hostility to her leg symptoms, and the need to do something about her marriage. The session that follows is the seventh.

Pt. I've decided that I've gotten myself in a bad situation. (*pause*)

Th. It's a situation you've been in or one you've gotten yourself into recently?

Pt. What I've gotten myself into, and I try to act nice, but so help me God I cannot say: "Well, look sweetie [*to Alfred her husband*] I love you, and we'll work this thing out." I can't do it. I'm nice to him, but it's a very impersonal "nice," and, of course, I'm terribly aware of it. I don't know how where he is, and again I may project and I'm more aware than he is. I try to do things that he wants done and so forth, the best I can, but it's hell. Brother, do I give myself the business! You talk about symptoms, then do I get them!

Th. Then you get them after that. How do you make the connection then? What happens to you?

Pt. Oh, then that's when I feel guilty. I feel so terribly guilty. I still do today. (*pause*)

Th. You feel evidence of guilt connected—connected to what?

Pt. The way I react to Alfred's illness and personality.

Th. And how does the guilt reflect itself in symptoms?

Pt. Feet and legs always. Well, not always, but mostly I get there.

Th. How do they seem now? Feet and legs.

Pt. Very bad.

Th. They do?

Pt. Today they're bad.

Th. You connect it up with your guilt feelings toward Alfred then.

Pt. Well, that's what I connect up with, but I can be wrong about that too, because in similar circumstances I usually get the same thing. But yet I know what I'm doing, so I don't feel as depressed. I don't have the depression that sometimes comes with it.

Th. The knowledge of what you are doing does that help lift the symptoms too?

Pt. Not so far. At least not immediately. I think it does after a while.

Th. How long?

Pt. Well, maybe 24 hours.

Th. And after 24 hours what do you notice?

Pt. Well, then I don't have the symptoms.

Th. And then you don't think about them.

Pt. That's right, but not immediately. Immediately knowing does not immediately relieve the symptoms, but immediately getting the reaction—whatever this thing is, this guilt thing or which is combined with superego and blah, blah, blah, but let's call it guilt—that will do. I immediately get symptoms. I get symptoms fast, but immediately knowing why I'm getting them is not immediately relieving. They don't cut off that fast.

Th. Yes.

Pt. Well, they're cut off in a hurry in this way. Probably tomorrow morning when I wake up, I won't have them—but that would be a period of 24 hours after I know what I'm doing. But you see, this terrific thing of hate this week. I can scarcely be in the same room with him. It's colossal, and I had it yesterday and it's all I can do to be decent. It is a superhuman effort.

Th. Have you noticed that the hate has been piling up on the surface more and more?

Pt. Sure, sure.

Th. There was a time when you didn't have any hate for him at all.

Pt. Oh, but you know that, yes. You see now, it gets closer and closer to the surface, and it's just almost physically impossible to control it.

Th. What do you feel like doing when you get this thing, this feeling?

Pt. Well, it's a peculiar thing, I would like to make him inanimate. I said the other day, to put him in his place, I would like to make him nonfunctional so that he couldn't bother me at all. The only reason I wouldn't want to kill him is because I know that that would be on my conscience. But I'd like to hit him physically at times. I look and lie in bed and I loathe him, oh, loathe him. Well, anyway, we'll quit this and go on to something else. Sort of the same subject. It's very interesting. Last night when I went to bed early and I consciously thought to myself, all right now, this leg department, because this thing kept mounting yesterday, you see.

Th. You noticed that the symptoms began piling up?

Pt. Worser and worser, and I'm going to dream what the hell is really wrong with my legs. Unconsciously I must know what the hell is going on; now I'm going to dream. My dream is the most fabulous thing you heard in your life. Wait until you hear. You better record this—uh, I wrote it in the dark. I think I can recall it, and then I'll go and check it and see if I'm right.

Th. All right.

Pt. I dreamed that I was in a bedroom and two women were in the room with me. Now they seemed to be in some capacity like a maid and a friend, or something like that—rather impersonal capacity—but they were there. And it was all very friendly, and I forget what we were doing, whether we were getting clothes ready to wear or something. But it was all a very pleasant atmosphere. And all of a sudden I saw this very strange little creature—animals again—about this big (*spreads fingers apart about 5 inches*), and it was a creature like I had never seen before, and it was sort of trying to get up my desk. There was a desk on the opposite wall and it was trying to get up on my desk. It could move somewhat like a squirrel or like a monkey, and I said, "Look at that thing—what is it?" And one of the women said, "Golly, I don't know what it is." "Well," I said, "that's the strangest creature I had ever seen." The other one said, "It looks like a bat, but it can't fly, it looks like a bat." And I said, "I don't want to see that thing, it is so odd." Then I sort of lay over. I was sitting up on top of the bed like I do so often—and then I sort of lay over there and I knew the creature was coming around. It came over the bed toward me and, Oh God, it was sort of a marked fear and a certain shudder. And one of the women said to me, "Well, you always said you weren't afraid of rodents." Of course, I'm not, for a long time I'm not afraid of rodents. And this little creature came over and got on me. It was only about so big—it had brown and white spots, not polka dots but mottled.

Th. Yes.

Pt. And it had arms and legs like a spider monkey. You know what a spider monkey is; its arms and legs are too long for it and very agile, and its nose and its head, well they looked like a frog. There was no differentiation between the head and the body, and its face looked somewhat froglike in that its face was flat and its snoot was square. It didn't have the face of a monkey at all, but I decided it belonged to the monkey family because of its movements. And let me see—something came in there between—oh, yes, some of the words I got were terrific. So I turned to one of the women and said, "I wonder what this thing is—and sitting up there on my shoulder." I wasn't frightened of it, but I didn't like it. I had no feeling of petting it.

Th. Yes.

Pt. You know my usual reaction about all animals. I mean if it's a cat, or a dog, or a horse, or a white mouse, or a guinea pig, or a rabbit—makes no difference to me—I would pet it. But this creature didn't particularly frighten me. I didn't have a feeling that it was a spider in the sense of my horrible feeling about insects, but I didn't want to touch it. It was just there.

Th. Uh-huh.

Pt. So this one woman said, "I wonder what it is." And she said, "It looks like an emu."

Th. An emu?

Pt. What she thought an emu is—soft American goat I think it is, I didn't look this up. I said, "No, it's an anus."

Th. It's an anus.

Pt. And then I said it was in the monkey family. So then it came over and it got on my right breast, and it jumped up and down like monkeys jump up and down and chattered, just chattered. Well, then the dream faded. And on the following day I'm on the same bed and talking on the telephone to my mother. I told her about this strange creature, and I thought about it and wondered what happened to it. It was there, I wonder what happened. I've got to find out what happened. It must be here in the house somewhere. So the maid said, "It's behind the door." So I got up and went over and behind the bedroom door—this all happened in the bedroom—this all happened in the bedroom—behind the bedroom door is this anus, I called it, folded up like a frog might fold up. Only the frog, I've never seen one that did, but they would be able to—folded up like this. Leaning up against the wall and next to it is a little anus. During the night it had had a baby. So I got off the telephone and took the two—they had awakened up and unfolded. The big anus immediately got over on my right breast and started jumping up and chittering and chattering, and the little one exactly the same was over here on this shoulder jumping up and down and chittering and chattering. And I was quite intrigued that this anus one day old could chitter. It had learned so fast. And I thought, my God, these things must reproduce, but with terrific rapidity. This would be awful, the whole house would be full. I've got to do something. And being as I don't dislike it and I hate killing creatures, what am I going to do? What was I going to do? And then my feelings, my emotional feelings were the thing in this dream, because usually I don't realize them so much, but I did in this. In looking for the anus, the combination of not wanting to see it but wanting to know where it was, and then my terrific feeling against killing any creature—any animal—or doing away with an animal. And I got this thing, and, of course, the baby of any animal is always cute. I don't care what it is, I got the thing, and I thought by golly the only thing to do is I have to dispose of one of them. Now I have to find out which one is the one that bears, which one is female, or whether they're both female or whether they're both male. Of course, that got mixed up there, but anyways one of them must have given birth to the other one. Maybe the big one was pregnant when it came into the room yesterday, which now should be logical, but I know that all animals do not mind incest. So, therefore, if this little one that she's had is a son, then at a given length of time whatever their period would be, why I'd have a lot more anuses around the house.

Th. The son would have relations with the mother? [*What the patient is implying is that her own relationship with her husband, symbolized by the monkey creature, is incestuous.*]

Pt. The son would have relations with the mother. Is this a lily? (*laughing*) And so I thought I'll see if I'm right now. So I started examining them, and they had no sexual organs at all. They were just in the light as silver dollars—they were the same on both ends except one end opened, which was obviously a mouth. They had no tails. They had these legs, so I gave that deal up and thought the god damned things don't have any sex. What am I going to do now, because I didn't want to kill both of them. I had this thing, and I didn't know what to do with it. Then something I missed in there was when I first asked what that thing was, and this is going way back, was that one of the women said, "I don't know what it is, but I always stay away from things that I don't know what they are." Then the two anuses (*laughing*) kept jumping up and down and chittering and chattering at me and chittering and chattering and that was the end of the dream.

Th. And that was the end of the dream. You were upset with both of them?

Pt. I was rather upset, but I wouldn't face this even in my dream; I was revolted with both of them or I was revolted with the idea of killing both because there was no way to determine whether or not they could conceive or produce maybe thousands of these little creatures. (*pause*)

Th. Well, that's rather an interesting dream.

Pt. And the fact that I let them jump up and down on me, I let them chatter at me. And it was interesting that they were very peculiar creatures that have never been seen the like of on this earth. But I did not want to touch them or pet them or fondle them, which I do all creatures. So if that isn't something, so that is the answer to what is wrong with my feet. Now you take it from there (*laughing*).

Th. You've thrown it my way.

Pt. (*laughing*)

Th. (*laughing*) Now where do the feet come into the picture? What do you make out of the dream incidentally?

Pt. Now, of course, that is Alfred. How in God's world I could ever. . . . In my conscious mind I could never get the attributes together that I really feel about him and put them in words—never—so practically completely in the dream.

Th. As you did in representing him as an anus. All right, what are your associations with that creature? What does that creature have that Alfred has?

Pt. Long arms and legs—monkeylike from the monkey family. I've always thought that Alfred was a rather queer-looking person. And I've often thought he looked rather froglike because of this great wide jaw and pop eyes. So I had this square nose on this creature. When I first see him, I don't know what it is. He's a hybrid of some type. The creature can't talk, chatters all the time and can't talk which is one of the things that aggravates me about Alfred.

Th. He chatters?

Pt. He chatters all the time, but he can't talk and jumps up and down on me.

Th. Is that what Alfred does?

Pt. Yes, I think so; it is the way I feel about what he does I'm telling you about.

Th. You also brought up from time to time that he's quite hairy.

Pt. Hairy? I could just simply fix him up for good.

Th. What about?

Pt. Then he's completely sexless.

Th. Sexless?

Pt. He wasn't male or female. I couldn't find out what he was; I looked him over and I couldn't find out what he was.

Th. That represents how you feel about Alfred? That's a pretty good description of how you feel about him?

Pt. Yeah, I don't think there's any doubt of it. When I woke up I thought, my God, that's a picture of Alfred and I couldn't believe it. Brown and white mottled. If you've ever noticed, people have colors to me. Now you're grey, and Alfred is brown, which might also cover the anus department, you see (*laughing*).

Th. Brown?

Pt. He's what I call a brown person. You're a grey person. Some people are pink people, and so forth. That may be a little farfetched, but I've always regarded people that way.

Th. Also you feel as if you are stuck with Alfred, the way you were stuck with these animals.

Pt. Yeah, I couldn't kill them. I was afraid there might get more of them, which would be terrible. He was dragging down on my breasts, which would mean put me in the mother role. In a way Alfred chatters exactly like monkeys. The monkeys chatter and climb over things and jump up and down, and these creatures had no tails. (*laughing*)

Th. Well, now how can you utilize this dream constructively for yourself? What does this explain to you that you could use in a constructive way?

Pt. Well, it explained this much to me: that as long as I feel this way about Alfred, which is the most graphic thing I've had—which doesn't necessarily say he's like that but I feel that way about him—I better do something about it.

Th. Well, how does that tie in with your legs?

Pt. Well, the way I find it—and maybe I'm fantastic on this and I wish you'd tell me (*laughing*). I tie it in with my leg symptoms because they arrived immediately upon marrying Alfred. So it makes some sense when I said to myself very powerfully last night before I went to sleep—because it was early and I hadn't had but a couple of drinks during the evening, one as a matter of fact—before I went to bed. I said I'm going to dream about this leg thing. What does give me these symptoms because I noticed the whole thing mount yesterday, particularly when I was kind of disgusted with the whole idea that he didn't go to work on Tuesday. Well, yesterday morning when he wakened up and saw that I was more disgusted than ever, I just thought I'll see if the old unconscious will unbutton by dreaming.

Th. Apparently it came through.

Pt. It did (*laughing*), and that's how I connect the leg symptoms with Alfred because if I had had the leg symptoms before I married Alfred, I wouldn't say that. That wouldn't make too good sense, but I got them immediately after marrying him. When I say immediately, I say within 4 weeks, and I never had trouble with my legs before. I danced, I walked, I'd done everything. And I've never been without trouble since the marriage.

Th. It sounds very suspicious.

Pt. It sounds more than suspicious doesn't it? And this dream was so vivid.

Th. It sounds very, very suspicious as if you've been living with it really.

Pt. This is my bedroom, in back of the door, and I had the feeling that I must know where it is a menace. It has a menacing quality, and yet I wasn't afraid of it from the standpoint of getting stunned.

Th. What do you think has tied you down to him, while really feeling this way about him as you obviously have felt? What has tied you down to him? You don't feel any differently toward him now than you did before for a long time, do you? At least you're more conscious of certain feelings.

Pt. I'm more conscious of them, and I suppose I don't feel any different, but I couldn't admit it to myself.

Th. But how come you are tied down with him for so long—3 years? That is a long time . . . to live with a monkey named anus.

Pt. I really think that's a quite brilliant dream

myself (*laughing*). I had to laugh the minute I realized what I had dreamed, and then I felt terribly guilty.

Th. Did you?

Pt. Yes, of course, the reason I've lived with him all these years is just that—guilt—that's the whole thing. I felt terribly guilty, and that's why my legs are bad.

Th. If you live with a person on the basis of guilt, what do you feel about yourself for doing a thing like that?

Pt. Well, you see, that I haven't disentangled myself yet.

Th. But if on the basis of guilt, you live with somebody, what do you feel might happen in your self evaluation, in your attitudes toward yourself? [*I feel I can use confrontation to challenge her defenses since she appears to have fairly good insight into what is happening. Also we have a good working relationship and she wouldn't feel I was putting her down.*]

Pt. Depreciation.

Th. Self-depreciation. How can you respect yourself under those circumstances? Wouldn't it be expecting the impossible of yourself? And then what would you do if you didn't respect yourself? There would be ways of covering yourself under the circumstances wouldn't there?

Pt. Yeah.

Th. Not being able to express hostility, what have you been doing with it?

Pt. Knocking the hell out of myself (*laughing*). [*Her laughter is actually a self-conscious defensive maneuver. It conceals a great deal of misery and self-concern.*]

Th. You mean you're an expert on punishing yourself, aren't you?

Pt. I'm an expert on hostility and what to do with it. Well, that's the story as plain as the nose on your face, and I can see it. I'm still reacting to it, but I can still see it.

Th. All right, the potentialities for doing something about it positively are limited to a number of things. One, either you're projecting into him attitudes and feelings that you have toward men in general, or toward certain men; or, two, he's a special kind of person whom you married on a fluke and therefore you're responding to him as a special kind of person. Three, there's a possibility you may feel that he may develop, he may change, and this may justify to yourself your living with him; or four, you could leave him, period. Are there any other possibilities you can think of?

Pt. No. Well, one, I may project some, I don't project completely because we know that he was a special kind of creature. Two, I married him on a fluke in an attempt to run away from my own superego thinking if I got away from control or anything representing a parent, I wouldn't feel the way I did, and suffer the way I did. So I chose a weak man, one who wouldn't control me.

Th. In other words, if you didn't marry your parent this time, like you did your previous husband, you'd be in control of the situation. You'd be able to manipulate and handle the situation.

Pt. Three, I was normal enough apparently to make some attempt at adjusting Alfred to some sense of normality otherwise I wouldn't have worked so hard on him. I didn't know that at the time, but I must have had a very strong drive, or, believe me, I wouldn't have put in the effort and time that I did in trying to make some sort of a man out of him.

Th. Well, what sort of a job have you done with that?

Pt. I have come to the conclusion that anybody, including you, could completely waste your time in trying to adjust a homosexual to normality. I do not think it is possible.

Th. You think all the effort you have made toward adjusting him to a heterosexual life has gone to waste?

Pt. I think I probably feel more strongly than that in the case of Alfred, because he was able to make a better adjustment probably than 9 out of 10, and it leaves him being nothing. God, the homosexuals that I know, and I know plenty of them, they are homosexuals and they love the fact that I'm a girl, and I love it. And they are better adjusted people than Alfred or the other boys that I have seen and have gotten married. Some of them had one child. Jesus, they get themselves into a thing where they never get themselves out of it.

Th. In what way?

Pt. They are nothing. They never become heterosexual—they don't. And if they do, they must be hanging in the Hall of Fame, because there aren't many of them. Alfred is not heterosexual, but neither are the homosexuals, and my guy can't accommodate himself to anything. We never have sex.

Th. He's neuter?

Pt. He becomes neuter.

Th. Just like that monkey.

Pt. Yeah, honestly, that's what I think today. Ask me another day, and I might have another idea. I don't think so—I've watched, so I guess that's one place my guilt feeling arrives.

Th. That you've taken him away from homosexual life?

Pt. I've taken him away from something that he obviously enjoyed. And the way he earns his living, it isn't looked down on too much. [*Alfred is a window designer.*] Most of them are—they have a terrific time. They have a lousy old age—that's true. When they get to be old, they have these—why it's pretty bad, but even that they adjust to. A bunch of them get old together. So what, they just don't grow up in one area, so they don't grow up in it. Or they're artists or singers, or they accommodate themselves to the feminine part of their nature. Why, they have a pretty good life. Only when they get so that they realize that they aren't living a full life that they suffer so damned much, and I think that's where I feel guilty about Alfred, I really do.

Th. You kind of feel that you weaned him away from that group and that he can't go back to it.

Pt. He'll go back, but that will be as much an adjustment as it was to adjust to a heterosexual situation. And with it he will have hellish guilt because he will know there's something better, because he will have glimpsed it. I think homosexuals—their mothers should be strangled point number one—they should be let alone—I'm speaking now not of kids in their young teens, but I'm talking about guys who get to be 25 and 28 and their pattern is pretty well set. It's a peculiar thing. I have them around the house all the time and I'm fairly observant; I can't help but be. It's a peculiar thing. It's true even with Alfred, and I know another one who had a similar experience—that's George who is married and has a child. He went back to homosexuality. George called me this morning, and I had a long talk with him. Nice guy, maladjusted as hell to every part of life. You get them in a room with other homosexuals, and the roving eye is really something. They can't help it; it's part of them—anymore than I can put Tiger, my male dog, with a little female dog and expect him to sit and look at her. I'm sitting and telling you about psychiatry. I love this. Anyway, it's my observation—see, you asked me what I've done to Alfred. See, that's what I think I've done, and that's why I feel so goddamned guilty about leaving him. You wanted to know why I didn't leave him earlier.

Th. It's quite possible that your guilt has been such that you felt it would practically kill him to leave him, and you know that he is a rather unstable person. He's unstable, and there is no telling what may happen in him whether you live with him or not.

Pt. My living with him, I've come to realize that now, my living with him will not prevent it, but I didn't realize that before.

Th. In other words, you're just not going to save him. If the process within him is a destructive one, it may defy anybody's ability to help him. On the other hand, you may want to handle whatever you decide to do in a careful way with him.

Pt. That's what will have to be because I don't think I know this, but it is something I feel intuitive about, if you believe in intuition. There have been a few times in my life with Alfred when I have seen him walk away from himself. That is the only way I can put it. Now he was starting to walk away from himself before he came up to see you yesterday—as if he wasn't here.

Th. That's sort of a psychotic-like retreat.

Pt. He gets what I call "over the border." (*pause*)

Th. Over the border?

Pt. Some damned thing that he will walk away from himself is the only way I can put it. He's not there—and that scares the hell out of me. Of course, I connect it with something I've done to him. Now, that may be very neurotic, but I apparently connect it with what I've done.

Th. Well, you happen to be the person he's living with now, and consequently his experiences with you can act as a trigger. But if it weren't you, it might be something else.

Pt. I realize that now, but I still blame myself on that score.

Th. Well, do you blame yourself so much that it's going to paralyze yourself from doing what you think is the best for you?

Pt. No, no, it's not going to stop me.

Th. What would be the best thing to do?

Pt. The best thing for me to do is to leave him, I'm sure of that. I don't know how the hell I'm going to do it right this minute. As you know what kind of spot I've gotten myself into financially.

Th. Financial circumstances are certainly such that you wouldn't want to do anything until you were more self-sufficient and secure?

Pt. That's right. Well, I can't, I don't know how to do it. So I've got myself in that kind of spot, and I think I feel guilty about that—getting myself in that kind of spot. But after marrying him I wanted to go down the road to destruction, and I played every card in such a manner that I did. Now, I don't feel that way about it anymore, and I can see what I've been doing to myself. But it lasted sufficiently until I was in physical pain. How I feel guilty that Alfred has to spend every cent he makes on me, which I know rationally I shouldn't because God knows he had the advantage of all the money I had for many years before our marriage. So he puts in a few months of forking up the dough and I don't see why I should feel too badly about it. But being the kind of creature I am, I act that way. I don't see anything to do except to wait until I can feel not even sure, but just even partly sure that what I'm working on now will have some merit.

Th. In terms of finances you mean?

Pt. That's right, I mean finances. If I find that it has even some merit—a limited merit—living alone, I can live on very little—why I would take the plunge then.

Th. You would?

Pt. Oh yes, I would. I really would because I don't think, I don't feel there is any foundation to build on for the two of us at all. I think it would be a crutch department from here on out for both of us. And if he's ever going to make anything of his life one way or the other—whichever way he decides to go it's high goddamn time he starts.

Th. Virtually, you know the character of his relationship with you.

Pt. The son and I'm the mother.

Th. He's the son, and the attitude and feeling he has toward you is as if you *are* his mother. Do you believe that?

Pt. That's why he vacillates so terrifically from this terrific love to just loathing me.

Th. And you're kind of fed up with that deal—you don't want to be his mother.

Pt. It's no decent relationship—if I'm going to be his mother I might as well really act like his mother (*laughing*). Right? It's just no good. So I can see the pattern cut out for what I have to do, and I'd rather stop beating myself on the head.

Th. Beating yourself on the feet.

Pt. During the time period that I have to go through to do it, that is something we can work out a little bit.

Th. And your own feelings about leaving him too.

Pt. That's beating myself on the feet, the guilt thing. And I don't quite know how to act with Alfred in that if I let my aggressive feelings come out, it would probably come out way overboard anyway. I've held them in a long time. I'm afraid I might do something awful to him so I keep sort of pretending around the house about this and that, and he'll say, "Oh, I love you so much." And I don't know what the hell to say to that—I mean I don't know—because what I say doesn't have any ring of truth, and that itself keeps me in an uproar. I get various reactions from it. Sometimes I shut up from anxiety. I feel very sorry, and then I look at him and think how in the hell I couldn't see it before. Now I see, I mean really see. Now little things like this are ridiculous, but they show how hard I react. We have this bed which is fixed just like your couch—it's got a back like this. It's a lounge. The bedroom is not fixed up like a bedroom; it's fixed up as another room. We sleep there and watch TV or read with our feet outstretched against this thing on my side, and he has his side. Alfred will never sit up straight in this thing; he will always lean over as close to me as he can get. My reaction is to take him and shove him away. When he gets in bed, he never lies straight he curves toward me and it just aggravates me.

Th. It does?

Pt. Sure, it aggravates the hell out of me.

Th. You don't want any monkeys jumping up and down on you.

Pt. (*laughing*) I don't want any spider monkeys

jumping up and down on me, anuses (*laughing*) in other words.

Case 2

One of the most difficult patients I have ever treated was a young college student who went into a negative transference even before she saw me at the first visit. A severe phobic reaction motivated her to seek help, but upon making the appointment she began to fantasy my forcing her to perform against her will. Sensing her resistance during the first session, I said, "I get the impression you find it hard to talk because you are afraid of my reactions." To this remark she exploded, "I feel people have no respect for me, if I show weakness especially. I'm getting angry at you. I think you get some satisfaction about humiliating me. Like my parents, my father especially. He gets some kind of thrill out of criticizing me. I think they say, "You are shy, weak. You are embarrassed. Get up there and perform and we'll watch!" But I feel so humiliated. My whole life is spent saving face. I never let them know. They always try to shame me." My reply was to the effect that she did not think I could accept her as she was with all her faults and problems. "How could you," she retorted. The problem really was, I countered, that she could not accept herself and therefore projected this feeling onto me. With this the patient stormed out of the room. She returned, nevertheless, for her next session, and she continued to upbraid and attack me. At the twelfth session she presented this dream which indicated the beginning of resolution of her negative transference.

Pt. I was coming back from a long trip during the summer. I had been hitchhiking. I talked to people and felt discouraged. Instead of engaging in normal activities, I withdrew and said I was dead, contrary to appearances. However, I saw a tall man with a moustache, and I began to assault him verbally. I said he was dictatorial like a Nazi in dealing with me. He had been oppressing me even though he was a stranger. After a few minutes of this, I got a sudden new idea largely because this man responded sympathetically. I felt I wasn't really dead, but suffered amnesia. I was extremely happy. I realized my disappearance for 2 to 3 months was that I was in amnesia, not dead. I started to tell people I had a weird experience in which I thought I was dead. I thought it was an amazing thing—bizarre and weird. I felt I was an expert on conformity, but I had just acted as a conformist in an unusual way. I had been submissive even though I knew all about what made for conformity. But I was happy about this, to realize that I felt discouraged because I felt nobody cared about me.

In her associations she said that being away was like nobody cared for her. As a child she felt this, and she was surprised when she had been away for 2 or 3 hours to discover that her mother and father had been worried. All of her life she had felt like a strange abnormal person, and this was like being dead. The tall man with the moustache was like her father when she was 6 or 7. "I remember accusing my father of indifference or dislike, of wanting to hurt me. He gradually convinced me I was wrong. I got a sudden feeling you are like my father."

Case 3

Frequently the transference elements are not as clearly obvious as they were in the foregoing dream, the identification of the theraist being more highly symbolized. The therapist who is on the watch for transference resistance will be alerted to translate dream symbols that forecast stormy weather ahead. Patients who have some psychological knowledge, or who have read psychological books, or who have had some therapy are often able to decode the disguised symbols themselves, operating as a cotherapist. This is illustrated by a patient with a problem of dependency who dreamt in oral terms and who wrote out the following:

Wednesday night

I am in a bakery with an unusually luscious-looking array of baked goods. I seem to remember that something I bought looked so good that I ate a piece while I was in the shop. Also, I vaguely remember arranging with the woman behind the counter to deliver some baked goods to my home later on. I remember giving her quite explicit directions about getting to my place. (My associations when I awoke went something like this, "The woman was a mother substitute. I was seeking from her the comfort I never got from my own mother. . . ." Then, "Dr. Wolberg is a mother substitute too. His voice was comforting, sympathetic; he was giving me something I'd wanted from my mother.")

Thursday or Friday night

I am in a cafeteria. Apparently I am early, for I am the only customer there. I walk down the long food table, but I can't seem to remember anything on it except a large roast turkey, which was almost at the very end of the table. When I come to the turkey, I decide that this is what I'd like, but I wonder if the cafeteria people will want to spoil its appearance by carving some off for me before the other customers get there. Someone—and again I have a vague feeling that it was a woman worker—assures me that it will be quite all right. (I don't remember any associations to this dream. As I type it now, it occurs to me that I want to be first—with my mother? perhaps with Dr. Wolberg?—but am afraid that it's not right that I should be.)

Case 4

Perhaps the most important use of dreams in short-term therapy is, as has been indicated, the signals that they emit pointing to the beginning development of a negative transference reaction that, if unheeded, may expand to block or destroy progress in therapy. Where a therapist does not encourage the patient to report all dreams, the patient may forget or repress them, and the only sign the therapist may notice that things are not going well is that the patient's symptoms return or get worse, that disturbing acting-out behavior appears, or, worse, that the patient simply drops out of therapy. Where dreams are regularly reported, the therapist will have available a sensitive barometer that indicates the oncoming of an emotional storm. A patient in the middle stages of therapy began coming late for appointments. Only upon urging did she report the following dream:

Pt. I was asleep on a desk or table in your office. I way lying on my side with my knees bent. You walked over to me. You were a shadowy figure that I could barely see through closed lids. I knew I should wake up, but I was curious to see what you would do and I lacked the will to awaken. You touched me. I had been covered, but you removed the cover and I remember thinking "I hope I have a pretty slip on." At first your touch was pleasant, sexual-like, and I felt rather guilty for not letting you know I was really awake. Gradually you began to turn into a sinister figure. You looked into my eyes with a light and said, "That's a lovely blue eye." I barely mumbled, "It's green," feeling that if you didn't know the color of my eyes it meant you didn't know me. I realized with a shock I didn't know the color of your eyes, either. Brown, I thought, but I wasn't sure. Then you said to me, "What are the things I've told you?" I started to mumble, "Many things." You said, "No, I have told you nothing." I took this to mean that you are absolutely not responsible for anything I might do. These things made you seem sinister to me. You slowly began to change into another man who seemed to be a derelict, and I knew I *must* get up. I struggled to awaken myself, and I finally succeeded. I ran to the door and ran out of the room, but there were a lot of people. In a mirror there I saw an utter ruin—I looked 80 years old and terribly ugly and I believe scarred. All the people were old and ugly. It was a village of discarded useless, and helpless people. A feeling of horror overcame me, and, as I stared at that face, I tried to comfort myself that it was only a nightmare and I would soon wake up, and I found it very difficult until I wasn't sure anymore if it was a nightmare or real.

I finally woke up from the dream so frightened that I wanted to wake my husband, but I decided to try to calm down. I fell asleep again and had a second dream. I dreamed I had stayed up all night writing a paper you asked me to do. I started to bring it into the room you told me to. It was locked. I decided to have some coffee and come back. I did. This time your wife was in the room. She told me who she was. I said I knew. Then she told me she was your daughter's mother as though this made her a figure of great importance and dignity. This made me feel guilty and gave me the feeling that I could not see you anymore. She didn't want me to and in respect to her sacredness as a mother I couldn't.

Had I not become alerted to the beginning transference, which certainly reflected an oedipal problem, I am convinced that my sinister qualities would have become so overwhelming in her unconscious mind that she would have discontinued therapy. As matters stood, we were able to engage in fruitful discussions following my interpretation of her dream.

Case 5

The following dream illustrates the eruption of negative transference in a young man with a problem of urinary frequency. This occurred at the tenth session and was related to his having met a young lady with whom he made a date. He had a penchant for meeting controlling women who dominated him and who finally frightened him off. The urinary symptom was associated in his mind with lack of masculinity. Our relationship had been going along well and the patient had been improving, but at the last session he spoke of the slowness of his progress. The dream that he related to me in the tenth session was in six parts:

Pt. (1) I met a friend in a laundramat. I told him I was engaged and he wanted to see pictures of my girl. I kept thumbing through a lot of boyish pictures and the last one was a good one, more feminine. My associations to this is that the new girl is a physical ed teacher and I wondered how feminine she is. I do meet different people in the laundramat I use.

(2) The second dream was that a math professor was trying to start my girl's car and he couldn't start it, but I could. [*I had a feeling here that he was being competitive with me and was putting me down for not making him well faster.*]

(3) Then I was looking for shoes in a window. I saw something I liked. I went in, and he didn't have my size. The shoes were nice masculine-looking ones. [*Was he really saying here that he couldn't fit into a man's shoes or that the storekeeper who might be me couldn't help him? Probably both.*]

(4) I was with a barber and he punched a hole in my head and he wanted to cover it with a toupe. I believe I said, "Nothing doing." I was angry at him. [*Apparently another reference to my ineffectuality and to his building resentment toward me.*]

(5) Then I was with one of the kids I grew up with. There was a toilet in the room. I was waiting for an opportunity to go. I decided to sit down—it wouldn't make me so self-conscious standing there and urinating only a few drops. But he got up and walked out.

(6) Then you were at dinner at my house. You had to go to the bathroom. You opened up the wrong door. Then you went into the bathroom and were away a long time. I wondered if you had the same problem I had.

In discussing his dream he stated that sitting down on a toilet was an escape from his embarrassment. Did it mean, I asked, also that it was a feminine gesture and a way of saying that he was not quite a man? And did he believe that I could not help him achieve his goals? The dream, I insisted, pointed out his feelings that I was ineffective. At this juncture I praised him for his ability to criticize me, and I asked him to associate to his feelings about me. This opened the door to his critical attitude toward his passive father for not doing more for him. For the next two sessions we worked on his negative transference; interestingly, his urinary symptom improved remarkedly. He was delighted also that he could act more aggressive toward his new girlfriend than he had toward any other woman in the past.

Case 6

Illustrative of the use of dreams to select a therapeutic focus as well as a measure of progress is the case of a young single woman of 30 who had been admitted to a mental institution after she had tried to commit suicide. At the end of 18 months of hospitalization she was taken out by her parents, and I was asked to see her in consultation with the object of deciding who the best therapist for her might be. Apart from a slight emotional dulling, I could find no active evidence of schizophrenia, which was the diagnosis given her at the hospital. The dream she revealed at the initial interview was the following:

Pt. I was on a date with a man and he proposed to me. I was frightened about going to bed with this man. Then I saw myself suckling at my mother's breast. I felt nauseated and ran away. I felt empty and helpless. Then I saw somebody holding up two fingers—one represented male and the other female. Somebody came along and took the male finger, and I was left with the female finger. I was upset at being forced to give up being a boy. I had to be a girl. This made me anxious.

The dream, which I recorded but did not interpret, gave me a clue as to her separation-individuation, dependency-independency problem, and I decided that this would be the dynamic focus in our therapy after we had worked out the time in my schedule. I saw her once weekly and I focused, whenever propitious, on her need for a mother figure, her fear of functioning like a woman, and her problem of identity. After 6 months of therapy at the twenty-fourth session she brought in the following two dreams:

Pt. The first dream was that I was having an affair with a teacher I had in high school. (I had a crush on this teacher when I was in school.) My mother found out and was furious. She wanted to kill me. She said I'd ruin my life. She pulled out a knife, and she told my brother and friends to get knives. I was going to get a knife and kill her. I said instead, "You really hate yourself and want to kill yourself." She tried to kill herself by throwing herself under a car. I grabbed her and said, "Please let me help you." She cried and cried and said she didn't want to live. She said she felt guilty for trying to take my life. [*The thought I had about this dream was that she felt that growing up and assuming a heterosexual role was forbidden by her mother, or rather the introjected mother within herself. Could her suicidal attempt be a desire to kill this introject?*]

The second dream was I was riding on a bicycle with my mother and brother. We stopped at a house with people I couldn't stand. Mother stayed there with a cousin Janet. My mother and my brother got on one bicycle. I was on another bicycle. They kept giving me directions, and I resented that. Then I was riding alone in the country and went over a cliff and died. [*The patient added*] I seem to be in terror of my new independence. It's like in the dream. Yet I feel a feeling of liberation. I know my relations with people since we began to talk about dependence are much better. I can get angry at my father and brother and at myself for building them up as those who can take care of me.

For the next 10 sessions we worked on her guilt feelings and killing fantasies in relation to her emerging independence. In the course of this the following dream occurred:

Pt. I am alone in a car, driving all alone. I am enjoying it. I knew where to go. My mother smiles at me and I am happy. [*Her associations follow*] Since coming to see you I feel my activity is released. Last week I had a date and I enjoyed myself. I know you feel I'm keeping myself in a box because of guilt and I know you are right. As you say, it's better for me to make mistakes and walk by myself than to have someone carry me.

The patient herself spontaneously terminated therapy after the forty-first session. She sent me an announcement of her marriage 11 months after this. I telephoned her to come to my office for a follow-up session. The change in the patient was striking—her posture, her poise, the confident manner in her speaking. Apart from a few minor rifts with her parents, there were no upsetting episodes to speak of. She avowed being happy and adjusted to marriage, which she described as a "give-and-take proposition." A telephone follow-up 5 years after her termination revealed that she had given birth to a child and had made an excellent adjustment.

Case 7

The working-through of a problem in identity through transference may be seen in another case of a 32-year-old married woman with an obsessive personality structure who periodically would get strong attacks of depression and anxiety. During these episodes she became riddled with great doubts about minor choices and would badger her husband, John, and her friends to make decisions for her, which she then would reject. An attractive feminine-appearing woman, she expressed at the initial interview concern about who she was and where she was headed. During the interview I asked her to tell me about any past dreams, and she stated she could not remember her dreams. At the third session she brought in the following dream which she had written down:

We were at a resort—John and I and another couple. I was attracted to someone there who seemed to change from a man to a woman, to a girl in her 20s. There were endless details about a carnival night with animals and all sorts of games. The night before we were leaving, this girl and I were going down the stairs and tripped. She stooped down to help me. I grabbed her, pulled her down, and kissed her (I was definitely a male at this point). I put my tongue in her mouth. I was still on the bottom and she was leaning over me, but I was a man. She asked me why I hadn't let on sooner that I cared for her. I told her it wouldn't work out because of John and it was just as well. I got up to leave. I ran down the stairs and said "goodbye." Then I changed it to "au revoir."

She reported that she felt terrible after this dream and that old fears of homosexuality came up. Her associations were to the effect that her sexual relations with her husband (toward whom she bore a great deal of hostility) had ceased. "When he is unhappy—which is most of the time—I have to make the first advances. But I refuse to because I don't feel like it. I'm not interested."

My interpretation of the dream was to the effect that she was striving to achieve strength and independence through masculinity—the symbol of strength in our culture. We discussed her anger at discovering as a child the fact that she lacked a penis and her envy of males for their sense of freedom and independence. Although she fantasied functioning like a male, she stated that there were no episodes of homosexuality. She fell in love with a young man whom she married and bore a child whom she cherished, but she continued to be dissatisfied with herself as a woman, believing that somehow she was damaged and inferior.

She developed a good relationship with me, and we continued to discuss her unhappy marital union and her conflict in relation to the dependency-independency imbalance. Evidence of transference followed the first hypnotic session, which was introduced at the sixth visit. The following dream is an example of how a response to a therapeutic technique (hypnosis here) may reveal a patient's struggle with resistance and how it helps the therapist to organize strategies to deal with emerging resistance.

Pt. I was in Dr.______'s office [*her general practitioner*] then somehow I left and it was more like a school building. I was in my old public school. I was hesitating about going back to school [*Could she be identifying me with her general practitioner and going back to school the treatment with me?*] Then the doctor saw me on the landing and told me to come in. This somehow solved the problem as it made me feel wanted and did not give me the feeling I have when I have to make the overtures. He tried to hypnotize me. [*This establishes me as* *the doctor in the dream.*] I started to go under deeply, but I suddenly caught myself. He tried again. He touched my breasts. When I pulled back, he got angry. I had the distinct feeling in the dream that he touched me not out of any desire, but only to make me realize that I had breasts just like any other woman and that I was like any other woman—no better, no worse. This attitude of complete lack of putting me on a pedestal gave me all at once a feeling of freedom and a feeling of intense sorrow. It was as though I was struggling for my right to be different, but at the same time I realized that my struggle was in a wrong direction. He tried to hypnotize me again. This time there were tricks involved, making me see colored balls coming out of a bag and so forth. My rational mind kept struggling against such a possibility, and even though I saw them, I felt they really weren't there. Again, I had this feeling of our wills being pitted against each other. I wanted so much to love, but I couldn't seem to give up the struggle.

My interpretations dealt with her resistance to giving up the kind of identity that made her feel safe, which she, of course, could do if this is what she wanted. I would like to help her, but she had a right not to change if she so wished. At this point the patient started crying, and she confessed being unhappy with the way she was, but she was afraid to change. At the ninth session she spoke of a dream that she had that appeared to indicate that she trusted me more and was utilizing her relationship with me as a growth vehicle:

Pt. I had a dream of someone running after me and making love to me in the sunlight. [*Her associations were to the effect that later the next morning she was reading Jung's* The Undiscovered Self.] This gave me a wonderful feeling of completeness and a sense of stimulation and peace at the same time. A feeling of well-being so strong that I really did not feel that angry feeling I usually have when John goes out. I really did not miss him; even my fear of being alone was somewhat stilled, not completely, but a great deal. I felt a wave of strong sexual desire and wished you were there with me. I wanted to talk to you about the book. I thought it would be so pleasant to have a cup of coffee with you, and I thought, although I supressed this thought, I wanted you to make love to me. But it was a quiet feeling with a feeling of softness, flirtatiousness, and even a little sadness. Not like the image I sometimes have of my making love to you because I want to see you aroused; I want to feel some form of passion from you just because your constant calmness seems a kind of rejection. This feeling has a great deal of hostility in it, but the feeling I had at home was different.

Why do I feel the sexual impulse when I am alone or when I feel my relatedness to the total world as when I looked in Brentano's window and saw reproductions of some of the art objects I love? The strength of the sexuality frightens me. If I had been with a man in my apartment, I do not think I could have resisted going to bed with him. In fact, the urge to adultery is very strong. I seem to want my sexual partner to aid me in keeping this relatedness to the world (to life, eternity, etc.). I know that I can't now have a complete and satisfying orgasm any other way. John's complete preoccupation with himself stands in my way so that love making becomes an erotic episode only. My soul is not released or nourished.

In our discussion we talked about her upbringing, her intensely close relationship with her mother, and the detachment of her father, who was a somewhat shadowy figure in her life.

Several sessions later she revealed this dream:

Pt. I came to your office which was somehow different. It had a bedroom. We walked into the bedroom. Somehow we were on the bed and we were kissing. You were on top of me, and I was happy to be in that position. I felt your tongue in my mouth, and I put my hands under your shirt and felt your back. For a split second, I had the fear that I would not find your back masculine feeling like, but it was. You refused to go any further, explaining that if we did, you would not be able to help me. You seemed sorry that it had gone that far, and I began to be frightened that it might in-

> fluence our relationship. However, I also felt quite happy, and then you came in I saw that it really would be all right. There was no real change in the relationship except that I felt more feminine and perhaps a little guilty as though I had seduced you. But I was really quite pleased.

Among her associations was her statement, "My relationship with John that day was easier, and I felt as though I wanted him." She avowed the need for a strong male figure in her life to help make her feel feminine.

Therapy was terminated against her wishes but at my insistence that it was necessary for her to continue working at her problem by herself. The patient accepted this. During the next few years she came in two times because of a brief obsessional episode when she could not make up her mind in relation to her continuing career as a book editor and the schooling of her child. No more than several sessions were needed on each occasion to get her to recognize that she was trying to make herself dependent again on an authority figure who would treat her like a child. Her marital and sexual adjustment improved constantly, and the image of herself as a female became increasingly consolidated.

Conclusion

Dreams, like conscious thinking, are dynamically motivated by urgent conscious and unconscious needs. Because reality testing, logic, and correct conceptions of time and space are more or less suspended in sleep and because repression is lowered, the dreamer may express basic wishes, conflicts, and fears that one would not ordinarily permit oneself to experience in waking life.

Dreams may thus serve not only as a revelatory screen for unconscious wishes and past memories, but also perhaps more importantly as a way of reflecting present adaptive and problem-solving activities, habitual character patterns, and the special ways an individual is interpreting and coping with current situations in the present. During therapy dreams are particularly important in (1) identifying conflicts and defenses toward providing a dynamic focus, (2) recognizing what immediate environmental events are so significant as to promote a dream and what meaning these events have for the patient, (3) understanding what is going on from the patient's standpoint in the relationship between the therapist and the patient, (4) detecting early resistances and transference distortions that potentially can block progress in treatment, (5) determining what progress the patient is making in therapy, and (6) providing a window into the patient's views of future problems and existing and latent capacities for adaptation.

In working with dreams the therapist has a tool applicable in all forms of short-term therapy that can lead to a better understanding of a patient's problems, to recognition of the quality of the working relationship, and to an overcoming of developing obstacles that threaten the effectiveness of the therapeutic process.

CHAPTER 13

Catalyzing the Therapeutic Process

The Use of Hypnosis

In therapy much time is consumed in coping with resistances to the yielding of ego-syntonic patterns. It is traditionally assumed that this extended period is inevitable as part of the process of "working-through." There is, however, some evidence that certain expediences may be employed to catalyze progress. One mode has a paradigm in crisis situations during which motivation has been created for change that otherwise would not have developed. Using this idea, some therapists attempt during therapy to create minor crisis situations for the patient by tactics such as aggressive confrontation and other ways of stirring up anxiety. The object is to convince the patient that pursuit of one's usual mode of behaving is offensive to others and unpleasant for oneself. In this way the therapists try to break through resistances to productive change.

In patients who are capable of countenancing challenge and confrontation such methods may prove successful. Unfortunately, where a weak ego structure exists, where the patient is hostile to or excessively defensive with authority, or where negative transference precipitates too readily, the relationship will not sustain the patient during the tumultuous readjustment period. The patient will either leave therapy or show no response to the procedures being used. With such patients it is better to employ an approach oriented around a deliberate maintenance of a positive relationship.

A search for other strategems that can hasten the therapeutic process has yielded a number of interventions that have, in the opinion of those skilled in their use, proven to be of special merit. Such vaunted catalysts are subject, however, to variables of therapist personality and patient response that can negate and even reverse their influence. Among the most commonly employed techniques utilized to accelerate treatment are hypnosis, narcoanalysis, emotive release strategies, guided imagery, behavior therapy, Gestalt therapy, experiential therapy, dream analysis, family therapy, and introduction of the patient into an active group.*

Certain ways of expediting insight have also been helpful, for example, citing specific episodes from the treatment of other patients (of course, anonymity is maintained) that in some respects relate to the patient's problem. This may serve as a projective technique to cushion the patient's anxiety and help maintain defenses that might otherwise be shattered by direct interpretations of the patient's personal reactions (A. Wolberg, 1973, pp. 185–234). Another method is the use of metaphors through relating stories or anecdotes that illustrate points the therapist wants to get across to the patient (De La Torre, 1972).

Therapists develop personal preferences in the choice of catalyzing techniques. These generally relate to their successes with the majority of patients. In my own experience I have found hypnosis of great value, and I recommend it with no illusion that it can be helpful to all therapists. It should be experimented with to see if it blends with one's style of working therapeutically.

* See Wolberg 1977, pp. 245–250, 685–740, and 761–823 for a full description of these methods.

When to Use Hypnosis

Hypnosis is particularly suited for the patient who is paralyzed by resistance. Resistance is embodied in overt or covert behavior patterns. Usually, the patient is unaware of such maneuvers. Resistance is particularly obstructive when it blocks the special techniques that are employed in psychotherapy. Hypnosis may help resolve such resistance and enable the person to respond better to treatment.

Hypnosis may be advantageously employed in the course of psychotherapy under the following conditions:

When the Patient Lacks Motivation for Treatment

Hypnotic techniques may be helpful in convincing an unmotivated patient that he can derive something meaningful from treatment. A patient may feel resentment toward those who insist that he get psychological help; he may be afraid of revealing secret or disgusting aspects of his life; he may feel distrust for the therapist or refuse to recognize an emotional basis for his complaints. These and other obstructions that contribute to the lack of incentive for therapy can usually be handled by a skilled therapist in the initial interviews without recourse to hypnosis. Occasionally, though, even skillful approaches do not resolve the patient's resistance to accepting help. At this point, if the patient permits induction, hypnosis may provide a positive experience that significantly alters recalcitrant attitudes.

For example, a patient who had great resistance to psychotherapy was referred to me by an internist. He suffered from urinary frequency, which had defied all medical intervention and had become so serious that it threatened his livelihood. He resented being sent to a psychiatrist and announced to me that there was no sense in starting what might prove to be a long and costly process when he was not fully convinced that he needed it. I accepted the patient's negative feelings, but I speculated that his tension might be responsible for at least some of his symptoms. I offerred to show him how to relax so that he might derive something beneficial out of the present session. He agreed, and I then induced a light trance, in the course of which I suggested a general state of relaxation. After the trance was terminated, the patient spontaneously announced that he had never felt more relaxed in his life and asked if he could have several more sessions of hypnosis. In the course of hypnorelaxation I casually suggested to him that there might be emotional reasons why his bladder had become tense and upset, and I inquired whether he would be interested in finding out whether this was so. When he agreed, I gave him a posthypnotic suggestion to remember any dreams he might have within the next few days.

He responded with a series of dreams in which he saw himself as a frightened person escaping from situations of danger and being blocked in his efforts to achieve freedom. His associations were about the democratic rights of oppressed people throughout the world and the futility of expressing these rights in the face of cruel and uncompromising dictatorships that seemed to be the order of the day. When asked how this affected him personally, living as he did in a democratic regime, he sarcastically replied that one could be a prisoner even in a democracy. Since his father had died, he had been obliged to take over the responsibility of looking after his mother. Not only did she insist that he stay in her home, but she also demanded an account of all of his movements. He realized that she was a sick, frightened woman and that consequently it was his duty to devote himself to her comfort for her few remaining years. These revelations were the turning point at which we were able to convert our sessions into explorations of his needs and conflicts. As he recognized his repressed hostility and his tremendous need for personal freedom, he realized that he himself was largely responsible for the condition that was virtually enslaving him. It was then possible for him to help his mother find new friends and to move into a retirement village. When he resolved some sources of his deep resentments, his bladder symptoms disappeared completely. More significant was a growth in assertiveness and self-esteem that improved the quality of his social relationships.

When the Patient Refuses to Begin Therapy Unless Assured of Immediate Relief of Symptoms

Symptoms may be so upsetting to the patient that therapy will be refused unless there is first a reduction or removal of symptoms. When symptoms are so severe that they create physical emergencies, as in cases of persistent vomiting, hiccuping, or paralysis, the therapist may be able to restore function through suggestions in hypnosis. After this the therapist may proceed with other psychotherapeutic techniques. In less severe cases, insistence on symptomatic relief may be a tactic for demonstrating the therapist as a sympathetic person concerned with the suffering of the patient. Hypnosis with suggestions aimed at relaxation, tension control, and symptom reduction can create an atmosphere conducive to a therapeutic working relationship. Hypnosis can also expedite the learning of new habit patterns through desensitization and reconditioning (behavior therapy).

A patient who came to me with an obsessional neurosis complained of belching and hiccuping after meals. This caused her great embarrassment and frequently forced her to skip meals. She was so preoccupied with whether or not her symptoms would overwhelm her that she could scarcely enjoy food when invited out to dine. Her symptoms forced her to seek medical help, in the course of which she was referred to me. At the initial interview she testily protested being sent for psychiatric treatments, particularly in view of a past unsuccessful psychotherapeutic experience. What she wanted, she insisted, was sufficient relief from physical distress to enable her to function at work and in her relationship with her family. In light of her disappointment with interview psychotherapy, I suggested hypnosis as a possible way of helping her to achieve some lessening of her trouble. She agreed to give it a trial. The next five sessions were spent in teaching her how to relax and how to control her symptoms. Her response was dramatic, and her attitude toward me changed from suspicion and hostility to friendly cooperativeness. She readily entered into a therapeutic relationship, and once therapy had started, there was no need for further hypnosis.

When the Patient has Such Deep Problems in Relationships with People that Therapy Cannot Get Started

A good working relationship between patient and therapist is mandatory for any kind of psychotherapy. This is particularly essential in therapy that tries to bring about modification of a personality that is prone to anxiety. This type of personality often feels great stress when the therapist probes for conflicts and challenges habitual defenses. With some sick patients the proper working relationship may never develop or may take many months to appear because of such factors as fear of closeness or intense hostility toward authority. Relaxation during hypnosis may resolve fears, reduce hostility, and cut down the time period required for the development of rapport. The patient often feels an extraordinary warmth and closeness toward the therapist even after only one or two hypnotic sessions. A therapeutic relationship may crystallize under these circumstances, and it will then be possible to proceed with psychotherapy without hypnosis.

One of the most severely disturbed patients I ever treated was a paranoidal man who upbraided me during our first session for my delay in arranging a consultation with him. He was upset, he said, because he was involved in litigious proceedings against his business partners, who had presumably deceived him about their business prospects when they first induced him to buy a share of the company. Another legal case was pending against a neighbor who had in a lot adjoining his house built a garage that the patient considered an eyesore. But what he most desired from the consultation with me was to determine the feasibility of hypnotizing his wife in order to obtain from her the truth of her exact whereabouts during an evening when he was out of town on business. He had carefully examined her tube of contraceptive jelly before his departure and again upon his return. At first he could see no difference, but he compulsively returned to it, ruminating about whether he had not made a mistake in his original conclusion about his wife's innocence. For weeks he had been subjecting her to cross-examinations, carefully tabulating contradictory remarks until he had convinced himself that she was concealing the truth about a rendezvous with her lover. The poor woman, protesting her innocence from the start, had become so confused by his confrontation that she desperately tried to make up stories to cover tiny discrepancies in her minute-by-minute account of activities on the fatal evening. With a sharp eye for her inconsistencies, the patient had seized on her flounderings to trap her into an admission of lying, which then convinced him all the more of her infidelity. A firm believer in the powers of hypnosis, he challenged her to submit to a hypnotic reliving of the evening in question in his presence.

Upon finishing this account, the patient inquired about my methods of trance induction since he had been reading about the subject. I volunteered to demonstrate the hand-levitation technique to him, and he cautiously agreed to be a subject. Before too long he entered into a trance, during which I suggested that he would soon begin to feel more relaxed, secure, and self-confident. If he visualized a happy scene or had a dream about the most wonderful thing that could happen to a person, he would probably feel free from tension as well as experience a general state of pleasure that would make him happier than he had ever been in his life. After an interval of 10 minutes he was brought out of the trance. Upon opening his eyes, he revealed, with humor, having had a dream of lying on a hammock while lovely slave girls circled around him with baskets of fruit. I suggested that he return in 2 days and bring his wife if she wished to accompany him.

During the second session, which was held jointly with his wife, his wife tearfully proclaimed her innocence, whereupon the patient petulantly asked her to leave my office if she was going to "act like a baby." When she promised to control herself, he requested that she wait for him in the reception room. He then told me he had felt so well since his first visit that he had decided that several more sessions of hypnosis would be valuable for his insomnia. His wife's problem could wait, he claimed, until he had healed his own "nerves." After this initiation into therapy, he underwent a number of sessions of psychotherapy with and without hypnosis, during which we worked on several problems that concerned him. He ended therapy when he had achieved a marked reduction of his symptoms, an easing of his tensions with his partners, and the reestablishment of a satisfactory relationship with his wife.

Another patient spent the first 3 months of treatment with me in fruitless associational explorations. He protested that "nothing was happening" in regard to his symptoms or "anything else." He did not have either a warm or hostile attitude toward psychotherapy. He appeared to resent any continued questioning concerning his feelings about me. There was a consistent denial reaction to my interpretations. After I induced him to try hypnosis, he was able to achieve a medium trance. From the very first hypnotic session his enthusiasm and energy increased. His activity and productivity also improved remarkably, and we were able to achieve a good therapeutic result. Without hypnosis, I am convinced that his detachment could not have been penetrated.

When the Patient is Unable to Verbalize Freely

When communication is blocked, there can be no therapy. Sometimes the usual unblocking techniques may fail to restore verbal communication. In such an event hypnosis can often be effective, although the way in which it is used will depend on the causes of the difficulty. The mere induction of a trance may uncork explosive emotions against which the patient had defended by refusing to talk in the waking state. Cathartic release in the trance may restore normal verbal expression. If the patient's silence is due to some resistance, it may be possible to explore and resolve it by encouraging the patient to talk during hypnosis. In speech paralysis (aphonia) resulting from hysteria these techniques may not suffice, and direct suggestion may be needed to lessen or eliminate the symptom. Speech disorders may be treated and sometimes helped by lessening tension during the trance, and there may then be a carryover into the waking state. When the speech difficulty is caused by needs that forbid the expression of painful sounds or ideas, an explosive outburst during hypnosis may not only release the capacity to talk freely, but will also open up areas of conflict that can be beneficially explored.

A young woman, a severe stammerer, came for therapy because of incapacitating phobias. Once she had established rapport with me, she expressed herself satisfactorily, but as we began to examine her fantasies and dreams, she experienced so pronounced a relapse in her speech disturbance that she was almost inarticulate. She complained that while she could talk better than ever before with her friends, she could scarcely communicate with me. Since progress had come to a halt, I suggested hypnosis as a way of helping her to relax. She reacted to this suggestion with anxiety but, nevertheless, agreed to try. During the process of deepening the trance she suddenly broke down and cried fitfully. Encouraged to discuss what she felt, she clenched her fists and shrieked, "No, no!" After exploding into a coughing spell, during which she could hardly catch her breath, she gasped over and over that she was choking. At my suggestion that she "bring it up," she broke into a torrent of foul language, pronouncing the word "shit" repeatedly and spitting with angry excitement. A few minutes of this frenzied behavior were followed by complaints of exhaustion. Thereupon she resorted to normal speech, which continued for the remainder of the session, even after she had been aroused. This performance was repeated in subsequent sessions, although the patient responded with diminished fury. The therapeutic process gained great momentum, and the young woman was able to curb her stammer. The experience opened the door to a discussion of her great concern over bowel activities. This was related to extremely rigid toilet training as a child by an obsessive, overdisciplinary mother who made her feel guilty and frightened about toilet activities. Feces, from early childhood on, were equated with poison and destruction. Our therapeutic sessions were largely concerned with clarifying her misconceptions. As she developed a more wholesome attitude toward her bowel functions, her general feelings about herself improved, and her speech difficulty practically disappeared.

When During Therapy the Patient is Unable to Engage in Unrestricted Exploration

A patient may maintain rigid control when he dreads psychological areas of conflict that may be exposed. He thus cannot permit his ideas to emerge freely and unrestrainedly in the process of exploring unguarded aspects of his psyche. When the patient is blocked because of resistance, hypnosis may be a possible solution. Not only may it bring the patient into contact with repressed emotions and thoughts, but it also may help him to analyze his blocks.

This was true of a patient who had retreated to a highly structured and rigidly directed form of verbal expression. Attempts to analyze his loss of spontaneity produced little response. After floundering, with no improvement and mere repetition of insignificant items, I induced hypnosis and encouraged the patient to talk about what really was bothering him. He revealed that he had felt guilty in the past few weeks for having masturbated in my office bathroom after one of our sessions. He had not wanted to tell me about this incident because he knew it was not an adult act. He then associated this action with having been caught as a child masturbating in his aunt's bathroom. Not only had he been reprimanded and warned by his aunt, but also his parents had promptly been told. The physician who referred the patient to me also frowned on his masturbatory practices, classifying masturbation as "idiot's delight, which is never indulged in by a mature person." Reassured by my handling of these revelations, the patient was able to continue with his associations in the waking state.

In instances where there is a dearth of dream material the patient may be trained to dream in the trance or through posthypnotic suggestions during normal sleep. General topics of specific topics may be suggested as the dream content. Once this process is started, it may be possible for the patient to continue dreaming without hypnosis. Hypnosis can also be used to restore forgotten elements of dreams, to clarify distortions elaborated to disguise their meaning (secondary elaborations), and to help the patient explore by means of dreams attitudes toward people and disturbing elements in everyday life. During hypnosis spontaneous dreams may occur reflecting unconscious attitudes, memories, emotions, and conflicts. Sometimes they reveal to the patient the meaning of the immediate hypnotic experience as well as distortions in relationship with the therapist, caused by confusing the therapist with early authority figures.

The improvement shown by one of my patients illustrates how valuable hypnotic dream induction can be. The patient came to me for psychotherapy when he could find no relief for severe rectal itching. He had tried every kind of medicinal oral and injection treatment. Although we soon established a good working relationship, he was unable to remember his dreams. In the trance I suggested that he would have a dream that would explain his rectal itching. He responded with an anxiety dream of a man with a huge penis approaching him from the rear. He was told to forget the dream or recall any part of it that he wished to remember after he had awakened. Upon opening his eyes, he complained of tension, but he did not remember his dream. He admitted some relief in his rectal itching. That same night he had a dream of riding a roller coaster with a male friend. His dream suggested concerns about homosexuality. In later dreams he was able to countenance homosexual impulses and to discuss them during the session. Hypnosis was responsible for opening up a repressed and repudiated area of guilt and conflict.

When the Patient Seems Blocked in Transferring to the Therapist Distorted Attitudes toward Parental and Other Early Figures of Authority

Childhood experiences, particularly relationships with parents and siblings, by their formative influence on attitudes, values, feelings, and behavior leave an indelible imprint and affect the way the adult responds not only to other people but also to oneself. Because some of the most important formative experiences are forgotten, or remain hazy, or are dissociated from the fears and anxieties with which they were originally linked, they subversively influence faulty ways of thinking and acting. Some of the transference distortions may be uncovered by hypnosis, and their interpretation may bring the patient to a realization that he also responds in destructive and unnecessary ways in many other situations. The lesson learned can serve as the basis of new, more wholesome attitudes to present-day authority, attitudes that fortunately will in all likelihood make life more comfortable and productive.

A patient who came for therapy entered easily into the hypnotic state but became more and more recalcitrant to suggestions. He had always been submissive to his father (and later to other male authorities). Along with this he felt great inner rage, turmoil, and depression, although he was outwardly calm. It seemed to me that his entering hypnosis was a means of pleasing me. This was the customary role with male authority, patterned after the way he reacted to his father. "For years, I hated my father," he said. "He couldn't stand being contradicted. I remember needing to lose at cards deliberately so that father would not get upset over my winning. I am never able to be successful: it makes me too anxious." When I interpreted to him the way that he was reacting to me, he at first denied it. But then he appeared to see the light, with the result that he challenged me first by resisting hypnosis and finally by manifesting a total inability to enter the hypnotic state, I accepted his refusal to comply, even encouraged it. At this phase the patient experienced dreams of triumph. "It's healthier to dream of feeling love rather than hate. For the first time, I realize I loved my father. I cried in my sleep. I felt my father really loved me, but we had this wall between us. I awoke feeling I really loved him." This change in feeling was accompanied by an abatement of symptoms and a capacity to relate more cooperatively. Soon the patient was able to enter hypnosis easily and without resentment, as a means of pleasing himself—not me.

Another patient, experiencing frigidity, was referred to me by her psychoanalyst for some hypnotic work. After the third induction she told me that she felt the need to keep her legs crossed during the entire trance state. So tightly did she squeeze her thighs together that they ached when she emerged from the trance. Before the next induction I instructed her to keep her legs separated. As I proceeded with suggestions, she became flushed, opened her eyes, and exclaimed that she knew what was upsetting her. I reminded her of her grandfather, she said, who, when she was a small child, had tossed her into bed and held her close to his body on several occasions. She had felt his erect penis against her body, and this had both excited and frightened her. It became apparent that the hypnotic experience represented for her an episode during which she hoped for and feared sexual seduction. Her leg crossing was a defense against these fantasies. Continued trance inductions with the patient diminished her fears, and she then revealed being able to have better sexual relations with her husband.

Another patient, who suffered from periodic attacks of nausea, vomiting, and gastrointestinal crises, was referred for hypnosis after two years of traditional psychoanalysis had failed to relieve her symptoms. Because she tended to shield herself from awareness of her problems with strong repressions, I felt that transference, which had not developed significantly during her previous therapy, might be important in helping her to gain insight into her problems. After she had been trained to enter a medium trance, I suggested that she would dream of her feelings about me. She failed to dream; instead she had a hallucination consisting of a peculiar taste in her mouth, which she described as "bittersweet." This taste persisted for several hours after her session. That evening she had a nightmarish dream in which a woman, whose handbag bore the initials B.S., took a small boy into the bathroom to help him to urinate and wash up. She was unable to interpret the dream. A trance was induced in which she recalled forgotten elements of the dream, namely that the sexes of the two participants had changed as they had entered the bathroom; the adult had been a man, the child a girl. The next few sessions were spent discussing a "reaction" to me that the patient had developed and that made her want to stop treatment. She was positive that I resented her, and she recounted several minor incidents indicating to her that I did not have her best interests at heart. She was positive that I preferred a young man whose sessions preceded hers because I once had kept him late, thus overlapping her time.

In the trance that followed, she broke into hysterical crying, identifying me as her father, whose nickname was Bing. (The initials B.S. in the dream stood for Bing. His last name began with an S. B.S. apparently was linked to the "bittersweet" taste she had in her hallucination.) He had been both father and mother to her (changed from male to female in the dream), had preferred her brother to her (her reaction to the male patient whose hour preceded hers), and had always reminded her that he regretted that she had not been born a boy (her being brought into the bathroom as a boy in the dream possibly indicated that she had finally succeeded in achieving a masculine status). Thereafter, she experienced strong sexual feelings toward me and shamefully asked if I did not have a preference for her among all my other patients. From then on it was possible to analyze the origins of these feelings in her relations with her father and to see that some of her symptoms were associated with fantasies of wanting to be a boy through acquiring a penis. Hypnosis succeeded rapidly in allowing us to understand what was behind her difficulty.

When the Patient has Forgotten Certain Traumatic Memories Whose Recall May Help the Therapeutic Process

In some emotional states memories may be submerged. Because they constantly threaten to come to the surface, anxiety and defensive symptoms, which bolster repression, affect behavior adversely. The trance can be instrumental in recalling the repressed experience, and the examination of the associated emotions helps to eliminate debilitating symptoms.

One patient suffered from periodic attacks of shortness of breath, an affliction that resembled asthma. He was given a suggestion in hypnosis that he would return (regress) to his first attack. In a scene in which he saw himself as a child of 3 standing in a snowdrift on a back porch, he described how he slipped and fell into a high snowdrift, gasping for breath as the snow filled his nose and throat. With panic, choking as he talked, he told of being rescued by his mother and father. This story was verified by his parents as a true experience. They were amazed that the patient remembered the exact details of the accident, and they confirmed that "asthmatic" attacks had begun soon after this incident. It was then established in therapy that interpersonal situations in which the patient felt trapped caused him to respond with the symptom of choking for breath. This pattern had originally been established when he actually had been physically trapped. With this recognition, the symptom was markedly alleviated.

When the Patient Seems to "Dry Up" in Conversations, Being Unable to Produce Any More Significant Material

Periods of resistance may develop during the course of therapy characterized by an almost complete cessation of activity. The patient will spend many sessions in fruitless attempts at conversation; he seems to be up against a barrier that he cannot break through. Attitudes of disappointment and hopelessness contribute to his inertia until he resigns himself to making no further efforts. He may even decide to abandon therapy. When such circumstances threaten, hypnosis may be tried to mobilize productivity. A variety of techniques may be used, including verbalizing one's thoughts without restraint (free association) in the trance, dream and fantasy stimulation, mirror gazing, automatic writing, play therapy, dramatic acting, regression and reliving (revivification), and the production of experimental conflicts (Wolberg, 1964). The specific method employed is usually determined by the therapist's experience and preference as well as by the patient's aptitudes in working with one or another technique.

A patient who had been working satisfactorily with me began to develop silences that greatly puzzled her since she had up to this time been quite garrulous in her ramblings. "When I try to think, my mind goes blank," she said. "Nothing comes to me." After several frustrating sessions, hypnosis was induced, and she was encouraged to talk about her mental meanderings. She began to moan and cry. "Grief, grief. It's all death—as if it's all over. It's my father; he died of cancer, and I took care of him. He keeps coming back. It chokes me up. It's as if it's all happening again." The patient then revealed, expressing great feelings of guilt, that while she had nursed her father during his illness, she had experienced tender and then voluptuous feelings for him. During his illness she was able to have him all to herself for the first time. Her mother was only too willing to let her take care of him. Sexual excitement was strong during this period, and she harbored guilt feelings during and after her father's death, scarcely daring to think about it. "I'm frightened. I know I felt guilty about my desire to be close to my father. After he died, I felt cold and detached. Maybe that is why I can't feel anything for men now. I realize I do this with all men, that is, I want to baby them, take care of them. I had been taking care of one man I know who got sick with the flu. I sponge-bathed him and got so sexually excited I could hardly stand it. The thought occurs to me that I would like to take care of you too. I'm so ashamed to talk about this." From this the patient stated she understood the reason for her guilt feelings and why they were causing resistance to therapy. She herself was able to interpret the transference to me of her feelings for her father. From then on she progressed satisfactorily in treatment.

When the Patient is Unable to Deal with Forces that Block the Transformation of Insight into Action

The mere development of insight is not enough to insure the correction of neurotic attitudes and patterns; it must be employed toward constructive action. Unfortunately, there are often anxieties and resistances that obstruct this process and bring therapy to an incomplete end. Hypnosis is sometimes useful in converting insightful perception into action, and it can achieve this goal in a number of ways. First, one may attempt by various techniques to explore resistance to change, the patient associating to fantasies or the dramatic acting-out of certain healthy courses of action. Second, posthypnotic suggestions can be made to the effect that the patient will want more and more to engage in actions that are necessary and that are being resisted. Third, role playing can be used, the patient dramatizing various situations in the present or future and verbalizing insights or fears to the therapist. Fourth, in somnambulistic subjects experimental conflicts may be set up to test the patient's readiness to execute necessary and desirable acts and to investigate reactions to their completion.

One of my patients, a man with a passive personality, had gained insight into some of the roots of his problem during therapy; he also realized the destructive consequences of his failure to be self-assertive. He wanted to change but was paralyzed at knowing how to begin. The best he could do was to fantasize walking into his employer's office and boldly asking for a promotion. In his fantasy he was rewarded with a higher position and a handsome raise in salary. But, he could not muster the courage to face his employer in real life, and he expressed fears of being turned down. In hypnotic role playing he took the part both of himself and his employer and vehemently discussed the pros and cons of his position. However, he still could not get himself to act. Since he was able to develop posthypnotic amnesia, I decided to try to set up an experimental conflict. I suggested that he imagine himself asking for a promotion. Then I told him to forget the suggestion but, upon emerging from the trance, to feel as if he had actually made the request. The first two attempts were followed by tension, headaches, and discouragement. This indicated that the patient was not yet prepared to take the necessary step forward. We, nonetheless, continued discussion and role playing, and a third experimental situation resulted in a feeling of elation and accomplishment. The next day the patient spontaneously approached his employer and was rewarded with success. Thereafter the patient began to act with more assurance, and his progress in therapy helped him to become more positive in his general behavior.

When the Patient has Problems in Terminating Therapy

Difficulties in ending therapy are sometimes experienced by patients who, having been freed of neurotic symptoms, are afraid of losing what they have gained and suffering a relapse. Patients with dependent personalities may resist ending treatment with astounding stubbornness. Contrary to what might be expected, the adroit application of hypnosis can help some of these patients toward self-reliance by relieving their tension at points where they try to act independently. The patient may also be taught self-hypnosis for purposes of relaxation and shown how to investigate spontaneously—through dreams, fantasies, and associations—the problems that arise daily from demands to adjust to specific situations. In this way responsibility is transferred to the patient toward becoming more capable of self-determination. Intervals between visits with the therapist are gradually prolonged. In the beginning the patient may resort to daily sessions of self-hypnosis because of anxiety. But as more confidence is developed in the ability to survive alone, self-hypnosis exercises become irregular, and finally they are resorted to only when tensions cry for relief. In many patients, however, regular relaxation exercises are an important part of adjustment and may be prolonged indefinitely with beneficial effect. In this respect a relaxing and ego-building cassette tape may be of help.

The situations just described are no more than brief outlines of how hypnosis may be effective in psychotherapy and only suggest the various ways in which the trance can be used as an adjunctive catalyzing procedure. Since all psychotherapy is a blend of the therapist's individual personality and techniques, no two therapists will operate identically. Each therapist has a particular philosophy about how people become neurotically ill and how they get well again. If a therapist believes that unconscious memories and conflicts are the basis for all neurotic ailments, digging will be indulged to uncover the emotional conflictual poison that has accumulated. Once it is released, the psyche will presumably heal. Freud and Breuer originally used hypnosis in this way and scored occasional success with some patients. They recorded their findings in *Studien über Hysterie,* the revolutionary book that was a precursor of psychoanalytic theories and methods. Although hypnosis used in this way may be instrumental in releasing repressed memories, we now know that the majority of patients are not helped by this process alone. Interesting and dramatic as are the results, additional techniques are necessary if we are to achieve lasting benefit.

There are other therapists whose theories about how people become emotionally ill involve the concepts of faulty learning and conditioning. They use hypnosis to reinforce their strategems of teaching their patients new patterns of habit formation, thinking, and action.

Although these "behavioral" methods are responsible for considerable progress in the treatment of some ailments, they are not successful in dealing with all problems. But neither is any other technique.

One of the most important points to be made about hypnosis is that it can be helpful as a catalyst irrespective of the method of psychotherapy. Some therapists are not able to use hypnosis with any measure of success, either for personality reasons or because of unresolvable prejudices. This does not invalidate hypnosis as a procedure. Hypnosis, like any other area of specialization, requires particular abilities and skills. Not every therapist is able to amalgamate hypnosis with one's personality and technical training.

It should be stressed again that hypnosis and any other catalyzing technique must be used intelligently within the context of a comprehensive treatment plan and with due regard for limitations. Applied indiscriminately such techniques not only fail to serve a therapeutic purpose, but their ineffectiveness tends to discredit them as worthwhile procedures and to impede their acceptance. Used at strategic points in psychotherapy, catalyzing methods may facilitate progress. In this way they can add an important dimension to the technical skills of the psychotherapist.

Case Illustration

The following is the fourth therapeutic session with a male patient who came to treatment because of work problems and terrifying nightmares of which the patient had no memory. These conditions had existed for several years, and after a period of psychotherapy with a psychoanalyst in the Midwest, he had derived some benefit from the sessions. However, he was unable to remember any dreams or to associate freely. The session that follows is the first one during which hypnosis was employed. It illustrates the use of various techniques in hypnoanalysis for the purpose of exposing a dynamic focus.

Pt. I am in good shape today, really, for no particular reason that I can think of, and yesterday I didn't feel so good. I had a fight with my wife where I came off very badly.

Th. Shall we go into that?

Pt. I was thinking the last time that this has degenerated into one session after another, my complaining about my wife. You know, I mean the material is all the same. When I think about it, I am really convinced the trouble is with me, not with her. Not that she doesn't have her troubles, don't mistake me; but I am really convinced if she had married a man, in every sense of the word, who really behaved as one, that many of her difficulties and hostilities would be erased.

Th. If she married a man? [*Obviously the patient has doubts about his masculinity.*]

Pt. If she had married a man—you know what I mean—a forceful guy who really ran the roost and her, who, well (*pause*).

Th. You mean, she would then straighten out?

Pt. Yes.

Th. So that the emphasis would be on whether you would like to be this kind of guy. Would you?

Pt. Yes. Yes. Yes.

Th. Do you think you would like to be a forceful guy?

Pt. Certainly. Well, I don't say that a man has to be—I don't mean he has to be brutish or stubborn or insensitive or unintelligent or dull. I don't think any of those things are necessary just to be a well-adjusted man. Don't you agree?

Th. Mm. All right, if you sense that there is a certain lack in you, that should be where we direct our therapeutic effort.

Pt. Right, I should say so; I agree a hundred percent. That is exactly my point, that, you know, I felt not much was accomplished last time, that I had spent all this time talking about my wife, what I said and what she said. What she said is not as important as what I did about it, or why the situation ever got to the point where she would say such a thing. She is not the patient. (*pause*)

Th. All right, then what would you like to talk about?

Pt. Well, I had a nightmare Tuesday night, that was the night. I had no memory of it, except when I woke up I thought I was choking; not exactly choking, but my throat was full of phlegm, or something. I had never had that one before, although, as you know, I have never been able to remember a nightmare. [*It is quite possible, I feel at this point, that the nightmare contains a core problem that he is repressing.*]

Th. It may be possible to catch it, to have it repeat itself and remember it in hypnosis.

Pt. That would be fascinating.

Th. We might be able to revive it so that you will be able to see the kind of nightmare that you repress, and maybe get some clues as to what these nightmares are all about. Now what was this fight all about? Just tell me very rapidly.

Pt. Very rapidly, last night, as you know, our house is in a big turmoil, without a kitchen really; we have a temporary kitchen, and so forth. I took a nap before dinner, before we went out to dinner last night. We go out to dinner almost every night because we have no kitchen. I said, "I actually am afraid that I am getting anemic again," because I was, and she said, "Are you taking your medicine?"—this is pills and stuff—and I said to her, "No, I am not, because I don't have enough for lunch." The point of it is, when I take this medicine, these pills, I have a ravenous appetite; I have to have for lunch a complete meal with potatoes and vegetables, the whole damned thing. This was a criticism of her and she blew sky-high, and I felt lousy anyway, and I did not come up to scratch at all. That is what it was all about. We went to dinner. Well, no, we had a fight a half hour later. We came home. She wanted to make love. I felt so lousy, I was really so tired, sick, tired.

Th. What day was this?

Pt. Oh, that was yesterday.

Th. That was yesterday?

Pt. That was yesterday, that was last night.

Th. Thursday?

Pt. Yes.

Th. What events happened on the day preceding your nightmare?

Pt. Well, I came here.

Th. You were here?

Pt. Yes.

Th. Anything else?

Pt. No. I haven't even done much work. I tried it. I have a very difficult time working. I tried reading, a romantic story, actually in romantic terms. It is about a woman who never thought she had any charm but plenty of character, and a guy with tremendous charm who thought he had no character. This, as I say, in fictional, dramatic, romantic terms are my wife and I. Now, my wife, she had done a tremendous lot for me, in many, many ways, tremendous therapy, and I actually have done a lot for her. She looks different. She walks into a room differently. She is an assured, attractive, charming woman. She is very well liked and admired, and she wasn't this when I met her.

Th. You have really helped her a great deal in this area.

Pt. Yes, and she helped me tremendously.

Th. Does she realize how much you have helped her?

Pt. Yes, sure she does.

Th. She realizes then this marriage has to go on?

Pt. Oh, yes; oh, yes. Actually this marriage will go on, no matter what I say. This marriage basically, basically is a good marriage. We need each other; we need each other very much. We give a lot to each other. It has been going to pieces a lot lately, but basically the foundation is good, I think; I am not sure. (*laughs*) I think I am sure. (*pause*)

Th. All right. Do you want to relax now?

Pt. Yes. Do you mind if I take my coat off? It's hot; it's tight; and I think I'll do better with it off. (*takes off coat.*)

The hypnotic induction process I will use is hand levitation. There are many methods of trance induction and a therapist may employ any of these, usually perfecting one technique. The relaxation method described in the chapter dealing with the making of a relaxing and ego-building cassette tape I find is the most suitable technique for most patients.

Th. Supposing you just lean back; stretch yourself out, and, for a moment, close your eyes and begin relaxing. Relax your forehead; purposely concentrate on your forehead, and your eyes, and your face, and your neck, and your shoulders. Let your arms relax. Relax your body. Then bring your hands, the palms of your hands, down on your thighs. Open your eyes; watch your hands. Just observe your hands. Concentrate on everything your hands do; sort of focus all your attention on your hands and keep all other sensations in the periphery. You may notice that your hands feel heavy as they press down on your thighs. Perhaps you notice the roughness of the texture of your trousers on your fingertips and palms. You may notice the warmth of your hands, or a little tingling in your hands. Notice whatever sensations there may be. Concentrate your attention on your hands; watch your hands. The next thing you will notice as you observe this over here, this right hand, is that very slowly your fingers will begin to spread, the spaces between the fingers will be wider and wider.

The spaces between fingers grow wider, and wider, and wider, just like that. And then you begin to notice that there will be a lifting of the fingers, slowly. One of the fingers will start lifting from your thigh, and then the rest of the fingers will follow, and then the hands will slowly begin to lift and move straight up in the air, moving, moving, and as they move, you will watch them, fascinated, as they move, slowly, automatically, without any effort on your part. Then your hand moves up, up. It moves toward your face; eventually it will touch your face, but only when it touches your face will you be asleep. [*The word "sleep" is used only because it signifies the deepest kind of relaxation. Obviously the patient will not be asleep*]. You will get drowsier and drowsier, but you will not fall asleep, and you must not fall asleep until your hand touches your face. And as your hand moves toward your face, you get drowsier, and drowsier, and drowsier, and just as soon as your hand touches your face, you will feel yourself dozing off and going to sleep, deeply asleep. You are getting very tired now, very, very drowsy; your eyes are getting heavier and heavier; your breathing is getting deeper and automatic; you feel yourself getting very, very tired, very drowsy; your hand is moving up, up, up toward your face. As soon as it touches your face, you will be asleep, deeply asleep. You will be very, very tired. Everything is floating off in the distance. You are getting very drowsy, very drowsy, drowsier, drowsier, drowsier. Your hand is moving up, up, up, up, toward your face; it approaches your face. Your eyes will soon close, and you will go deeply to sleep; but do not fall asleep until your hand touches your face. Your breathing is getting deep; you are getting very tired; everything is slipping away into the distance. Your eyes are shutting. You are going into a deep, deep, deep sleep; you are very drowsy now. You are very tired, very sleepy. Your hand is coming toward your face; now it touches your face. Now you are going to sleep, and you are going to stay asleep until I give the command to wake up. Your sleep is getting deeper, and deeper, and deeper. [*The patient's hand touches his face; his eyes close; and he is breathing deeply and regularly.*]

I am going to take your hand over here and bring it down to your thigh, just like this. You keep getting drowsier, and drowsier, and drowsier. Listen carefully to me. I am going to stroke your left arm, and your forearm and your hand, and as I stroke them, I am going to count from one to five. You will notice that as I count, you get the feeling as if your arm has become just as stiff and heavy as a board. As I stroke it, the arm gets heavier, and heavier, and heavier. Your arm is getting heavy and stiff, heavy and stiff, heavy and stiff, just like a board. The arm is getting heavier, heavier, stiff, stiff, stiff, stiff. One, it gets stiff and heavy like a board. Two, just as stiff as a board. Three, stiffer and stiffer; the arm is getting stiff. Four, stiff and heavy. Five, stiff, heavy; when I try to bend it, it will resist motion. The harder you try to move it, the heavier and stiffer it becomes. It will be impossible to raise it no matter how hard you try. However, when I snap my fingers, when I snap my fingers, your arm will relax. (*pause, then sound of fingers snapping*) Now you can raise your arm, if you wish. (*The patient lifts his arm slightly.*)

Now, relax yourself all over and fall asleep, even deeper. Your eyes are glued together, very, very, very tightly glued together, as if little steel bands bind them together. They are very tightly bound together. The harder you try to open your eyes, the heavier your lids are. Finally together, and you feel yourself dozing off, going into an even deeper sleep. You are getting drowsier, drowsier, very tired, very, very sleepy. (*long pause*)

Listen carefully to me. I am going to stroke your hand, and your forearm, and your arm, and as I do that, it will become just as light as a feather. As a matter of fact, it may start swinging up in the air spontaneously; it will become so light that it will almost automatically swing straight up in the air, just as light as a feather, straight up. It floats around in the air now, floats around in the air, just as light as a feather. It floats around in the air, just as light as a feather, until I snap my fingers. (*The patient easily lifts his arm and waves it.*) Then it will slowly come down, slowly down. Now it slowly comes down, right down to your thigh, and you slip off into a deeper sleep, a deeper sleep. (*The arm comes down.*) When I talk to you next, you will be still more deeply asleep. (*long pause*)

Now, I want you to imagine yourself walking outdoors. As soon as you see yourself walking outdoors, raise your left hand about 6 inches. (*Hand rises.*) Now bring it down. Again visualize yourself walking outdoors, raise your left hand about 6 inches. (*Hand rises.*) Now bring it down. Again visualize yourself walking outdoors on the street, and see yourself entering an alley between two buildings. You turn into the alleyway and you walk slowly, and, as you do, on the right-hand side of the alleyway you notice a pail of water, steaming hot water. As soon as you see that, raise your hand about 6 inches. (*Hand rises.*) Good. Now bring it down. Listen carefully to me. Try now to test how hot that water is. See yourself walking over to the pail of water. You take your right hand and plunge it into the water, and as you do, you get a sensation of scalding, of heat. As soon as you feel that, indicate it to me by your hand rising about 6 inches. (*Hand rises.*) The hand feels tingly and sensitive and tender. I am going to show you how tender. I am going to show you how tender it is by poking it with a pin.

As soon as I poke your hand with a pin, it may feel very, very painful and tender. I will show you. Very, very painful, just like that. (*Patient withdraws hand.*) In contrast, this other hand is normal. (*Touched with a pin, the hand does not withdraw.*) Now your hand returns to normal sensation. Now the left hand is going to start getting numb. It is going to have a feeling, a peculiar feeling, almost as if I had injected novocain all the way around the wrist. This gives you a sensation of numbness that increases to a point where you get the feeling you are wearing a stiff, heavy, leather glove. There is a sense of feeling, but no real sense of pain, a sense of feeling, but no real sense of pain, a sense of feeling, but no real sense of pain. As soon as you feel your hand growing numb and you have a sensation as if you are wearing a stiff, heavy, leather glove, indicate it to me by raising your hand about 6 inches. (*Hand rises.*) Good. Now bring it down.

I am going to poke this hand with a pin, and you will notice, in contrast to your right hand, which is rather tender, that this left hand will be numb; there will be no real pain. You will have a sensation of feeling, but no real pain. I will show you, no pain even when I poke it very deeply, no pain. You notice the difference when I touch this hand over here and the hand here. You notice that, don't you?

Pt. Yes.

Th. All right, now go to sleep, more deeply alseep. When I talk to you again, you will be even more deeply asleep, more deeply asleep. (*long pause*)

Now listen carefully to me. Even though you are asleep, it will be possible for you to talk to me just like a person talks in his sleep. You will be able to talk loudly and distinctly, but you will not wake up. I want you to imagine yourself walking outdoors again, but this time you walk out into a courtyard and you see a church, a beautiful church, steeple, spire, and a bell. As soon as you see the church, indicate it by your hand rising. (*Hand rises.*) Good. Now bring it down. Next you see the bell; the bell begins to move; the bell moves, and it starts clanging. You hear the clang clearly. As soon as you hear the bell clanging, indicate it to me by your hand rising about 6 inches. (*Hand rises.*) Now bring your hand down.

You turn around from the courtyard, and you go back to your home. You walk into the living room. You go over to the radio. You turn your radio on, and you hear a symphony orchestra. Beautiful music comes from the radio. As soon as you hear it, indicate this to me by your hand rising about 6 inches. (*Hand rises.*) Good. Now bring it down. Can you recognize the music?

Pt. Uh-huh.

Th. What was the music?

Pt. It is something by Bach.

Th. Good. Next, you decide to go to the theater. You walk along the street. Then you notice a theater; you have a hunch that you want to see something in this particular theater, but you don't know exactly what it is you want to see. You don't even look at the billboard to see what may be playing. You walk right into the theater, down to the fourth row orchestra and sit down. You look up and notice that the curtain is down. There are very few people in the theater. You are rather curious as to what is behind that curtain.

Pt. Uh-huh.

Th. As soon as you observe yourself sitting in the theater, indicate it to me by your hand rising about 6 inches. (*Hand rises.*) Good. Now bring it down.

In your curiosity you notice that there is a man with a gray suit, a tall young man, up there on the platform. [*To enhance identification, this person is of the same sex and attire as the patient.*] He seems to be peering behind the curtain as if his patience has almost come to an end and he would like to see what is going on backstage. But as he turns around, you notice that he has a horrified expression on his face as if he has seen something horrible, about the most horrible thing that could happen to a person. As you observe that, you begin to absorb some of that feeling. [*This is a technique of imagery evocation often useful in many ways.*] And you wonder what is behind that scene. I am going to count from one to five, and then snap my fingers. At the count of five, as I snap my fingers, the curtain will suddenly rise and you will see a scene that is what this man saw, the most horrible thing that can happen to a person. (*counting to five, then sound of fingers snapping*) Tell me about it as soon as you see it.

Pt. No, no (*crying*); no, no, no (*crying*); no, no, no, no, no; I don't know; I don't know (*screams with anguish*).

Th. Tell me.

Pt. I don't know; I don't know.

Th. What has frightened you?

Pt. Oh (*crying*), oh, no, no, no.

Th. The curtain is down.

Pt. Yes.

Th. Something frightened you.

Pt. Yes. (*crying*)

Th. The curtain goes down.

Pt. (*crying*) Oh, oh, oh.

Th. You saw something that frightened you.

Pt. I don't know; I don't know what I saw.

Th. All right, now listen carefully to me. I am going to help you. Something frightened you; something continues to frighten you all the time, and we have got to liberate you from that. You want to be liberated from that fright, don't you?

Pt. Yes, yes, yes.

Th. You would like to get over that fright. That fright makes you insecure. That fright may hold the key to your trouble.

Pt. Yes, yes, yes, yes, to the nightmare.

Th. And when we uncover that fright and see what it is and get it out of your system, get rid of it, we'll solve your nightmares.

Pt. Yes, that will be good.

Th. Now listen carefully to me. You don't know when this is going to happen. I am going to help you. You want to be helped?

Pt. Yes, yes.

Th. All right, now listen to me. As you sit there, the scene is going to change completely. Instead of being a horrible scene, it will change to a happy scene. You are going to notice the same man peering behind the curtain again, but this time when he turns around, he has a happy expression on his face. The whole atmosphere has changed. He feels very happy, very contented. As you see this wonderful expression on his face, you too feel a part of it. You realize he has seen the most wonderful thing that can happen to a person. You feel as if it is about to happen to you. You watch that curtain very closely. At the count of five, I will snap my fingers and you will see the most wonderful thing that can happen to a person. (*counting to five, then sound of fingers snapping*) As soon as you do, I want you to tell me about it without waking up.

Pt. It is a play. No, no. (*crying*)

Th. It is a play?

Pt. No. It is a play (*crying in an agitated way*).

Th. It is a play?

Pt. I am not happy—oh, oh. [*Apparently the nightmarish image is still with the patient, neutralizing the happy scene.*]

Th. You are not happy. The other thing bothers you, doesn't it?

Pt. I don't know what is behind that curtain. I don't know. I don't want to know. (*crying in anguish*)

Th. You don't know?

Pt. No.

Th. Listen carefully to me. You don't know what is behind it, but you would like to know and get rid of it?

Pt. Yes.

Th. I am going to try to help you now so you will get rid of it once and for all. (*Patient continues crying.*) Listen.

Pt. Yes, yes.

Th. I am going to count from one to five. At the count of five, suddenly a number is going to flash into your mind.

Th. The number will be the number of letters in the word that holds the clue to what is behind the curtain that frightens you. It may hold the clue to what is behind the nightmare that frightens you. As I count from one to five, a number will suddenly flash into your mind as if it has been etched out. That number will be the number of letters in the word, the key word, which contains a clue to this whole thing.

Pt. Uh-huh.

Th. And the letters all taken together, unscrambled, will give us the clue to the word that is so significant, that has within it the core of your problem. Do you understand me?

Pt. Yes, yes.

Th. Give me the first number that flashes in your mind when I count to five. One, two, three, four, five.

Pt. Eleven.

Th. Eleven. All right, now rapidly from one to five, when I reach the count of five, a letter will flash into your mind. Give me the letters, regardless of the order. One, two, three, four, five.

Pt. H.

Th. One, two, three, four, five.

Pt. P.

Th. One, two, three, four, five.

Pt. R.

Th. One, two, three, four, five.

Pt. M.

Th. One, two, three, four, five.

Pt. I.

Th. One, two, three, four, five.

Pt. L.

Th. One, two, three, four, five.

Pt. E.

Th. One, two, three, four, five.

Pt. H.

Th. One, two, three, four, five.

Pt. O.

Th. One, two, three, four, five.

Pt. A, m, n—I don't know.

Th. I will do it again. One, two, three, four, five.

Pt. A. O.

Th. All right, now listen carefully to me. I am going to count from one to five, and this time when I reach the count of five, all these letters will just scramble together and make a word that will give you a clue. You understand me?

Pt. Yes.

Th. One, two, three, four, five.

Pt. Oh, oh, homophrile, homophrile.

Th. Homophrile? [*This word, it was determined later, was "friend and lover of men," a designation of "homosexual." The patient's concern of his wife not being married to a man is somehow related to the fear that he is a homosexual.*]

Th. Now, you have a clue. You are going to have a dream. The dream will not be too scary a dream, but it will be a first step in coming to an understanding of what this fear is. Do you understand me? The dream will be the first step.

Pt. Yes.

Th. It will have within it the essence of the word that you just spelled out for me. As soon as you have this dream, which may or may not be like the nightmares you have, you will open your eyes and wake up. As soon as you awaken, everything will be blotted out of your mind. It will be as if you are waking from a sound sleep. Then what I will do is tap three times on the side of the desk, like this. (*three taps*) With the third tap you will suddenly remember the dream that caused you to wake up. Do you understand me?

Pt. Yes.

Th. You will have a dream. The dream will contain a clue, and then, as soon as you have had the dream, you will wake up. But you will blot the dream from you mind, or it will be very vague in your mind. You won't remember, but on the third tap the whole thing will pop into your mind. Do you understand me?

Pt. Yes.

Th. Go to sleep and have a dream, and then wake up. [*The object in having the patient repress the dreams is to protect him from any associated anxiety. The tapping signal may release the dream if the anxiety is not too great.*]

Th. (*After several minutes the patient awakens.*) How do you feel?

Pt. A little tired.

Th. A little tired. What are you thinking about?

Pt. Well, well, I know I cried. But . . .

Th. Anything else? (*pause and three taps*)

Pt. Oh, yes, I was on that stage.

Th. Yes.

Pt. And only I came into—it was—there was a woman seated at a desk and she had her hair tied on top of her head, and the whole thing was so red, damask, a red house on the stage, a sort of a whorehouse. This woman I guess was sort of a madame; and there is a painting by Toulouse-Lautrec, that is who her face was. She had a very sharp nose. Maybe it was one of the entertainers. Anyway, she was seated at her desk, and this is on the stage, red lights, and I walked in and she gets up and greets me; and she is an older woman, sort of, and she begins to caress me. Only it gets too much, clutching at my clothes. And then about five girls come out, and they begin caressing me, but then after their caresses started, they start to bite me, to attack me, to tear off my clothes. I am surprised, a little frightened, turn almost into harpies actually, in the classical sense of the word. I back away from them and back away from them, and I fall over the footlights into the orchestra pit. That was the dream I just had.

Th. I see.

Pt. The whole thing is red. Oh, boy, what did I go through today?

Th. You seemed to go through plenty.

Pt. I remember crying, and I couldn't stop. I remember what I went through, actually. I remember you told me to look behind that curtain, and, you know, I couldn't see behind it. I don't know why I cried though. I was scared.

Th. Something scared you. You have gotten a clue as to what the essence of your nightmares might be. It is just the first clue, the first breaking down of your repression. As we keep at this, you should gradually be able to lift your repressions and become liberated from this monster that has you by the throat.

Pt. I can't explain it to you. I don't know what made me cry because I didn't see anything. I know you said it was pleasant as I approached that curtain again. What made me cry, I have no idea.

Th. Mm, hmm.

Pt. I certainly had a strange experience.

Th. Do you feel you were in a trance?

Pt. I must have been. It is a funny thing, I could hear you, I knew what was happening. I can remember. I am sure I recall the thing, and yet there is no question that I was hardly myself, like in the crying.

Th. I am sorry that it had to be as painful as it was.

Pt. Strangely enough, I can't explain it to you. I can't remember. It was almost a release.

Th. Yes.

Pt. And that is true.

Th. Uh-huh.

Pt. The crying, and it wasn't (*pause*).

Th. It should make you feel better, and it should possibly enable you to remember your dreams or nightmares. How do you think you would feel if a thing like your dream happened in reality? Supposing you were to walk into a house and were greeted by these clawing harpies who came at you and started tearing at your skin? How do you think you would feel in a situation like that?

Pt. I was frightened, frightened; I wanted to get out of the whorehouse.

Th. There is a sexual tinge to this?

Pt. Oh, yes, very definitely; yes, very definitely.

Th. Do you remember anything about letters?

Pt. I remember all the letters, but it didn't come out with anything, did it?

Th. You came out with a group of letters that start with h-o-m-o.

Pt. I didn't use all the letters, did I?

Th. Not all.

Pt. I am not very good at anagrams, but I will try to figure out what this means.

At the next session the patient reported another dream that he actually remembered, the hypnotic experience apparently having resolved the resistance to dreaming. A woman wearing a red gown descended a flight of stairs. He noticed with terror her exposed pubic area, which consisted of an open gaping mouth. As he watched, the woman changed into a threatening tiger with a fierce open mouth. At this point the patient began to discuss his feelings about his mother, whom he remembered as wearing a red gown. He was overprotected by his mother, his father having been an extremely passive person who died when the patient was young. He remembered with guilt having some vague sexual feelings toward her. When he married, there were some problems with impotence and sexual indifference, but his wife wooed him out of his apathy. But this seduction apparently opened up a pocket of oedipal anxieties. Occasional homosexual fantasies were not acted out. It is interesting that he began to remember his nightmares which were patterned after the hypnotic dream and dealt with his fears of women. Soon he identified his wife in his dreams. After a quarrel he would almost always have a nightmare that evening. At around the fifteenth session he started complaining that his symptoms were not being relieved as rapidly as he wished, and he associated this with the fact that his father did not help him much. The transference elements were exposed in his dreaming about me as being ineffectual like his father. I interpreted his transference feelings, and the interpretations had a dramatic effect on him, enabling him to see how he was translating what had happened before in the here and now. From this point on we were able to establish excellent rapport. He was able to relate spendidly to his wife and his children, his work block disappeared, and his nightmares vanished.

Hypnotic induction techniques are illustrated in Chapter 15, which deals with the making of a cassette tape, as well as in the case illustration in this chapter. Other techniques may be found elsewhere (Wolberg, 1948).

Conclusion

In most cases interview psychotherapy will proceed satisfactorily without needing to resort to catalyzing techniques. However, when certain blocks to treatment develop or when it is difficult to define a dynamic focus, measures to resolve resistance or to accelerate progress may be of value. Here a wide range of methods is available, including confrontations, hypnosis, narcoanalysis, behavior therapy, Gestalt therapy, guided imagery, emotive release strategies, experiential therapy, dream analysis, family therapy, and analytic group therapy. Preference for techniques is generally determined by the therapist's training and experience with certain modalities. Resistance, of course, can also develop with these catalyzing interventions, and the manifestations of resistance may serve as a dynamic focus, the understanding and working through of which may be of consequence for both symptom relief and personality change.

Certain advantages accrue to the use of hypnosis as an accelerating technique where (1) incentives for interview therapy are lacking, (2) symptom relief is an exclusive motivation, (3) rapport is delayed in developing, (4) verbalization is blocked or impoverished, (5) dreams and fantasies are forgotten, (6) transference arousal is deemed essential, (6) repressed memories require recall, (7) greater activity is essential in the interview, (8) little material is forthcoming, (9) insight is not being converted into action, and (10) when there are problems in termination. Hypnosis also enhances the placebo effect in therapy, intensifies the force of suggestion, and opens the floodgates of emotional catharsis. Some therapists may not be able to utilize hypnosis as an adjunct in therapy because they fear its effects or are skeptical of its value. In such cases they may be more amenable to other accelerating techniques (Wolberg, 1977, pp. 761–833).

CHAPTER 14

Crisis Intervention

In recent years a great deal of planning has been conducted in the United States in an attempt to lower the rate of admissions to mental institutions, diminish the incidence of suicides, quiet the outbreak of violence in the streets, and in general reduce psychiatric morbidity. One of the main developments toward these goals has been the evolvement of methodologies in the area of crisis intervention. The recognition that crises are so common in the lives of all people has encouraged the growth of walk-in clinics, psychiatric emergency units in general hospitals, suicide prevention hot-line telephone services, and a variety of other facilities whose aim is restoring, in as few sessions as possible, the psychological balance of persons in states of emotional excitement or collapse.

What has become painfully apparent is that practically every individual alive is a potential candidate for a breakdown in the adaptive equilibrium if the stressful pressures are sufficiently severe. A crisis may precipitate around any incident that overwhelms one's coping capacities. The crisis stimulus itself bears little relationship to the intensity of the victim's reaction. Some persons can tolerate with equanimity tremendous hardships and adversity. Others will show a catastrophic response to what seems like a minor mishap. A specifically important event, like abandonment by a love object, can touch off an explosive reaction in one who would respond much less drastically to bombings, hurricanes, cataclysmic floods, shipwreck, disastrous reverses of economic fortune, and major accidents. The two important variables are, first, the *meaning* to the individual of the calamity and, second, the *flexibility of one's defenses,* that is, the prevailing ego strength.

The immediate response to a situation that is interpreted as cataclysmic, such as the sudden death of a loved one, a violent accident, or an irretrievable shattering of security, is a dazed shock reaction. As if to safeguard oneself, a peculiar denial mechanism intervenes accompanied by numbness and detachment. This defensive maneuver, however, does not prevent the intrusion of upsetting fantasies or frightening nightmares from breaking through periodically. When this happens, denial and detachment may again intervene to reestablish a tenuous equilibrium, only to be followed by a repetition of fearsome ruminations. It is as if the individual is both denying and then trying somehow to acquire understanding and to resolve anxiety and guilt. Various reactions to and defenses against anxiety may precipitate self-accusations, aggression, phobias, and excessive indulgence in alcohol or tranquilizers. Moreover, dormant past conflicts may be aroused, marshalling neurotic symptomatic and distorted characterologic displays. At the core of this confounding cycle of denial and twisted repetitive remembering is, first, the mind's attempt to protect itself by repressing what had happened and, second, to heal itself by reprocessing and working through the traumatic experience in order to reconcile it with the present reality situation. In an individual with good ego strength this struggle usually terminates in a successful resolution of the crisis event. Thus, following a crisis situation, most people are capable after a period of 4 to 6 weeks of picking up the pieces, putting themselves together, and resuming their lives along lines similar to before. People who come to a clinic or to a private practitioner are those who have failed to achieve resolution of stressful life events.

In some of these less fortunate individuals the outcome is dubious, eventuating in prolonged and even permanent crippling of functioning. To shorten the struggle and to bolster success in those who otherwise would be destined to a failing adaptation, psychotherapy offers the individual an excellent opportunity to deal constructively with the crisis.

In the psychotherapeutic treatment of crisis situations (crisis therapy) the goal is rapid emotional relief—and not basic personality modification. This does not mean that we neglect opportunities to effectuate personality change. Since such alterations will require time to provide for resolution of inner conflicts and the reshuffling of the intrapsychic structure, the most we can hope for is to bring the patient to some *awareness* of how underlying problems are related to the immediate crisis. It is gratifying how some patients will grasp the significance of this association and in the post-therapy period work toward a betterment of fundamental characterologic distortions. Obviously, where more than the usual six-session limit of crisis-oriented therapy can be offered, the greater will be the possibility of demonstrating the operative dynamics. Yet where the patient possesses a motivation for change—and the existing crisis often stimulates such a motivation—even six sessions may register a significant impact on the psychological status quo.

Variables Determining the Mode of Crisis Therapy

Catastrophic Symptoms Requiring Immediate Attention

Selection of techniques in crisis therapy are geared to four variables (Wolberg, 1972). The first variable we must consider relates to catastrophic symptoms that require immediate handling. The most common emergencies are severe depressions with strong suicidal tendencies, acute psychotic upsets with aggressive or bizarre behavior, intense anxiety and panic states, excited hysterical reactions, and drug and alcoholic intoxications. Occasionally, symptoms are sufficiently severe to constitute a portentous threat to the individual or others, under which circumstances it is essential to consider immediate hospitalization. Conferences with responsible relatives or friends will then be essential in order to make provision for the most adequate resource. Fortunately, this contingency is rare because of the availability of modern somatic therapy. Consultations with a psychiatrist skilled in the administration of somatic treatments will, of course, be in order. Electroconvulsive therapy may be necessary to interrupt suicidal depression or excitement. Acute psychotic attacks usually yield to a regimen of the neuroleptics in the medium of a supportive and sympathetic relationship. It may require almost superhuman forebearance to listen attentively to the patient's concerns, with minimal expressions of censure or incredulity for delusional or hallucinatory content. Panic reactions in the patient require not only fortitude on the part of the therapist, but also the ability to communicate compassion blended with hope. In an emergency room in a hospital it may be difficult to provide the quiet objective atmosphere that is needed, but an attentive sympathetic doctor or nurse can do much to reassure the patient. Later, frequent visits, even daily, do much to reassure a frightened patient who feels himself or herself to be out of control.

Less catastrophic symptoms are handled in accordance with the prevailing emotional state. Thus during the first stages of denial and detachment, techniques of confrontation and active interpretation of resistances may help to get the patient talking. Where there is extreme repression, hypnotic probing and narcoanalysis may be useful. On the other hand, where the patient is flooded by anxiety, tension, guilt, and ruminations concerning the stressful events, attempts are made to reestablish controls through relaxation methods (like meditation, autogenic training, relaxing hypnotherapy, and biofeedback), or by pharmacological tranquilization (Valium, Librium), or by rest, diversions (like social activities, hobbies, and occupational therapy), or by behavioral desensitization and reassurance.

The Nature of the Precipitating Agency

Once troublesome symptoms are brought under reasonable restraint, attention can be focused on the second important variable in the crisis reaction, the nature of the precipitating agency. This is usually in the form of some environmental episode that threatens the individual's security or damages the self-esteem. A developmental crisis, broken love affair, rejection by or death of a love object, violent marital discord, persisting delinquent behavior and drug consumption by important family members, transportation or industrial and other accidents, development of an incapacitating or life-threatening illness, calamitous financial reverses, and many other provocative events may be the triggers that set off a crisis. It is rare that the external precipitants that the patient holds responsible for the present troubles are entirely or even most importantly the cause.

Indeed, the therapist will usually find that the patient participates actively in initiating and sustaining many of the environmental misfortunes that presumably are to blame. Yet respectful listening and questioning will give the therapist data regarding the character structure of the patient, the need for upsetting involvements, projective tendencies, and the legitimate hardships to which the patient is inescapably exposed. An assay of the existing and potential inner strengths in relation to the unavoidable stresses that must be endured and identification of remediable problem areas will enable the therapist better to focus the therapeutic efforts. Crucial is some kind of cognitive reprocessing that is most effectively accomplished by interpretation. The object is to help the patient find a different meaning for the upsetting events and to evolve more adequate ways of coping.

The Impact of the Family on the Patient

The third variable, the impact on the patient of the family system, is especially important in children and adolescents as well as in those living in a closely knit family system. The impact of the family may not be immediately apparent, but a crisis frequently indicates a collapsing family system, the end result of which is a breakdown in the identified patient's capacities for adaptation. Crisis theory assumes that the family is the basic unit and that an emotional illness in any family member connotes a disruption in the family homeostasis. Such a disruption is not altogether bad because through it opportunities are opened up for change with potential benefit to each member. Traditional psychotherapy attempts to treat the individual patient and often relieves the family of responsibility for what is going on with the patient. Crisis theory, on the other hand, insists that change must involve more than the patient. The most frequently used modality, consequently, is family therapy, the object of which is the harnessing and expansion of the constructive elements in the family situation. The therapist does not attempt to halt the crisis by reassurance but rather to utilize the crisis as an instrument of change. During a crisis a family in distress may be willing to let a therapist enter into the picture, recognizing that it cannot by itself cope with the existing emergency. The boundaries are at the start fluid enough so that new consolidations become possible. The family system prior to the crisis and after the crisis usually seals off all points of entry. During the crisis, before new and perhaps even more destructive decisions have been made, a point is reached where we may introduce some new perspectives. This point may exist for only a short period of time; therefore it is vital that there be no delay in rendering service.

Thus a crisis will permit intervention that would not be acceptable before nor subsequent to the crisis explosion. One deterent frequently is the family's insistentence on hospitalization, no longer being able to cope with the identified patient's upsetting behavior. Alternatives to hospitalization will present themselves to an astute therapist who establishes contact with the family. Some of the operative dynamics may become startingly apparent by listening to the interchanges of the patient and the family.

The most important responsibility of the therapist is to get the family to understand what is going on with the patient in the existing setting and to determine why the crisis has occurred now. Understandably there is a history to the crisis and a variety of solutions have been tried. The therapist may ask himself why these measures were attempted and why they failed, or at least why they have not succeeded sufficiently. The family should be involved in solutions to be utilized and should have an idea as to the reasons for this. Assignment of tasks for each member is an excellent method of getting people to work together and such assignments may be quite arbitrary ones. The important thing is to get every member involved in some way. This will bring out certain resistances which may have to be negotiated. Trades may be made with the object of securing better cooperation. Since crisis intervention is a short-term process, it should be made clear that visits are limited. This is to avoid dependencies and resentments about termination.

The Patient's Behavior and Its Roots

The fourth variable is often the crucial factor in intiating the crisis situation. Unresolved and demanding childhood needs, defenses and conflicts that obtrude themselves on adult adjustment, and compulsively dragoon the patient into activities that are bound to end in disaster, would seem to invite explorations that a therapist, trained in dynamic psychotherapeutic methodology, may with some probing be able to identify. The ability to relate the patient's outmoded and neurotic modes of behaving, and the circumstances of their development in early conditionings, as well as the recognition of how personality difficulties have brought about the crisis, would be highly desirable, probably constituting the difference between merely palliating the present problem and providing some permanent solution for it. Since the goals of crisis intervention are limited, however, to reestablishing the precrisis equilibrium, and the time allotted to therapy is circumscribed to the mere achievement of this goal, we may not be able to do much more than to merely point out the areas for further work and exploration. Because crisis therapy is goal limited, there is a tendency to veer away from insight therapies organized around psychodynamic models toward more active behavioral-learning techniques, which are directed at reinforcing appropriate and discouraging maladaptive behavior. The effort has been directed toward the treatment of couples, of entire families, and of groups of nonrelated people as primary therapeutic instruments. The basic therapeutic thrust is, as has been mentioned, on such practical areas as the immediate disturbing environmental situation and the patient's disruptive symptoms, employing a combination of active procedures like drug therapy and milieu therapy. The few sessions devoted to treatment in crisis intervention certainly prevent any extensive concern with the operations of unconscious conflict. Yet a great deal of data may be obtained by talking to the patient and by studying the interactions of the family, both in family therapy and through the observations of a psychiatric nurse, caseworker, or psychiatric team who visit the home. Such data will be helpful in crisis therapy planning or in a continuing therapeutic program.

In organizing a continuing program we must recognize, without minimizing the value of depth approaches, that not all persons, assuming that they can afford long-term therapy, are sufficiently well motivated, introspective, and possessed of qualities of sufficient ego strength to permit the use of other than expedient, workable, and goal-limited methods aimed at crisis resolution and symptom relief.

Technical Suggestions

The average patient applying for help generally complains about a disturbing symptom such as tension, anxiety, depression, insomnia, panicky feelings, physical problems, and so on. Associated life events are considered secondary circumstances even though it may become obvious that they are the primary etiological precipitating agencies. Sometimes the patient recognizes the importance of a traumatic situation, such as separation, divorce, death of a family member, an accident, or financial disaster, and will focus discussions around painful associations to these. In approaching such a patient, empathic listening is the keynote. The most that can be done during the first two sessions is to identify the key trouble areas, and perhaps reassure the patient that there *are* ways of coping with the difficulty since others have also gone through similar upsetting events and with proper therapy have overcome them and even have gotten stronger in the process. The following is an excerpt from an early interview with a woman suffering from a reactive depression.

Pt. It all seems hopeless. I just can't seem to pull myself together after Jack left me. I keep falling apart and can't interest myself in anything.

Th. Your reaction is certainly understandable. Why shouldn't you feel indignant, hurt and angry, and depressed. But you would like to get over Jack, wouldn't you, and go on to be happy again?

Pt. (*pause*) Do you think that's possible?

Th. If I didn't, I wouldn't be sitting here with you. Other women have gone through similar desertions and have come out on top. And you can too.

Pt. I'd like to start.

Th. We have started.

In allowing a patient to focus on his presenting problem the therapist must always attempt to answer the questions Why now? Why did the difficulty break out at this time? Did the patient in any way participate in bringing about the crisis? Though the latter may seem obvious, the patient may not see this clearly, but through interviewing and clarification he may be helped to identify the sources of the crisis and one's personal participation in it.

It is important to be alert to how the crisis can be converted into an opportunity for change. Appraisal of the patient's ego strength, flexibility, and motivation are helpful, though this assay at first may not be entirely accurate. The patient when first applying for help is at low ebb and may not present an optimistic picture of latent potentialities. These may filter through later on as hope penetrates the depressive fog in which the patient is enveloped.

As problems become clarified and identified

through interviewing, the patient and the family in family therapy will better be able to deal with such problems constructively. The therapist may sometimes do nothing more than facilitate ventilation of thoughts and feelings among the family members. Verbalization and communication have great powers of healing. The therapist need not sit in judgment over what is being said nor always offer golden words of advice. By keeping communication open, by asking the right questions, one may help the family to productive decisions that will lead to problem solving and resolution. It may be difficult at the start to get the family members to open up after years of withdrawal and secret manipulations. A simple invitation like "I believe you will all feel better if you each tell me what is on your mind" may get the conversational process going. If none starts, the therapist may ask a pertinent question as an opener or make a simple statement such as "I'll bet each of you feels worried about what has happened. Why don't you each talk about this."

Some patients are extremely concerned with their physical symptoms that accompany or are manifestations of anxiety, and they may be convinced, in spite of negative physical findings, that they have a terminal disease. Where there is a preoccupation with these symptoms, an explanation such as the following may help:

Th. When a person is upset emotionally every part of the body is affected. The heart goes faster; the muscles get tenser; headaches may occur; or the stomach may get upset. Practically every organ in the body may be affected. Fortunately, when the emotional upset passes, the organs will tend to recover.

Should the patient wonder why other people react less intensely to troubles than he does and blame himself for failing, he may be told that he can do something about it:

Th. Children are born different—some are active, some less active. You have a sensitive nervous system, which is both good and bad; good because you are a responsive person to even nuances, but also bad for you since you react very actively to stress and suffer a good deal. You can do something about this to reduce your overreaction to stress.

The following is a summation of practical points to pursue in the practice of crisis intervention.

1. *See the patient within 24 hours of the calling for help* even if it means canceling an appointment. A crisis in the life of an individual is apt to motivate one to seek help from some outside agency that otherwise would be avoided. Should such aid be immediately unavailable, one may in desperation exploit spurious measures and defenses that abate the crisis but compromise an optimal adjustment. More insidiously, the incentive for therapy will vanish with resolution of the emergency. The therapist should, therefore, make every effort to see a person in crisis preferably on the very day that help is requested.

2. At the initial interview *alert yourself to patients at high risk for suicide.* These are (a) persons who have a previous history of attempting suicide, (b) endogenous depression (history of cyclic attacks, early morning awakening, loss of appetite, retardation, loss of energy or sex drive), (c) young drug abusers, (d) alcoholic female patients, (e) middle-aged men recently widowed, divorced, or separated, (f) elderly isolated persons.

3. *Handle immediately any depression in the above patients.* Avoid hospitalization if possible except in deep depressions where attempts at suicide have been made recently or the past or are seriously threatened now. Electroconvulsive therapy is best for dangerous depressions. Institute antidepressant medications (Tofranil, Elavil, Sinequan) in adequate dosage where there is no immediate risk.

4. *Evaluate the stress situation.* Does it seem sufficiently adequate to account for the present crisis? What is the family situation, and how is it related to the patient's upset? What were past modes of dealing with crises, and how successful were they?

5. *Evaluate the existing support systems available to the patient* that you can utilize in

the therapeutic plan. How solid and reliable are certain members of the family? What community resources are available? What are the strengths of the family with whom the patient will live?

6. *Estimate the patient's ego resources.* What ego resources does the patient have to depend on, estimated by successes and achievements in the past? Positive coping capacities are of greater importance than the prevailing pathology.

7. *Help the patient to an awareness of the factors involved in the reaction to the crisis.* The patient's interpersonal relations should be reviewed in the hope of understanding and reevaluating attitudes and patterns that get the patient into difficulty.

8. *Provide thoughtful, empathic listening and supportive reassurance.* These are essential to enhance the working relationship and to restore hope. The therapist must communicate awareness of the patient's difficulties. The patient should be helped to realize what problems are stress related and that with guidance one can learn to cope with or remove the stress.

9. *Utilize tranquilizers only where anxiety is so great that the patient cannot make decisions.* When the patient is so concerned with fighting off anxiety that there is no cooperation with the treatment plan, prescribe an anxiolytic (Valium, Librium). This is a temporary expedient only. In the event a schizophrenic patient must continue to live with hostile or disturbed parents who fail to respond to or refuse exposure to family therapy, prescribe a neuroleptic and establish a way to see that medications are taken regularly.

10. *Deal with the immediate present and avoid probing of the past.* Our chief concern is the here and now. What is the patient's present life situation? Is trouble impending? The focus is on any immediate disruptive situation responsible for the crisis as well as on the corrective measures to be exploited. Historical material is considered only if it is directly linked to the current problem.

11. *Avoid exploring for dynamic factors.* Time in therapy is too short for this. Therapy must be reality oriented, geared toward problem solving. The goal is restoration of the precrisis stability. But if dynamic factors like transference produce resistance to therapy or to the therapist, deal rapidly with the resistances in order to dissipate them. Where dynamic material is "thrown" at the therapist, utilize it in treatment planning.

12. *Aim for increasing self-reliance and finding alternative constructive solutions for problems.* It is essential that the patient anticipate future sources of stress, learning how to cope with these by strengthening adaptive skills and eliminating habits and patterns that can lead to trouble.

13. *Always involve the family or significant others in the treatment plan.* A crisis represents both an individual and a family system collapse, and family therapy is helpful to alter the family system. A family member or significant friend should be assigned to supervise drug intake where prescribed and to share responsibility in depressed patients.

14. *Group therapy can also be helpful* both as a therapy in itself and as an adjunct to individual sessions. Contact with peers who are working through their difficulties is reassuring and educational. Some therapists consider short-term group therapy superior to individual therapy for crises.

15. *Terminate therapy within six sessions if possible and in extreme circumstances no later than 3 months after treatment has started* to avoid dependency. The patient is assured of further help in the future if required.

16. *Where the patient needs and is motivated for further help for purposes of greater personality development after the precrisis equilibrium has been restored, institute or refer for dynamically oriented short-term therapy.* In most cases, however, further therapy is not sought and may not be needed. Mastery of a stressful life experience through crisis intervention itself may be followed by new learnings and at least some personality growth.

Common Questions About Crisis Intervention

What would you consider a crisis by definition?

What constitutes a crisis varies in definition. Some restrict the definition to only violent emergencies. Others regard a crisis as reactions to any situation that upsets the adaptive balance. Many consider that any individual applying for help is actually in some state of crisis.

How far back was crisis intervention organized as a structured technique? Are there useful readings?

Eric Lindemann (1944) was among the first to recognize the value of crisis intervention in his work with the victims of the Coconut Grove (Boston) fire disaster. The organization of emergency services in hospitals and community mental health centers to help persons undergoing critical adaptive breakdowns has contributed a body of literature out of which may be mined valuable ideas about short-term intervention (Butcher & Maudal, 1976; Caplan, 1961, 1964; Coleman & Zwerling, 1959; Darbonne & Allen, 1967; Harris et al, 1963; Jacobson, 1965; Jacobson et al, 1965; Kalis et al, 1961; Morley, 1965; Rusk, 1971; J. Swartz, 1971).

Can one apply the principles of crisis intervention to conditions other than emergencies?

Emergencies constitute only a small proportion of the conditions for which people seek help. Crises for the most part are of a lesser intensity, but, nonetheless, are in need of immediate services to insure the highest degree of therapeutic effectiveness.

Are one-session contacts for crisis intervention of any value?

Very much so, but most patients will require more sessions for an adequate work-up, institution of treatment, and follow-up. The average number of sessions is six; sometimes a few more sessions are given.

Are community mental health concepts of any use in crisis intervention?

Drawing on community mental health concepts is considered by some to be of inestimable help in crisis intervention (Silverman, 1977), particularly when the goal is a servicing of sizable populations. Here a public health orientation employing systems theory and an ecological point of view may reduce the incidence of future crisis among target populations. Identification of potential users of mental health services, exploration of the kinds of problems that exist, and an assay of available support systems and service providers are important in planning educational programs as well as in fostering political activity to meet existing needs.

Is there any way of solving the waiting-list problem, which in many clinics prevents seeing crisis patients immediately?

How to reduce waiting lists is a problem in most clinics. Converting long-term therapeutic services to short-term services and the use of group therapy are often helpful. Some innovative programs have been devised to deal with this situation, for example, the screening evaluation technique described by Corney and Grey (1970) that allows in all cases an immediate access to professional help, eliminating the waiting list and serving as the first step in a crisis-oriented program.

What has the experience been with walk-in clinics as to the kinds of patients who seek crisis intervention?

There is general agreement on the need for a flexible policy of admitting patients for crisis therapy without exclusion irrespective of diagnosis, age, and socioeconomic status. Citing their experience in operating the Benjamin Rush Center, Jacobson et al (1965) list some interesting statistics. About one-third of the patients were diagnosed psychoneurotic, one-third personality disorders, one-fifth psychotic, and somewhat less transient situational disorders. Approximately 15 percent had mainly acute problems, and 63 percent had chronic problems with acute difficulties superimposed. In the first year and one-half of operation, 56.6 percent of patients saw their therapist for less than four sessions, almost one-half having one session. Only 1.8 percent had more than six visits. The improvement rate was estimated at two-thirds of those treated. More data on this question may be found in Chapter 1, "Models of Short-term Therapy."

Don't social caseworkers do a good deal of crisis intervention in social agencies?

Crisis therapy is often appropriately managed by trained social workers, and its theoretical concepts as conceptualized by Lindemann (1944) Caplan (1961), and others are compatible with general social work theory (Rapaport, 1962). In many cases social casework by itself is more adequately designed for certain problems than psychiatry. Tyhurst (1957) has remarked that "turning to the psychiatrist may represent an impoverishment of resources in the relevant social environment as much as an indication of the type of severity of disorder."

Is behavior therapy ever used in family therapy for crisis?

A wide variety of techniques have been used many of them behaviorally oriented, for example, feedback, modeling and role playing, rehearsal, and reciprocal reinforcement (Eisler & Herson, 1973). Videotape replays are also used showing interactive sequences.

What team members are best in crisis intervention?

In a clinic setup a team approach is ideal. A good team for the handling of emergencies is a psychiatric nurse, a psychiatrist, and a psychiatric social worker who have had training in emergency psychiatry and crisis intervention. A multidisciplinary team can also include psychologists and members of other disciplines, such as rehabilitation workers, provided they are trained to work with people in crises.

Has anything been done with crisis intervention groups, and are there any leads as to technique?

Some work has been done with crisis intervention in a group setting (Berlin, 1970; Crary, 1968; Strickler & Allgeyer, 1967; Trakas & Lloyd, 1971). At the Benjamin Rush Center–Venice Branch (a division of the Los Angeles Psychiatric Service) crisis group therapy is instituted with walk-in patients. The groups are open-ended and heterogeneous (Morley & Brown, 1969). The format allows one individual pregroup interview followed by five group sessions. Excluded from group therapy are serious suicidal or homocidal risks and overt psychoses. At the first group session the patient is asked to tell the group what brought him to the clinic. The therapist encourages the patient to discuss the precipitating factor, the events of the crisis and what measures have been taken to solve it. The group explores alternate coping measures. Group support and the expression of opinions are often helpful. Unlike traditional group therapy there is no analysis made of the group process. Most of the time is spent focusing on each individual's presenting problem. A "going-around" procedure is employed to give each person a chance to talk. Transference interpretation is minimized due to the lack of time. In reviewing results with 1,300 patients it is claimed that a number of advantages are available to a crisis group as compared to individual therapy. Group support and reassurance have been valuable. Social relationships have developed between the members and good alternate coping measures seem to be more palatable to a patient when offered by a member who comes from the same subcultural milieu with knowledge of problems and defenses exploited within the culture that are better known to the group members than to the therapist. Expression of significant feelings is greater in the group than in individual therapy. The forces of modeling and desensitization are also more potent. One disadvantage is the greater difficulty of keeping discussions in focus.

Is it possible to select techniques in crisis intervention that are specially suited for certain patients?

Some attempts have been made to correlate responses to stressful events with the character structures of the victims (Shapiro, 1965) and then to choose techniques best suited for character styles. Horowitz (1976, 1977) has outlined the various ways that hysterical, obsessional, and narcissistic personalities respond to stress as a consequence of their unique conflicts, needs, and defenses. For example, preferred techniques in the hysteric are organized around dealing with impediments to processing; in the obsessive, with methods that support maintenance of control and substitution of realistic for magical thinking; in the narcissistic personality, with interviewing tactics that cautiously deflate the grandiosity of the patient and at the same time build up self-esteem.

In many cases, however, it is difficult, particularly in severe crises, to delineate sharply habitual personality styles that would make preferred techniques possible since the patient may be responding with emergency reactions that contaminate or conceal his basic patterns. All that the therapist may be able to do is to try to help the patient develop a clearer idea of the stress incident and its meaning to him, with the hope of helping him understand his defensive maneuvers. The patient is encouraged to put into words his feelings and attitudes about the traumatic incident and its implications for him. Support, reassurance, confrontation, interpretation, and other techniques are utilized in relation to existing needs and as a way of countering obstructive defenses. The aim is to put the patient into a position where he can embark on a constructive course of action in line with the existing reality situation, hoping that he will accept the therapist's offerings irrespective of his personality style.

Doesn't a short period of hospitalization provide a breathing space for the patient in a crisis?

Hospitalization should be resorted to only as a last resort recognizing that it will solve little in the long run. Indeed, it will probably be used by the family as an escape from facing their involvement in the crisis and from altering the family climate that sponsored the crisis in the first place.

Since crisis intervention is a kind of holding operation to defuse a critical situation, shouldn't all cases receive more thorough treatment after the crisis is resolved?

It is a misconception to conceive of crisis intervention as a holding operation. Limited as it seems, it is a substantial form of treatment in its own right, and it may for many patients be the treatment of choice. The experience is that only a small number of patients receiving adequate crisis intervention need seek more intensive therapy, satisfactory results having been obtained with crisis therapy alone. Indeed, there is evidence that in some instances deep and lasting personality changes have been brought about by working through a crisis. Often the patient has gained enough so that there is no future incidence of crises.

Does crisis therapy require special training?

The key factor in this model of mental health service is the availability of trained and skilled personnel. Unfortunately, crisis intervention has been regarded as a second-best form of treatment that can be done by relatively untrained paraprofessionals. Appropriate professional training in this model is rarely given and is an essential need in psychiatric and psychological training programs. The usual training does not equip a professional to do crisis intervention. Additional skills related to the crisis model are required. As a matter of fact, the crisis model is best learned by professionals at an advanced stage of training and supervision. Excessive anxiety and an erosion of confidence is often precipitated in students at lower levels of training when handling the problems of highly disturbed people in crisis. Supervision by experienced crisis therapists is also most important. Some literature on training methods and directions may be found in the writings of Baldwin (1977), Kapp and Weiss (1975), and Wallace and Morley (1970).

Isn't the main goal of crisis intervention namely the bringing of a person back to a previous dubious precrisis stability too superficial?

When one considers that a patient may reach habitual stability in from one to six sessions, we may consider such a goal quite an achievement. This is usually all a patient seeks from therapy. But in a considerable number of patients the working-through of the crisis starts a process that can lead to extensive change in patterns of behavior and perhaps even in alterations of the personality structure. And the fact that a patient stops therapy in six sessions or less does not mean that he cannot later seek further treatment aimed at more extensive goals, should he so desire.

Isn't the time devoted to therapy too limited in crisis intervention?

Experience shows that most people can be helped to resolve a crisis within the traditional time limitation of six sessions. A good therapist can accomplish more with a patient in six sessions than a bad therapist can in six hundred.

If a patient comes to an emergency room in a hospital in an agitated state saying he is afraid of giving in to an impulse to kill someone, what is the best way of handling this?

First, assure the patient that he will receive help to protect him from these fears. In an acute state it is obviously difficult to probe the sources of his fears of violence. Bringing him to some immediate stability is the aim. For this purpose neuroleptics should be administered in proper dosage to calm the patient down. The therapist will be wise to summon security personnel to aid him if violence breaks through. This measure not only can allay the therapist's fears, but also the patient often realizes that he will be protected from acting out his impulses, and this helps calm him down. The greatest help is rendered by the patient's ability to communicate to an understanding person; therefore, prior to giving the patient intensive tranquilization, he should be allowed to verbalize freely. Hospitalization must be considered to protect the patient should violent tendencies reappear. Too frequently the patient's threats are taken lightly. The patient should be assured that it is essential that he be temporarily hospitalized for his own protection and that he will not need to stay in a hospital longer than is necessary. Even where the patient does not agree to hospitalization, he may still be willing to accept it if he feels that the therapist is sincere and concerned about his welfare. Transportation to another hospital should be done by ambulance with enough security attendants to manage violent displays should they occur. A proper diagnosis is necessary. Is the violence a manifestation of a neurological condition like a brain tumor or epilepsy, a breakthrough of psychosis, a consequence of a recent head injury, an indication of excessive alcohol or drug intake? Continuing therapy will be contingent on the proper diagnosis.

Even in crisis therapy of a very brief nature some therapists claim that it is possible to influence deeper parameters of personality. Are there techniques that can bring this desired result about?

No better way exists than to study the reactions of the patient to the techniques that are being utilized in the effort to resolve the crisis. The patient's reactions to the therapeutic situation, irrespective of the specific techniques employed, will reflect basic needs, defenses, and reaction patterns that embody interpersonal involvements dating back to formative experiences in the past. Responses to the current treatment experience, if one understands psychoanalytic theory and methodology and has the motivation to use this knowledge, are like a biopsy of the smoldering psychopathology. Patterns excited by therapy and the therapist will reveal both the sources and effects of faulty early programming. These effects are often expressed in the form of resistance. Because the patient has learned to operate with a social facade and because the more fundamental operations of repression shield him from anxiety, he may not manifest resistances openly. It is here that the trained and experienced therapist operates with advantage. From the patient's gestures, hesitations, manner of talking, slips of speech, dreams, and associations, one may gather sufficient information to help identify and deal directly and actively with resistances to techniques. These resistances embody fundamental defensive operations, and their resolution may influence many intrapsychic elements, initiating a chain reaction that ultimately results in reconstructive change. This change, started in relatively brief therapy focused on the existing crisis, may go on the remainder of the individual's life. If the patient has been able to establish a continuity between the crisis situation, his active participation in bringing it about, the forces in his character organization that sustain his maladjustment, and their origin in his early conditionings, the opportunities for continued personality maturation are good.

Should time limits be set in advance in crisis intervention even if you don't know the direction treatment will take?

Definitely. Crisis intervention is one situation where advance setting of the number of sessions is required. Inexperienced therapists are usually hesitant about doing this. Where a termination date is not agreed on, the patient will usually settle back and wait for a miracle to happen no matter how long it takes.

What about the advance setting of goals in crisis intervention?

It is important to project achievable goals and to get the patient to agree to these. Where goals are too ambitious and will require extensive time to reach, or where they are unreachable irrespective of time, the therapist may undershoot his mark and at termination be left with a disgruntled and angry patient.

If on termination the patient still has unresolved problems, what do you do?

The goal of crisis intervention, from a purely pragmatic viewpoint, is to bring a patient to precrisis equilibrium. Once this is achieved, the chief aim of this model of therapy has been reached. Inexperienced therapists especially have difficulty discharging patients because the patients have some unresolved problems at termination. While goals are modest in crisis therapy, and while we may terminate therapy abruptly, it is often gratifying to see on follow-up how much progress has actually occurred after treatment as a result of the learnings acquired during the active treatment period. The therapist, therefore, should learn to handle his own separation symptoms and fears and let the patient go at the proper time. Naturally, if the patient is still seriously and dangerously sick, further treatment will be necessary.

Doesn't the traditional limited goal of crisis intervention in itself circumscribe the therapeutic effort and prevent more extensive personality growth?

This is an important point. The goal of precrisis homeostasis is, for better or worse, pragmatic; cost effectiveness is the cursed term. Being pragmatic, however, does not mean that one cannot proceed beyond the patient's established precrisis neurotic homeostasis. If one accepts the dictum that a crisis is an opportunity for growth, a means of transgressing modes of coping that have failed, and an invitation to release spontaneous growth processes, it is possible *within the prescribed few sessions available* to bring an individual in crisis as well as the family to new potentialities. I believe this is where a dynamic orientation is so helpful. It is not necessary to delve too deeply in the unconscious during crisis; the unconscious with its wealth of encrusted needs and conflicts is already near the surface with the defenses shattered as they are. And latent creative drives may also be trying to surface. The therapist can, if alert, harness these forces and bring the patient to an awareness of how and why he is being victimized by some of his distortions and interpersonal shortcomings. If interpretations are presented skillfully in the context of the here and now, and identified underlying nuclear problems are related to the crisis situation, the therapist may promote changes far beyond pragmatic barriers.

Have telephone hot-lines for crises proven successful? Have any books been written on this subject?

On the whole, yes. But the adequacy of the service is entirely dependent on the quality of volunteer help available. Where volunteers are untrained and unskilled, the effect can be antitherapeutic. A book on the subject has been edited by D. Lester and G. W. Brockopp (*Crisis Intervention and Counseling by Telephone,* Springfield, Ill., Thomas, 1976).

What is the best tactic in the case of a suicide risk?

A person who really is intent on taking his life will manage to do so stealthily. Endogenous depressions are especially disposed to do this; therefore, where in a depression there is a past history of a genuine suicidal attempt, or the patient has expressed a threat of suicide, electroconvulsive therapy should be instituted without delay. Temporary hospitalization may be essential in these cases unless the patient is consistently watched 24 hours a day. Suicide is especially possible as the patient begins to feel better and has more energy at his disposal.

Does a suicide threat call for immediate use of crisis intervention?

Suicide is often an angry communication and reflects an inability to resolve a personal crisis. Ruben (1979) reports a study of 151 suicidal patients at the emergency department of a large general hospital over a 2-year period, 56 percent of whom acted impulsively and had no previous history of an emotional problem. He suggests that two-thirds of suicidal patients are excellent candidates for crisis intervention.

In the event of an actual suicidal attempt how should one proceed?

An assessment of the suicidal attempt is necessary. Was it motivated by a truly genuine desire to kill oneself or was it an appeal for understanding or help? Was there a revenge motif? If so, against whom—the people the patient is living with, parents, or whom else? Had there been threats of suicide prior to the attempt? What immediate events, if any, prompted the attempt? If the patient suffered a loss, is the loss permanent (such as the death of a mate)? Is there a chronic debilitating physical illness present, a desire to escape intractable pain, or evidence of a terminal illness like cancer? Was the method employed a well-designed and truly lethal method? Or was it poorly organized, and if so, was the attempt made with a hope to be rescued? How deeply depressed is the patient now? Is the depression recent, one of long-standing, or one that periodically appears? Has the patient received psychiatric help in the past, and if so, what kind of help and for what? What kind of support is now available to the patient (relatives, friends, organizations, etc.)? Is it possible for the therapist to establish a good contact with the patient and to communicate with him? How are relatives and friends reacting to the patient's attempt (angry, frightened, desire to be helpful, etc.)? Once answers to these questions are obtained, the therapist will be in a better position to deal constructively with what is behind the attempt. Should hospitalization be decided on, as when there is a possibility that the attempt may be repeated, the therapist should see to it that a responsible member of the family is brought into the picture immediately and follows through on recommendations protecting the patient from any lethal objects (drugs, knives, razors, etc.) and not permitting the patient to be alone until the patient is actually hospitalized. In the event hospitalization is not deemed necessary, the principles of crisis intervention with the patient and the family should immediately be instituted.

Are there any data on what happens to patients in a crisis who cannot be seen immediately and are put on a waiting list?

According to one study, fully one-third to one-half of the patients on a waiting list when contacted later on will no longer be interested in treatment (Lazare et al, 1972). The reasons for this generally are that the patient having come for help in a crisis finds other resources to quiet him down or he works out the problems by himself even though some of the solutions prove to be poor compromises. Thus a man suffering from intense anxiety finds that drinking temporarily abates his suffering with the consequence that he becomes an alcoholic. A depressed woman who seeks companionship gets herself involved with and so dependent on a rejecting exploitative psychopath that she cannot break the relationship. A man having experienced several episodes of impotency detaches himself from women to avoid the challenge of sexuality. A youth out of college fearful of failing in an executive post with a good future decides to give up his job in favor of work as a laborer. To forestall such compromises it is important to interview the applicant if possible within 24 hours of the request for help. One way of circumventing a waiting list is to organize an intake group pending an opening in a therapist's schedule. Such an interim provision may surprisingly be all that some patients need.

Conclusion

Disruptive as a state of crisis may be, it can offer the victim an opportunity to develop new and healthier coping mechanisms. In initiating a state of disequilibrium that fails to clear up with habitual problem-solving methods, the crisis may energize old unresolved conflicts, reactivating regressive needs and defenses. Working out solutions for the crisis often will encourage more appropriate ways of coping. Thus, "the crisis with its mobilization of energy operates as a 'second chance' in correcting earlier faulty problem-solving" (Rapaport, 1962).

Studies of crisis states indicate that they usually last no longer than 6 weeks, during which time some solution, adaptive or maladaptive, is found to bring about equilibrium. The initial dazed shock reaction to a crisis is usually followed by great tension and mobilization of whatever resources individuals have at their command. Should efforts at resolution fail, they will exploit whatever contrivances or stratagems they can fabricate to resolve their troubles. The more flexible the person, the more versatile the maneuvering. Abatement of tension and cessation of the crisis state may eventually result in the restoration of the previous adaptional level and hopefully in the learning of more productive patterns of behavior. Failure to resolve the crisis, however, or continuance of unresolved conflicts may ultimately lead to more serious neurotic or psychotic solutions. Therapeutic intervention through crisis intervention is required when patients cannot overcome difficulties by themselves and before there is entrenchment in pathological solutions.

Crisis therapy incorporates a number of active techniques implemented in the medium of a directive therapist relationship with the patient. It is essentially short term, oriented around two goals: (1) the immediate objective of modifying or removing the critical situation or symptom complaint for which help is being sought, and (2) the hoped-for objective of initiating some corrective influence on the individual's and family's customary behavior. The unbalancing of the family equation will optimistically institute changes in the behavioral patterns that have led up to the crisis. The theoretical framework governing the approach is problem solving. The methodologic strategies are eclectic in nature and recruit sundry tactics including interviewing, confrontation, environmental manipulation, drug therapy, hypnosis, group therapy, family therapy, and behavior therapy, depending on the needs and problems of the patient and the particular aptitude for working with a selected method.

The technique or techniques employed, while aimed at relieving the immediate crisis situation or symptomatic upset, will often set into motion certain resistances and defensive operations that if detected must be managed to prevent sabotage of the treatment process. In other words, even though the tactics may be nonanalytic, the patient's response to the techniques and to the therapist become a focus for exploration for the purpose of detecting and resolving resistances to change. Extensive personality modifications are not expected, but some modifications may eventuate as a serendipitous dividend, which often expands after therapy has ended. Follow-up interviews over a period of years have shown that this approach can score sustained symptomatic relief, freedom from further crises, and in some cases actual constructive personality alterations.

CHAPTER 15

Making a Relaxing and Ego-Building Tape

One of the simplest ways of promoting relaxation and enhancing morale is through the employment of a cassette recording. Among the advantages of this adjunct is that the patient can use it away from the therapist's office. Too often treatment begins and ends with each weekly or biweekly therapeutic session. The only carryover is the memory of the patient, which tends to be blunted by resistance and by the intrusion of everyday distractions and responsibilities. By playing the tape at least twice daily, the patient reenforces and consolidates the lessons learned in the therapeutic session.

Other tangible dividends accrue too: (1) The tape is material evidence that something definite and palpable is being done for the patient. Some persons consider the "talking cure" temporary and flimsy. They seek something more substantial. This, in part at least, is why demonstrable techniques, such as those used in behavior therapy, make a greater impact on certain patients than simply verbalizing. It may be that the placebo effect is also enhanced through the instrumentality of a tape. (2) A relationship with the therapist becomes more intensified. Listening to someone who soothes, quiets, relaxes, and reassures solidifies rapport. The idealized image of empathic authority is augmented. Even when the voice on the tape is not that of the therapist, it becomes identified with the therapist. A relationship that may not develop in the brief time devoted to treatment will have a better chance of evolving because of the more intensive contact with an extension of the therapist. (3) Tensions and anxieties become alleviated through relaxing and reassuring suggestions. This subdues defensive maneuvers that have diverted the patient from putting into practice more adaptive patterns. (4) A more constructive self-image is encouraged through positive persuasive suggestions neutralizing negative suggestions with which the patient has been habitually preoccupied. (5) Termination is more easily achieved since a token of the therapist, embodied in the cassette, remains with the patient, and this ameliorates separation anxiety. (6) After therapy the patient has a helping resource to turn to in the tape should anxiety emerge, symptoms return, or critical situations arise that threaten to overwhelm coping capacities.

Understandably, several questions arise regarding limitations, disadvantages, and dangers of supplying the patient with an ersatz therapist in the form of a tape.

Does not a tape enhance the patient's dependency and provide him with a crutch he can use instead of standing on his own feet?

In follow-ups, which have extended in some cases over 15 years, I have not encountered a single patient who has become dependent on a tape or in whom dependency has increased as a consequence of having a tape available to him or her. The problem is not that patients will overuse the tape; rather, it is that they will stop using it when they start feeling better, putting it aside before they have achieved its full benefit. Some tape suggestions are akin to forms of assertive training, and they lead to greater, not lesser, self-sufficiency.

Doesn't a tape, which contains supportive and reeducative suggestions, take away from a dynamic approach that deals with deeper and more fundamental issues?

On the contrary, it adds to a dynamic approach. Transference may be enhanced through the patient's reactions to the tape (as will be illustrated later in the chapter), and characteristic resistances may surface—that is, if one watches for these responses and if the patient is encouraged to report dreams. Several reasons account for this. Contact with the therapist through the tape is on a daily basis, thus preventing the patient from avoiding or repressing emerging destructive feelings, which can happen when therapeutic contact is minimal. Moreover, inducing relaxation results in an altered state of consciousness that invigorates regressive phenomena. How one handles transference, resistance, emergence of archaic emotions, and the elicitation of memories should these erupt will determine whether or not a therapeutic effect will be registered. Of course, the therapist may choose to ignore these manifestations. But where resistances are powerful enough to block the therapeutic effort, learning about them expeditiously (which can occur by studying the patient's responses to the tape) may enable the therapist to deal with them and thus salvage treatment that otherwise would end in failure.

In the event the tape breaks or is lost, won't the patient's symptoms return?

An adjunctive cassette tape is no substitute for psychotherapy. It supplements and expedites psychotherapy. There is no reason why symptoms should return if psychotherapy has dealt satisfactorily with the patient's problems.

Preliminary Preparations

The equipment for making a tape is simple. A good cassette recorder and a microphone that has a start and stop switch are essential. It is best not to rely on the patient's recorder, with which idiosyncrasies the therapist may not be acquainted. A metronome is optional. I use an electonic metronome that is tuned to a base tone at a speed of about one beat per second. A metronome may be purchased in any music store. A small bottle of rubbing alcohol, some Q-tips and a needle should be available in the event the therapist wishes to test for glove anaesthesia. In making a tape the suggestions should be given fluently, with conviction and without stumbling for words. To prevent omissions and embarrassing speech blunders, a prepared script is essential, one that is sufficiently general so that it applies to practically all patients, yet into which the therapist can interpolate special suggestions that are applicable to specific patients. The script in this chapter has been tested over a number of years, and it has many advantages. The therapist may copy it on cards and experiment with it. It is best to rehearse the making of a tape with pauses and emphasis at certain points so that when it is played back it sounds like natural talk. Performers on radio or television have mastered the skill of reading a script so that it sounds spontaneous. The therapist should practice by dictating several tapes, trying to articulate naturally, then listening to what has been dictated, and continuing to recite until the art of talking casually from script has been mastered. Some therapists prefer to give their patients a prerecorded tape made by another person.* It may also be help-

* A prerecorded relaxing and ego-building tape was made from the script in this chapter and may be obtained from Elba Industries, 491 Seventh Ave., New York, N.Y. 10018.

ful for a therapist to secure a tape that can serve as a model to follow.

When to introduce the desirability of making a tape is a concern. I usually decide to do this if I have the time at the end of the first session after collecting data about the patient and presenting a hypothesis of the problem. However, it may be done at the second or a later session. The patient may be approached as in the following excerpt:

Th. I believe you would benefit if I make a relaxing cassette tape for you. Understandably, with what you have gone through, you have a lot of tension, and the tape should help.

Pt. I see.

Th. Have you ever noticed how much better you feel when you are free from tension and relaxed?

Pt. Yes, but that's the trouble. I can't relax.

Th. For that reason I'm going to teach you a method that will help you relax. You know when you are tense, every organ in your body is keyed up. This makes it hard for you to heal. By learning how to relax your muscles and breathe easily you should begin to notice an improvement. This will give you the best chance to overcome tension.

Pt. That's good. Is that like meditation?

Th. Meditation is one form of relaxation. Hypnosis is another. There are other forms too. I will show you one that should be suitable for you. Do you have a tape recorder—a cassette recorder? [*If the patient has no recorder, it is best that he purchase one, preferably one that has an automatic shutoff with the ending of the tape.*]

Pt. Yes, I play music on it.

Th. Fine, I'll make a relaxing tape for you that should be of help. The next time you come here bring a blank 1-hour tape, that is, 30 minutes on each side. Get a good quality tape so that it will last. It is not necessary to bring your recorder since I'll use mine.

Pt. All right.

It is usually best to employ the word "relaxation" rather than "hypnosis" since the latter may have connotations for the patient that will complicate matters. People are acquainted with the symptoms of relaxation, but they may anticipate some mysterious, extramundane phenomenon in hypnosis, which when not experienced will inspire disappointment and a sense of failure. In the course of responding to the relaxing exercises many patients will actually enter a state of hypnosis. For practical purposes it is not necessary to differentiate relaxation from hypnosis in making a tape since the suggestions that are given are effective in both states. Indeed, it may be wise to minimize the need for hypnosis by stating that all we wish to do is to practice relaxation. If the patient asks whether what will be done is a form of hypnosis, he may be advised: "Some people relax so deeply that they may go into hypnosis, and some actually doze off. But this is not important. How deep you go makes little difference. The suggestions I will give you can be equally effective whether you are lightly relaxed or close to sleep."

It is often expedient at the end of the initial interview to have a preparatory session of relaxation as a preliminary to making a tape, which is done at the next session. The reason this is helpful is that it enables the therapist to observe how the patient responds to suggestions. It also prepares the patient for what will happen at the tape-making session.

The patient is made comfortable in a chair that should be sufficiently high so that it provides support for the head. An ottoman, if available, provides support for the feet. The patient may be told the following:

Th. Prior to making a relaxing tape for you, which we will do next time, I would like to see how you relax. What I would like to have you do is just lean back, close your eyelids and keep them closed until I give you the command to open them. Remember you will not be asleep and you will not be hypnotized, just pleasantly relaxed.

The following script is then slowly read in a kind of drawling, chanting tone as if lulling a person to sleep.

Now just settle back and shut your eyes. Listen comfortably to the sound of your breathing. Breathe in right down into the pit of your stomach. D-e-e-p-l-y, but gently, d-e-e-p-l-y. Just deeply enough so that you feel the air soaking in. In . . . and out. D-e-e-p-l-y, d-e-e-p-l-y. In . . . and out. And as you feel the air soaking in, you begin to feel yourself getting pleasantly tired and r-e-l-a-x-e-d, very r-e-l-a-x-e-d. Even d-r-o-w-s-y, d-r-o-w-s-y and relaxed. Drowsy and relaxed.

Now I want you to concentrate on the muscle groups that I point out to you. Loosen them, relax them, all while visualizing them. You will notice that you may be tense in certain areas and the idea is to relax yourself completely. Concentrate on your forehead. Loosen the muscles in your forehead. Now your eyes. Loosen the muscles around your eyes. Your eyelids relax. Now your face, your face relaxes. And your mouth . . . relax the muscles around your mouth. Your chin; let it sag and feel heavy. And as you relax your muscles, your breathing continues r-e-g-u-l-a-r-l-y and d-e-e-p-l-y, deeply within yourself.

Now your neck, your neck relaxes. Every muscle, every fiber in your neck relaxes. Your shoulders relax . . . your arms . . . your elbows . . . your forearms . . . your wrists . . . your hands . . . and your fingers relax. Your arms feel loose and relaxed; heavy and loose and relaxed. Your whole body begins to feel loose and relaxed. Your neck muscles relax; the front of your neck; the back muscles. If you wish, wiggle your head to get all the kinks out. Keep breathing deeply and relax. Now your chest. The front part of your chest relaxes . . . and the back part of your chest relaxes. Your abdomen . . . the pit of your stomach, that relaxes. The small of your back, loosen the muscles. Your hips . . . your thighs . . . your knees relax . . . even the muscles in your legs. Your ankles . . . your feet . . . and your toes. Your whole body feels loose and relaxed. And now as you feel the muscles relaxing, you will notice that you begin to feel relaxed and pleasantly tired all over. Your body begins to feel v-e-r-y, v-e-r-y relaxed . . . and you are going to feel d-r-o-w-s-i-e-r, and d-r-o-w-s-i-e-r, and d-r-o-w-s-i-e-r, from the top of your head right down to your toes. Every breath you take is going to soak in deeper and deeper and deeper, and you feel your body getting drowsier and drowsier. (*pause*)

And now I want you to imagine, to visualize the most relaxed and quiet and pleasant scene imaginable. Visualize, a relaxed and pleasant quiet scene. Any scene that is comfortable. Drowsier, and drowsier, and drowsier. You are v-e-r-y weary, and every breath will send you into deeper and deeper and deeper. [*If a metronome is to be used the patient may be told,* "I am going to turn on a metronome and every beat of the metronome will send you in deeper and deeper."] As you visualize this quiet scene, I shall count from one to twenty, and when I reach the count of twenty, you will feel yourself in deep, sufficiently deep to absorb the suggestions I'm going to give you. One, deeper and deeper. Two, deeper, and deeper, and deeper. Three . . . drowsier and drowsier. Four, deeper and deeper. Five . . . drowsier, and drowsier, and drowsier. Six . . . seven, very tired, very relaxed. Eight, deeper and deeper. Nine . . . ten, drowsier and drowsier. Eleven, twelve, thirteen, deeper and deeper, d-r-o-w-s-i-e-r and d-r-o-w-s-i-e-r. Fourteen, drowsier, and drowsier, and drowsier. Fifteen . . . sixteen . . . seventeen, deeper and deeper. Eighteen . . . nineteen . . . and finally twenty. (*pause*)

I want you (*the patient's first name may be mentioned*) for the next few minutes, to continue visualizing a quiet and wonderfully relaxed scene, and, as you do, you will get more, and more, and more, and more relaxed. Your body will begin to get more pleasantly tired and more relaxed, and you will get drowsier and drowsier; your arms may feel heavy, your hands tingly. When I talk to you next, you'll be more deeply relaxed. Deep, d-r-o-w-s-y and relaxed; d-r-o-w-s-y, and deep, and relaxed; deep, d-r-o-w-s-y, and relaxed; relaxed, and deep, and drowsy. (*pause for about 30 seconds*)

Now I'd like to have you concentrate on your left arm. I am going to stroke the arm and as I stroke it, the muscles get firm and rigid and the arms get stiff. Every muscle, every fiber in the arm stiffens, and the arm will feel as if it is glued right down to the side of the chair. (*The therapist at this point may walk over to the patient and while suggestions are given stroke the left arm. The intonation should now change from a lulling chant to a firmer more commanding tone.*) Every muscle, every fiber feels stiff and firm and rigid. The arm feels as if a 100-pound weight presses on the arm (*the therapist may press the arm down*) as if a suction pad holds the arm down, as if steel bands bind the arm down to the chair. The arm seems glued to the chair, and when I try to lift it, it feels heavy and rigid, glued against the chair. (*The therapist then lightly tries to lift the arm.*) Heavy and stiff and rigid. [*This is the first test as to whether the patient is responding to suggestions. The great majority of patients will exhibit a stiffness of the arm. Those who show no stiffness and rigidity are resisting for some reason. In the latter event the therapist may remark,* "It is a little hard to do this the first time. Next time you will probably find it easier." *Then the therapist may go on uninterruptedly.*] And now I'm going to stroke the arm, and whatever stiffness is there will leave. In fact, the arm will feel light as a feather. (*The arm is stroked and then rapidly lifted.*)

Feel your eyelids glued together now. Your eyelids feel tight, tight and when you try to lift them, they feel as if they are glued together. Tight, tight, tight. [*This is the next test, and most patients will comply with the suggestions. In the event the patient is in resistance and lifts the eyelids, simply press them down to close them and say,* "It is a little difficult now. Next time it will be easier," *and continue with the suggestions.*]

Now what I'd like to have you do is to picture things in your mind as I describe them, and, as you do, indicate it by lifting this finger an inch or so in the air. (*The index finger of the left hand is touched.*) For example, imagine yourself walking outside on the street, and when you see yourself walking on the street, indicate this by lifting up your finger. [*These suggestions are aimed at training the patient in imagery. Most patients easily visualize themselves walking on the street. Occasionally, a patient will block doing this for one reason or another. Where this occurs and after a minute or so has passed without the finger lifting, the therapist may say:* "It is a difficult to do this. So now picture yourself sitting in the chair and you are in looking at me. In your imagination see me as I talk to you, and when you do, lift the finger." *This usually brings a positive response since the image of the therapist is fresh in the patient's mind. Once the patient has lifted the finger, the suggestion about picturing oneself walking on the street is made and should be successfully executed. In the very unusual event the patient resists all these suggestions, or later suggestions during the session, the therapist may say*: "It is a little difficult now. You will find it easier next time." *The hope is that the patient will eventually work through the resistance.*]

Visualize yourself walking into an alleyway between two buildings. See yourself stepping into this alleyway. And you walk right into an open courtyard. See yourself walking into this courtyard, and right in front of you you see a tall church—the steeple, spire, and bell. Then lift the finger. (*The therapist continues suggestions.*) Now watch the bell. Now watch the bell. It will begin to move from one side to the next, from one side to the next, and as it does, you get the sensation of a clanging, c-l-a-n-g-i-n-g in your ears. As soon as that happens, as soon as you see the bell move, lift your finger. [*It is possible that the patient may be an excellent hypnotic subject and actually hallucinate ringing of the bell at this point. This is, however, not questioned so that in the event no auditory hallucinations exist the patient does not infer he has failed. Actually, it makes no difference whether or not the patient hallucinates insofar as the later making of the tape is concerned.*] (*pause, until the finger lifts*)

Turn away from the church building now and see yourself walking back through the courtyard into the alley. Over the right-hand side of the alley, on the ground, you see a pail with steaming water. Lift your finger when you see this. (*pause, until finger lifts*)

Now see yourself taking your right hand and waving it through the steam. As you do this, your hand will get tingly and tender and sensitive as if it has been soaked in steam. When you see yourself doing this, lift your finger. In a moment your hand will become sensitive and tender as if you have waved it in steam. (*pause, until finger lifts*)

In contrast to your sensitive right hand, your left hand is going to get numb and insensitive. It will feel as if I have created a wrist block with novocaine (*The therapist may touch the patient's left wrist with his finger in a number of spots, circling it as if novocaine is being injected.*) As a matter of fact, you are now going to imagine yourself wearing a thick heavy leather glove on your left hand, and as soon as you see yourself in your imagination wearing a thick heavy leather glove on your left hand, indicate it by lifting your finger. (*pause, until finger lifts*)

Now I am going to show you the difference between the sensitive right hand and the left hand enveloped in a glove. [*In most cases a partial glove anaesthesia will be obtained, and this more than any other phenomenon during the present relaxing session will impress the patient that something important may be accomplished with suggestion. After the session is over, many patients express surprise or incredulity that anaesthesia has occurred. Some doubt that the therapist actually touched the hand with the needle, and the therapist will have to assure them this was so.*] I am going to touch your left hand with a sterilized needle, and it will feel as if I am touching it through a thick, heavy leather glove. You will feel touch, but no pain; touch but no pain. Touch, but no real pain. (*A needle, a small bottle of alcohol and a swab of cotton or Q-tip being available, the needle is wiped with alcohol, and the alcohol-soaked swab is applied to the back of the hand in the triangle between the thumb and forefinger. The therapist should then touch the skin with the needle lightly to avoid drawing blood*). On the contrary, the other hand, the right hand, will be very sensitive and tender and painful even to the slightest touch. (*The same process with the needle is repeated with the back of the right hand to demonstrate the difference in sensation between the two hands.*)

What we have done is to produce an anesthesia, which is sometimes used in minor surgical operations. But what it indicates is the power of the mind in controlling physical functions. And if the mind can do this with a fundamental function like pain, it can also control your symptoms (*these may be mentioned*).

I am now going to count slowly from one to five. When I reach the count of five lift your eyes and you will be out of it. One . . . two . . . three . . . four . . . five.

Most patients will slowly lift their eyelids and spontaneously comment on how relaxed they feel. They may inquire if the therapist really touched the left hand with a needle. If the patient does not present his comments spontaneously, the therapist may inquire about his personal reactions. In the event the patient resisted certain suggestions (which as has been mentioned before is not unusual), the therapist may ask whether the patient was upset or had any other feelings or thoughts during the relaxing exercises.

In one patient, for example, when asked what thoughts came to him when he could not visualize a church when asked to do so, he replied: "I had a peculiar fantasy, visionlike. There was a manhole in the street, and I was walking toward it. And there was a machine with teeth in it ready to grind me up." At this point, the patient smiled and he said; "I knew a man who went for analysis and referred to his analyst's office as a hell hole." The fantasy and his association provided a dynamic focus for our interviews, which dealt with transference feelings that I, like his father, was a dangerous authority who, if he relaxed his guard, might injure him.

In most cases resistances will not be encountered and the therapist may then proceed with these instructions: "The next time you come here bring a 1-hour blank cassette tape of good quality, 30 minutes on each side. It is not necessary to bring your recorder since I will use my own machine."

At the next session, if the patient does not spontaneously report dreams, the therapist should inquire about them. Following the relaxing session, many patients are apt to have dreams that relate to their relaxation experience and that expose transference as well as resistance maneuvers. These reactions may be very important because not only do they open a window into the underlying dynamics, but they are warning signals of problems that will have to be handled that may sabotage the benefits of the recorded tape.

Thus a male patient brought in this dream after the first session: "I was ill in bed. Friends were visiting me. It's grandpa's house, and my mother is there. She talks about helping me, but she gets me pink ribbons for my bed and tells me to sleep. I say, 'This is for girls.' She tries to persuade me it's all right. But I don't want to believe her. Then I had another dream. There was a rope around my penis; it changed to ribbons and it was choking my penis." The transference elements came out rapidly after the relaxation session. Had I not been alerted to the patient's fear of castration (which apparently stemmed from his unresolved oedipal fantasies and which he was projecting onto me) I would not have been able to deal with his core problem. I delayed the making of the tape until we had worked sufficiently on this material so that he would not interpret my tape-making activities as a castrating threat.

In the great majority of patients the dreams and fantasies that follow the first relaxing session are pleasant ones and do not indicate any need for delay in dictating the cassette.

Making the Tape

The patient is made comfortable in a chair (some patients prefer lying on a couch since they are more relaxed in it), and the blank cassette is put into the therapist's recorder. It is wise to test the voice level, counting from one to ten in the microphone, at the volume that one will use during the dictation, and then listening to the playback. After the proper adjustments have been made, the therapist says to the patient, "If you hear some rustling it is because I may refer to my cards and to the case record to make sure I include all the material that is important. Now I want you to shut your eyelids and keep them shut until I give you the command to open your eyes."

The script, which has been copied on cards, is essentially similar to that in my book, *The Technique of Psychotherapy* (1977, pp. 795–796). The first part is identical with that of the beginning of the preliminary session, but to avoid confusion the complete script will be included here. Dictation should be slow, with proper pauses and emphases much as in the first session. The patient's first name may be interpolated in certain spots to make the tape more personal. The patient having shut the eyes, the recorder is turned on and the script dictated.

Now just settle back and shut your eyes. Listen comfortably to the sound of your breathing. Breathe in right down into the pit of your stomach. D-e-e-p-l-y, but gently, d-e-e-p-l-y. Just deeply enough so that you feel the air soaking in. In . . . and out. D-e-e-p-l-y, d-e-e-p-l-y. In . . . and out. And as you feel the air soaking in, you begin to feel yourself getting pleasantly tired and r-e-l-a-x-e-d, very r-e-l-a-x-e-d. Even d-r-o-w-s-y, d-r-o-w-s-y and relaxed. Drowsy and relaxed.

Now I want you to concentrate on the muscle groups that I point out to you. Loosen them, relax them, all while visualizing them. You will notice that you may be tense in certain areas and the idea is to relax yourself completely. Concentrate on your forehead. Loosen the muscles in your forehead. Now your eyes. Loosen the muscles around your eyes. Your eyelids relax. Now your face, your face relaxes. And your mouth . . . relax the muscles around your mouth. Your chin; let it sag and feel heavy. And as you relax your muscles, your breathing continues r-e-g-u-l-a-r-l-y and d-e-e-p-l-y, deeply within yourself.

Now your neck, your neck relaxes. Every muscle, every fiber in your neck relaxes. Your shoulders relax . . . your arms . . . your elbows . . . your forearms . . . your wrists . . . your hands . . . and your fingers relax. Your arms feel loose and relaxed; heavy and loose and relaxed. Your whole body begins to feel loose and relaxed. Your neck muscles relax; the front of your neck; the back muscles. If you wish, wiggle your head to get all the kinks out. Keep breathing deeply and relax. Now your chest. The front part of your chest relaxes . . . and the back part of your chest relaxes. Your abdomen . . . the pit of your stomach, that relaxes. The small of your back, loosen the muscles. Your hips . . . your thighs . . . your knees relax . . . even the muscles in your legs. Your ankles . . . your feet . . . and your toes. Your whole body feels loose and relaxed. And now as you feel the muscles relaxing, you will notice that you begin to feel relaxed and pleasantly tired all over. Your body begins to feel v-e-r-y, v-e-r-y relaxed . . . and you are going to feel d-r-o-w-s-i-e-r, and d-r-o-w-s-i-e-r, and d-r-o-w-s-i-e-r, from the top of your head right down to your toes. Every breath you take is going to soak in deeper and deeper and deeper, and you feel your body getting drowsier and drowsier. (*pause*)

And now I want you to imagine, to visualize the most relaxed and quiet and pleasant scene imaginable. Visualize, a relaxed and pleasant quiet scene. Any scene that is comfortable. Drowsier, and drowsier, and drowsier. You are v-e-r-y weary, and every breath will send you into deeper and deeper and deeper. [*If a metronome is to be used the patient may be told,* "I am going to turn on a metronome and every beat of the metronome will send you in deeper and deeper."] As you visualize this quiet scene, I shall count from one to twenty, and when I reach the count of twenty, you will feel yourself in deep, sufficiently deep to absorb the suggestions I'm going to give you. One, deeper and deeper. Two, deeper, and deeper, and deeper. Three . . . drowsier and drowsier. Four, deeper and deeper. Five . . . drowsier, and drowsier, and drowsier. Six . . . seven, very tired, very relaxed. Eight, deeper and deeper. Nine . . . ten, drowsier and drowsier. Eleven, twelve, thirteen, deeper and deeper, d-r-o-w-s-i-e-r and d-r-o-w-s-i-e-r. Fourteen, drowsier, and drowsier, and drowsier. Fifteen . . . sixteen . . . seventeen, deeper and deeper. Eighteen . . . nineteen . . . and finally twenty. (*pause*)

I want you (*the patient's first name may be mentioned*) for the next few minutes, to continue visualizing a quiet and wonderfully relaxed scene, and, as you do, you will get more, and more, and more, and more relaxed. Your body will begin to get more pleasantly tired and more relaxed, and you will get drowsier and drowsier, your arms may feel heavy, your hands tingly. When I talk to you next, you'll be more deeply relaxed. Deep, d-r-o-w-s-y and relaxed; d-r-o-w-s-y and deep and relaxed; deep, d-r-o-w-s-y, and relaxed; relaxed, and deep, and drowsy. (*pause for about 30 seconds*)

Relax and feel drowsy. As you begin to feel more drowsy, you have a sort of floating sensation and you relax more. Things seem to fade a little and lose their immediacy—any anxiety and depression fade. A sort of fuzzy and tingling sensation and a feeling of welcoming sleep, yet different from the reaction to ordinary sleep.

The mind is like a sponge. It soaks up suggestions. In your case it has been filled with negative suggestions that have piled up in you over the years. [*These may be enumerated. For example, if the patient has a feeling that he cannot get better, or is unable to succeed at anything or if he has a devalued self-image, these may be mentioned as negative thoughts.*]

I shall now give you a number of suggestions and you may utilize those that apply to you at this moment and put aside those that do not, which may apply at some other moment.

Every day . . . you will become physically *STRONGER* and *FITTER*. You will become *MORE ALERT . . . MORE WIDE AWAKE . . . MORE ENERGETIC*. You will become *MUCH LESS EASILY TIRED . . . MUCH LESS EASILY FATIGUED . . . MUCH LESS EASILY DEPRESSED . . . MUCH LESS EASILY DISCOURAGED*. Because of resolution of your troubles [*specific symptoms that have burdened the patient may be mentioned here if desired*]. Every day . . . you will become . . . *SO DEEPLY INTERESTED IN WHATEVER YOU ARE DOING . . . SO DEEPLY INTERESTED IN WHATEVER IS GOING ON . . . THAT YOUR MIND WILL BECOME MUCH LESS PREOCCUPIED WITH YOURSELF AND YOUR PROBLEMS . . . AND YOUR OWN FEELINGS.*

Every day . . . *YOUR NERVES WILL BECOME STRONGER AND STEADIER . . . YOUR MIND WILL BECOME CALMER AND CLEARER . . . MORE COMPOSED . . . MORE PLACID . . . MORE TRANQUIL*. You will become *MUCH LESS EASILY WORRIED . . . MUCH LESS EASILY AGITATED . . . MUCH LESS FEARFUL AND APPREHENSIVE . . . MUCH LESS EASILY UPSET*. You will be able to *THINK MORE CLEARLY* . . . You will be able to *CONCENTRATE MORE EASILY. YOUR MEMORY WILL IMPROVE* . . . and you will be able to *SEE THINGS IN THEIR TRUE PERSPECTIVE . . . WITHOUT MAGNIFYING THEM . . . WITHOUT ALLOWING THEM TO GET OUT OF PROPORTION.*

Every day . . . you will become *EMOTIONALLY MUCH CALMER . . . MUCH MORE SETTLED . . . MUCH LESS EASILY DISTURBED*. Every day . . . you will feel a *GREATER FEELING OF PERSONAL WELL-BEING . . . A GREATER FEELING OF PERSONAL SAFETY . . . AND SECURITY AND CONTROL* than you have felt for a long, long time.

Every day . . . *YOU* will become . . . and *YOU* will remain . . . *MORE AND MORE COMPLETELY RELAXED . . . AND LESS TENSE EACH DAY . . . BOTH MENTALLY AND PHYSICALLY* . . . And, *AS* you become . . . and, *AS* you remain . . . *MORE RELAXED . . . AND LESS TENSE EACH DAY . . . SO,* you will develop *MUCH MORE CONFIDENCE IN YOURSELF. MUCH* more confidence in your ability to *DO . . . NOT ONLY* what you *HAVE* to do each day, . . . but *MUCH* more confidence in your ability to do whatever you *OUGHT* to be able to do . . . *WITHOUT FEAR OF CONSEQUENCES . . . WITHOUT UNNECESSARY ANXIETY . . . WITHOUT UNEASINESS*. Because of this . . . every day . . . you will feel *MORE AND MORE INDEPENDENT . . . MORE ABLE TO STAND*

UPON YOUR OWN FEET WITHOUT PROPS [*If the patient is utilizing props, like tranquilizers or pills, these may be mentioned,* "Like tranquilizers and sleeping pills."] *AND WITHOUT WORRYING.* TO *HOLD YOUR OWN* . . . no matter how difficult or trying things may be.

And, because all these things *WILL* begin to happen . . . *EXACTLY* as I tell you they will happen, you will begin to feel *MUCH HAPPIER . . . MUCH MORE CONTENTED . . . MUCH MORE CHEERFUL . . . MUCH MORE OPTIMISTIC . . . MUCH LESS EASILY DISCOURAGED . . . MUCH LESS EASILY DEPRESSED.*

Now relax and rest for a minute or so, going deeper, d-e-e-p-e-r, d-e-e-p-e-r, and in a minute or so I shall talk to you, and you will be more deeply relaxed. (*pause about 10 seconds*)

There are four things we are going to accomplish as a result of these suggestions. I call them the four S's: symptom relief, self-confidence, situational control, and self-understanding. First, your various symptoms (*enumerate*) are going to be less and less upsetting to you. You will pay less and less attention to them because they will bother you less and less. You will find that you have a desire to overcome them more and more. And as we work at your problems, you will feel that your self-confidence grows and expands. You will feel more assertive and stronger. You will be able to handle yourself better in any situations that come along, particularly those that tend to upset you (*enumerate*). Finally, and most importantly, your understanding of yourself will improve. (*pause*)

I want you to continue to listen to this recording as often as possible and as practical. It makes no difference how deep you go. Even if you feel you are conscious, or if your mind wanders off while listening, or if you fall asleep, the suggestions will penetrate. (*pause*)

Relax and rest and, if you wish, give yourself any additional suggestions to yourself to feel better, or suggestions to handle an immediate problem, using the word "you" as if you are talking to yourself. Then relax, go to sleep or arouse yourself. Take as long as you like. When you are ready you will arouse *yourself* no matter when that is by counting slowly to yourself from one to five. You will be completely out of it then—awake and alert. Remember the more you practice the more intense will be your response, the more easily will your resistances give way.

Keep on practicing: and now go ahead . . . relax . . . and *when* you are ready . . . wake *yourself* up.

After the patient lifts the eyelids, he may be asked how he feels. Generally, the reply will be "Relaxed." The therapist then plays back the last sentence and then rewinds to the beginning and plays back the first few words to make sure the tape contains the start and end of the script. The patient is given the tape with the injunction; "If you can borrow another recorder, it is best to copy the tape. Use the copy so that if the tape breaks or is lost you have a master to copy from."

Reactions to the Tape

The patient's experiences in playing the tape should be reviewed at the next session. A number of questions may concern the patient, such as the following:

Q. I fall asleep before the tape ends. Does this matter?

A. No. The suggestions will still get through. All it means is that you are a good subject.

Q. Should I count out loud before I come out of it?

A. It is best to count to yourself.

Q. Supposing someone is at the door buzzing or the telephone rings while the tape is playing, what do I do?

A. If you wish to interrupt the session, just count to yourself from one to five and tell yourself to lift your eyelids.

Q. At the end of the tape before I come out of it, what suggestions should I give myself?

A. Whatever your immediate problems are, tell yourself you will work them out. If you are anticipating difficulties in facing a situation, try to outline in advance the best way of handling it and tell yourself you will do it.

Q. If my mind wanders and I am not concentrating on what the tape says, what then?

A. Let it wander. Some of the suggestions will still get through even if you fall asleep. There are peripheral areas of attention that still are absorbing the suggestions that are being made.

Q. What are the best times to use the tape?

A. If convenient the first thing in the morning and the last thing at night before going to sleep. Some people put themselves to sleep with the tape. The tape should be played daily.

Q. When I use the tape at night my wife listens to it. I think she gets as much out of it as I do.

A. Your problems are different than hers. But you probably do share some common problems. You can get an ear plug [*one usually comes with a recorder*] to let you listen privately without disturbing your wife.

Q. How often shall I use the tape?

A. At least twice a day, every day.

The patient's reactions to the tape are important because they may reveal some basic problems, transference manifestations, resistances, and the movement in therapy. Occasionally a patient will become quite argumentative after listening to the tape a few times. For example, one patient at the third session (the tape had been made at the second session) handed me the following typewritten comments:

The tape—questions and reactions.

"*Lean back*" Must I sit? I have no chair where I can rest my head. If I do get drowsy I get to be like a Japanese wobblehead doll, and the sudden jerk of the head distracts. Can I lie down? (Then I tend to fall asleep.)

"*In and out*"—I don't breathe that fast, and the in and out never coincide.

"*Tired and relaxed.* Very tired, very relaxed." A total contradiction, and I must add "pleasantly," and it's distracting. To me "tired" means extreme tension and collapse, tension to the point of violent pain.

Cannot relax, not most of the time (or much of the time. Not really relax). And cannot follow the points enumerated so fast. Arms never feel loose. Neck is most difficult. And—how can anyone relax on order?

Can't "wriggle my head" if I lie down.

Enumeration of parts of body is felt like physical touch—an intrusion, an invasion of my private self—with erotic undertones—and resented.

Cannot visualize a "pleasant, quiet, wonderfully relaxed scene." Every time respond with bitterness—I've never experienced one.

When you mention my name it always surprises and touches me—a recognition of me (unworthy of notice).

"*Floating sensation . . . things fade a little and lose their immediacy. Anxiety and depression fade . . . a sort of fuzzy and tingling sensation and a feeling of welcoming sleep.*" It does not happen. Also "sleep." Why sleep?

"*Negative suggestions that piled up in you over the years.*" If the thoughts and feelings are suggestions, they must have come from somewhere or someone. From where? From whom?

"*We must replace them with positive suggestions.*" My reaction—a bitter and angry "the power of positive thinking," "every day in every way I get better and better."

Description of how I've felt brings me to the point of tears. "Every day now, etc., etc."—promises that are not being fulfilled (too good to be true, unattainable—to me). None of it is happening. How long must it take to take effect?

"*You'll be much less easily tired.*" "Tired" again. Contradiction is disturbing. I was urged to feel tired before. Are there different kinds of "tired"? "Every day, you will become so deeply interested . . . " Felt as a derogation. I've always been deeply interested—in what I was doing, in people, in so many things, except when the depression got so bad that I didn't *want to do* anything or see anyone. And this persists, even though to a lesser degree. Enough to keep me stuck and paralyzed. The "what the hell for?" still operates. I don't, or almost don't work. I cannot answer letters. I am not functioning *from within* (only, to some extent, in response to outside stimuli and people), either emotionally or creatively. Whatever potential is there, is still locked up tight. And when I say I am nothing, I am not self-depreciating, I am merely describing the awful sense of emptiness within.

I don't want to be "*much less conscious of myself and my feelings.*" I want to be conscious, but I want the feelings to change. I want to *feel* (and not only pain and rage). I want to be able to feel love. To feel joy. To *have* a "feeling of personal well-being." "See things in their true perspective." What the devil is "true perspective?" There is no such thing.

"*More relaxed, less tense each day.*" It isn't happening.

"*Not only what you have to do each day, but what you ought to be able to do.*" (Meaning? But, of course, *I* am to supply the meaning.)

"Without fear of consequences." (Meaning?)

"More and more able to stand on your own feet without props." Is the tape a prop? Are the W's props?

"They will happen, exactly as I tell you they will happen." When?

Cannot stand "*I call them the four S's.*" I can scream whenever I hear a formula. Can it be omitted, please? (If another tape is made).

"*As we work on your problems*" (? Do we?)

"*In situations that upset you.*" Situations don't upset me. (Of course not. I avoid what I fear).

"*It makes no difference how deep you go. Even if you feel you are conscious*" (Am I supposed to be unconscious? I am conscious every time—not every time or all the time. At times I've fallen asleep).

"*Make your own suggestions.*" Among them: Stop rejecting yourself. Stop rejecting life. Be glad you are alive. Feel good. Feel alive. Don't feel worthless. You are worthwhile. You are intelligent. You are talented. You have accomplished much. Relax, feel rested. Feel bright. Feel alert. Feel. Remember—this or that.

"*Go to sleep. Or arouse yourself.*" Confusing each time. Is this deliberate?

Fortunately, it is rare that one encounters so negative a reaction. In this case I listened silently to her objections and merely told the patient to continue listening to the tape, promising that if she needed a new tape in the future I would make one. I then discussed her dreams and her feelings about me. Her response was a good one, and she did not request another tape, benefiting from the one I had dictated to which originally she had so many negative reactions. She seemed to be fighting off closeness to me as indicated in this dream:

Pt. A herd of wild hogs across the field, moving rapidly, full of wild angry energy, but rather small. I wonder—I thought they were bigger. They are dangerous.

Back to where I came from. Mother says I shouldn't have gone. That area is very dangerous. I am frightened in retrospect. I look across the water at the distant, green land. It seems peaceful from here. But no, it is very dangerous.

Total loneliness. I can see strangers to whom I mean nothing. Aside from that—nothing. I can run and run. When I stop, there is nothing. I love no one, and no one loves me.

I walk with my hand in Dr. Wolberg's arm. Somewhat behind us walks his wife. Will she feel jealous? I am mildly anxious. (There was more, but I can't recall it.)

I was listening to the tape and I kept thinking maybe you didn't hate me. But I pushed it out of my mind. Because I couldn't tolerate that because it would make me vulnerable. I said, "I'm going to ask him if he is sure he approves me." I had another dream:

I was on a stage giving a performance, and I felt I could do it. I wanted everybody to like me, and I wanted to put on a pose of confidence. I kept saying, "Dr. Wolberg says I'm not bad." Then I was in an embryonic saclike a ballonlike I was giving birth to a baby. A man was blowing on it as if he was helping me.

The positive aspects of the dream predicted the responsive relationship the patient developed with me.

Another patient with a strong fear of authority had the following reaction and dream after the playback of the tape.

Pt. I felt comfortable and protected and I thought maybe I can stand up to my supervisor. That night I dreamed, that there was a woman at a campsite. She was a cross between a fury and a witch. There was also a man and a child. I was coming for help. As I approached the campsite, this woman came forward. I was supposed to have inner conviction, the strength of will to overcome this specter. She comes toward me—awful looking, pale. I awoke in a cold sweat. Then I fell asleep again and the dream resumed. The director came in and said: "This thing is not real—all imaginary—no reality." I went in again to the campsite. This time it is not so bad, but I sweat and have anxiety and I woke up. Again I went to sleep and the dream continued. The director said, "O.K. Look at it as it is. Recognize the reality for what it is and face it." I did it and that was it. I looked at the vision and the dream ended.

I awoke relaxed and happy. Played the tape again. I have had recurrent dreams all my life of a child or baby. Must be some aspect of myself, I'm sure. The child is usually dying or sick or in danger. A burden. And I as an adult am saving it. The woman in this dream, the fury-witch, the awful—looked like a combination of my mother, the woman analyst I had once seen, and myself. The man I'm not sure—my stepfather? The director looks like you and the man I live with. This week I was able to face and talk to my supervisor without shaking.

It may not always be possible to get dreams or associated feelings from patients in reponse to the tape, but the therapist will be able to deduce the responses from behavioral and other clues. In the event the patient does not bring up the matter, the therapist should inquire as to how the patient feels listening to the tape. It is rare that objections to some aspects of the tape are so strong that a new tape deleting these sections will be needed.

Conclusion

A cassette tape containing relaxing and ego-building suggestions offers the patient a continuing means of supportive and educational help away from the therapist's office. Responses to the tape provide transference and resistance material for a dynamic focus that may be explored and interpreted. Upon termination of therapy the tape may serve as an important aid toward furthering the objectives of treatment.

CHAPTER 16

Homework Assignments

One of the most neglected aspects of short-term therapy is assigning homework through which patients can facilitate means of controlling or eliminating self-defeating patterns. It is often assumed that the lessons absorbed in the therapist's office will automatically carry over into everyday life. This cherished hope does not always come to pass. The average patient generally dissociates the learnings in the therapist's office from behavior at home, at school, at work, and in the community. After psychologically stripping oneself during a session, outside the patient puts back on the familiar neurotic suit of clothes. It can be helpful, therefore, in consolidating therapeutic gains to insist that therapy does not stop with the exit from the treatment room. The patient must put into practice what is learned during the sessions in order for any change to register itself permanently. And when treatment has ended, the patient will certainly need to reinforce new modes of coping by continuing homework; otherwise, in returning to the customary environment, relapse may be inevitable.

Instructions may thus be given the patient along the following lines:

1. *Look squarely at your immediate life situation.* What elements are to your liking? Are these elements good for you and constructive, and do they need reinforcement? Or should they be minimized or eliminated because they get you into problems? What elements are destructive? What can you do to make them less destructive? Should they be eliminated completely? How can you go about doing this? Once you have decided on a plan of action, proceed with it a step at a time, doing something about it each day.

2. *What patterns of behavior would you like to change, patterns that should be changed?* How far back do they go? Do you see any connection between these patterns and things that happened to you as a child? Realize that you may not have been responsible for what happened to you as a child, but you are responsible for perpetuating these patterns now, for letting these patterns ruin your happiness at the present time. *You can do something about them.* When you observe yourself acting these patterns out, STOP. Ask yourself are you going to let them control you? Say to yourself, "I am able now to stop this nonsense," *and do it.* For example, every time you beat yourself and depreciate yourself, or act out a bad pattern and say you are helpless to control it, are you doing these things to prove that you are defenseless and that therefore somebody should come along and take care of you? Are you punishing yourself because you feel guilty about something? It is easy to say you are a crippled child and that some kind person must take care of you. But remember you pay an awful price for this dependency by getting depressed, feeling physically ill, and destroying your feelings of selfworth. Every time you control a bad pattern, reward yourself by doing something nice for yourself, something you enjoy and that is good for you.

3. *What patterns of behavior would you like to develop that are constructive?* Would you like to be more assertive for instance? If so, plan to do something that calls for assertiveness each day.

These assignments may be given verbally to the patient in the therapist's own words. If a relaxing and ego-building cassette tape (see preceding chapter) has been made, remind the patient that results are contingent on utilizing the tape preferably at least twice daily.

In addition to the above, some patients may benefit from a printed or typewritten set of directions, such as suggested below. These may be adapted to specific problems. The list may be given to and discussed with the patient shortly before termination.

1. *Whenever you get upset or your symptoms return or get worse, ask yourself why this is so.* Try to establish a relationship between the symptoms and happenings in your environment. Did something occur that made you feel guilty or angered you or that you didn't like? Are you punishing yourself because you feel guilty? Is something going on in your relationship with a person who is close to you or with the people who are around you that is hard for you to take? Or is something bothering you that you find difficult to admit even to yourself? It is often helpful to keep a written record of the number of times daily that your symptoms return and approximately when they started and when they stopped. If you jot down the things that happened immediately before the symptoms started, and the circumstances, if any, that relieved them, you may be able to learn to control your symptoms or eliminate them.

2. *What are the circumstances that boost and the things that diminish the feelings about yourself?* When do you feel good about yourself and when do you feel bad? Are these feelings connected with your successes or your failures? What makes you feel inferior, and what makes you feel superior? Do you feel better when you are alone and away from people, or do you feel better when you are with people? What kind of people?

3. *Observe the form of your relationship with people.* What tensions do you get with people? What kind of people do you like and dislike? Are these tensions with all people or certain kinds of people? What do people do to upset you? In what ways do you get upset? What do you do to upset them or to get yourself upset when you are with them? What do you do and what do they do that tends to make you angry? What problems do you have with your parents, mate, children, boss, associates at work, authorities, people in general? Do you tend to treat anyone in a way similar to the patterns that you established with your father, mother, siblings? How is your reaction to people above you, below you, equal to you? What are your expectations when you meet a very attractive person of the opposite sex? Do you try to make yourself too dependent on certain people?

4. *Observing daydreams or night dreams.* A useful outline for observing the meaning of one's day or night dreams includes these three questions: What is your feeling about yourself in the dream? What problem are you wrestling with in the dream? By what means do you reach, or fail to reach, a solution to the problem that presents itself in the dream?

Recurring dreams are particularly significant because they represent a continuing core problem in one's life. Again, whenever possible, you should attempt, if you can, to relate the content of your dreams to what is happening in your life at that time. One man found that he had recurring dreams of bloodshed but that those dreams only occurred after he had made an attempt to assert himself by asking for a raise in pay or by going out with a girl that he liked. He was much surprised to discover that his frightening dreams were actually evidence that he still had some old childish fears about standing up for himself.

5. *Observing resistances to putting understanding into action.* Expect inevitable resistance when you try to stop neurotic patterns. And there can be tension and fear when one faces a challenge that formerly has been evaded. When delaying and avoidance continue to occur, it is well to question the reasons for the delay and ask why one is afraid—and then to take heart and deliberately challenge the fear to see if it can be overcome.

The disciplined practice of these principles of self-observation can lead to progressive growth. Patterns have to be recognized and revised if one is to achieve more satisfying goals in life. But as everyone knows, the habits of years give ground grudgingly and slowly. Ideally, however, the process of personality understanding and growth is marked by several discrete features: There is the awareness that one's problems do not occur fortuitously but are intimately connected with the events (especially the human interactions) of one's life. For a given individual there is a certain quality of human event that generates anxiety, conflict, and stress. These phenomena, once detected, may lead next to a searching for the origin and history of these patterns. It is not impossible to see how these patterns operated as far back as a person can remember—

perhaps even the very earliest memory contains something of the same thing. Seeing the conditions under which fears originated, and under which they are not retriggered, one may next determine whether one can be more the master of one's life rather than a victim of it. Could we be different from the way we have always known ourselves to be? And ever so slowly, we may challenge one habitual childish fear at a time, pushing ourselves to break out of the prison of our neurotic self-defeating patterns. Success breeds success, and victory leads to victory. Defeats are reanalyzed in accord with their place in the psychic structure. Seeing ourselves defeated by the same old enemies, we are buoyed up in knowing that formulations about our personalities are correct, and we are then encouraged to fight on. Increasingly, we can express a claim to a new life; we find ourselves able to be more expressive. Self-recriminations diminish. Our capacities expand, and we gratify more of our needs. Feeling less frustrated in life, and therefore less angry, we can enter into relationships with people with more openness and a greater ability to share.

These are idealistic goals, but they represent a guide along the way toward greater self-observation and richer living. Fidelity to the practice of self-observation, together with the actual translation of understanding into action, can be a lifelong quest marked by high adventure and notable results.

The knowledge of oneself and how one reacts continues to constitute the surest path to health and to mature behavior.

Evolving a More Constructive Life Philosophy

One of the ways psychotherapy influences people is by helping them to develop new values and philosophies of living. However, the history of the majority of patients, prior to their seeking therapy, attests to futile gropings for some kind of philosphical answer to their dilemmas. The search may proceed from Christian to Oriental philosophies, from prurience to moralism, from self-centeredness to community mindedness. What at first seems firmly established soon becomes dubious as new ideas and concepts are proffered by different authorities. It is far better to evolve philosophies that are anchored in some realistic conception of one's personal universe than to accept fleeting cosmic sentiments and suppositions no matter how sound their source may seem. Even a brief period of psychotherapy may till the soil for the growth of a healthier sense of values. We may be able during this span to inculcate in the person a philosophy predicted on science rather than on cultism.

The question that naturally follows in a short-term program is: Can we as therapists expedite matters by acting in an educational capacity, pointing out faulty values and indicating healthy ones that the patient may advantageously adopt? If so, what are the viewpoints to be stressed?

Actually, no matter how nondirective a therapist may imagine himself to be, the patient will soon pick up from explicit or implicit cues the tenor of the therapist's philosophies and values. The kinds of questions the therapist asks, the focus of his interpretive activities, his confrontations and acquiescences, his silences and expressions of interest, all designate points of view contagious to the patient, which he tends to incorporate, consciously and unconsciously, ultimately espousing the very conceptual commodities that are prized by the therapist. Why not then openly present new precepts that can serve the patient better? Superficial as they sound, the few precepts that can be tendered may be instrumental in accelerating a better adjustment. Among possible propositions are the following:

Isolating the Past from the Present

All persons are victimized by their past, which may operate as mischief mongers in the present. A good adjustment presupposes modulating one's activities to present-day considerations rather than resigning to promptings inspired by childish needs and misinterpretations. In therapy the patient may become aware of what early patterns are repeating themselves in his adult life. This may provide him with an incentive for change. On the other hand, it may give the patient an excuse to rationalize his defections on the basis that unalterable damage has been done to him by his parents, who are responsible for all of his trouble. The therapist may remind the patient that he, like anyone else, has a tendency to project outmoded feelings, fears, and attitudes into the present. His early hurtful experiences undoubtedly contribute to his insecurity and to his devalued self-esteem. They continue to contaminate his adjustment *now*, and he, therefore, must try to overcome them. Thus, the therapist would make a statement similar to the following:

Th. Ruminating on your unfortunate childhood and bitter past experiences are indulgences you cannot afford. These can poison your present life if you let them do this. It is a credit to you as a person to rise above your early misfortunes. Attempt to restrain yourself when you fall back into thinking about past events you no longer can control or when you find yourself behaving childishly. Remember, you may not have been responsible for what happened to you when you were a child, but you *are* responsible for perpetuating these patterns in the present. Say to yourself, "I'm going to release myself from the bonds of the past." And work at it.

Handling Tension and Anxiety

The patient may be reminded that tension and anxiety may appear but that he can do something positive about them.

Th. Everytime you experience tension, or any other symptoms for that matter, ask yourself why? Is it the immediate situation you are in? Is it something which happened before that is stirring you up? Is it something you believe will happen in the future? Once you have identified the source of your tension or trouble, you will be in a better position to handle it. The least that will occur is that you will not feel so helpless since you know a little about its origins. You will then be in a better position to do things to correct your trouble.

The idea that one need not be a helpless victim of symptoms tends to restore feelings of mastery. A patient who has given this suggestion went to a new class. While listening to the lecturer, she began to experience tension and anxiety. Asking herself why, she realized she was reacting to the presence of a classmate who came from her own neighborhood and knew her family. She then recognized that she felt guilty about her interest in one of the men in the class. This happened to be the real reason why she registered for the course. She realized that she feared the neighbor's revealing her interest in the man to her parents if she sat near him or was friendly to him. She then thought about her mother who was a repressive, punitive person who had warned her about sexual activities. With this understanding, she suddenly became angry at her classmate. When she asked herself why she was so furious, it dawned on her that she was actually embittered at her own mother. Her tension and hostility disappeared when she resolved to follow her impulses on the basis that she was now old enough to do what she wished.

Tolerating a Certain Amount of Tension and Anxiety

Some tension and anxiety are inherent parts of living. There is no escape from them. The patient must be brought around to accept the fact that he will have to tolerate and handle a certain amount of anxiety.

Th. Even when you are finished with therapy, a certain amount of tension and anxiety are to be expected. All persons have to live with some anxiety and tension, and these may precipitate various symptoms from time to time. If you do get some anxiety now and then, ride it and try to figure out what is stirring it up. But, remember, you are no worse off than anyone else simply because you have some anxiety. If you are unable to resolve your tensions entirely through self-observation, try to involve yourself in any outside activities that will get your mind off your tensions.

Tolerating a Certain Amount of Hostility

If the patient can be made to understand that he will occasionally get resentful and that if he explores the reason for this, he may be able to avoid projecting his anger or converting it into symptoms.

Th. If you feel tense and upset, ask yourself if you are angry at anything. See if you can figure out what is causing your resentment. Permit yourself to feel angry if the occasion justifies it; but express your anger in proportion to what the situation will tolerate. You do not have to do anything that will result in trouble for you; nevertheless, see if you can release some of your anger. If you can do nothing more, talk out loud about it when you are alone, or engage in muscular exercises to provide an outlet for aggression, like punching a pillow. In spite of these activities you may still feel angry to a certain degree. So long as you keep it in hand while recognizing that it exists, it need not hurt you. All people have to live with a certain amount of anger.

Tolerating a Certain Amount of Frustration and Deprivation

No person can ever obtain a full gratification of all of his needs, and the patient must come to this realization.

Th. It is important to remember that you still can derive a great deal of joy out of eighty per cent rather than one hundred percent. Expect to be frustrated to some extent and learn to live with it.

Correcting Remediable Elements in One's Environment

The patient may be reminded of his responsibility to remedy any alterable factors in his life situation.

Th. Once you have identified any area of trouble, try to figure out what can be done about it. Lay out a plan of action. You may not be able to implement this entirely, but do as much of it as you can immediately, and then routinely keep working at it. No matter how hopeless things seem, if you apply yourself, you can do much to rectify matters. Do not get discouraged. Just keep working away.

Adjusting to Irremediable Elements in One's Life Situation

No matter how much we may wish to correct certain conditions, practical considerations may prevent our doing much about them. For example, one may have to learn to live with a handicapped child or a sick husband or wife. One's financial situation may be irreparably marginal. There are certain things all people have to cope with, certain situations from which they cannot escape. If the patient lives in the hope of extricating himself from an unfortunate plight by magic, he will be in constant frustration.

Th. There are certain things every person has to learn to accept. Try your best to alter them as much as you can. And then if some troubles continue, just tell yourself you must live with some of them, and resolve not to let them tear you down. It takes a good deal of courage and character to live with your troubles, but you may have a responsibility to carry them. If you start feeling sorry for yourself, you are bound to be upset. So just plug away at it and build up insulation to help you carry on. Say to yourself: "I am not going to respond to trouble like a weather vane. I will remedy the trouble if I can. If I cannot, I will adjust to it. I will concentrate on the good things in my life and minimize the bad."

Using Will Power to Stop Engaging in Destructive Activities

One of the unfortunate consequences of a dynamic approach is that it gives the patient the idea that he is under the influence of unconscious monsters he cannot control. He will, therefore, justify the acting-out on the basis of his "automatic repetition-compulsions." Actually, once he has a glimmer of what is happening to him, there is no reason why he cannot enlist the cooperation of his will power to help inhibit himself.

Th. If you know a situation will be bad for you, try to divert yourself from acting it out even if you have to use your will power. There is no reason why you can't work out substitute solutions that are less destructive to you even though they may not immediately be so gratifying. Remember, a certain amount of deprivation and frustration is normal, and it is a compliment to you as a person to be able to give up gratifications that are ultimately hurtful to you. Remember, too, that some of the chief benefits you get out of your symptoms are masochistic, a kind of need to punish yourself. You can learn to overcome this too. When you observe yourself acting neurotically, stop in your tracks and figure out what you are doing.

A woman, living a conventional life as a housewife, was involving herself sexually with two of her friend's husbands. She found herself unable to resist their advances, even though the sexual experiences were not particularly fulfilling. She felt ashamed and was guilt-ridden by her actions. There was obviously some deeper motive that prompted the patient to act out sexually, but the threat to her marriage and relationship with her husband required an immediate halting of her activity. I remarked to her: "Until you figure out some of your underlying feelings, it is best for you to stop your affairs right now. How would you feel about stopping right now? Let's give ourselves a couple of months to figure out this thing. Frankly, I don't see how we can make progress unless you do." The patient reluctantly acquiesced; but soon she was relieved that somebody was supporting her inner resolution to resist. The interval enabled us to explore her disappointment with her husband, her resentment toward him, and to find outlets for her desires for freedom and self-expression in more appropriate channels than sexual acting-out. If the patient has been given a chart detailing the interaction of dependency, low feelings of independence, hostility, devalued self-esteem and detachment, their manifestations as well as reaction formations to neutralize them, he may be enjoined to study the chart and see how his own drives and needs, with their consequences, fit into the overall design.

Stopping Unreasonable Demands on Oneself

If the patient is pushing himself beyond the limits of his capacities or setting too high standards for himself, it will be essential for him to assess his actions. Are they to satisfy his ambitions or those of his parents? Are they to do things perfectionistically? If so, does he feel he can achieve greater independence or stature as a person when he succeeds?

Th. All people have their assets and liabilities. You may never be able to accomplish what some persons can do; and there are some things you can do that others will find impossible. Of course, if you try hard enough, you can probably do the impossible, but you'll be worn down so it won't mean much to you. You can still live up to your creative potentials without going to extremes. You can really wear yourself out if you push yourself too hard. So just try to relax and to enjoy what you have, making the most out of yourself without tearing yourself to pieces. Just do the best you can, avoiding using perfectionism as a standard for yourself.

Challenging a Devalued Self-image

Often an individual retires on the investment of his conviction of self-devaluation. What need is there for him to make any effort if he is so constitutionally inferior that all of his best intentions and well-directed activities will lead to naught? It is expedient to show the patient that he is utilizing his self-devaluation as a destructive implement to bolster his helplessness and perhaps to sponsor dependency. In this way he makes capital out of a handicap. Pointing out realistic assets the patient possesses may not succeed in destroying the vitiated image of himself; but it does help him to reevaluate his potentialities and to avoid the despair of considering himself completely hopeless. One may point out to the patient instances of his successes. In this respect, encouraging the patient to adopt the idea that he can succeed in an activity in which he is interested, and to expand a present asset, may prove to be a saving grace. A woman with a deep sense of inferiority and lack of self-confidence was exhorted to add to her knowledge of horticulture with which she was fascinated. At gatherings she was emboldened to talk about her specialty when an appropriate occasion presented itself. She found herself the center of attention among a group of suburbanites who were eager to acquire expert information. This provided her with a means of social contact and with a way of doing things for others that built up a more estimable feeling about herself.

Logic obviously cannot convince a person with devalued self-esteem that he has merit. Unless a proper assessment is made of his existing virtues, however, the person will be retarded in correcting his distorted self-image.

Th. You do have a tendency to devalue yourself as a result of everything that has happened to you. From what I can observe, there is no real reason why you should. If you do, you may be using self-devaluation as a way of punishing yourself because of guilt, or of making people feel sorry for you, or of rendering yourself helpless and dependent. You know, all people are different; every person has a uniqueness, like every thumbprint is unique. The fact that you do not possess some qualities other people have does not make you inferior.

Deriving the Utmost Enjoyment from Life

Focusing on troubles and displeasures in one's existence can deprive a person of joys that are his right as a human being. The need to develop a sense of humor and to get the grimness out of one's daily life may be stressed.

Th. Try to minimize the bad or hurtful elements and concentrate on the good and constructive things about yourself and your situation. It is important for every person to reap out of each 24 hours the maximum of pleasures possible. Try not to live in recriminations of the past and in forebodings about the future. Just concentrate on achieving happiness in the here and now.

Accepting One's Social Role

Every adult has a responsibility in assuming a variety of social roles: as male or female, as husband or wife, as a parent, as a person who must relate to authority and on occasions act as authority, as a community member with obligations to society. Though he may feel immature, dependent, hostile, and hypocritical, the individual still must try to fill these roles as completely as he can. If the patient is destructively involved with another person with whom he must carry on a relationship, like an employer, for example, he must attempt to understand the forces that serve to disturb the relationship. At the same time, however, he must try to keep the relationship going in a way that convention dictates so that he will not do anything destructive to his security.

Th. One way of trying to get along with people is to attempt to put yourself in their position and to see things from their point of view. If your husband [wife, child, employer, etc.] is doing something that is upsettting, ask yourself: "What is he [she] feeling at this time; what is going on in his [her] mind? How would I feel if I were in his [her] position?" At any rate, if you can recognize what is going on, correcting matters that can be resolved, adjusting to those that cannot be changed; if you are able to relate to the good rather than to the bad in people, you should be able to get along with them without too much difficulty."

The form by which the above guidelines are verbally or graphically communicated to the patient will vary, and each therapist may decide whether they are useful in whole or in part for specific patients. Reading assignments may also be given and suggestions for continued self-education made after therapy has ended. A full list of reading materials will be found elsewhere (Wolberg, 1977, pp. 816–833).

Conclusion

It is important to supply patients with homework assignments to reinforce the value of their sessions. These tasks are usually related to what is immediately going on in therapy, whether they involve exploring the nature of one's problems, charting the frequency of symptoms and recording the circumstances under which they appear, recognizing the constructive and destructive elements in the immediate environment, observing behavioral patterns and reinforcing those that are adaptive, picking out situations that enhance or lower self-esteem, studying one's relationships with people, examining dreams and fantasies, or seeing what resistances block the putting of understanding into productive action. Practice sessions devoted to assertive and other constructive forms of behavior are especially helpful. Some of the assigned exercises strive to inculcate new values and philosophies that contribute to a more productive adjustment. A relaxing and ego-building cassette tape as well as assigned readings are additional useful accessories.

CHAPTER 17

Termination of Short-term Therapy

Proper termination of treatment is one of the most neglected aspects of the therapeutic process. Ideally, it should start in the initial interview during which the limited time span is emphasized. Even though the patient immediately accepts this provisional arrangement, later, as the therapeutic relationship crystallizes, its ending can pose a threat.

Termination of therapy is no problem in most patients who are adequately prepared for it, or who are characterologically not too dependent, or who are seen for only a few sessions and discharged before a strong relationship with the therapist develops, or who are so detached that they ward off a close therapeutic contact. It may, however, become a difficult problem in other cases. Patients who in early childhood have suffered rejection or abandonment by or loss of a parent, or who have had difficulties in working through the separation-individuation dimensions of their development are especially vulnerable and may react with fear, anger, despair, and grief. A return of their original symptoms will tend to confound the patient and inspire in the therapist frustration, disappointment, guilt feelings, and anger at the patient for having failed to respond to therapeutic ministrations.

Resistance to termination affects not only the patient; it is present also in the therapist who for conscious or unconscious reasons may not be willing to let his patient separate. Therapists countertransferentially form attachments to some of their patients, and they may resent sending them away. Sometimes monetary factors influence delays in termination, particularly during periods when new referrals are sparse. Sometimes the projected goals of therapy have been set too high, and both patient and therapist are disappointed with what seem meager results. They will then eagerly cancel the termination contract and hopefully embark on a search for a cure with a fresh series of sessions that will usually eventuate in long-term and in some cases interminable treatment.

The word "cure" is an ambiguous expression when related to emotional problems. Most optimistically it designates an elimination of pathology and the induction of a total and robust state of well-being. To anticipate such a goal in short-term therapy excites unrealistic hope and optimism. Many of the imprints of unfortunate life experience, particularly those compounded in early childhood, are more or less indelible and cannot be eliminated completely by any method known today. Nor can all characterologic deficits be totally regenerated, residual distortions often obtruding themselves impertinently at unguarded moments even in the most successfully treated individual. On the other hand, it is possible to neutralize the effects of inimical past experience, to enhance security, to bolster self-esteem, and to improve adaptation and problem solving through well-conducted short-term psychotherapy. The objectives that we may practically achieve are these:

1. Modification or removal of symptoms and relief of suffering.
2. Revival of that level of functioning that the patient possessed prior to the outbreak of the illness.
3. Promotion of an understanding that there are patterns indulged that sponsor symptoms, sabotage

functioning, and interfere with a more complete enjoyment of life.

4. Attainment of some idea of how to recognize the existence of self-defeating patterns and how to explore their consequences.

5. Provision of useful ways of dealing with such patterns and their effects in order to rectify and replace them with more constructive coping measures.

Termination Procedures

Following the suggestions detailed in Chapter 4 "A General Outline of Short-term Therapy," the patient is apprised of the limited number of sessions that will constitute treatment, either by designating the exact number in advance and setting a termination date or, after indicating that the number of sessions will be circumscribed, by postponing announcing the ending date until after therapy has started. Once the target date is settled, the patient is periodically reminded of it and responses to this briefing handled (see pp. 45–46). With rare exceptions therapy should be ended on the agreed-upon date (p. 46). The need to work on oneself is stressed (p. 47), and arrangements for further treatment made if necessary (p. 47).

The question is often asked as to whether symptomatic improvement by itself without some understanding of the underlying sources of the current upset is sufficient justification for the termination of therapy. Ideally the answer would be no. Symptomatic relief may occur as a consequence of the placebo effect and may expend itself rapidly unless changes are brought about in the environment as well as in the self. Nevertheless, we should not minimize the importance of symptom removal since without it no therapy can justify itself. Relief of symptoms can restore important defenses that are a part of the individual's habitual adaptive machinery. In this way we may best achieve the objective of restituting the optimal past adjustment. Most patients are satisfied with this accomplishment, but occasionally some individuals expect more extensive results within a few sessions.

It is manifestly impossible to uproot personality difficulties that date back to childhood in a short period, and quite likely even intensive prolonged treatment will fail to budge some patterns. The patient will therefore have to be prepared for termination with the achievement of only less than a complete cure. A patient who came for treatment with a problem of obesity, depression, and strong feelings of inferiority was helped in 10 sessions to correct his food habits and to lose weight. His depression lessened to a great extent, but there was no change in the sleazy image he had of himself. I reminded him that our agreed-upon goal in therapy was to help him develop better food habits and moderate his depression. An excerpt follows:

Pt. I feel a lot better, the weight and all, but I still feel like I don't amount to much.

Th. We've gone over some of the reasons why you always have felt this way.

Pt. But can't I be cured of this?

Th. Your problem goes so far back that a complete cure would take a long time. Even then a few residues of your childhood may pop up from time to time. This isn't important because you can still keep growing and developing on your own with what you have already learned in therapy. Right now you can overcome your symptoms, like overeating and depression, and function a lot better in spite of how you feel about yourself. The reality is that you are not an inferior person even though you feel you are. Over a long period applying the understanding you now have will wear out this delusion about yourself. But expect no miracles. It will take time. The important thing is to keep working at yourself. Suppose you try things on your own, and in about 3 months we will make another appointment to see how you are doing.

Pt. That's great. Maybe I can work at this by myself, and if I need further help, I'll call you.

Th. Fine. Don't hesitate to call me if any further problems develop.

In avoiding the patient's request for longer-term therapy, we indicate that it is essential for the patient to try to resolve his problems by himself. This is done with no illusion that a cure will come about in any characterologic distortions, but rather to avoid becoming dependent on therapy. Proceeding on one's own, progress may be made with interim sessions of short-term therapy if necessary. In this case two such brief periods of five and six sessions each were used the first year and three sessions the second year. Single follow-up sessions the third and fifth years revealed extensive and gratifying personality changes.

This does not imply that long-term therapy may not be the treatment of choice in some cases. But the selection of patients must be carefully made.

Another common question that confronts the therapist is if at the end of the alloted treatment time a patient feels better but has not reached the goals set by the therapist originally, should termination then be delayed? It is difficult to generalize an answer to this question other than to say that certain patients will benefit from further therapy and others will not. Much as we would like to continue working with a patient, the danger of interminable therapy must be kept in mind. Some patients will not, for sundry reasons, be able to achieve the objectives that the therapist has anticipated or that they themselves covet, no matter how long we keep them in treatment. Indeed, continued therapy may dissipate the gains achieved in the preliminary short-term treatment period, the patient becoming steeped in a negative transference and in crippling dependency from which he cannot liberate himself. The way this problem is best handled is to terminate therapy, enjoining the patient to continue working on his own (with the assigned homework) listening regularly to the cassette tape if one is given him, and reporting back for a session in 2 weeks, then once a month, and after a while once every 3 months. It is not unusual for a patient to have achieved considerable progress by himself after formal therapy has ended once the momentum has been started during the short-term span. Should no progress have occurred several months after termination, and should the patient be dissatisfied with his status, another intensive short-term treatment can be instituted, during which an assay is made of the kind of therapy best to use, the capacity of the patient to change, and realistic goals that may be achieved. Sometimes the second brief treatment trial does the job without further formal therapy being needed. On the other hand, we may not be able to avoid resorting to long-term therapy, and here the kind of therapy and the depth of therapy will suggest itself from the data already obtained.

We must, nevertheless, brace ourself to the possibility of failure no matter what we do. Inevitably there will be persons who do not well with any kind of therapy. Many of these individuals go on to prolonged treatment with the object of achieving reconstructive change through the alchemy of time. The idea that long-term therapy will inevitably succeed where short-term approaches have failed is deceptive. There are some patients who seem doomed to a perpetual immature adjustment, clinging to a parental figure in a dependent way the remainder of their lives. Some theories of why this is so have been presented. One speculation for a certain type of patient is that in treatment the patient is unable "to bring about the internalization of the therapist as an object-anchor around which the patient can organize himself" or to maintain an equilibrium "in the face of the anxiety released by interpretive work" (Appelbaum, 1972). There are other surmises too, but some sicker patients will respond much more to adjunctive environmental manipulation, rehabilitative treatment, social therapy, and pharmacotherapy than to formal psychotherapy, although periodic psychotherapeutic sessions with a skillful and empathic therapist along with adjunctive approaches should produce optimal results.

Most patients, fortunately, may be helped—and significantly helped—by dynamic short-term therapy. Even deep personality difficulties may be influenced. Because entrenched character patterns are dislodged reluctantly, however maladaptive they may be, it is assumed that character alterations while *initiated* during the formal treatment period will need to continue to develop in the post-therapeutic span over an extended interval, even over years, before *permanent* altered imprints are etched into the personality structure.

Managing Untoward Reactions to Termination

In patients who have been in therapy for more than a handful of sessions and who have established a good therapeutic alliance, stormy clouds may gather as the termination date draws near. The fact that the ending of therapy brings out unresolved issues related to the separation-individuation theme is not entirely a liability. Indeed, as Rank (1936, 1947) insisted years ago it may become the most important aspect of the helping process by forcing the patient to face paralyzing dependencies and to assume the responsibilities of individuation. Many other authorities affirm Rank's belief that the working-through of residues of childish helplessness is essential toward sponsoring greater personality maturation. It is, however, naive to assume that adulthood will break out in a flash solely as a consequence of being evicted from therapy. It will require perhaps years before the fruits of maturity can mellow. The therapist should not deceive himself into believing that individuation is easy to achieve and that with termination the patient, sword in hand, can happily saunter out to conquer the world. Nevertheless, the seeds of self-reliance have a greater chance of germination in the soil provided by the proper management of the terminal phases of the patient–therapist relationship.

How intense the reactions to termination become will depend on the patient's residual dependency needs, how thoroughly these needs have been supported during treatment, the way that the patient was prepared for termination, and bringing into the open the patient's feelings about termination. Often these feelings are not explicit, the patient being afraid to express anger or grief openly and the therapist avoiding areas that might be upsetting or embarrassing to him. It is important, consequently, to face the fact that termination can be difficult for the therapist also and because of this may require some soul searching on his part. Will the therapist be relieved in getting rid of a burdensome patient and consequently facilitate the easing of the patient out of his office? Will he feel guilty at discharging a patient who still suffers from residuals of the problem for which help was originally sought? Will he resent the financial loss created by a hole in his caseload? Will he himself suffer separation anxiety caused by his own unresolved separation-individuation problems? It will take a good deal of courage to face up to these issues.

Where dreams and exploration of acting-out tendencies are employed, the patient's feelings about termination will be most readily available. A patient was asked at the tenth session how she felt about terminating treatment the following month. She admitted feeling better and said that she was happy that I considered her well enough to be on her own. The next session she admitted feeling a "bit shaky" about handling matters by herself and that this reaction lasted for several hours after she left my office. She denied any feelings of resentment or depression. At the following session she brought in this dream: "I am attending a funeral. A girl with arms cut off in a coffin. She looks like me. I am frightened and run home." For the next few sessions we focused on her feelings of helplessness and fears of what might happen to her after she stopped, as well as her anger at me. Early dependencies fostered by an overprotective mother were explored. No revision of the termination time was made. At the fourteenth session she admitted feeling a great deal better, and she presented this dream: "I am sliding down a chute and falling down, then standing up, then falling down, then standing up, then falling down. Mother and father run up to pick me up. I push them away and I stand alone. I walk unsteadily but under my own power." In her associations she stated that at work she had taken a definite stand. She was proud of herself because she refused to go to her employer for advice. "I know more about these things than he does." Termination occurred after the next session. A 2-year follow-up showed continuing and extensive improvement in her adjustment.

The importance of allowing patients to express their feelings of disappointment, anger, and sadness cannot be overemphasized. The therapist will especially be alerted for problems where, as has been mentioned before, the patient as a child experienced a death of or separation from a parent or where in later life a catastrophic reaction followed the loss of or separation from a parent or mate. Patients with a high level of characterologic dependency may regard termination as a personal injury, an unwarranted desertion, or a sign of their lack of importance or self-worth. It is essential not to act defensive or guilty about terminating treatment. Explanations should focus on the need to protect the patient from getting locked into a dependency situation in treatment that will prove crippling and infantalizing. Most patients will handle the termination experience when given a chance to express themselves freely. Occasionally, though, the patient may become so angry or distrustful as to break appointments. If this occurs, the therapist should contact the patient by telephone and discuss what is happening. The fact that sufficient interest exists to induce the telephone call in all probability will motivate the patient to return for the remaining sessions.

I have found that the use of a cassette tape helps the termination process immeasureably pp. 223–234). The patient does not experience the shock of being left alone on his own devices. He has a tool that he can utilize by himself to expand the gains that he has derived from treatment. Therapists who imagine that the individuation process is expedited by abruptly tossing patients out of treatment after the last session on the theory that the absence of the therapist and the presence of insight are remedial will encounter a rude shock when adqequate follow-ups are done. A surprisingly large number of patients, who presumably had achieved maturity at discharge, sooner or later lock themselves into new paralyzing dependencies with some surrogate parental figure or exploit successive offbeat treatment modalities once they reexperience tension or anxiety. The use of the tape makes these feckless resources unnecessary. Speculation that the patient may get dependent on the tape and that this will thwart the individuation process is completely groundless. On the contrary, the tape enjoins the patient to continue the working-through process toward greater self-sufficiency.

No short-term treatment program is complete without some provision for this or some other type of self-help as well as maintenance of proper vigilance to prevent slipping back to the previous state. The patient should be enjoined to pursue "homework" assignments given him during the active treatment period (see Chapter 16) and invited to return to see the therapist briefly should serious problems develop in the future that he cannot manage by himself (p. 46).

An aspect in therapy that is also neglected is providing patients with some means of correcting distorted cognitions. Supplying them with a way of looking at life and at their own experiences, in short with a proper life philosophy, may add to their enhancement of well-being. We might consider this a kind of cognitive therapy. The spontaneous evolution of more wholesome ways of looking at things often occurs subtly as a result of the cogent application of principles that the patient has learned in therapy. Life is approached from an altered perspective. What was at one time frightening or guilt inspiring is no longer disturbing; what brings insecurity and undermines self-esteem ceases to register such effects. This revolution takes time. Value change may not be discernible until years have passed beyond the formal treatment period.

It is often helpful to warn the patient that, while one may feel better, there will be required a consistent application of what has been learned in therapy to insure a more permanent resolution of deeper problems. The need for self-observation and for the active challenging of neurotic patterns is stressed. The patient is also enjoined not to get upset if a setback is experienced.

Th. Setbacks are normal in the course of development. After all, some of these patterns are as old as you are. They will try to repeat themselves even when you have an understanding of their nature. But what will happen is that the setbacks will get shorter and shorter as you apply your understanding to what produced the setback. Gradually you will restructure yourself. In a way it is good if a setback occurs, for then you will have an opportunity to come to grips again with your basic problems to see how they work. This can build up your stamina. It is like taking a vaccine. Repeated doses produce a temporary physical upset, but complete immunization eventually results. In other words, if your symptoms come back, don't panic. It doesn't mean anything more than that something has stirred up powerful tensions. Ask yourself what has created your tensions. Is there anything in your immediate situation that triggered things? Relate this to what you know about yourself, about your personality in general. Eventually, you will be able to stop your reaction. But be patient and keep working at it.

Another neglected aspect of therapy are follow-up sessions. Prior to his discharge the patient may be told that it is customary to have a follow-up session 1 year after treatment, then yearly thereafter for a few years. Most patients do not object to this; indeed, they are flattered by the therapist's interest. An appointment for a session is best made by a personal telephone call. Where the patient, for any reason, finds it impossible to keep the appointment, a friendly letter may be sent asking him to write the therapist detailing his feelings and progress if any.

Conclusion

The termination phases of short-term treatment are often minimized, many therapists imagining that the end of therapy will come about automatically. Left to their own resources, a considerable number of patients, if they can afford it, or if treatment is paid for by a third party, will want to continue in treatment indefinitely. The goals of short-term therapy are often set too high by both patients and therapists. Realistically, it is a forlorn hope that patients can undo in a few sessions a lifetime bundle of personality immaturities they could not eliminate with long-term treatment over an indefinite period. It will be essential, therefore, for the therapist to accept modest attainable goals within the brief span of treatment, while alerting the patient to problems to be worked on by oneself after therapy has ended. Therapy with a few exceptions should be terminated at the designated set time limit.

Termination, however, can be a problem for

both patient and therapist. As the termination date approaches, the patient may experience a regression with symptom revival. The therapist will then be tempted to proceed beyond the termination date hoping that a few more sessions will save the day. Instead of yielding to this temptation, the therapist more propitiously should examine what termination means to the patient and to himself. Usually it will have stirred up the old dependency-autonomy conflict in the patient. And the fact that the patient has not achieved the entire hoped-for cure may, in turn, open old unhealed wounds in the therapist, including grandiosity and narcissistic need to prove invincibility as a therapist. It may also kindle the separation anxiety sparked by the patient's threatened departure. Both transference and countertransference will require exploration at this point to help the separation process toward allowing patients to stand on their own feet, putting into practice the lessons learned in therapy. The therapist must accept the fact that no patient can be completely cured at the termination of short-term therapy. The most that can be hoped for is that enough has been gained in treatment to have achieved symptom relief, abandonment of an old destructive pattern or two or at least some understanding of these patterns, and ideas of how one can keep working on oneself to assure continuing improvement.

Therapeutic change does not cease at the termination of therapy. It may continue long after treatment has ended, perhaps the remainder of the individual's life. Indeed, follow-up studies of patients who stopped therapy in a stalemate or because of no apparent improvement have revealed gratifying alterations that seem to have required the ripening effects of time.

Too frequently therapy is presumed to terminate with the last interview. The fact that over 60 percent of patients who have completed short-term therapy seek out further treatments (Patterson et al, 1977) indicates that an ongoing therapeutic experience of some kind, formal or informal, is deemed necessary by the great majority. If the therapist does not provide a direction, the patient will search for one personally, perhaps blundering into adventures that are unrewarding to say the least.

One way to foster continued improvement is to prepare the patient to work toward altering a destructive environment so that it ceases to impose strains on adjustment. The lines along which such modulations may be made will be determined during the active treatment phase. "Homework" should be encouraged. These may embody (1) tension reduction and ego-building through self-relaxation exercises or listening to a cassette tape, (2) inculcation of a proper philosophical outlook by imparting new meanings to one's existence, (3) observation of one's behavior to detect patterns that provoke problems, and (4) the studied practice of more constructive modes of coping with essential responsibilities.

Lest we chide ourselves at not having achieved with dynamic short-term therapy a completely "analyzed" patient on termination, we may heed the wise words of Freud who wrote: "Our aim will not be to rub off every peculiarity of human character for the sake of a schematic normality, nor yet to demand that the person who has been thoroughly analyzed shall feel no passions and develop no internal conflicts. The business of the analysis is to secure the best possible psychological conditions for the functions of the ego; with that it has discharged its task." We are, of course, hopeful that with continued work on themselves our patients will proceed beyond this objective.

References

Adler A: The Individual Psychology of Alfred Adler. New York, Basic Books, 1956.

Adler G, Buie DH: The misuses of confrontation with borderline patients, in Masserman JH (ed): Current Psychiatric Therapies, Vol 14. New York, Grune & Stratton, 1974.

Adler G, Myerson PG: Confrontation in Psychotherapy. New York, Aronson, 1973.

Adler KA: Techniques that shorten psychotherapy: Illustrated with five cases. J Ind Psychol 28(21):155–168, 1972.

Akiskal HS, McKinney WT, Jr: Psychiatry and pseudopsychiatry. Arch Gen Psychiatry 28:367, 1973.

Alexander F: The brief psychotherapy council and its outlook. Proc Brief Psychother Council 2:14, 1944.

Alexander F, French TM: Psychoanalytic Therapy. New York, Ronald Press, 1946.

Alexander JF, Parsons BV: Short-term behavioral intervention with delinquent families: Impact on family process and recidivism, J Abnorm Psychol 81:219–225, 1973.

Alger I: Television image confrontation in group therapy, in Sager CJ, Kaplan HS (eds): Progress in Group and Family Therapy. New York, Brunner/Mazel, 1972.

Amada G: Crisis-oriented psychotherapy: Some theoretical and practical considerations. J Contemp Psychother 9:104–111, 1977.

Annexton M: Treatment for delayed stress response. JAMA 240:1948, 1978.

Ansbacher HL: Adlerian psychology: The tradition of brief psychotherapy. J Ind Psychol 28:137–151, 1972.

Appelbaum SA: How long is long-term psychotherapy? Bull Menninger Clinic 36:652, 1972.

Argyle M, et al: Social skills training and psychotherapy: A comparative study. Psychol Med 4:435–443, 1974.

Aronson ML: A group program for overcoming the fear of flying, in Wolberg LR, Aronson ML (eds): Group Therapy 1974: An Overview. New York, Stratton Intercontinental, 1974.

Avnet HH: Psychiatric Insurance: Financing Short-term Ambulatory Treatment. New York, Group Health Insurance, 1962.

Ayllon T, Azrin NH: The Token Economy: A Motivational System for Therapy and Rehabilitation. New York, Appleton-Century-Crofts, 1968.

Bach GR: The marathon group: Intensive practice in intimate interaction. Psychol Rep 18:995–1002, 1966.

Bach GR: Marathon group dynamics: I. Some functions of the professional group facilitator. Psychol Rep 20:995–999, 1967 (a).

Bach GR: Marathon group dynamics: II. Dimensions of helpfulness: Therapeutic aggression. Psychol Rep 20:1147–1158, 1967 (b).

Bach GR: Marathon group dynamics: III. Disjunctive contacts. Psychol Rep 20:1163–1172, 1967 (c).

Bach GR: Group and leader phobias in marathon groups. Voices 3:41–46, 1967 (d).

Back KW: Beyond Words: The Story of Sensitivity Training and the Encounter Movement. New York, Russell Sage Foundation, 1972.

Bakker CB, Bakker-Rabdau MK: No Trespassing, Explorations in Human Territoriality. Corte Medera, Calif, Chandler & Sharp, 1973.

Baldwin BA: Crisis intervention in professional practice. Am J Orthopsychiatry 47:659–670, 1977.

Bandura A: Principles of Behavior Modification. New York, Holt, Rinehart & Winston, 1969.

Barten HH: The coming of age of the brief psychotherapies, in Bellak L, Barten HH (eds): Progress in Community Mental Health. New York, Grune & Stratton, 1969.

Barten HH: Brief Therapies. New York, Behavior Publications, 1971.

Barten HH: Comments on Adlerian psychology: The tradition of brief psychotherapy. J Ind Psychol 28:152–153, 1972.

Bartoletti MD: Conjoint family therapy with clinic team in a shopping plaza. Group Psychother 22:203–211, 1969 (a).

Bartoletti MD: Conjoint family therapy with clinic team in a shopping plaza. Int J Soc Psychiatry 15:250–257, 1969 (b).

Beck AT: Reliability of psychiatric diagnosis. I. A critique of systematic studies. Am J Psychiatry 119:210, 1962.

Beck AT: Cognition, affect, and psychopathology. Arch Gen Psychiatry 24:495–500, 1971.

Beck AT: Cognitive Therapy and Emotional Disorders. New York, International Universities Press, 1976.

Beck AT, Ward CH, Mendelson M, et al: Reliability of psychiatric diagnosis. 2. A study of consistency of clinical judgments and ratings. Am J Psychiatry 119:351, 1962.

Beck D: Treatment techniques in short-term psychoanalytic therapy. Z Psychosom Med Psychoanal 14(2):125–136, 1968.

Beck DF: Research findings on the outcome of marital counseling. Soc Casework 56:153–181, 1975.

Beck SJ: Rorschach's Test, Vols 1–3. New York, Grune & Stratton, 1944–1952.

Becker A, Goldberg HL: Home treatment services, in Grunebaum H (ed): The Practice of Community Mental Health. Boston, Little, Brown, 1970.

Bellak L: Handbook of Community Psychiatry and Community Mental Health. New York, Grune & Stratton, 1964.

Bellak L: Combined psycho and pharmacotherapy with special reference to short-term therapy and emergency therapy. Psychiatr Clin (Basel) 10(1–3):102–112, 1977.

Bellak L, Small L (eds): The choice of intervention, in Emergency Psychotherapy and Brief Psychotherapy. New York, Grune & Stratton, 1965; 2nd ed, 1978.

Bellak L, Small L: Emergency Psychotherapy and Brief Psychotherapy. New York, Grune & Stratton, 1965; 2nd ed, 1978.

Bellville TP, et al: Conjoint marriage therapy with a husband-and-wife team. Am J Orthopsychiatry 39:73–83, 1969.

Bender L: A Visual Motor Gestalt Test and Its Clinical Use. New York, American Orthopsychiatric Association, 1938.

Benjamin J: A method for distinguishing and evaluating formal thinking disorders in schizophrenia, in Kasanin JS (ed): Language and Thought in Schizophrenia. Berkeley, University of California Press, 1944.

Benson H, Beary JF, Carol MP: The relaxation response. Psychiatry 37:37–46, 1974.

Bention AL: Psychological tests for brain damage, in Freedman AM, Kaplan HI, Sadock BJ (eds): Comprehensive Textbook of Psychiatry, Vol 2, 2nd ed. Baltimore, Williams & Wilkins, 1975, pp. 757–768.

Berenbaum HL, et al: Massed time-limited therapy. Psychother Theory Res Prac 6:54–56, 1969.

Berger MM: Videotape Techniques in Psychiatric Training and Treatment. New York, Brunner/Mazel, 1970.

Berger MM: Self-confrontation through video. Am J Psychoanal 31:48–58, 1971.

Bergler E: The Basic Neuroses, Oral Regression, and Psychic Masochism. New York, Grune & Stratton, 1949.

Berlin IN: Crisis intervention and short-term therapy: An approach in a child psychiatric clinic. J Am Acad Child Psychiatry 9:595–606, 1970.

Berne E: Games People Play. New York, Grove Press, 1964.

Bierer J: Therapeutic Social Clubs. London, Lewis, 1948.

Bijou SW, Redd WH: Behavior therapy for children, in Arieti S (ed): American Handbook of Psychiatry, Vol 5, 2nd ed. New York, Basic Books, 1975.

Binder JL: Modes of focusing in psychoanalytic short-term therapy. Psychother Theory Res Prac 14:232–241, 1977.

Blanchard EB, Young LD: Clinical applications of biofeedback training: A review of evidence. Arch Gen Psychiatry 3:573–589, 1974.

Bleeker JA: Brief psychotherapy with living cancer patient. Psychother Psychoanal 29:282–287, 1978.

Bloch DA: Techniques of Family Psychotherapy: A Primer. New York, Grune & Stratton, 1973.

Borghi J: Premature termination of psychotherapy and patient-therapist expectations. Am J Psychother 22:460–473, 1968.

Bragan K: Time-limited psychotherapy with university students. Aust NZ J Psychiatry 12(3):151–155, 1978.

Brechenser DM: Brief psychotherapy using transactional analysis. Soc Casework 53:173–176, 1972.

Brown JS, Kosterlitz N: Selection and treatment of psychiatric outpatients. Arch Gen Psychiatry 11:425–438, 1964.

Buck JN: The-House-Tree-Person Test. Colony, Va, Lynchburgh State Colony, 1947.

Buda B: Utilization of resistance and paradox communication in short-term psychotherapy. Psychother Psychosom 20:200–211, 1972.

Budman SH, et al: Adult mental health services in a health maintenance organization. Am J Psychiatry 136:392–395, 1979.

Burdon AP, Neely JG: Chronic school failure in boys: A short-term group therapy and educational approach. Am J Psychiatry 122:1211–1220, 1966.

Burke JD, White HH, Havens LL: Matching patient and method. Arch Gen Psychiatry 35:177–186, 1979.

Burton A: Encounter: The Theory and Practice of Encounter Groups. San Francisco, Jossey-Bass, 1969.

Butcher JH, Maudal GR: Crisis intervention, in Weiner IB (ed): Clinical Methods in Psychology. New York, Wiley, 1976.

Campbell DD: A short-term psychotherapy for depression: A second controlled study. Dissertation Abstracts Int 35(2-B):1039, 1974.

Campbell RJ: Facilitation of short-term clinic therapy, in Masserman JH (ed): Current Psychiatric Therapies, Vol 7. New York, Grune & Stratton, 1967.

Caplan G: An Approach to Community Mental Health. New York, Grune & Stratton, 1961.

Caplan G: Principles of Preventive Psychiatry. New York, Basic Books, 1964.

Carr AC: Instruments commonly used by clinical psychologists, in Freedman AM, Kaplan HI, Sadock BJ (eds): Comprehensive Textbook of Psychiatry, Vol 2, 2nd ed. Baltimore, Williams & Wilkins, 1975, pp. 768–771.

Carr AC: Psychological testing of intelligence and personality, in Freedman AM, Kaplan HI, Sadock BJ (eds): Comprehensive Textbook of Psychiatry, Vol 2, 2nd ed. Baltimore, Md. Williams & Wilkins, 1975, pp. 736–757.

Carrington P: Freedom in Meditation. New York, Doubleday, 1977.

Carrington P, Ephron HS: Clinical use of meditation, in Masserman JH (ed): Current Psychiatric Therapies, Vol 15. New York, Grune & Stratton, 1975.

Casriel D: A Scream Away from Happiness. New York, Grosset & Dunlap, 1972.

Casriel D, Deitch D: The marathon: Time extended group therapy, in Masserman JH (ed): Current Psychiatric Therapies, Vol 8. New York, Grune & Stratton, 1968.

Castelnuovo-Tedesco P: Decreasing the length of psychotherapy: Theoretical and practical aspects of the problem, in Arieti S (ed): The World Bienniel of Psychiatry and Psychoanalysis, Vol 1. New York, Basic Books, 1971, pp 55–71.

Castelnuovo-Tedesco P: Brief psychotherapy, in Arieti S, Freedman DX, Dyrud JE (eds): American Handbook of Psychiatry, Vol 5, 2nd ed. New York, Basic Books, 1975, pp. 254–268.

Chiles JA, Sanger E: The use of groups in brief inpatient treatment of adolescents. Hosp Community Psychiatry 28:443–445, 1977.

Clark CC: A social systems approach to short-term psychiatric care. Perspect Psychiatr Care 10(4):178–182, 1972.

Coleman MD, Zwerling I: The psychiatric emergency clinic: A flexible way of meeting community mental health needs. Am J Psychiatry 115:980–984, 1959.

Conroe RM, et al: A systematic approach to brief psychological interaction in the primary core setting. J Fam Pract 7:1137–1142, 1978.

Corney RT, Grey WH: Toward removing the barricade to psychiatric clinic availability. Am J Psychiatry 126:144–148, 1970.

Corsini RJ: Role Playing in Psychotherapy: A Manual. Chicago, Aldine, 1966.

Cramer B: Brief therapy interventions with parents and children. Psychiatrar enfant 17(11):53–118, 1974.

Cramond WA: Psychotherapy of the dying patient. Br Med J 3:389–393, 1970.

Crary WG: Goals and techniques of transitory group therapy. Hosp Community Psychiatry 19:389–391, 1968.

Crasilneck HB, Hall JA: Clinical Hypnosis: Principles and Applications. New York, Grune & Stratton, 1975.

Crosa G: The Schultz method of autogenous training: Global therapeutic technique. Riv Psichiatria 2(6): 534–539, 1967.

Crowe MJ, et al: Time-limited desensitization, implosion and shaping for phobia patients. Behav Res Theory Prac 10:319–328, 1972.

Dahlstrom G, Welsh GS, Dahlstrom LE: An M.M.P.I Handbook. Vol I, Clinical Interpretation. Minneapolis, University of Minnesota Press, 1972.

Danner J, Gamson R: Experience with multi-family time-limited, outpatient group at a community psychiatric clinic. Psychiatry 3:126–137, 1968.

Darbonne AR, Allen R: Crisis: A review of theory, practice and research. Psychother Theory Res Prac 4(2):49–56, 1967.

Dasberg H, Van Praag HM: The therapeutic effect of short-term oral diazepam treatment on acute clinical anxiety in a crisis center. Acta Psychiatr Scand 50(3):326–340, 1974.

Davanloo H (ed): Short-term Dynamic Psychotherapy. New York, Spectrum, 1978.

Davanloo H, Benoit C: Transference in short-term dynamic psychotherapy. Psychother Psychosom 29:305–306, 1978.

Davis AE, Dinitz S, Pasamanick B: The prevention of hospitalization in schizophrenia five years after an experimental program. Am J Orthopsychiatry 42:375–388, 1972.

Dean SR: Self-help group psychotherapy: Mental patients rediscover will power. Int J Soc Psychiatry 17:72–78, 1970–1971.

Deatherage G: The clinical use of "mindfulness" meditation techniques in short-term psychotherapy. J Transpersonal Psychol 7:133–143, 1975.

Decker B, Stubblebine JM: Crisis intervention and prevention of psychiatric disability: A follow-up study. Am J Psychiatry 129:725–729, 1972.

Deeths A: Psychodrama crisis intervention with delinquent male drug users. Group Psychother 23:41–44, 1970.

De La Torre JC: The therapist tells a story: A technique in brief psychotherapy. Bull Menninger Clin 36:609–616, 1972.

Deutsch D: Group subgroup and individual therapy combined to treat the family. Roche Report 3:3, 1966.

Deutsch F: Applied psychoanalysis. New York, Grune & Stratton, 1949.

Dickes RA: Brief therapy of conversion reactions: An in-hospital technique. Am J Psychiatry 131:584–586, 1974.

Doll E: Measurement of Social Competence: Vineland Social Maturity Scale. Minneapolis, Educational Test Bureau, 1947.

Donner J, Gamson A: Experience with multifamily, time-limited, outpatient group at a community psychiatric clinic. Psychiatry 31:126–137, 1968.

Donovan WB, et al: The crisis group—An outcome study. Am J Psychiatry 136:906–910, 1979.

Dressler D, et al: The development of a mental health entry service. J Community Psychol 3:88–92, 1975.

Druck AB: The role of didactic group psychotherapy in short-term psychiatric settings. Group 2:98–109, 1978.

Durell VG: Adolescents in multiple family group therapy in a school setting. Int J Group Psychother 19:44–52, 1969.

Eisenberg M: Brief psychotherapy: A viable possibility with adolescents. Psychother Theory Res Prac 12:187–191, 1975.

Eisler RM, Herson M: Behavioral techniques in family-oriented crisis intervention. Arch Gen Psychiatry 28:111–116, 1973.

Ellis A: Outcome of employing three techniques of psychotherapy. J Clin Psychol 13:344–350, 1957.

Ellis A: An answer to some objections to rational-emotive psychotherapy. Psychother 2:108–111, 1965.

Ellis A: My philosophy of psychotherapy. J Contemp Psychol 6:13–18, 1973.

Elmore JL, Saunders R: Group encounter techniques in the short-term psychiatric hospital. Am J Psychother 26:490–500, 1972.

Epstein N: Brief group therapy in a child guidance clinic. Soc Work 15:33–38, 1970.

Epstein N: Techniques of brief therapy with children and parents. Soc Casework 57:317–323, 1976.

Erikson EH: Childhood and Society. New York, Norton, 1963.

Errera P, Braxton MC, Smith C, Gruber R: Length of psychotherapy. Arch Gen Psychiatry 17:454–458, 1967.

Feighner JP, Robins E, Guze SB et al: Diagnostic criteria for use in psychiatric research. Arch Gen Psychiatry 26:57, 1972.

Fensterheim H: Help Without Psychoanalysis. New York, Stein & Day, 1971.

Ferber H, Keeley SM, Shemberg KM: Training parents in behavior modification. Behav Ther 5:415–419, 1974.

Ferster CB: Positive reinforcement and behavioral deficits of autistic children, in Franks CM (ed): Conditioning Techniques in Clinical Practice and Research. New York, Springer, 1964, pp 255–274.

Fitzgerald RV: Conjoint marital psychotherapy: An outcome and follow-up study. Fam Process 8:260–271, 1969.

Fleischl MF, Wolf A: Techniques of social rehabilitation, in Masserman JH (ed): Current Psychiatric Therapies, Vol 7. New York, Grune & Stratton, 1967.

Flomenhaft K, et al: Avoiding psychiatric hospitalization. Soc Work 14:38–46, 1969.

Frances A, et al: Focal therapy in the day hospital. Hosp Community Psychiatry 30:195–199, 1979.

Frank JD: Persuasion and Healing: A Comparative Study of Psychotherapy, 2nd Ed. Baltimore, Johns Hopkins Press, 1973.

Frankel BL, et al: Ineffectiveness of electrosleep in chronic primary insomnia. Arch Gen Psychiatry 29:563–568, 1973.

Frankl VE: Fragments from the logotherapeutic treatment of four cases, in Burton A (ed): Modern Psychotherapeutic Practice. Palo Alto, Calif, Science & Behavior Books, 1965.

Frankl VE: Logotherapy and existential analysis—A review. Am J Psychother 20:252–260, 1966.

Franks CM: Conditioning Techniques in Clinical Practice and Research. New York, Springer, 1964.

Franks, CM, Wilson GT: Annual Review of Behavioral Therapy, Theory and Practice, Vol 3. New York, Brunner/Mazel, 1975.

Freud S: On Beginning the Treatment (1913). The Standard Edition of the Complete Psychological Works, Vol 12. London, Hogarth Press, 1958, pp 139–142.

Fulchiero CF: Evaluation of a therapeutic paradox technique in brief psychotherapy. Dissertation Abstracts Int 36(8–13):4153, 1976.

Fulkerson SC, Barry JR: Methodology and research on the prognostic use of psychological tests. Psychol Bull 58:197–204, 1961.

Garner HH: Brief psychotherapy and the confrontation approach. Psychosomatics 11:319–325, 1970 (a).

Garner HH: Psychotherapy: Confrontation Problem-Solving Techniques. St. Louis, Green, 1970 (b).

Gelb LA, Allman M: "Instant psychiatry" offered at an outpatient psychiatric clinic. Roche Report, Vol 4, Aug 1, 1967.

Gerber I: Bereavement and the acceptance of professional services. Community Ment Health J 5:487–495, 1969.

Gerber I: Bereavement and the acceptance of professional advice, in Barten HH (ed): Brief Therapies. New York, Behavioral Publications, 1971, pp 236–245.

Ghadirian A: Two cases of phobia treated according to a dynamic behavior approach. Laval Med 42(3):242–244, 1971.

Gillman RD: Brief psychotherapy: A psychoanalytic view. Am J Psychiatry 122:601–611, 1965.

Glasser W: Reality Therapy: A New Approach to Psychiatry. New York, Harper & Row, 1965.

Glasser W, Zunin LM: Reality therapy, in Masserman JH (ed): Current Psychiatric Therapies, Vol 12. New York, Grune & Stratton, 1972.

Glicken MD: A rational approach to short-term counseling. J Psychiatr Nurs Ment Health Serv 6:336–338, 1968.

Glueck BC, Stroebel CF: Biofeedback and meditation in the treatment of psychiatric illnesses, in Masserman JH (ed): Current Psychiatric Therapies, Vol 15. New York, Grune & Stratton, 1975.

Godbole A, Falk M: Confrontation—Problem-solving therapy in the treatment of confusional and delirious states. Gerontologist 12:151–154, 1972.

Goldberg HL: Home treatment. Psychiatr Ann 3:59–61, 1973.

Goldberg PA: A review of sentence completion methods in personality assessment. J Proj Tech Pers Assess 29:12, 1965.

Goldfarb AI, Turner H: Psychotherapy of aged people: II. Utilization and effectiveness of brief therapy. Am J Psychiatry 109:916–921, 1953.

Goldstein D: Crisis intervention: A brief therapy model. Nurs Clin N Am 13:657–663, 1978.

Goldstein K, Gelb A: Ueber Farbennamenamnesie. Psychol Forsch 6:127, 1924.

Goldstein K, Scheerer M: Abstract and concrete behavior. Psychol Monograph 53:239, 1941.

Gonen JY: The use of psychodrama combined with videotape playback on an inpatient floor. Psychiatry 34:198–213, 1971.

Goodenough F: Measurement of Intelligence by Drawings. Yonkers, NY, World Book, 1926.

Goodwin JM, Goodwin JS, Kellner R: Psychiatric symptoms in disliked medical patients. JAMA 241:1117–1120, 1979.

Goolishian HA: A brief psychotherapy program for disturbed adolescents. Am J Orthopsychiatry 32:142–148, 1962.

Gottschalk LA, Mayerson P, Gottlieb AA: Predictions and evaluation of outcome in an emergency brief psychotherapy clinic. J Nerv Ment Dis 144:77–96, 1967.

Graham P: Management in child psychiatry: Recent trends. Br J Psychiatry 129:97–108, 1976.

Grayson H (ed): Short-term Approaches to Psychotherapy. New York, Human Sciences Press, 1979.

Greenblatt M: Mental health consultation, in Freedman AM, Kaplan HI, Sadock BJ (eds): Comprehensive Textbook of Psychiatry, 2nd ed. Baltimore, Williams & Wilkins, 1975.

Greene BL: Treatment of mental disharmony when the spouse has a primary affective disorder (manic-depressive illness). I. General review—100 couples. J Marr Fam Counsel 1:82–101, 1975.

Greenwald H: Decision therapy. Personal Growth, No. 20, 1974.

Gross WF, Deridder L: Significant movement in comparatively short-term counseling. J Counsel Psychol 13:98–99, 1966.

Guernsey BG, Stollack G, Guernsey L: The practicing psychologist as educator—An alternate to the medical practitioner model. Prof Psychol 2:276–282, 1971.

Gurman AS: Some therapeutic implications of marital therapy research, in Gurman AS, Rice DG (eds): Couples in Conflict. New York, Aronson, 1975.

Hagelin A, Lazar P: The Flomp method. Int Ment Health Res Newsletter 15:1–18, 1973.

Haley J, Hoffman L: Techniques of Family Therapy. New York, Basic Books, 1967.

Hammer EF (ed): The Clinical Application of Projective Drawings. Springfield, Ill, Thomas, 1958.

Hand I, LaMontagne Y: Paradoxical intention and behavioral techniques in short-term psychotherapy. Can Psychiatr Assoc 19:501–507, 1974.

Hansell N: Casualty management method: An aspect of mental health technology in transition. Arch Gen Psychiatry 19:281–289, 1968.

Harris MR, Kalis BL, Freeman EH: Precipitating stress, an approach to brief therapy. Amer J Psychother 17:465–471, 1963.

Harris MR, Kalis MB, Freeman EH: An approach to short-term psychotherapy. Mind 2:198–207, 1964.

Harris T: I'm OK—You're OK. New York, Harper & Row, 1967.

Haskell D, Pugatch D, McNair DM: Time-limited psychotherapy. Arch Gen Psychiatry 21:546–550, 1969.

Hathaway SR, McKinley JC: Minnesota Multiphasic Personality Inventory. New York, Psychological Corporation, 1951.

Haug M: Focal therapy of the family: An application of psychoanalysis to child guidance. Psyche Stuttgart 25(8):595–602, 1971.

Hayworth RM: Positive outcome in psychiatric crisis: Evaluation of Thioridazine concentrate in an intensive, short-term psychiatric program. Psychosomatics 14:42–45, 1973.

Heine R, Trosman H: Initial expectations of the doctor-patient interaction as a factor in continuance in psychotherapy. Psychiatry 23:275–278, 1960.

Herschelman P, Freundlich D: Large group therapy with multiple therapists, in Masserman, JH (ed): Current Psychiatric Therapies, Vol 12. New York, Grune & Stratton, 1972.

Hitchcock J, Mooney WE: Mental health consultation. A psychoanalytic formulation. Arch Gen Psychiatry 21:353–358, 1969.

Hofmeister JF, et al: A behavioral program for the treatment of chronic patients. Am J Psychiatry 136:396–400, 1979.

Hollensbe SM: Script enactment as a technique for brief psychotherapy. Dissertation Abstracts Int 36(8-B):4160, 1976.

Hollister LE: Clinical use of psychotherapeutic drugs. Postgrad Med 47:100–105, 1970.

Holt RR (ed): Diagnostic Psychological Testing. New York, International Universities Press, 1968.

Horowitz MJ: Stress Response Syndrome. New York, Aronson, 1976.

Horowitz MJ: Stress Response Syndromes and Brief Psychotherapy. Strecker Monograph Series No. 14. Philadelphia Institute of the Pennsylvania Hospital, 1977.

Imber SD, et al: Uses and abuses of the brief intervention group. Int J Group Psychother 29:39–49, 1979.

Ishida R: Naikan-analysis. Psychologia: Int J Psychol in the Orient 12(2):81–92, 1969.

Jacobson G: The briefest psychiatric encounter. Arch Gen Psychiatry 18:718–724, 1968.

Jacobson GF: Crisis theory and treatment strategy: Some sociocultural and psychodynamic considerations. J Nerv Ment Dis 141:209–218, 1965.

Jacobson GF, et al: The scope and practice of an early-access brief treatment psychiatric center. Am J Psychiatry 121:1176–1182, 1965.

Janov A: The Primal Scream: Primal Therapy. The Cure for Neurosis. New York, Putnam, 1970.

Johnson RL, Chatowsky AP: Game theory and short-term group counseling. Personnel Guidance J 47:758–761, 1969.

Kalina E: Psychoanalytic psychotherapy of the couple: A brief psychotherapy approach, in Wolberg LR, Aronson ML (eds): Group Therapy 1974: An Overview. New York, Stratton Intercontinental, 1974.

Kalinowsky LB, Hippius H: Pharmacological, Convulsive and Other Somatic Treatments in Psychiatry. New York, Grune & Stratton, 1969.

Kalis L, Harris MR, Crestwood AK, et al: Precipitating stress as a focus in psychotherapy. Arch Gen Psychiatry 5:219, 1961.

Kanfer FH, Saslow G: Behavioral diagnosis, in Franks CM (ed): Appraisal and Status. New York, McGraw-Hill, 1969.

Kaplan HS: The New Sex Therapy. New York, Brunner/Mazel, 1974.

Kapp RA, Weiss SD: An interdisciplinary crisis-oriented graduate training program with a student health service mental health clinic. J Am Coll Health Assoc 23:340–344, 1975.

Karpman SB: Developments in transactional analysis, in Masserman JH (ed): Current Psychiatric Therapies, Vol 12. New York, Grune & Stratton, 1972.

Kaswan J, Love LR: Confrontation as a method of psychological intervention. J Nerv Ment Dis 148:224–237, 1969.

Kerns E: Planned short-term treatment. Soc Casework 51:340–346, 1970.

Kettle J: The EST Experience. New York, Kensington, 1976.

Killeen MR, Jacobs CL: Brief group therapy for women students. Soc Casework 21:521–522, 1976.

Kimbro EL, et al: A multiple-family group approach to some problems of adolescence. Int J Group Psychother 17:18–24, 1967.

Kirchner F, et al: Identification and management of the anxious patient with a model family practice unit. J Fam Pract 6:533–540, 1978.

Klapman JW: The case for didactic group psychotherapy. Dis Nerv Syst 11:35–41, 1950.

Klapman JW: Objective appraisal of textbook mediated group psychotherapy with psychotics. Int J Group Psychother 2:116–126, 1952.

Knobloch F: Czech-type therapeutic unit successfully used in Canada. Psychiatr News 8:32–33, 1973.

Koch W: Short-term therapy of obsessive compulsive neuroses with guided affective imagery. Z Psychother Med Psychol 19(5):187–191, 1969.

Kramer M: Cross-national study of diagnosis of the mental disorders: Origin of the problem. Am J Psychiatry 125:1 (Suppl), 1969.

Kraus AS, Lilienfeld AM: Some epidemiological aspects of the high mortality rate in the young widowed group. J Chron Dis 10:207–217, 1959.

Krimmel HE, Falkey BD: Short-term treatment of alcoholics. Soc Work 7:102–107, 1962.

Kusnetzoff SC: Communication theory and brief psychotherapy: Its application in therapy of children and adolescents. Am J Psychoanal 34:141–149, 1974.

La Ferriere L, Calsyn R: Goal attainment scaling: An effective treatment technique in short-term therapy. Am J Comm Psychol 6(3):271–282, 1978.

Langsley DG, Kaplan DM: The Treatment of Families in Crisis. New York, Grune & Stratton, 1968.

Langsley DG, et al: Family crisis therapy—Results and implications. Fam Process 7:145–148, 1968.

Langsley DG, et al: Follow-up evaluation of family crisis therapy. Am J Orthopsychiatry 39:753–759, 1969.

Langsley DG, Machotka P, Flomenhaft K: Avoiding mental hospital admission: A follow-up study. Am J Psychiatry 127:1391–1394, 1971.

Laqueur HP: General systems theory and multiple-family therapy, in Masserman JH (ed): Current Psychiatric Therapies, Vol 8. New York, Grune & Stratton, 1968.

Laqueur HP: Mechanisms of change in multiple-family therapy, in Sager CJ, Kaplan HS (eds): Progress in Group and Family Therapy. New York, Brunner/Mazel, 1972, pp 400–415.

Lazare A, Cohen F, Jacobson AM, et al: The walk-in patient as a "customer": A key dimension in evaluation and treatment. Am J Orthopsychiatry 42:872–883, 1972.

Lazarus AA: Behavior therapy in groups, in Gazda G (ed): Basic Approaches to Group Psychotherapy and Group Counseling. Springfield, Ill., Thomas 1968.

Lazarus AA: Multimodel Behavior Therapy. New York, Springer, 1976.

Leiblum SR, Rosen RC: The weekend workshop for dynamic dysfunctional couples: Assets and limitations. J Sex Marital Ther 5:57–69, 1979.

Lester D, Brockopp GW: Crisis Intervention and Counseling by Telephone. Springfield, Ill., Thomas, 1976.

Leuner H: Guided affective imagery (GAI): A method of intensive psychotherapy. Am J Psychother 23:4–22, 1969.

Levin RE, Rivelis de Paz, L: Contributions to the theory of the technique for group psychotherapy: Short-term groups for children in latency age. Acta Psiquiatr Psicol Am Lat 16(3):265–268, 1970.

Levinson DJ: The mid-life transition. A period of adult psychosocial development. Psychiatry 40:99–112, 1977.

Lewin KK: Brief Encounters. St. Louis, Green, 1970.

Lewis AB: Brief psychotherapy in the hospital setting: Techniques and goals. Psychiatr Q 47:341–352, 1973.

Lewis J, Mider PA: Effects of leadership style content and work styles of short-term therapy groups. J Counsel Psychol 20:137–141, 1973.

Liberman RA: Behavioral approach to group dynamics. I. Reinforcing and prompting of cohesiveness in group therapy. Behav Ther 1:141–175, 1970.

Lick JR, Bootzin RR: Expectancy, demand characteristics, and contact desensitization in behavior change. Behav Ther 1:176–183, 1970.

Lindemann E: Symptomatology and management of acute grief. Am J Psychiatry 101:141–148, 1944.

Lipkin S; Round robin time-limited therapy. Am Acad Psychother Newsletter 2:37–42, 1966.

Loreto G: Mental health for university students. Neurobiologia 35(4):253–276, 1972.

Louis P: Crisis intervention. Ment Hygiene 50:141–145, 1966.

Lowen A: Physical Dynamics of Character Structure. New York, Grune & Stratton, 1958.

Luber RF, Wells RA: Structured, short-term multiple family therapy: An educational approach. Int J Group Psychother 27:43–58, 1977.

Ludwig AM, Levine J: Hypnodelic therapy, in Masserman JH (ed): Current Psychiatric Therapies, Vol 7. New York, Grune & Stratton, 1967.

Luria A: Higher Cortical Functions in Man. New York, Basic Books, 1966.

Luthe W: Autogenic training: Method, research and application in medicine. Am J Psychother 17:174–175, 1963.

McGee TE, Meyer W: Time-limited and time-unlimited group psychotherapy: A comparison with schizophrenic patients. Comp Group Studies 2:71–84, 1971.

MacGregor R: Multiple impact psychotherapy with families. Fam Process 1:15–29, 1962.

Machover K: Personality Projection in the Drawings of the Human Figure. Springfield, Ill., Thomas, 1949.

Maizlish L, Hurley JR: Attitude changes of husbands and wives in time-limited group psychotherapy. Psychiatr Q Suppl 37:230–249, 1963.

Malan DH: A Study of Brief Psychotherapy. London, Tavistock, 1963. (Also Springfield, Ill., Thomas, 1964.)

Malan DH: The Frontier of Brief Psychotherapy. New York, Plenum, 1976 (a).

Malan DH: Toward the Validation of Dynamic Psychotherapy. New York, Plenum, 1976 (b).

Malan DH, Bacal HA, Heath ES, et al: A study of psychodynamic changes in untreated neurotic patients. I. Improvements that are questionable on dynamic criteria. Br J Psychiatry 114:525, 1968.

Malan DH, Heath ES, Bacal HA, et al: Psychodynamic changes in untreated neurotic patients. Arch Gen Psychiatry 32:110–126, 1975.

Maltz M; Psycho-cybernetics. Englewood Cliffs, NJ, Prentice-Hall, 1960 (paperback: New York, Pocket Books, 1973).

Mann J: Time-limited Psychotherapy. Cambridge, Harvard University Press, 1973.

Marmor J: Theories of learning and the psychotherapeutic process. Br J Psychiatry 112:363–366, 1966.

Marmor J: Dynamic psychotherapy and behavior therapy. Arch Gen Psychiatry 24:22, 1971.

Marmor J: Short-term dynamic psychotherapy. Am J Psychiatry 136:149–155, 1979.

Marrone RL, et al: A short duration group treatment of smoking behavior by stimulus saturation. J Behav Res Theory 8:347–352, 1970.

Martin B: Family interaction associated with child disturbance: Assessment and modification. Psychother Res Prac 4:30–35, 1967.

Martin PA, Bird HW: An approach to the psychotherapy of marriage partners: The stereoscopic technique. Psychiatry 16:123–127, 1963.

Martin PA, Lief HI: Resistance to innovation in psychiatric training as exemplified by marital therapy, in Usdin G (ed): Psychiatry: Education and Image. New York, Brunner/Mazel, 1973.

Martin RC: The acute situational crisis and communication theory. Dissertation Abstracts 29(4–A):1296, 1968.

Matarazzo JD: Wechsler's Measurement and Appraisal of Adult Intelligence. Baltimore, Williams & Wilkins, 1972.

Meacham ML, Wiesen AE: Changing Classroom Behavior: A Manual for Precision Teaching, 2nd ed. New York, Intext Educational Publishers, 1974.

Mears E: Sexual problem clinics: An assessment of the work of 26 doctors trained by the institution of psychosexual medicine. Public Health 92:218–223, 1978.

Melnick J, Tims AR, Jr.: Application of videotape equipment to group therapy. Int J Group Psychother 24:199–206, 1974.

Mentzel G: Goal-directed short-term therapy with functional disturbances. Z Psychosomat Med Psychoanal 15(1):37–44, 1969.

Merrill S, Cary GL: Dream analysis in brief psychotherapy. Am J Psychother 29:185–193, 1975.

Meyer E, et al: Contractually time-limited psychotherapy in an outpatient psychotherapy clinic. Am J Psychiatry 124(Suppl):57–68, 1967.

Meyer R: The psychosomatic patient in analytic brief psychotherapy. A follow-up study. Psyche (Stuttg) 32(10):881–928. 1978.

Meyer R, Beck D: The outcome of brief psychotherapy in 28 psychosomatic patients (author's trans). Praxis 67(39):1434–1439, 1978.

Miller WB: A psychiatric emergency service and some mental concepts. Am J Psychiatry 24:924–933, 1968.

Millman RB: An editorial reply. The Bulletin (Area II, American Psychiatric Association) 21(4):1, 1979.

Mone LC: Short-term group psychotherapy with postcardiac patients. Int J Group Psychother 20:99–108, 1970.

Moreno JL (ed): The International Handbook of Group Psychotherapy. New York, Philosophical Library, 1966.

Moreno M: Perspectives of analytic psychology for short-term psychotherapy. Riv Psichiatria 2(6):488–491, 1967.

Morley WE: Treatment of the patient in crisis. West J Medicine 6:77–87, 1965.

Morley WE, Brown VE: The crisis intervention group: A natural mating or a marriage of convenience. Psychother Theory Res Prac 6:30–36, 1969.

Morra M: Ambulatory short-term psychotherapy: Theoretical principles and some experiments. Riv Psichiatria 2(6):491–498, 1967.

Morrison JK, Cometa MS: Emotive-reconstruction psychotherapy: A short-term cognitive approach. Am J Psychother 31:294–301, 1977.

Moser AJ: Structural group interaction: A psychotherapeutic technique for modifying focus of control. J Contemp Psychother 7:23–28, 1975.

Muench GA: An investigation of the efficiency of time-limited psychotherapy. J Counsel Psychol 12:294–299, 1965.

Murray HA: Explorations in Personality. New York, Oxford University Press, 1938.

Negele RA– A study of the effectiveness of brief time-limited psychotherapy with children and their parents. Dissertation Abstracts Int 36(8–B):4172, 1976.

Neu C, et al: Measuring the interventions used in the short-term interpersonal psychotherapy of depression. Am J Orthopsychiatry 48:629–636, 1978.

Nichols MP: Catharsis in brief psychotherapy: An outcome study. Dissertation Abstracts Int 35(1–B):520, 1974.

Nichols MP, et al: The study of brief psychotherapy in a college health setting. J Am College Health Assoc 22:128–133, 1973.

Nicol AR: Psychotherapy and the school. J Child Psychol Psychiatry 20:81–86, 1979.

Normand WC, Fensterheim H, Schrenzel S: A systematic approach to brief therapy for patients from a low socioeconomic community. Community Ment Health J 64:349–354, 1967.

Ostow M: The Use of Drugs in Psychoanalysis and Psychotherapy. New York, Basic Books, 1962.

Palmer RD: Desensitization of the fear of expressing one's own inhibited aggression: Bioenergetic assertive techniques for behavior therapists. Paper presented at the Association for the Advancement of Behavior Therapy, Washington DC, September 1971.

Parsons BV, Alexander JF: Short-term family intervention: A therapy outcome study. J Consult Clin Psychol 41:195–201, 1973.

Patterson GR: Retraining of aggressive boys and their parents. J Can Psychiatr Assoc 19:142–158, 1974.

Patterson GR, et al: A social engineering technology for retraining the families of aggressive boys, in Adams HE, Unikel IP (eds): Issues and Trends in Behavior Therapy. Springfield, Ill., Thomas, 1973 (a).

Patterson GR, Reid JB: Intervention for families of aggressive boys: Replication study. Behav Res Theory 11:383–394, 1973 (b).

Patterson V, Levene H, Breger L: A one year follow-up of two forms of brief psychotherapy. Am J Psychother 31:76–82, 1977.

Paul GL: Experimental-behavioral approaches to schizophrenia, in Cancro R, Fox N, Shapiro L (eds): Strategic Intervention in Schizophrenia. New York, Behavioral Publications, 1974.

Peck H: An application of group therapy to the intake process. Am J Orthopsychiatry 23:338–349, 1953.

Peck H, Kaplan S, Romar M: Prevention, treatment and social action: A strategy of intervention in a disadvantaged urban area. Am J Orthopsychiatry 36:57–59, 1966.

Perls FS: Gestalt Therapy Verbatim. Moab, Utah, Real People Press, 1969.

Phillips EL, Johnston MS: Theoretical and clinical aspects of short-term parent child psychotherapy. Psychiatry 17:267–275, 1954.

Pittman FS: Managing acute psychiatric emergencies: Defining the family crisis, in Bloch DA (ed): Techniques of Family Psychotherapy: A Primer. New York, Grune & Stratton, 1973.

Pittman FS, DeYoung C, Flomenhaft K, et al: Crisis family therapy, in Masserman JH (ed): Current Psychiatric Therapies, Vol 6. New York, Grune & Stratton, 1966.

Pittman FS, et al: Work and school phobias: A family treatment approach. Am J Psychiatry 124:1535–1541, 1968.

Preston BH: Class method in treatment of psychotic patients. Int J Group Psychother 4:321–330, 1954.

Pruch D, Brody B: Brief relationship therapy in the military setting. Am J Orthopsychiatry 16:707–721, 1946.

Quaytman W: Impressions of the Esalen (Schutz) phenomenon. J Cont Psychother 2:57–64, 1969.

Rabin AI: Projective Techniques in Personality Assessment. New York, Springer, 1968.

Rabin HM: Any answers to the compelling arguments against encounters and marathons? Psychother Bull 4:16–19, 1971.

Rabkin R: Strategic Psychotherapy: Brief and Symptomatic Treatment. New York, Basic Books, 1977.

Rada RT, Daniels RS, Draper E: An outpatient setting for treating chronically ill psychiatric patients. Am J Psychiatry 126:789–795, 1969.

Rank O: Will Therapy. New York Knopf, 1936.

Rank O: Will Therapy and Truth and Reality. New York, Knopf, 1947.

Rapaport D, Gill MM, Schafer R, et al: Diagnostic Psychological Testing. New York, International Universities Press, 1968.

Rapaport L: The state of crisis: Some theoretical considerations. Soc Sci Rev 36:211–217, 1962.

Raskin DE: Problems in the therapeutic community. Am J Psychiatry 128:492, 1971.

Reder P: A case of brief psychotherapy. Br J Med Psychol 51(2):147–154, 1978.

Rees WD, Lutkins SG: Mortality of bereavement. Br Med J 4:13–16, 1967.

Regan PF: Brief psychotherapy of depression. Am J Psychiatry 122:27–32, 1965.

Reid WJ, Epstein L: Task Centered Casework. New York, Columbia University Press, 1972.

Reid WJ, Shyne A: Brief and Extended Casework. New York, Columbia University Press, 1969.

Reynolds DK: Morita Psychotherapy. Berkeley, University of California Press, 1976.

Rhodes SL: Short-term groups of latency-age children in a school setting. Int J Group Psychother 23:204–216, 1973.

Richardson FC, Suinn RM: Effects of two short-term desensitization methods in the treatment of test anxiety. J Counsel Psychol 21:445–458, 1974.

Rivera GG, Battaggia PG: Considerations in different types of short-term psychotherapeutic treatment. Riv Psichiatria 2(6):498–503, 1967.

Robbins OS: Crisis theory and its relation to psychotherapy. Psychother Psychosom 29:288–292, 1978.

Robkin R: Strategic Psychotherapy. New York, Basic Books, 1977.

Rolf I: Structural Integration. San Francisco, Guild for Structural Integration, 1958.

Rorschach H: Psychodiagnostic. Bern, Bircher, 1921.

Rosenthal AJ, Levine SV: Brief psychotherapy with children: A preliminary report. Am J Psychiatry 127:646–651, 1970.

Rosenthal AJ, Levine SV: Brief psychotherapy with children: Process of therapy. Am J Psychiatry 128:141–147, 1971.

Rosenthal D, Frank JD: The fate of psychiatric clinic outpatients assigned to psychotherapy. J Nerv Ment Dis 127:330–343, 1958.

Rosenwald AK: The psychological examination, in Arieti S (ed): American Handbook of Psychiatry. New York, Basic Books, 1974, pp 1181–1199.

Ruben HL: Managing suicidal behavior JAMA 241:282–284, 1979.

Rubenstein D: Rehospitalization versus family crisis. Am J Psychiatry 129:715–720, 1972.

Rush AJ: Cognitive Therapy. Weekly Psychiatry Update Series. Lesson 52, 1978.

Rush AJ, Beck AT: Cognitive therapy of depression and suicide. Am J Psychother 32:201–219, 1978.

Rush AJ, Beck AT, Kovacs M, et al: Comparative efficacy of cognitive therapy in pharmaco therapy in the treatment of depressed outpatients. Cognitive Ther Res 1:17–37, 1977.

Rusk TN– Opportunity and technique in crisis psychiatry. Compr Psychiatry 12:249–263, 1971.

Sadock B, Newman L, Normand WC: Short-term group psychotherapy in a psychiatric walk-in clinic. Am J Orthopsychiatry 38:724–732, 1968.

Safer DJ: Family therapy for children with behavior disorders. Fam Process 5:243–255, 1966.

Sager CJ, et al: The married in treatment. Arch Gen Psychiatry 19:205–217, 1968.

Sarvis MA, Dewees S, Johnson RF: A concept of ego-oriented psychotherapy. Psychiatry 22:277–287, 1958.

Satir VM: Conjoint Family Therapy. Palo Alto, Calif, Science & Behavior Books, 1964 (a).

Satir VM: Symptomatology: A Family Production. Palo Alto, Calif, Family Project Institute, 1964 (b).

Satir VM: Conjoint marital therapy, in Green BL (ed): The Psychotherapies of Marital Disharmony. New York, Free Press, 1965.

Schafer R: The termination of brief psychoanalytic psychotherapy. Int J Psychoanal Psychother 2:139, 1973.

Schreiber KA: Does training prepare for practice: A case

in point. The Bulletin (Area II, American Psychiatric Association) 21(4):1, 1979.

Schultz JA, Luthe W: Autogenic Training—A Psychophysiologic Approach in Psychotherapy. New York, Grune & Stratton, 1959.

Schutz W: Interpersonal Underworld. (Original title: Firo: A Three-dimensional Theory of Interpersonal Behavior.) Palo Alto, Calif, Science & Behavior Books, 1967.

Seibovich MA: Short-term insight psychotherapy for hysterical personalities. Psychother Psychosom 24: 67–78, 1974.

Selye H: Stress, The Physiology and Pathology of Exposure to Stress. Montreal, Acta, 1950.

Shafii M, et al: The development of an acute short-term inpatient child psychiatric setting: A pediatric-psychiatric model. Am J Psychiatry 136:427–429, 1979.

Shapiro D: Neurotic Styles. New York, Basic Books, 1965.

Sharpe KM: A study of the influence of transactional analysis on ego structure. Dissertation Abstracts Int 37(1–A):137–138, 1976.

Shaw R, et al: A short-term treatment program in a child guidance clinic. Soc Work 13:81–90, 1968.

Shlien JM: Cross-theoretical criteria in time-limited therapy. Paper presented at the Sixth International Congress of Psychotherapy, London, 1964.

Shlien JM, et al: Effects of time limits: A comparison of two psychotherapies. J Counsel Psychol 9:31–34, 1962.

Shorr JE: Psycho-imagination Therapy. New York, Stratton Intercontinental, 1972.

Shrader WK, et al: A didactic approach to stimulus in short-term group therapy. Am J Orthopsychiatry 39:493–497, 1969.

Sifneos PE: Seven years' experience with short-term dynamic psychotherapy, in Proceedings of the Sixth International Congress of Psychotherapy, Part IV. Basil, Karger, 1965, pp 127–135.

Sifneos PE: Psychoanalytically oriented short-term dynamic or anxiety-provoking psychotherapy for mild obsessional neurosis. Psychiatr Q 40:271–282, 1966 (a).

Sifneos PE: Two different kinds of psychotherapy of short duration. Paper presented at the 122nd Annual Meeting of the APA. Atlantic City, NJ, May 1966. (Also in Am J Psychiatry 123:1069–1074, 1967) (b).

Sifneos PE: The motivational process: A selection and prognostic criterion for psychotherapy of short duration. Psychiatr Q 42:271–279, 1968 (a).

Sifneos PE: Learning to solve emotional problems: A controlled study of short-term anxiety provoking psychotherapy, in Porter R (ed): The Role of Learning in Psychotherapy: A Ciba Foundation Symposium. London, Churchill, 1968, p 87 (b).

Sifneos PE: Short-term Psychotherapy and Emotional Crisis. Cambridge, Harvard University Press, 1972.

Sifneos PE: An overview of a psychiatric clinic population. Am J Psychiatry 130:1033, 1973.

Sifneos PE: Motivation for change: A prognostic guide for successful psychotherapy. Psychother Psychosom 29:293–298, 1978.

Silk S: The use of videotape in brief joint marital therapy. Am J Psychother 26:417–424, 1972.

Silver GA, Cherkasky M, Axelrod J: An experience in group practice, Montefiore Hospital Medical Group, 1948–1956. N Engl J Med 256:785–791, 1957.

Silverman PR: Services to the widowed: First steps in a program of preventive intervention. Community Ment Health J 3:37–44, 1967.

Silverman WH: Planning for crisis intervention with community mental health concepts. Psychother Theory Res Prac 14:293–297, 1977.

Simon L: Marital counseling: A dynamic-holistic approach. Am J Psychoanal 38:243–254, 1978.

Skynner ACR: School phobia: A reappraisal. Br J Med Psychol 47:1–16, 1974.

Sletten I, Altman H, Ulett G: Routine diagnosis by computer. Am J Psychiatry 127:1147, 1971.

Sloane RB, Staples FR, Cristol AH, et al: Short-term analytically oriented psychotherapy versus behavior therapy. Am J Psychiatry 132:373–377, 1975.

Sloane RB, Staples FR, Whipple K, et al: Patients' attitudes toward behavior therapy and psychotherapy. Am J Psychiatry 134:134–137, 1977.

Small L: The Briefer Psychotherapies. New York, Brunner/Mazel, 1971.

Smallwood JC: Dance-movement therapy, in Masserman JH (ed): Current Psychiatric Therapies, Vol 14. New York, Grune & Stratton, 1974.

Smith AC: Identity in transformation: A study of individual change in the Fischer-Hoffman process of psychotherapy. Dissertation Abstracts Int 37(2–B):990, 1976.

Smith W: A model for psychiatric diagnosis. Arch Gen Psychiatry 14:521, 1966.

Sokol RJ: A short-term technique of psychotherapy for psychotic depressive reactions. Int J Psychoanal Psychother 2:101–111, 1973.

Speers RW: Brief psychotherapy with college women: Technique and criterias for selection. Am J Orthopsychiatry 32:434–444, 1962.

Sperber E, Feitas R, Davis D: Bulletins of Structural Integration, Vols I, II, 1969.

Spiegel H: A single treatment method to stop smoking using ancillary self-hypnosis. Int J Clin Exp Hypn 18:235–250, 1970.

Spiegel H, Spiegel D: Trance and Treatment: Clinical Uses of Hypnosis. New York, Basic Books, 1978.

Spitzer RL, Endicott J: Can the computer assist clinicians in diagnosis? Am J Psychiatry 131:523, 1974.

Spitzer RL, Wilson PT: Nosology and the official psychiatric nomenclature, in Freedman AM, Kaplan HI, Sadock BJ (eds): Comprehensive Textbook of Psychiatry, Vol 2, 2nd ed. Baltimore, Williams & Wilkins, 1975, pp 826–845.

Spivack G, Platt JJ, Shure MB: The Problem-Solving Approach to Adjustment; A Guide to Research and Intervention. San Francisco, Calif, Jossey-Bass, 1976.

Sprince MP: Work with adolescents: Brief psychotherapy with a limited aim. J Child Psychother 2(2):31–37, 1968.

Springman RR: Single session psychotherapy in secondary male impotence. Ment Health Soc 5:86–93, 1978.

Stainbrook E: The hospital as a therapeutic community, in Freedman AM, Kaplan HI, Sadock BJ (eds): Comprehensive Textbook of Psychiatry. Baltimore, Williams & Wilkins, 1967, pp 1296–1300.

Standish CT, Semrad EV: Group psychotherapy with psychotics, in Rosenbaum M, Berger M (eds): Group Psychotherapy and Group Function. New York, Basic Books, 1963.

Stein C: Hypnotic projection in brief psychotherapy. Am J Clin Hypn 14:143–155, 1972.

Stein EH, Murdaugh J, MacLeod JA: Brief psychotherapy of psychiatric reactions to physical illness. Am J Psychiatry 125:1040–1049, 1969.

Stekel W: Conditions of Nervous Anxiety. New York, Liveright, 1950.

Stone A, Parloff M, Frank J, et al: The use of diagnostic groups in a group therapy program. Int J Group Psychother 4:274–284, 1954.

Straker M: Brief psychotherapy in an outpatient clinic: Evolution and evaluation. Am J Psychiatry 124: 1219–1225, 1968.

Strickler M, Allgeyer J: The crisis group: A new application of crisis theory. Soc Work 12:28–32, 1967.

Stroebel CF, Glueck BC: Biofeedback treatment in medicine and psychiatry: An ultimate placebo? Semin Psychiatry 5:379–393, 1973.

Strupp HH: On the technology of psychotherapy. Arch Gen Psychiatry 26:270–278, 1972.

Stuart RB: Operant-interpersonal treatment for marital discord. J Consult Clin Psychol 33:675–682, 1969.

Stuart RB, Tripodi T: Experimental evaluation of three time-constrained behavioral treatment for predelinquents and delinquents, in Rubin RD, Brady JP (eds): Advances in Behavior Therapy, Vol 4. New York, Academic Press, 1973.

Suess JF: Short-term psychotherapy with the compulsive personality and the obsessive-compulsive neurotic. Am J Psychiatry 129:270–275, 1972.

Suinn RM, et al: Accelerated massed desensitization: Unmotivation in short-term treatment. J Behav Ther 1:303–311, 1970.

Swanson MG, Woolson AM: Psychotherapy with the unmotivated patient. Psychother, Theory Res Prac 10:175–183, 1973.

Swartz J: Time-limited brief psychotherapy. Semin Psychiatry 1:380–388, 1969.

Swartz J: Time-limited brief psychotherapy, in Barten HH (ed): Brief Therapies. New York, Behavioral Publications, 1971.

Swenson WM, Martin HR: A description and evaluation of an outpatient intensive psychotherapy center. Am J Psychiatry 133:1043–1046, 1976.

Szasz TS: The Myth of Mental Illness. New York, Harper & Row, 1961.

Taft J (ed): Family Casework and Counseling: A Functional Approach. Philadelphia, University of Pennsylvania Press, 1948.

Teicher A, de Freitas L, Osherson A: Group psychotherapy and the intensive group experience: A preliminary rationale for encounter as a therapeutic agent in the mental health field. Int J Group Psychother 24:159–173, 1974.

Terman LM, Merrill MA: Measuring Intelligence. Boston, Houghton, Mifflin, 1937.

Tien HC: From couch to coffee shop: A new personality via psychosynthesis. Roche Report 2(18,19), 1972.

Tolor A: Teachers evaluation of children in short-term treatment with subprofessionals. J Clin Psychol 24:377–378, 1968.

Tomkins SS: The Thematic Apperception Test: The Theory and Technique of Interpretation. New York, Grune & Stratton, 1947.

Tracey J: Parent guidance groups: Is this therapy? J Psychiatr Nurs Ment Health Services 8(3):11–12, 1970.

Trakas D, Lloyd G: Emergency management in a short-term open group. Compr Psychiatry 12:170–175, 1971.

Tuckman AJ: Brief psychotherapy and hemodialysis. Arch Gen Psychiatry 23:65–69, 1970.

Tyhurst JS: The roles of transition states—including disasters in mental illness. Symposium on Preventive and Social Psychiatry. Washington, DC, Walter Reed Army Institute of Research, 1957.

Upham F: Ego Analysis in the Helping Professions. New York, Family Service Association of America, 1973.

Ursano RM, Dressler DM: Brief vs. long-term psychotherapy: A treatment decision. J Nerv Ment Dis 159:164–171, 1974.

Verhulst J: Marital change: An intensive, short-term approach. Int Ment Health Res Newsletter 17(2):7–10, 1975.

Vernallis FF, et al: Saturation group psychotherapy in a weekend clinic: An outcome study. Psychother Theory Res Prac 7:144–152, 1970.

Vernallis FF, et al: The treatment process in saturation group therapy. Psychother Theory Res Prac 9:135–138, 1972.

Visher JS, O'Sullivan M: Nurse and patient responses to a study of milieu therapy. Am J Psychiatry 127:451, 1971.

Volkan V: A study of a patient's "re-grief work" through dreams, psychological tests and psychoanalysis. Psychiatr Q 45:244–273, 1971.

Volkan V, Showalter CR: Known object loss, disturbance in reality testing, and re-grief work as a method of brief psychotherapy. Psychiatr Q 42:358–374, 1968.

Wahl CW: The technique of brief psychotherapy with hospitalized psychosomatic patients. Int J Psychoanal Psychother 1:69–82, 1972.

Walker RG, Kelley FE: Short-term psychotherapy with hospitalized schizophrenic patients. Acta Psychiatr Scand 35:34–56, 1960.

Walker RG, Kelley FE: Short-term psychotherapy with schizophrenic patients evaluated over a three-year follow-up period. J Nerv Ment Dis 137:349–352, 1963.

Wallace MA, Morley WE: Teaching crisis intervention. Am J Nurs 70:1484–1487, 1970.

Walter H, Gilmore SK: Placebo versus social learning effects in parent training procedures designed to alter the behavior of aggressive boys. Behav Ther 4:367–370, 1973.

Wattie B: Evaluating short-term casework in a family agency. Soc Casework 54:609–616, 1973.

Watzlawick P: A review of the double-bind theory. Fam Process 2:132–153, 1963.

Watzlawick P, Beaven JH, Jackson DD: Pragmatics of Human Communication: A Study of Interactional Patterns, Pathologies, and Paradoxes. New York, Norton, 1967.

Waxer PH: Short-term group psychotherapy: Some principles and techniques. Int J Group Psychother 27:33–42, 1977.

Wayne GJ: Clinical aspects of short-term hospitalization. J Natl Assoc Private Psychiatr Hospitals 9:21, 1976.

Wechsler D: Intelligence Scale for Children: Manual. New York, Psychological Corporation, 1949.

Wechsler D: The Measurement and Appraisal of Adult Intelligence, 4th ed. Baltimore, Williams & Wilkins, 1958.

Weinberger G: Brief therapy with children and their parents, in Barten HH (ed): Brief Therapies. New York, Behavioral Publications, 1971.

Weisenberg T, McBride KE: Aphasia. New York, Hafner, 1964.

Weisman G, Feurstein A, Thomas C: Three-day hospitalization—A model for intensive intervention. Arch Gen Psychiatry 21:620–629, 1969.

Wells RA: Structured Short-term Therapeutic Intervention. Leonia, NJ, Behavioral Sciences Tape Library, 1974.

Wells RA: Group facilitative training with conflicted marital couples, in Gurman A, Rice D (eds): Couples in Conflict. New York, Aronson, 1975.

Wells RA: Short-term Treatment: An Annotated Bibliography 1945–1974. (Catalog of Selected Documents in Psychology) 6(1), 13 MS 1189, 1976.

Whittington HG: Transference in brief psychotherapy: Experience in a college psychiatric clinic. Psychiatr Q 36:503–518, 1962.

Wilder JF: Roche Report: Frontiers of Psychiatry, 9(1), 1979.

Wilkens GD, et al: A therapeutic community development in a state psychiatric hospital. Med J Aust 2:220–224, 1963.

Wiltz NA, Patterson GR: An evaluation of parent training procedures designed to alter inappropriate aggressive behavior in boys. Behav Ther 5:215–222, 1974.

Wolberg A: The Borderline Patient. New York, Stratton Intercontinental, 1973.

Wolberg A, Padilla-Lawson E: The goals of community mental health consultation, in Masserman JH (ed): Science and Psychoanalysis, Vol 8. New York, Grune & Stratton, 1965, pp 243–261.

Wolberg LR: Medical Hypnosis, Vols 1, 2. New York, Grune & Stratton, 1948.

Wolberg LR: Hypnoanalysis, 2nd ed. New York, Grune & Stratton, 1964.

Wolberg LR: Short-term Psychotherapy. New York, Grune & Stratton, 1965.

Wolberg LR: Psychiatric technics in crisis therapy. NY State J Med 72:1266–1269, 1972.

Wolberg LR: The Technique of Psychotherapy, 3rd ed. New York, Grune & Stratton, 1977.

Wolf A: Short-term group psychotherapy, in Wolberg LR (ed): Short-term Psychotherapy. New York, Grune & Stratton, 1965, pp 219–255.

Wolpe J: Behavior therapy in complex neurotic states. Br J Psychiatry 110:28–34, 1964.

Wolpe J: The effects of psychotherapy. Int J Psychiatry 1:175–178, 1965.

Would RL, Reid R: A study of group psychotherapy results with youthful offenders in detention. Group Psychother 17:56–60, 1964.

Young H: A Rational Counseling Primer. New York, Institute for Advanced Study in Rational Psychotherapy, 1974.

Young M, Benjamin B, Wallis C: The mortality of widowers. Lancet 2:454–456, 1963.

Zwerling I, Wilder JF: Day hospital treatment of psychotic patients, in Masserman JH (ed): Current Psychiatric Therapies, Vol 2. New York, Grune & Stratton, 1962.

Author Index

Subject Index